You´re on track, keep going...

Basoit int Hald is the aptronym pseudonym for the authors real name which in abbreviation is TFD, a.k.a. Bisse(n), a.k.a. Don Dahl.

ISBN: 978-87-975005-0-7

TABLE OF CONTENTS

Dedicated to my unborn child(ren), and everyone else

Preface

"Life´s a bitch and then we die…". This sentence, from the song by the same name on rapper Nas´ Illmatic-album, keeps repeating in my head, as it has done it so very often when I catch myself questioning the meaning and thus purpose of life. Not because I usually attach too much importance to song-lyrics in my search for answers, but anyway, still I can´t help but to consider if this sentence in a general context really *do* make sense, and is hitting the bullseye when boiling life down to only one sentence? Of course, we throughout life can experience moments of pleasure if we e.g. succeed in something we find important, if we taste something we adore, if we have passionate sex, etc., but from a macro (zoom out) perspective, here high above our world as a whole, as if observing and analyzing the current state of our planet, Earth, from outer space – or theoretically observing it from the heights of utopia, then this sentence might not be all crazy after all. Among others, for all and any reason – including none – we´re warring each other, we allow for the suffering of both ourselves and others, and we´re killing each other, we´re doing a "great" job destroying our planet and our mental health, ergo our home and ourselves. Short and mildly said, we humans are some quite self-destructive creatures – largely non compos mentis (a.k.a. pretty fucking insane).

Every large scale negative condition on Earth has its root-cause in human behavior, human made pollution – in more than one sense, human made ideologies, cultures, religions and worldviews moreover, human made borders, laws and currencies, which thus all are infrastructure institutions under the umbrella term of social structures, which hence further constitute our societies, currently overall run by mainly human greed, power lust and thereof selfishness. The fact that we humans in the current Anthropocene

Epoch[1] actually are in the process of destroying the incredibly beautiful and superhuman strong nature, should abundantly clearly illustrate how destructive we humans really are, while additionally question if the term of superhuman even still has its place on Earth, and if, then for how long?
We humans clearly are responsible for just about all of our own tragedy, and it´s thus thereby only us humans who have the ability and hence potential to turn things positively around, to change our damaging direction, to make things right in order for us to reach the utopia that´re just laying waiting for us to arrive; depending on human priorities, faith and willpower, the notion of a real life utopia is by many considered to be extremely naïve – a pure fantasy unicorn mirage, while it for others are considered highly plausible, and why the fuck not? "Only" stupidity – pure plain and thereof also Kafkaesque[2], so far prevent you-me-we from actually getting there where we need to be to peel off the evil shit of the mean shit to feel that the shit without bullshit ain´t really shit but *the* shit.
Personally, my ideological creed is based upon getting as close to the optimal utopia as possible, the potential is de facto already here, and my elixir of life is as a minimum bound to a hope of the better – in regard to both life itself and our world as a whole. The needed changes of direction for the better in almost all aspects of our world damn well must be possible, I believe, our actions for the better can and must be raised to a higher level, I say, everything is possible for the one who carry the will in their heart and puts their mind into it, I´ve learned. All Earth-related life is pretty much in our own hands – hopefully for the next billions of years to come (unless *we* fuck up), and who the shizzle are we to blow this miraculous crazy amazing

---

[1] The epoch of significant human impact on Earth´s geology and ecosystem, a.k.a. the time period we today live in.

[2] Nightmarish bureaucratic absurdity as described in Franz Kafka's (1883-1924) fictional world.

opportunity; we´ve a responsibility to do great, and self-inflicted fatal failure isn´t an acceptable option.
Justice to the seriosity and importance of now and beyond is so cosmic that it even can seem pointless expressing in words, however, as I on some parameters in my believe tend to kiss the limit of fantasism – all too often impossible "just" covers what hasn´t been proven possible yet, I hence hereby intend to give it a go and bring you my humble (as if) attempt of an initial confessing assertion.
This book addresses all people, it might can appear pretty basic and elementary for some while challenging complex to others, in either or any third way don´t quit, I´m sure you´ll benefit.
From most to everybody likes simple answers to complex questions, and some pretentiously tries to sound smart by giving overcomplicated complex answers to even the banally simplest of questions. Pretentious behavior can make even the clever seem stupid, and despite wishing for simple, then sometimes simplifying an answer too much simply doesn´t justify the question, why the answer to *this* "question" probably is to be found somewhere in the midst – depending on the concrete context. Hence, against my nature (I normally talk like an ol´ school dockworker from the gutter, and writes like a steroided stiff upper lip Lord), I exceptionally language-wise in this piece of writing aim to go somewhat down the middle, to thereby allow for anyone and everyone to feast; no matter what ethnicity or gender or sexuality you have, if you´re a yuppie, if you´re an academic, if you´re a working-class hero, an authority or a thuggin' rebel, a pacifist or a warrior, young or retired or both, short or tall, powerful or weak, if you're a space traveller chillaxing in your spaceship or reading in the sun or cozy at home or an inmate reading behind the steel curtains on your bunk in the pen, blue collar, white collar, brown collar, green collar, red collar, orange collar, checkered collar, striped collar, no matter what color collar you wear or no collar at all, whoever you are – wherever you

are, fuck limiting talk about segments, specific target groups, and a precise sought audience; entrée, this book is for *you*.
Buckle up, the best karma and happy reading *your* way!

Prologue: The Third Pill

"Let me tell you why you´re here. You´re here because you know something. What you know you can´t explain, but you feel it. You felt it your entire life, that there´s something wrong with the world... ...like a splinter in your mind, driving you mad. It is this feeling that has brought you to me".

The splinter-based spirit in this quote taken from the first Matrix movie partly somewhat describes you, and why you´re now reading this book. In the movie-scene – following the above mentioned citing, the protagonist, a.k.a. the main character of the movie, Neo, The Chosen One, and in this context *you*, is being given the choice between a blue pill that will erase from the memory what was just presented and thus allow for a return to the continuation of a blindfolded life, or a red pill that will open the rabbit hole gate to a "wonderland" of truths.

The fact that you´re now – still – reading this book, already reveals about you that you most probably in a "Matrix-ish-kinda-context" is a red-pill kind of person, that you´re one of the chosen ones, and that you by choice are ready to enter *this* book´s "wonderland" of truth – the whole truth and nothing but the truth so help me love.

Though, to be fair, and immediately set truth straight by popping a truth (Spoiler alert!): In somewhat line with relativism and realism and pretty fucking close to the core essence of perspectivism, there almost are no truths, almost only perspectives[3]. It´s e.g. a true fact that we´ve been created and brought to life (and *that* even if you e.g. vow to the simulation theory[4]), and that we as individuals

[3] Although slightly less ultimate than his approach, then of course still inspired by what the French novelist, Gustave Flaubert (1821-1880), expressed: *"There is no truth. There is only perception"*.

[4] Some people believe that we live in a simulation, that all current existence – including Earth and the rest of the universe – could in fact be an artificial simulation, e.g. a virtual reality computer simulation.

eventually will pass away (at least say goodbye to our common perception of physical existence), but almost everything else in between creation and death (the concept of an ending which we define as death) surely is up for debate and interpretation, and hence do not stand out as single handed truth.

Therefore, I cannot promise you that you´ll receive all the truths of your desire, but what I *can* promise is that you from my vantage point will receive some of *my* truths about our internal and external worlds, and that this book for sure will help to open your eyes in relation to certain topics, maybe remind you about what you already know, and as a minimum give you plenty of contemplation for the creation of your own truths. Thus, to be crystal clear, I´m not necessarily giving you all of *your* answers, I´m the humble facilitator nourishing *your* process of finding *your* answers, so that *you* can grow, tap in, showcase, and thus participate in making *your* surroundings to grow with you.

I´ve thought about which jokes to include in this book to make the reading process as entertaining as possible. However, even though I enjoy spicylicious jokes, and even more so dry humor, then I also have to admit that I find many of the topics in this book to be too serious, and too important, to use as just fuel for a cheap laugh, and if I *have* to choose, then I most often prefer interesting over funny – if I can´t have both. Hence, this book will not quite present itself as a script to a stand-up comedy show, although I cannot completely turn my back on and refuse the use of irony.

For sure I´ve gone through the full spectrum of emotions during the process of writing this book, from excitement to frustration, from happiness to anger, and back, and from melancholia to literally crying from laughter to the point where also my one-eyed friend[5] involuntarily had to surrender and squeeze a drop or two (and no, I´m not suffering with enuresis[6]).

---

[5] Slightly NSFW (Not safe for work): My dick.

[6] Inability to control urination.

I know that my humor sometimes might can appear a bit dry, and that it can be dangerous to be too sophisticated humor-wise in written words, as "things" and points easily can be misinterpreted and misunderstood in a word "only" setting without a proper supplementation of mimics, tones of voice, etc., to underline my sometimes pubic-hair thin line between irony, tragicomic, and dead serious.

Thus, I hope that you´ll be able to navigate, demarcate, and thus appreciate, my both ironic and serious points as they purposely come flying in from all directions on your travel from cover to cover. Of course, some topics are heavier than others, and perhaps you´ll find some of the passages or chapters a bit hard to cope with – to grasp at first read. *If* so, and only if (I´m definitely not trying to talk down to the brilliance of you), fear not, it´s okay, simply read it again, read slower, work with it, do whatever you have to do, but don´t tap out, don´t fucking quit. What I´ve written I wrote for *you*, it´s love damn too important for you to miss out on, and for sure you´ll prosper your way through it as long as you invest yourself into it.

Anyway, as I was saying, inspired by the before mentioned Matrix-pill-choice (the choice between the red and the blue pill), which metaphorically is equal to the overall two choices democracies most often in the "real world" has to offer (at least in the western part of the world where we somewhat tells ourselves that we´re fortunate enough to not directly have a autocracy psycho dictator behind the wheels, where we at least still have a senate or a parliament of "only" partly psychos to curb our actual psychos in charge of our plutocratic [7] idiocracies in which the extremity of the present stupidity exponentially is getting out of hand), I cannot help to transfer the pill-choice example to the current political landscape wherein the red pill represents the political left-wing, and the blue pill represents the political right-wing.

---

[7] Elitist (in a primarily economic sense) ruling.

Stuck with only these two choices of either red or blue, left or right, any electoral decision-making suddenly can seem like a forced choice between two evils with the overall same denominator – two sides of the same coin, as the political horse-trading compromises which democracies most often tend to accumulate more or less most often overall seems to show the somewhat same result and end-product anyway; perhaps a sexy ladyboy isn´t to sneeze at, but purple – in all respect – nevertheless aren´t really my color; notwithstanding a red or blue colored flag fluttering in the wind above the high castle, notwithstanding a red or blue toastmaster at the end of the table, what we see, what constantly is maintained, and what thus is the outcome – until further, is an overruling capitalistic direction at the expense of humanism; the only difference between the red and the blue pill, left- and right-wing policies and hence politics, seems to be the speed of which capitalism considerably accelerates during periods under right-wing hegemony[8], and how it slightly decelerates during periods under left-wing hegemony.

Surely, it shouldn´t be denied that some politicians are good people, and that we occasionally do get to see some great greater good things being achieved politically. Though, opposed to the political power hierarchy, the most noticeable political achievements mostly seem to showcase themselves in and around local communities bound to local policy, a lot less on a national level, while it compared to the dirt pile of bullshit that´re taking place in our world requires a quite powerful magnifying glass to spot the great achievements on an international global scaled level of politics.

Of course, the larger the scale the more complex and complicated politics become, but from a spectator perspective, how can the world ever accomplish remarkable achievements of peace, health,

---

[8] A.k.a. being in power, a.k.a. being in office.

and harmony, universally (a la one size fits all[9]), through a somewhat one-sided doomsday system in which the will to groundbreaking altruistic orientated actions on an international global scale almost seems paralyzed, as if we collectively "just" continue to either tread water to save ourselves or drown, and in doing so likewise continue to float offshore with the human made offshore wind and waves, although our only option and solution to save the situation is to swim ashore, and where those who *can* swim offers help to those who *cannot* swim. Unfortunately, those individuals who thus actually manage to get solid ground under their feet, and maybe even manage to get their hands on a boat, should thus focus on helping the individuals still treading water before they drown, rather than having their heads so far up their own asses that they most often selfishly prefer to use their boats for merely personal pleasures – (still) figuratively speaking as e.g. a place to sunbathe and yacht party from, in a sea of dead or half-dead bodies. The world is not a good place just because you wear a fire protecting suit in a fire where everyone and everything else still burns, at least use your advantage to help put out the fire, and rescue as many as possible in the process. Inspired also by words from the British writer and broadcaster, Damian Barr (1976-): We´re in the same storm, some have yachts, some canoes, some tread water, and some are drowning. Be kind and help whoever you can. In lack of better, many of us, the voters, in spite of witnessing how one electoral promise after the other is being broken, clings to a diminishing hope of a political and thereby social structural change for the better, and in doing so, we´re obligated to support either the one or the other, left or right, red or blue. Cause, if we don´t use our righteous one given electoral vote on election-day, then we as

[9] The term of universal here covers everything within the human cognitive ability (unlike what e.g. the French philosopher and mathematician, René Descartes (1596-1650), believed, when he qualified *everything* as object for reason in his use of the term universal).

citizens are missing out on our one and only official minimal saying – our only official "chance of change", without successive formal right to in hindsight complain about the political and social structural outcomes.

Due to this narrow ultimate deal or no deal – or rather deal or go fuck yourself as compensation-ish – scenario, too many have simply completely given up on their hopes of influence in our world; "my vote is just one vote and thus won't make any difference in the overall result anyway", said millions of nonvoters on elections which often proves to be decided by a margin of a relatively few thousand votes. Instead, as a result, people tend to take out their frustrations on each other and our environments to an extend that matches the also politically created downward state of the human mental health, or rather lack of same.

As of now, all we – the multitude people – at the very best can do is to stay strong in our believe of the better, plant mental seeds around us favoring the better, and by our actions lead by example for the better. What we at least need instead of a weak choice between a red or a blue pill, is the third pill.

What the third pill is, how it plays out, and how we get to have it, is partly what this book is all about, although the main focus will be on you, our shared social sphere, and the parts of our world which we can see, feel, touch, hear, and smell, short said percipere, a.k.a. sense. We´re literally going to operate in the time span from before the genesis of everything, and to pursuing to look into the future. Thus, if you´re now worrying that this´ll be yet another political "walk in the desert" then fear not, we´ll definitely not going to waste our time fly-fucking (a.k.a. nitpicking) circular letters or treaties or any boring bureaucratic shit like that, life´s already short enough as it is. And yes, I´ve also studied law – including constitutional law, so I also in this context *do* know a bit of what I´m talking about.

We of course *cannot* change human nature overnight, but we *can* change parts of ourselves, our modus operandi – and thereby approach, thereby our surrounding others, our cultures, our social constructions[10], and thereby our way of life, etc., to catalyze processes of future positive changes to the world in which we live, and therein small important changes to human nature included – which by time can lead to big important changes all over; in our personal sphere of control we have the power, empowerment, to constantly work with ourselves to become the best versions of ourselves, and therethrough thus contribute to our social sphere – fellowships and communities – to the best of our abilities. We are all a part of a larger fellowship, humanity, and even all life on Earth and beyond, and we are thus not exactly entirely in ourselves the main goal; the main goal is hence not only about you or me winning as much as it´s about all of us succeeding together, and this as much as possible in the fulfilment of our potential – which is a process that of course starts with ourselves, goes through ourselves, and hence happens from ourselves.
"This project has absolutely no deeper meaning, and I´m only making it because I feel like it". Those were the exact words from a world renowned (some say global top five) Danish film director[11] in *the* Directors Intentions Statement I was handed from him when I some years back worked in the movie business and was helping out with the official application to have one of his movies partly financed through the DFI (Danish Film Institute). "Normally", the Directors Intentions Statement is of vital importance for the odds of receiving funds through the DFI, but in this particular case, despite – from mainly economic reasons – refusing many applications with

[10] By social constructions is meant those society systematic, institutional and interpersonal both written and unwritten laws, rules and customs, requirements, demands and expectations, which we´re all subject to.
[11] I´m not mentioning his name simply because I´m not about to promote myself through his name, and because I do not wish to name shame him.

equally many well written Directors Intentions Statements from other talented up-coming film directors, the DFI film consultants anyway – despite the "I don´t give a fuck Directors Intention Statement" – chose to suck up to our famed director by granting *his* movie the largest movie budget ever given by the DFI to any film (at least up until that moment in time).
I´m not mentioning this to bitch about us landing the budget we back then were aiming for, and despite in fact not always having the best report with this particular director then I still very much respect much of his art and courage to be unbendingly honest (although some of his courage probably prosper from a side-effect of his excessive (ab)use of pills and booze). Rather, I mention this because it really was one of the first times I in a professional context noticed how the mechanism of nepotism – or here favoritism now since we´re talking about a non-family relation – unreasonably unfolded itself at the expense of others, who probably de facto deserved it more. Sure, I´ve been privileged with having pretty cool jobs in e.g. the businesses of first class premium concerts and movies, etc., and "right" enough I got at least one of those jobs by knowing someone – a friend or a friend of a friend, but never had I in my immature mind really considered the related aspect of unfairness up until that point.
The very same mechanism often plays out when e.g. trying to enter the job market or change career, the employers tend to demand of applicants that they´re young and submissive enough to be molded, that they´re highly educated, and that they unrealistically have twice as many years of relevant work experience within some very specific field than they realistically have actual years in the field; I e.g. recently saw a job advert wherein it was wanted by an applicant to have a minimum of eight years of experience in working with a specific computer-program that in fact had only existed for little less than three years. When you´re young everybody expects you to have a strong portfolio, but almost nobody´s willing to add anything

to it, and when you´re older then nobody cares about your portfolio compared to how much they consider your age – the higher your age the most often harder to land the job. *"If youth knew, if age could"* [12]. Unless you know somebody, or know somebody who knows somebody, unless you roll with the right network – are born into it or lick enough ass to walk around with a shitty taste in your mouth, then most most likely can go whistle for "that dream job" – and perhaps even any job for that matter, which even goes in relation to the usually unpaid internships which often can be the only entrance to get your feet inside the door, together with all other "accepted" setups where employees tend to take advantage and the rich – again – are being favored as only they can afford to work for free. Even a legit job of digging diches now requires of you to be certified with a diploma from a technical school, *and* have plenty of relevant experience within the field of digging, and if you as an alternative to a fancy education try to apply for a less prestigious job, then you most likely will find yourself to be found too overqualified to be hired anyway – what should´ve been to your advantage thus suddenly becomes your disadvantage (as they fear (Ed. know) that you most likely will bounce at first chance to advance).

To exemplify, "telling for a friend" (wink wink); I e.g. know a Danish guy who went and did his postgraduate abroad at a global top 10 university, and he´s the first and only person in Denmark to hold that exact education he has. Within his field he received schooling from some of the best professionals in the world, his specialization is highly relevant for areas which certain public institutions needs expertise in, he graduated with good results, he has relevant personal experiences, a deep professional understanding, contacts to just about everything of everything, and hence a network beyond "normal" (which he though based on integrity and ethical reason

[12] Quote by the Austrian neurologist and founder of psychoanalysis, Sigmund Freud (1856-1939).

just aren´t revealing and handing out already in the application process (he wants employment for him because he deserves it, and not because of who he knows)), his record´s clean, he was ready to climb a steep learning curve, and on top of that he´s "just simply" one hell of a great guy – outstanding personality and social skills. However, simply because he aren´t born with a silver spoon up his ass, and neither are the superficial ass-licking type or hide behind the names of others, because he literally declined to fuck his way in and up (yea, that´s a true story), and not least because the recruiters (HR-departments or whoever) clearly didn´t understand what capacity they had in between their hands, then all of the 100+ job applications (which in quality was applauded by job-coaches) he sent out was rejected without even a shortlisting, and the applied jobs – confirmed by in-house sources – instead went to someone who either are only half of the capacity he sure is, simply because that hired someone had been namedropped and promised the job by someone within the incestuous organization even before the job add officially was posted (a posting which was just a formality because the democratic rules (at least in Denmark) dictate that all jobs are to be publicly posted), or because that someone who got hired didn´t mind to give the "right" individual an undreamt-of amount of thorough rim-jobs to get the job that my guy in a decent setting should and would´ve had. Yea, he could´ve used his contacts, and told them what they didn´t but surely would like to know, but without even being invited in the door then that itself simply would conflict with and compromise some of his greatest – both personal and external – assets, and thus also his high loyalty and strong integrity.

"To be fair", to prove a point, he finally pulled some strings in his network and thus got shortlisted and hence was invited to an interview for a position in a special intelligence unit, where he together with four others had been "picked" from field of 250+ applicants. But at the job interview, *all* his potential "superior"

wanted to know was whether or not he literally would be willing to be the "superior´s" personal punching bag bitch, to which my man in all honesty replied, that he would be willing to take all the critique coming his way, and work round-the-clock without time for sleep if necessary, as long as the critique would be merited *and* constructive, and as long as the work tasks would be meaningful, and that that promise would stand for at least as long as he didn´t have a family at home to also take good care of. Guess that "superior" didn´t found that answer to be submissive enough, a point was proved, and "my friend" moved on to other battle fields – on which he anyway later for the record – according to himself – unfortunately had to surrender and give up on his own heroic values, and as a sellout now finds himself trapped in "the hamster wheel" without space to be and nurture himself, in another position as an Intelligence Analyst specialized in the fields of Countering Organized Crime and Terrorism, at least up until his hopefully next adventure which hopefully awaits, in hopefully more creative and less squared settings, when he hopefully manages to break free and find back home to his own self again, hopefully before his "democratic" indoctrination prevails. And now, until further, only hope(fully) of something else is what keeps him going.
And that´s "just" a "tiny teaser" piece of example of how e.g. honesty by far doesn´t always pay off in the current social structures, and a sneak peek into a few general mechanisms of the so called democracy right there for you (without – of course – that one "superior" representing all of democracy), a system which seemingly one way or the other either practice (im)morally reprehensibility, or at the expense of a good-natured moral heart doesn´t mind to undermine a thus unfulfilled – hence somewhat wasted – potential. And with "only" one world at hand, our forced only choices hence are to live with, fight to change, or die from it.
As the American journalist, Ezra Klein (1984), wrote: "*Corruptive systems overcome good individuals with ease*", and unfortunately

nepotism and favoritism (in mechanism a.k.a. corruption) is just one of several unhealthy issues haunting our current social structures – our cultures, and thus only one "minor" example to now leave behind as we move on to take on other presumably even vitally more unhealthy issues thoroughly under treatment in the following chapters.

In honor of my old profession in the movies, also I here *could* try to state an '*Authors* Intentions Statement' in the same fashion as the before mentioned 'Directors Intentions Statement', but since the book then thus would finish now even before it really started, and due to me not being famous with crack licking fans on my side, at least not yet, then I – in that case deserved – probably would just be taken a joke in doing so, and for sure I then also – opposed to reality – would be straight up lying, as I unlike the mentioned director, *do* feel to have plenty of meaningful intentions and good non-selfish reasons for writing this book.

Shit´s about to get real, it´s time for a serious showdown with the so called competition state – first and foremost the mindset favoring the competition state, which is a term for how some people (and thereof states) in our post-modern world battles and competes each other – and drags everybody else into their dirty battle – on e.g. economic growth for primarily an ego based sake of growth, etc. In doing so, a multi-levelled unhealthy competition has been created, and as a result our natural environment and otherwise healthy human values are being neglected at the expense of paltry materialism, cold-hearted selfishness, and not least greedy hunger for money and power, as a resource to control in a world thus currently dominated by small-minded people with big egos.

Simultaneously with the decreasing lack of humanity that are spreading (diffusing) like rings in water among us humans, the post-modern humans, the people, we are commonly degrading to be just individuals. The individuals are to a corresponding increasing extend collectively stroke by individual inferiority complexes, a.k.a.

low self-worth, and are thus driven by a compensating eagerly strive for asserting themselves through selfish gain and personal status in their constant pursuit to buff and boost their vain egos. Sadly, in our current societies, such an unhealthy strive isn´t really possible without compromising certain core moral values, including *honesty, kindness, solicitude, respect,* and *compassion* for others. This development is growingly embedded into the majority of the individuals and has thus led to a situation where that minority who still firmly believes in and lives by the principles of those core moral values in general by the majority are being perceived to be naïve cheesy hippies, and in even more extreme cases as carriers of a "loser-mentality". However, in reality, if lowering the guards and strike and light a match to narrowminded primitive prejudices, then who are de facto the real losers here, is it the ones who *thinks* that they´re tough while blindfoldedly presenting themselves as a predatorial product who shortsighted only cares about themselves and their own personal "winnings" at the expense of everything and everyone else, or is the ones who actually truly cares about a greater good for all and everything – the ones who with open eyes are tough enough to go up against the stream by actually being honest, kind, respectful, and compassionate, even when others around them aren´t? Au contraire of the somewhat common perception of success, there should be no doubt about the answer to this question, and if you don´t have it yet, then – unless you´re an idiot – I´m sure you at the latest will be closer to the better answer by the end of this book; stay tuned.

Despite I've travelled to many places around the world, then most of my life has played out in a western world context which thus of course rubs off on my approach, but since I likewise of course am very aware about the many differences in the landscapes around the globe, then I nevertheless in the following intend and hence aim to address my words to as far as possible fit a general context in the representation of those relevant mechanisms which somewhat

universally are valid across all continents, and hence more or less all cultures of our planet – despite it might go beyond common praxis of all.
Hardly any topic is small enough to fit only one book if to be taken thoroughly under care in all its detail, why I therefore base much of the following journey on certain selected impacting nodal points. And so, should you by any chance have a problem with my chain of equivalence, or feel that I am not being specific or detailed enough in some of my social relevant, psychological, philosophical, technological, or scientific examples, points and explanations, should my semantics play with your perception and conceptual framework, or should any of the non-personal narratives and topics raise concrete questions within yourself, then as a start feel free to view every incident of question as an open invitation for you to later look further into the specific topic(s) on your own.
You have a free will to the third pill.
Hit it.

1. Enlightenment is Key

Like many before and after me, in my younger days (although I still as a 'generation Y (millennial)'[13] am "only" in my late thirties (Ed. "the new twenties" – when I wrote this that is)) I immaturely used to believe in the need for a global physical revolution, a need for overthrowing the world´s ruling powers by physical force to thereby end their demonized tyranny which throughout history and still today is the root-cause to the skewed uneven distribution of wealth and wellbeing in the world. And should you in this regard by any chance think that this uneven distribution "just" is a natural consequence of the masses not standing up for themselves, then yes, you´re partly right, although it still is no excuse for anyone to take advantage of anybody less fortunate. However, although revolutions throughout history have proven to be an effective mean to overthrow ruling powers, at least on a regional scale, e.g. the Russian revolution, the French revolution, the Cuban revolution, parts of the Arab spring, etc., then they still didn´t really impact enough to convincingly accumulate a much better outcome on a global scale.

Today, approximately 868 million people in the world on a daily basis suffers from hunger, approximately 25 thousand people die every day because of hunger, approximately every 12. second a child starves to death, and never before in the history of the world has hundreds and hundreds of millions of people been killed in less than 100 years in the names of a few (relatively speaking) men´s war-thirst and greedy hunger for power. The world´s richest and hence – in some ways – most powerful one percent currently holds approximately half of the world, while more than half of the world´s population live in poverty or even extreme poverty. On top of that, we´re now witnessing critically global climate changes which

[13] A term for people born in the years between 1980-1994.

potentially can have ultimate fatal consequences for all life on Earth, and still the ruling powers are not taking the significantly needed actions because what has to be done to save our planet obviously conflicts with their own personal – selfish and – power-related interests; some diabolic individuals don´t care about the nature of the world and future generations, and obviously driven by stupidity still perversely thinks that they can eat, drink, and breathe money. I mean, if these facts which sadly are just small drops in an ocean of hard facts doesn´t stir up and invite for the masses to take action, then It definitely should be fair to state that *if* the masses, the people of the world, would ever come together and stand up and organize a physical revolution against the world´s oppressing ruling powers, then they probably already would have done it by now.
Other thoughts I had, as alternatives to the thought of a global physical revolution, was e.g. the advantages of a global deadly biological virus pandemic, a nuclear war to also confirm our stupidity, or major natural catastrophes – e.g. volcanic eruptions, massive earthquakes, or a meteor[14] (or asteroid[15] or comet[16]) impact bigger than the one which eradicated the dinosaurs, and hence one that would make sure to wipe out all current human existence. One such could then reset our whole world and give it a fresh start and a new chance to recover from the human destruction to once again blossom in all its beauty, and thereby by evolution give future life – a.k.a. future civilizations – a new chance to do better than we do with what we amazingly got. However, on a second reflection, history has a way of repeating itself, so who knows if life with a fresh start anyway would "just" relapse and evolve into making the exact same mistakes all over again – "we"

---

[14] What´s left of a Meteoroid after burning up through the Earth´s atmosphere, primarily of rocky material.

[15] A large rocky body, smaller than a planet but considerably larger than a Meteoroid.

[16] A cosmic snowball of frozen gasses, rock and dust.

probably would. Also, for the record, I of course have absolutely no wish of seeing all life vanish on a "no-reassurance-chance", as life truly is one of few – if not the one and only – existing miracles which we´re blessed and honored enough to take part in and witness the beauty of. Just imagine how powerful living creatures on Earth are, that we not only are a proof of intelligent life in the universe, but that we also have the ability to actually create life ourselves. If that´s not truly amazing in all its glory, then I don´t know what is. For sure, the world would be a better place if certain individuals were no longer here, e.g. those with 'destructivity' "as middle name", active pedophiles, dangerous psychopaths, and other cruel and disrespectful individuals, no doubt, but to wish for all life on Earth to end for the sake of life on Earth immediately seems like quite a contradictory and less desirable solution to the problems[17] in our world. Nevertheless, with our current destructive behavior – in fact the presumably most destructive force to ever hit Earth, human destructivity, the conditions surrounding this question might change in the future if we e.g. eventually succeed in ruining and making our beautiful planet uninhabitable, or if – more likely when – something else beyond our knowledge and control happens.

But until further, we for now surely have all reason to fight for life, our existence, and hence the preservation of civilization, cause, if we fail to secure consciousness, then also everything our lifeline stand for will be futile, together with everything the future can still achieve to become based on same.

My above presented thoughts of physical revolutions, pandemics, and natural catastrophes though changed when I in my early thirties by choice finally had a serious revival at university, and only just then finally came across one of my now all-time favorite authors, the man, the myth, the legend, I kid you not, the German philosopher, Immanuel Kant (1724-1804).

---

[17] Despite me using the word 'problem' for the sake of common lingual simplicity, then remember that problems doesn´t really exist, challenges only.

On a side note, to elaborate on why it from an old-fashioned perspective untraditionally took me more than thirty years to finally enroll and do great at university: I´m not from a family with piano, some would say I had a troublesome upbringing, and academia were definitely not in my blood – I´m the first ever on both sides of my bloodline. I never took school seriously, I hardly ever opened a book until after my teen years, and yet here I am. Thus, feel free to use my narratives as inspiration, don´t allow for social heritage to define you, with the right mindset you surely can go from ghetto through growth to glory; life´s a lifelong learning process, and since we should all strive to live our lives until the very last moment, then it´s *never* too late to learn, to educate yourself, to overcome your fears, and to change lane in life if that´s what it takes for you to grow and realize yourself – liberate and redeem yourself; one of my biggest worries is to become one of those people who hates their lives, who e.g. calls their wife the "bitch at home" or their husband the "wussy son of a bitch they should never have betted on", and who without passion in life are spending most of their time counting the days up until their retirement – although such a depressing lifestyle paradoxically entails strongly reduced chances of even making it through to retirement.

Many have a tendency of creating negative thoughts, not only toward their external world but also their internal, they might think about themselves as no good for nothing, that they´re forced to work the shitty job they hate instead of sticking their necks out for what they rather want. They might be afraid to try new things, to take a chance, and to risk anything, to e.g. parachute themselves into realizing that idea they might dream about, or to ask that special someone out on a date, or to say something as simple as 'no' if merited, or whatever the fuck it is. What´s the worst that can happen, and is that then really worse than "living" a life where you aren´t really living – according to *your* passion? Inspired by words from the legendary Danish Author, Theologist, Poet, Teacher, Priest,

Philosopher, Historic, Bishop, Philologist, Debater, and Politician, N. F. S. Grundtvig (1783-1872), hang onto passion all throughout life, as life´s a long process towards becoming human. Make the switch from "I got to, to I get to" – from I do wish to I did; dare to follow the dream rather than bowing down for the fear.

From a metacognitive [18] standpoint, at large our sometimes interfering worries are rooted in mere hypotheses we´ve build up within ourselves, hypotheses that dictates that we aren´t able stop or at least control our worries, and thus hypotheses through which we hence like enforce upon ourselves a locked position. However, questioning the utility of our hypotheses, our worries, it often shows that it actually isn´t our worries that is the actual problem, the problem is that we fool and thereby convince ourselves that our worries are uncontrollable, and that we thus *have* to keep hanging on to ´em to fight and pursue to control ´em, rather than actually learning how to overcome ´em and "just simply" to let go of ´em. Not that you should stop caring, and of course not all worries are useless, but when innate rationality becomes irrational, then *"what is it good for, absolutely nothing"*[19].

If you´re not pleased with where you are in life then see to make the necessary changes, release yourself from your invisible chains, and repeat after me: "Wishes do come true, but only if I actively make an effort to follow them". No obstacles or tribulations are unsurpassable, and no excuses are acceptable. Be curious, courageous[20], and indomitable, always.

Backtrack to what I was saying related to Immanuel Kant; luckily, Kant´s words came into my life as one of my "roads to Damascus", and thus partly became my rescue from my desperate thoughts of

---

[18] Cognitive is our thoughts, and metacognitive is thinking about what we´re thinking.

[19] As song by Edwin Starr in War.

[20] *"Courage is resistance to fear, mastery of fear – not absence of* fear", as explained by Mark Twain (1835-1910).

violence as the only solution capable of providing the needed changes to the world´s social structures – at least his words helped to catalyze my thoughts towards convincing myself about Enlightenment as being the most lacking yet wisest and most sufficient and sustainable feature needed in order for us humans to regain our agency and autonomy, simplified a.k.a. self-determination, and the strength and ability to act accordingly.
As the master himself, Kant, opens one of his masterpieces, 'An Answer to the Question: What is Enlightenment? (1784)':
"Enlightenment is man´s emergence from his self-incurred immaturity. Immaturity is the inability to use one´s own understanding without the guidance of another. This immaturity is self-incurred if its cause is not lack of understanding, but lack of resolution and courage to use it without the guidance of another. The motto of enlightenment is therefore: Sapere aude! [Dare to be wise!] *Have courage to use your own understanding!*
Laziness and cowardice are the reasons why such a large proportion of men [and all other genders], *even when nature has long emancipated them from alien guidance (naturaliter maiorennes* [Those who have come of age by virtue of nature]), *nevertheless gladly remain immature for life. For the same reasons, it is all too easy for others to set themselves up as their guardians. It is so convenient to be immature! If I have a book* [or any other kind of media for that matter, I say, in a 21st century context] *to have understanding in place of me, a spiritual advisor to have conscience for me* [e.g. related to a religious authority, or perhaps a life coach or so], *a doctor* [or e.g. a dietitian or a nutritionist or a personal trainer, etc.] *to judge my diet for me, and so on, I need not make any efforts at all. I need not think, so long I can pay; others will soon enough take the tiresome job over for me. The guardians who have kindly taken upon themselves the work of supervision will soon see to it that by far the largest part of mankind (including the entire fair sex) should consider the step forward to maturity not only as difficult*

but also as highly dangerous. Having first infatuated their domesticated animals, and carefully prevented the docile creatures [a.k.a. sheep, as I clarify shortly] *from daring to take a single step without the leading-strings to which they are tied, they next show them the danger which threatens them if they try to walk unaided. Now this danger is not in fact so very great, for they would certainly learn to walk eventually after a few falls. But an example of this kind is intimidating, and usually frightens them off from further attempts".*

1.2. Sheep or Shepherd

We´re all subjects to power structures, since we were kids we have been taught when, where, and how to do what. This is broadly considered a "normal" part of an "cultivated" upbringing, and for many this learning process in itself paradoxically probably constitutes the foundation for why they never learned to take charge of and responsibility for their own life, and partly why it has become their nature to partake in an unnecessary latter of hierarchy whereon they sadly spend their lives licking upwards and kicking downwards.

We´re all born into 'du contrat social', a.k.a. 'the social contract', an unwritten collective agreement which in thought state that people as part of a society automatically but still willingly should have to give up part of their personal freedom and hand it over to a superior ruler, elitist guardians, shepherds, or whatever else you wish to call those "in charge" of our world, in return for "protection" and other various "benefits" that thus comes from being a member of a society. We´re hence born as constrained people, a.k.a. sheep, ergo sheeple (hybrid of sheep and people), and it´s therefore entirely up to ourselves to renegotiate or completely cancel this catbird seat contract.

The only difference between a shepherd and an idiot with a stick is whether or not the sheep(le) follows him.
You have to wake up and understand and realize and make up with the fact that you have to engage yourself in yourself, and then – in the names of solidarity and compassion – also positively and unselfishly in others for that matter, depending on how much they welcome your engagement, and not least depending on how much you´re able to give of yourself without compromising, breaking, or slaying your own peace (balance is legend (as treated in a later chapter)). We all need a safe-haven, and if you have no better nouns to turn to then at least as far as possible try to make 'yourself' yours. Too many people don´t look further than the tip of their own nose (feel free to feel the reproof merited), and they either lack the ability or simply refuse to mentalize[21], a.k.a. to put themselves in the shoes of others to thereby better understand what they might immediately cannot see, the motivation, frustration, tribulation, struggle and pain, within others around them; the anxious find everyone else wild, and the wild find everyone else boring. Even a happy face can be a cover for sorrow, the tears which you cannot see are the ones that hurts the most, and the ones which obviously are the hardest to wipe away. Just because you don't see and feel what I feel – my pain, it doesn't give you "carte blanc" to mock or walk all over me, and to rub salt in my wound. Maybe it´s asking for too much, for the impossible for some, but I so much would wish for these non-mentalizing people, and not least their surroundings, that they would be able to expand and broaden their horizon and understanding, at best all the way and at least a little, and then their kids a bit more, and then their kids´ kids (grandkids) a little more again, and so on, until we eventually get "there".

[21] Mentalization is by sympathetic insight to put yourself in the shoes of another or others, to thereby better understand and thus hopefully achieve empathy for that or them or theirs.

Too many people are always negatively on the hunt for weakness in others because they themselves in their own character – or lack of same – are too weak to feel powerful enough from within. They like to see you a mess simply to pray on your misery as company for their own ditto. Only too often such people are deceived by their own ignorant eagerness which misleadingly guides them to misinterpret and take advantage of a kind heart and good intentions, and they among others – as the human amateurs they are – tend to expose themselves by an unfair and unhealthy habit of mistaking kindness for weakness. As a mean to boost their own low self-confidence, low self-worth, and hence weak egos, a.k.a. to elevate themselves, it becomes like an obsession for these pitiless individuals – even subconsciously – to feast from others like boundless bloodthirsty freeloading vampires, who without scruples constantly seeks to suck all life out of their philanthropical surroundings; it´s the cup inside that is – at least close to – empty, and no matter how much you fill in it, then you´ll never be able to sustainably fill up the cup if there´s hole in the bottom, and even more impossible if your own resources has already been drained. The thing is, these people simply – and sadly – lost their spark (a.k.a. mojo) somewhere along the way, they might lost it before they even remember, they might lost it little by little on their journey in life, they might lost it as a consequence of a specific incident or situation, they might or might not be able to find it again (hopefully they will), they might need help to find it, they might need *your* help to find it. Nevertheless, none of us has any right to claim anyone else´s spark, and ruthless exploitation on a spark helps at max no more than peeing your own pants for heat – a quick fix which (likewise in a setting of more wanting more) quite quickly will worsen whatever was aimed to solve; the junkie way won´t make your day, at least not in the long run, okay; true you should live every day as if it´s your last, but remember to keep in mind that there´s a day yet again tomorrow. What feeds your soul probably isn´t letting other people

feed on it, and you losing your spark surely won´t in any way help either them or you – Definitely with a big D not you; sometimes you might even have to burn a bridge of strife to make a positive switch in life. Don´t allow for other people to eat you up, don´t let them kill your spark, especially not if you´re an highly (a.k.a. hyper) sensitive empath, cause then you´re unfortunately directly playing with fire in the shape of your own fatality; listen to yourself, be good to yourself, stand up for yourself, and *then* with generosity help others as much as you possibly can without losing yourself – without exceeding your own boundaries and limitations, and thus thereby abusing yourself; in the same spirit as with the safety-instructions we´re taught on board airplanes (and yea yea yea, I know that it´s one of the most used examples in modern literature – ad nauseam, but it´s nevertheless still one of the best examples in this context): "In case the cabin pressure drops, oxygen-masks will drop down from the panels in the ceiling above your seat, and it´s thus essential that you make sure to don and adjust your own mask before helping others put on *their* mask". Because, if you don´t, and instead prioritize to help others before helping yourself, if you allow for others to take advantage of you, you in fact might end up compromising the whole situation by losing your own consciousness – yourself – or worse, and your potential to do a difference that matters for both yourself and others thus simply vanish, and hence goes to waste.
Thus, most often in life you´re like obliged to help and be for yourself before you´re able to help and be anything for anyone or anything else, just like you also have to be able to love and validate yourself before you properly are able to validate and love any other – cause how can *you* anyway do anything as you if you already lost yourself. And for the very same reason, as well as you being the only one truly feeling what you feel, you should not always look externally to fix whatever is troubling you internally, introspection and connected reflection is a paramount must. Although I agree

that it often is easier to look out than in (guess the eyes point out for a reason), that self-knowledge is harder to obtain than it is to have opinions about everything and everyone other than yourself, which I assume has to do with our integrated emotional filter, then the easy way is not always the right way, especially not if the view out causes the ability to look in to be caught in a blind angle – by hypocritically judging others for what you should but don´t see in yourself.
Of course, you can seek for and make use of your entrusted, experts, or sponsors, to guide you in whatever specific area you might need help, and for sure your self-revelation shouldn´t turn into unnecessary selfishness, but the message here rather is that you-me-we should never allow for anyone other than ourselves to be in charge of our motivational driving forces in life, a.k.a. who we are and what we stand for, a.k.a. ourselves; you can marinade yourself in external advises and inspiration all you want, but be cautious about not drowning your internal "I" in the marinade.
When people submit themselves to their paternalistic shepherds and degrades to sheeple the mechanism is e.g. the same as when a long-term prisoner or someone who served in the military for a long time is being released, they suddenly find themselves too institutionalized to grasp how to deal with their own free choice. They´ve been used to prison guards, higher ranking prison gang members, or higher ranking commanding officers, like grownups to a child, down to even the smallest detail telling them how, where, and when they had to do what, which moreover likewise easily applies to many 'boss-employee' and "romantic" relationships as well. Same sadly in general goes for conform sheeple in society – in the institution society has become, although they "only" more hiddenly are being manipulated and guided, a.k.a. indoctrinated, a.k.a. brainwashed; as times goes by the sheeple increasingly sees freedom as exponentially more scary than restraints, and their increasing urge for being in cahoots with (a) rigorous system(s) thus

equally increasingly as an often unaware compensation for lost autonomy makes them extremely obstinate – to pull their own lacks and limitation down over the head(s) of their surroundings, the surroundings which represent what they´ve lost themselves, and what they thus aren´t capable of handling and hence digesting; if only they could and would accept that and what they don´t understand, work on their weaknesses, and grow according to natures plan – the greater good positive potential through their personal ditto.

Unfortunately, the majority of the people – the sheeple – in our world seems to have become only passengers in their own existence – like plastic bags in the wind. They underperform in stepping up and being true to their own authentic a-game, they hate it when real authenticity outshines their conformity, herd-ish populism, and futile personalities, and with a chip on their shoulder tops widespread many – warmongers – in frustration attempt to compensate their impotence by showcasing a self-nominated and self-appointed title of "street-sheriff" – which in term covers how their own neurotic apprehensive anxiety according to their manipulated messed up mind through a self-imagined alpha-mandate obliged by force has to be normative on all and everything in the world around them. Hence, from a somewhat indoctrinated rigid fascistic mindset, the main concern for the majority thus sadly have become to impose and enforce their own self-inflicted miserable limitations down on every genuine automotive free-spirit coming their way, those who the majority outside their own strongly limited and stringent comfort zone of tension in their own thus overt ignorance ridiculed in fallacy tend to view as provocatively apathetic laissez-faire, dishonorable, and unethical rioting insubordinates; it´s easy to hate (or fear or both) what you don´t understand – what´s outside the limited echo chamber of your comfort zone, and envy is an ugly feature, "street-sheriff", you might fight to see yourself as a hero in your own story but your inhibition secure you status of no more than a pathetic choleric hemorrhoid in everyone else´s; I understand that you fear changes, and I´ll help protect you where I can, but no need to pursue universal limitations according to your own ditto. And no, the 'gabos' ('Game Ain´t Based on Sympathy') code ain´t cool, rather it´s a human tragedy, to be ruthless or to be or behave like a psycho ain´t cool, it´s a transparent cover for mental damage and weakness, an unprofitable and unsustainable poor substitute for accepting and dealing with whatever demons are made of. I understand why some feel it a necessity to make a mark of themselves to fit in and to not be perceived an easy target bitch – to not carry an asshole open for business – in a dog-eat-dog environment where the rules of norms in more than one sense might be to fuck or be fucked. Nevertheless, only few in "'gabos dominated environments" actually are and like how they behave anyway, most merely are sorry ass products of the seriously sick sorry ass few tyrants who in their behavior analogically scratches their knuckles on the ground when they walk, and here weakness thus is to bow down for the primitivity rather than showing true power by overcoming and hence not becoming what you damn well deep down know ain´t right; from fatal position when no one´s looking to bullying playing hardball when others are around, only to impress the few or your own low level, or simply don´t own sympathy at all, overcompensation or not, you know it ain´t right, cuz. And every excuse e.g. involving "the pain I´ve gone through" is straight up worthless if that "excuse" is just an excuse to cause pain, just as every call for respect is like eating water with a fork (a.k.a. a damn joke) if the sought respect relies on disrespect; "*Whoever fights monsters should see to it that in the process he* [or she, or whatever gender] *does not become a monster*"[22]. Cool if you really are on top of your game – where you-me-we all at best always should find ourselves to be, but no need to be putting anyone down

[22] Quote by Friedrich Nietzsche (1844-1900).

for the exact same reason. I e.g. have authentic 1:1 four starred general (the highest rank in Denmark) shoulder marks tatted on my shoulders, not because I per se am above anyone, but because I most definitely ain´t under. There´s the queen bee, and there´re the working bees, and I´ve not been brought into this world to be anyone´s working bee; I´ve not been brought into this world to act fluffer for anyone. Trying to showcase strength by unmerited peace preventing infliction is in action just personal exposure of the antonym [23] of genuine strength, as with quicksand, the more disturbing and stirring you are the more you sink and the lower you are; add ease, "street-sheriff". Even if a tyrant might be nice to you then still remember: *"A person who is nice to you, but rude to the waiter, is not a nice person"*[24], and *"Being kind to someone, only to look kind to others, defeats the purpose of being kind"*[25].

One thing is that a riveting leading alpha is somewhat important in laying the foundation for a movement, but it´s the first follower (or sceptic) who legitimate (or illegitimate) the movement who is the most important – the potentially single point of failure. Therefore, be aware of your power, and of who and what you support.

The right move leads toward a combo of peace, compassion, and freedom, the real ballsy move is the right route to secure the right move, and to shut down only them who prevent it, to take the stand of turning a negative atmosphere of a bad environment into ambience of what right is – to turn a bad environment from bad back to good, to make good better, or at a minimum to make sure that an already healthy environment *stays* healthy. Not that you should "street-sheriff" the "street-sheriffs", or become one of the sorry ass few tyrants – no one owns patent on the right to opinions and personal procedures, rather you should have the mindset of and be a role model example of a respectful game changing

---

[23] The diametrical opposite of something (here of strength, hence weakness).

[24] Quote by the American writer, Dave Barry (1947-).

[25] Quote by the American writer, Shannon L. Alder.

freedom-fighter, in the sense of the word certified fight for equitable freedom all across the board; don´t be scared nor supercilious, don´t be subservient nor disrespectful, be humble without being shy, be proud without being arrogant, own confidence without haughtiness, respect all, fear none, fearless justice and righteousness. If you don´t stand up for yourself, you´re easily giving in to everything. Fine you´re among the few, but let it be the present day few who actually believe in and defend compassioned freedom; unnecessary restraints are de facto *un*healthy, *"Not because I´m unfit for punishment/But because I´m too fit for it"*[26] – a.k.a. not because I´m too insane not to be curbed but because I´m too sane to be, and still "they" (society and tyrants (hence including shepherds and whoever following their footsteps)) without understanding it yet again, and again, and again, and what feels like infinite again, tries to tame and tie me down; don´t restrain, attack, and antagonize my health, don´t diminish my worth, I die before surrendering, I think to myself, cause if not I´m already dead, and instead of not living, I rather die trying.

Don´t lose your internal control, just make sure to be free from "their" external control, and despite there of course is a moral limit to acceptable behavior then there´s also a threshold of de minimis – a limit to your unnecessary perfidiousness, "street-sheriff", no need to be the "human" version of an unnecessary migraine; *"You want it to be one way* [...] *But it´s the other way"*[27], and not rarely that´s the third way.

Some might now think that I´m a bit hypocritical in the way I criticize "streets-sheriffs" while almost in the same breath likewise are telling you what to and don´t do. Well, here the main difference is

[26] My directly translated quotation from words by the Danish-Palestinian poet, Yahya Hassan (1995-2020).

[27] Spoken by the drug kingpin character, Marlo Stanfield, to a working-class security guard watching and confronting him, in the g.o.a.t. (greatest of all time) tv-show, 'The Wire' (2002-2008).

that while "street-sheriffs" – and all kinds of unhealthy shepherds – lives to limit or completely block other people´s personal unfolding, then I reversed aim to create passage and encourage people, you, and especially sheeple, to break down barriers, to break out, and to unfold – as long as it doesn´t directly cause any avoidable damage, suffering, and despair, on anyone else than those who otherwise immorally gain from your defeat.

In regard to "street-sheriffs", what many tend to overlook – especially themselves – is that many of them – if not all – are radicalized extremists associated with and connected to some of the same mechanisms as other kinds of terrorists, the only thing that really separates them from the "common" perception of a deadly terrorists is that they instead of killing people directly most often more slowly do it with psychological violence, a.k.a. psychological terrorism. A bit like when perpetrators of physical or sexual abuse often proves to have been victims of same themselves, instead of recognizing that what they with horror were exposed to was wrong, they confused inflict and pass on the same suffering to *their* victims. Again, the motivational mechanisms are the same.

Humans are habitual creatures, and on top of that they (a.k.a. we) in a general context are comfort addicted; in relation to the majority´s "own personal" lives, too many are too lazy to think for themselves, too many are too much of a coward to take proper responsibility for themselves and to support their surrounding innovativeness, and too many are too frighten to step up and forward in making any unconventional decisions and take any groundbreaking actions of and on their own. Instead, they immaturely, as the apathetic degenerate sheep they are, find it pleasantly convenient to entrust their tiresome troubles to what can be perceived their dictating aristocratic elitist guardians, and their thus thereby paternalistic shepherds, e.g. their superior, religious, or spiritual authorities, governmental leaders and their henchmen, greedy banks, large corporations, biased medias, and corrupt scientists (yea, many scientists are actually on the payroll and in the pocket of certain political forces and businesses who thus pay these scientists to tailor their speculations and results to favor certain interests and agendas), etc. – the mechanisms of power lust and greed can be found across just about all settings and branches where humans are involved. I´m hereby not saying that all superiors and spiritual authorities have a bad influence, or that all politicians have bad intentions, or that all scientists are corrupt – cause they´re not, all I´m saying is that this surely without a doubt is the case for an overwhelming too huge proportion of them. Unlike with large commercial corporations, and especially the banks, cause yea, no known exceptions, they sadly are all greedy embezzling rascal bastards, who literally couldn't´ t care less about anything else than the smell of profit and realization of their infinite cynical "ambitions", and their ill lust for profit and power indeed debauch their sense of humanity and morality – which in this context is as good as non-existing. And in relation to biased medias, obviously most medias are quite transparent in regard to their political or ideological stands – open eyes and ears are most often all it takes, and even if they´re not, then still no one genuinely are objective enough to go free from the inevitable biased subjectivity literally involved whenever and wherever humans are involved (and this book thus obviously is no exception). Hence, be aware of your sources, and for the love of love don´t let merely shitty journalism – with click-bate articles and infomercials being among the worst (probably only topped by disguised adverts and commercials, which by the way almost always makes me defiant enough to not even wanna touch the commercial product with a fire-tongs) – or purely personal interpretations and thus distortions of e.g. "holy" scripts, to be the defining factor for your entire world view; don´t believe everything you hear and read, source criticism and not least a healthy skepticism is key. A 2018 study from Massachusetts Institute of Technology (MIT) e.g. *"found that falsehood diffuses significantly farther, faster, deeper, and more broadly than the truth, in all categories of information*" on social medias, that "*false news stories are 70 percent more likely to be* [forwarded[28]] *than true stories are*", and that "*it takes true stories about six times as long to reach 1500 people as it does for false stories to reach the same number of people*". Like the Colombian philosopher, Nicolás Gómez Dávila (1913-1994), expressed it: "*In a century where the media publish endless stupidities, the cultured man* [or any cultured gender] *is defined not by what he knows but by what he ignores*"; not enough equals uninformed, too much equals misinformed. Enlightenment isn´t merely about amount of information, it´s about – useful – wisdom, quality above quantity.

Moreover, you generally always should be wary of written communication (ironically hereby stated in a piece of writing), as various studies has found that approximately a quarter of all SMS[29] is misunderstood by the receiver, and that almost half of all e-mails can be misunderstood, which thus also besides keeping a critical approach to what you read further should be an extra reason for you to perhaps consider to be even more clear in what you write, and to exert yourself in how you read and interpret text(s) before making your conclusive judgements.

The German philosopher, Friedrich Nietzsche (1844-1900), once said: "*A politician divides mankind into two classes: tools and enemies*". Apart from a very, very, *very* few exceptions (those exceptionally few who actually do value and favor common goods over personal "winning"), I without hesitation am more than willing to agree with Nietzsche on this matter, while further addingly having to emphasize that the very same most certainly goes in every single case of an unhealthy shepherd.

---

[28] An easy recognizable term of a specific social media has been excluded here to not render unnecessary marketing.

[29] Short message service, ergo text-messages.

Indubitably, there´s always going to be a catch when the elitist guardians, the shepherds, offers their "assistance" without openly asking for an exchange of "favor", although they undoubtedly would wish you to believe that "catch" is just a "potty deserted ghost town in Russia". Ironically speaking, all you humbly have to give the shepherds in return is your submission, subjection, and obedience, perhaps your electoral vote, or perhaps to buy their product, or to "just" pay what they consider to be minor inconsiderable economical fees – e.g. unreasonable interest rates (which morally illogically improves the more resources you have, and worsen the less you have), campaign contributions, or perhaps underserved fines, for their troubles of saving you from yourself; after all, they *do* work intensively to control you, to keep you down, or at least to stay above you, and their special privileges, golden handshakes, and extravagant lifestyles, for sure doesn´t "come cheap" or pays themselves.

Hence, while the ignorant people from almost all walks of life deceive themselves to believe that they through their own submission are as cozy as a plum in an toasty egg, they in fact are mere self-inflicted slaves of their own dosser laziness and cowardice, a.k.a. stupidity, whom easily are being pimped and played by their shepherds like cheap hoe chess-pieces in a red-light game of chess. As the French Psychologist and Philosopher, Michel Foucault (1926-1984), once spoke: *"A stupid despot may constrain his slaves with iron chains; but a true politician binds them even more strongly by the chain of their own ideas* [...] *on the soft fibers of the brain is founded the unshakable base of the soundest of Empires"*.

This is roughly more or less how the pyramid of our current social structures are constructed, and hence how the wheels of the world run. Sadly, this currently is the rule rather than the exception.

If you freely give away your autonomy, then *you* as you simply are in control of fuck all, and that even include every cheap excuse of hypocritically blaming anyone else for your self-inflicted misery; in spirit of O.G. indigenous “mythological goddess symbol” of the Americas, Corn Mother[30], you reap as you sow. And when accepting for such devasty to thrive, by letting a contemptible immoral bunch of perfidious, abhorrent, and deceitful Machiavellian[31] and Sun Tzu[32] inspired shepherds to dictate and control every step of your sacred one and only life – without sequels or after life, then instead of allowing for your own full personal potential to blossom through the fertilizer of freedom, your world is being reduced to nothing less than what figuratively speaking can be associated with and described as a big open prison, or a – mazed – sheepfold if you prefer, and this in a both physically and mentally sense, in which you as a part of the herd are the woolen inmate (sheep) controlled by fear and guilt, guarded by a maintaining sophisticated[33] agitating vocabulary as a substitute for the traditional rod and staff, and all in the name of the sophisticating warden´s (shepherd´s) and guards´ (shepherd henchmen´s) covert greed for power and hence control. Again, rather than being a person of the people you´re hence reduced to a sheep of the sheeple.

---

[30] Among indigenous agricultural tribes in North America, the mythological figure of ‘Corn Mother’ was believed to be responsible for the origin of corn (maize), and she´s the conceptual representation of “you reap as you sow”.
[31] Without eating its calculated immorality raw, check out the book, ‘The Prince’, by Niccolò Machiavelli (1569-1527), if you want to know more of what I refer to (the book has a reputation as the unofficial gangster bible, but while being a gangster then obviously is connected to cynical machoism – in the mind of those wankstas who missed the point, a real man should be man and clever enough to non-enemy leniency, which hence also better matches “the men of honor” predicate authentic gangsters sworn to live by).
[32] ‘The Art of War’, a book by the Chinese general, Sun Tzu (approximately 500 BCE) (the book is by many considered a strategic masterpiece useful in e.g. warfare, politics, sports and business).
[33] From sophism: An imposter pretending to be smart by giving a preposterously “clever” but false arguments by e.g. a subtle language of fashionable fancy words deliberately used to deceive the receiver. Short said, a bullshitter offering nicely wrapped bullshit.

“What the fuck are you saying about me, what is this shit, I for sure ain´t no sheep, and I don´t allow for anyone to boss me around, hell no, and I don´t fear anybody or even anything at all”, you might think, and I then based on your self-proclaimed no-fear hallmark feature then could be prone enough to either find you completely blind, abnormally brave, or accuse you of being a stone cold fearless psychopath and whatnot, if it wasn´t because I luckily know better than that. Cause yea, if you´re blind there´s still hope and you just need to start listening – not just hearing but actually listen in order to understand. If you´re abnormally brave, I salute you while sending a warm warning of hubris. And although personality types that fits the human made criteria for defining a fearless psychopath (‘f60.2’, as the antisocial personality disorder (APD, or ASPD) diagnosis is called nowadays)[34] unfortunately do exist, and in spite of my degree in psychology – with highest honor, and despite my prior work with psychopathy, then I naturally could never from the distance or in advance tell whether or not you actually *are* among the two to four percent of all people who actually *are* considered psychopathic, or if you just like most simply don´t yet know yourself well enough to actually know all of your own fears.
Of course, it´s very important for us humans to possess fear as an innate defense-system against potential danger, cause if we don´t have fear we´ll most likely quite quickly die as a consequence of the

[34] Very simplified, there´s overall two ways to psychopathy: 1) Something or someone literally driving your mind mad. 2) Psychopathy is partly hereditary, if e.g. one of your parents has the psychopathy DNA then there´s approximately a 50% chance that you inherit the DNA as well, and no, even if both of your parents have the psychopathy DNA then it still isn´t certain that you inherited it. Furthermore, a but – a big but (for you not to worry if one of your parents actually are a psychopath), even though you have the psychopathy DNA then it still doesn´t mean that you actually are or will become a psychopath. To become a full-blown psychopath is most often a process where genes and environment comes together, an interaction wherein your environment might or might not trigger your innate genes to unfold.

damage we thus then probably constantly would expose ourselves to. However, on the contrary, being overly anxious definitely doesn't do much good either. Without neglecting our feelings, we have to train the strength of our minds to be able to handle our emotions in order for us to not lose ourselves; some fear death so much that they forget how to live – from time to time myself included, which paradoxically almost costed me my life, while also saved my life more than once. Like the Chinese martial artist, Bruce Lee (1940-1973), once spoke: "[...] *here is the natural instinct and here is control. You are to combine the two in harmony*". We surely would be better off if we consistently rationally would be able to understand and control our fear internally, and then only canalize it to where it makes the most rational sense according to the concrete situation instead of it occasionally take on character of an ingrown irrational burden – a strong currency of external control. By means of this, your own fear unfortunately can become a very useful and effective both strategical and tactical tool to use against you, "the people" – "the sheeple", which the ultraconservative former Chair of the Federal Reserve of the United States from 1987 to 2006, Alan Greenspan (1926-), in relation to manipulation and control of the people – again the sheeple – thus formulates as follows: "*Fear is a far more dominant force in human behavior than euphoria* [...] *it shows up in the data in so many ways*". Talk about cynicism... – and understand what you´re up against, when knowing Greenspan uses his data as a tool to manipulation[35].

[35] Try to consider that Greenspan actually has been honored by the Presidential Medal of *Freedom* (the highest civilian award in the US) – which among others is given for contribution to '*world peace*'. On top of everything else, this also should help illustrate how insane the world currently is.

"*If being a puppet of your lowest instincts* [including fear] *you´re easily puppeteered by whoever able to provoke them*"[36].
Let me give you some examples:
Several European studies independently concludes that what European citizens in a public setting fear more than anything else, except for the current catastrophic climate-changes, are Islamic terror-attacks, and that refugee migration will lead to more Islamic terror-attacks.
Thus, to put this fear to the test, I conducted a study – in fact my honored dissertation which concluded my Master of Science degree, and which became the first rigorous study to search and test for systematic relationships between drug crime (quite many terrorists tend to use drug crimes to finance their terror) and terrorism (terror-attacks, and terror-related-arrests), and migration and terrorism (terror-attacks and terror-related-arrests), in a Western European context. The data used in my study I mainly got from major players like Europol (The European Union Agency for Law Enforcement Cooperation), the UNODC (United Nations Office on Drugs and Crime), and the UNHCR (United Nations High Commissioner for Refugees), and the data covers the period from the year 2000 to 2017 (i.e. including post 9/11, the Arab spring, the Daesh caliphate, the war in Syria, etc.).
Among other groundbreaking conclusions, my study clearly illuminates statistically significant systematic relationships, a.k.a. significantly strong correlations, between drug crime and terrorism, and migration and terrorism. However, as opposed to the above mentioned fear, the study also surprisingly clearly reveals that despite seeing an increase in terror-attacks (or attempts of same) when drug crimes increases, and despite seeing an increase in terror-attacks (or attempts of same) when the numbers of migrants

[36] As spoken by The Stoic Emperor (some social media profile promoting self-made new thoughts which I couldn´t confirm the human identity of as the person behind the profile never replied my reaching outs).

– from mainly the Middle East and thereby Islam dominated countries – increases, then these terror-attacks (or attempts of same) are not mainly jihadi (Islamic) terror-attacks. Instead, these terror-attacks (or attempts of same) at large mainly are separatist and left- and right-wing terror-attacks (or attempts of same), and the attacks are thus to a larger extend rather politically motivated than rooted in religious motives – including the typically common denominator, Islam.

These results hence contradict the then quite irrational fear among the European citizens, and to further elaborate on the irrational aspect of the fear, then it should be useful to apply some perspectival and supporting numbers here: The chances of dying in a terror-attack has over the last decade in the United Kingdom been approximately one in 11.4 million per year, and in the United States approximately one in 20 million. By comparison, the risk of being killed by lightning is one in 10 million, the risk of drowning in your own bathtub is one in 800.000, and the risk of being killed in a car crash is one in 19.000.

I´m not saying that lethal terror-attacks are not extremely horrific, because they obviously are, and not to say that Islamic terror-attacks has never been carried out by refugee immigrants, cause they have – just as they´ve also been carried out by western coalitions or "friends" of same, etc. (to play it "fair"). Of course, some people actually are unfortunate enough to die in terror-attacks, and no doubt that every single person who´s killed in a terror-attack for sure is one too many; a BIG heartfelt rest in peace shout out to all innocent victims and their love ones (and here I´m not "only" referring to women and children, innocence is innocence), and love bless their souls.

Nonetheless, except if you´re actually living in a warzone or whatnot, then the chances of dying in a terror-attack still are so minimal compared to other lethal dangers and thus risk-factors that it seems quite irrational to have fear of Islamic terror to dominate our list of fears. The main "rational" root-cause reason behind this huge fear of being killed in specifically Islamic terror-attacks, and of refugee migration, hence hugely must be ascribed to the sophisticating work that e.g. governmental leaders and biased medias – shepherds and henchmen of same – distortedly puts in to popularize exactly this fear, and thereby create a public consensus about Islamic terror and migration being the general prime targets when talking about the greatest fears in the west.

In addition to the mentioned European example, the present biggest fear recorded among Americans is in a general context corruption of government officials. Yet, instead of acknowledging the problem and seriously take action against their present living nightmare, the Americans still remains passive spectators to all the lobbyism that are currently taking place in American politics (as is the case in and around politics all over the world), how politicians and their campaigns are sponsored and thereby bought by large corporations and rich people to favor certain agendas and personal interest, and how officials shuttle between official positions and top positions in the private sector – e.g. corrupt companies and thinktanks. At the top of "the power pyramid", everything and everybody coalesces while being an incestuous well-composed window-dressing ran by shady commissions. I mean, if this isn´t the essence of corruption, and if corruption is thus not already here, there, and everywhere, if the feared corruption is not already playing out in front of your very eyes, then the meaning of corruption *has* to be rephrased in the dictionary. In sum, this fear of corruption of government officials thus isn´t only irrational, it´s rather pathetic.

Another fear-related example to illustrate how irrational our rational fear in a postmodern context is, deals with the general number one personal fear among humans, nyctophobia, a.k.a. being afraid of the dark.

I personally don´t think I know a single person who would not have their amygdala – a.k.a. the brain´s fear and defense center – tricked at least a slightly bit if they e.g. found themselves walking around in a completely dark forest alone at night, even if they have a flashlight to see where they´re stepping. When the shadows get long, majestic trees that are amazingly beautiful in daylight quickly can transform into unrecognizable shady figures in the dark, especially when fear runs high.
The reason for this fear to be so widespread among humans dates all the way back to the stone age, approximately 100.000 years ago, which is when the basic features of the human brain evolved to become as they still are today. Although we humans have gained a lot more knowledge over the years then our brains still hasn´t developed much further since, and for this reason our brains rightfully today still have to be perceived as pretty ol´ school. Our "mental software" related to fear is thus still to this day programmed to run at a stone age level, which thus genetically still today causes us people to fear the same kinda things as we feared in the stone age, and back in the stone age the biggest threat to safety were wild nocturnal hunting animals lurking in the dark – nights simply meant terror in those days. Nevertheless, these days wild animals by far are no longer to be considered the biggest threat to humans, at least not for most of us who are not living in the "uncivilized" wilderness or on the savannah, and while most humans don´t really hang out or wanders around in the dark anyway, then the chances of actually bumping into life-threatening dangers in the woods at night – or in your dark basement, or in your dark closet, or wherever else your fear of darkness normally kicks in – are almost as good as zero. Talking from a Danish perspective, we don´t even have a single dangerous animal in our nature anymore – at the top of our animal food chain we have wolfs who runs off even before humans get to lay eyes on them, and next in line deers who are just about as harmless as brown eyed Bambi herself. And still

fear of darkness continuously dominates the Danish statistics of personal fears.

From a rational perspective, what we e.g. *should* be more worried about is traffic, the number one non-disease-related killer in the world (add to that that industrial air pollution (including pollution from fossil fueled traffic) actually according to new studies currently kills even more people than car crashes (we´ll touch upon pollution in a later chapter)). To check out how real danger looks like, then you just have to take a look at the post-modern jungle of rush hour traffic, how cyclist and motorcycles rushes in and out between moving cars that are often driving too fast with inattention behind the wheels, while the real predators of today, trucks and busses, are only one misjudgment or overlooked detail away from making mincemeat out of everything coming their way. And still hardly no one thinks twice about going into traffic – notwithstanding day or night.

Postmodern humans, you-me-we, generally don´t understand the most relevant dangers of our surroundings, and we´re thus not really on top of our own fears. If we *truly* understood how savagely dangerous traffic is, then nobody in their right mind who has their life dear, would ever dare to neglect and move around in it.

I´m of course not advocating for us not to move around in the public sphere, and that we instead would be better off isolating ourselves, definitely not, I´m just pinpointing how our brains are not fully updated, and how the developments in our world are moving too fast for our stone-age brains to keep up.

With that said, I endorse development, and I would almost always encourage you to go out in the world to discover, feel, even smell, and thus experience your growth. Like my Danish compatriot, the Poet Hans Christian Andersen (1805-1875), wrote it: *"To move, to breathe, to fly, to float, To gain all while you give, To roam the roads of lands remote, To travel is to live"*. And related to almost all aspects of life, as the Persian Poet, Jalal ad-Din Rumi, a.k.a.

Mawlana, a.k.a. Rumi (1207-1273), said: "*When setting out on a journey do not seek advice from someone who never left home*"
To further exemplify our misconception about fear, and how our fear affects us to easily being played like manipulated sheep by shepherds in the context of our current social structures, a final cavalcade of examples for this time around takes off with some of my personal narratives; I used to work 15-20 hours a day, seven days a week, for years in a row, a life by appointments and forced upon obligations, while at the same time still socializing in the processed sinsemilla gangzta grass 420 mistress Mary Jane kush-fog with my homiez, being the go-to guy of whatever you need and thus made it my business to profit from having connections many others didn´t. Most days I was out drinking like a barfly sponge (beers for warmup, wine for dinner, and a couple of bottles of dark rum on a good night), and constantly hunting I busy chasing tails and conquering punani, a.k.a. female genitalia – and then on to the next like the fuck-boy stud and merited Playas Club playa I once were (without stating that I no longer own sexual lust, the game were just massively different back then when "we rode the women and raped the horses" (aaand before I get lynched here, no I´m not promoting rape, rape is bad)); like my papa used to say, "You always have to be nice to kids, you never know if they´re your own". Within a relatively short time frame, I was busy enough to meet thousands of different people that I had to relate to, and while humans from a psychological perspective on average only are capable of having approximately 130 relations at the same time (+/- some, depending on the concrete person), then also this immediate innocent aspect was further oil to the fire of a lurking mental disaster waiting to strike. Furthermore, I´ve been "fortunate" enough to experience two handfuls of crazy shootings – with everything from hand guns to AK-47 (Kalashnikov), a guy having his head chopped wide open with a samurai sword, two different people on two different occasions being killed – that I´m sure of (although I´m not sure

about the exact number of wounded and the death tolls across all of the incidents, then at least one was shot less than two meters (approx. six feet) away from me and I was the last person there when he took his last breath, and right in front of my eyes another one was smashed down by a train), a third kill I "only" heard. I know the sound of bullets whistling *very* close by, I know the smell of ignited gunpowder, I´ve experienced a restaurant being blown up with a bomb, and on top of that plenty of stabbings and crazy street fights, and much much *much* more. With nice and easy the pedal to the metal and a frustrating dissatisfaction about not having 72 hours a day, I lived a long life in a relatively short time, and already from an early age I guess you can say that I forcedly matured beyond the "normal" steps of maturity – it came with the territory of my upbringing, and the life I´ve lived. I paid the cost to be the top don dog boss, for years my lifestyle of being invincible rewarded me with only two to three hours of sleep a night, and I never really got to digest and process my external caused increasing internal overload; I failed to comprehend my mortality, and I failed to appreciate it; downtime was primitively a sinful crime exclusively reserved for boring people to commit. And should you by any chance now wonder why I just used the term 'fortunate' in the context of the severe harsh realities of the life I´ve lived, then it´s because I´m referring to all the personal growth I in hindsight have been privileged enough to gain by going through all these experiences. Cause, even though they´re a bitch to process, even though I don´t wish for others to go through the same shit, and even though I of course would prefer if the involved were never harmed in the first place, then as the situation is, I still wouldn´t be without most of my experiences however tragic they might be.
Nevertheless, quite opposite of Nietzsche´s famous quote, "*what doesn´t kill me* [you], *makes me* [you] *stronger*", science clearly shows that the more trauma and pain we´re exposed to, the more our threshold weakens. Still though, while truly wishing good karma

and happiness to others, I firmly believe that one learns more from defeat, pain, and adversity, than one does from success, pleasure, and prosperity, as long as one manages to overcome the con-side of the coin – which unfortunately but naturally not all do. You can compare it with e.g. being a brawler, e.g. a boxer or an MMA-fighter[37], the more beating you receive in a fight the more your threshold against being beaten weakens, but learning- and experience-wise, strategically, tactically, technically, how you should defend, attack, and strike strengthens, although still not posing any bulletproof guarantee for unambiguously all to not experience to be knocked the fuck out.

Hence, to cope with the danger and thus fear of defeat, many people have as an ingrown defense (a.k.a. coping) mechanism developed a tendency of ignoring or to forcibly forget less lucky memories – in somewhat line with what in psychology is called a trauma membrane[38] – in hope of them vanishing by themselves – a kinda spineless attempt of resilience. However, take it from me, they most often don´t just vanish, and they don´t solve themselves either, and if you don´t continuously deal with – by working to process – your problems, then there´s a big chance of them one unprocessed unfortunate memory after another adding weight to your mental backpack up until that point where you eventually can´t carry – yourself – anymore; the risk is that your unsolved problems eventually catch up with and break you, and unless you work to deal with your shit then everything eventually *will* catch up. Hence, the more of your problems you solve along the way, the more relieved and thus lighter you´ll feel, the more surplus you´ll have, the better you´ll sleep, the happier you´ll be, the more you move forward, the

[37] Mixed Martial Art fighter.

[38] A membrane against talking or even thinking about what they wish to forget – what they against psychological evidence think serves them the best to forget; "*Insane in the membrane, insane in the brain*" (Cypress Hill).

more you grow, the more we grow. Almost whatever negativity you carry, your past is “just” a lesson, don´t make it a life sentence.

I almost agree to what the Bohemian-Austrian Poet, Rainer Maria Rilke (1875-1926), wrote: *“Let everything happen to you. Beauty and terror. Just keep going. No feeling is final”*, albeit don´t just keep going without solving what solved can; embrace life while seeking to find order in your mess to sort your soul, the universe doesn´t stagnate and so neither should you; get to know and caress your limits without unnecessarily limiting yourself. One step back and two steps forward is still forward, just as uphill likewise is; sometimes many small steps cover more distance than a few bigger steps, recovery is no less important than performance, and thus backing up for a better run-up might sometimes be a necessary precondition for a better drift, traction, and the furthest distance forward.

As said by the Danish former pilot, Stefan G. Rasmussen (1947-), who by an emergency landing on a field surrounded by trees in 1991 managed to save the lives of 129 people, and here are reflecting on the importance of valuing the lessons in and life itself: *“Life is full of coincidences, but it might not be a coincident, how the coincidences by coincidence arrive”*.

In the same essence as when saying that every cloud has a silver lining, when you overcome your struggles, they become part of your most valuable assets, they become wisdom, they become strength. As served by the German philosopher, Hans-Georg Gadamer (1900-2002), on experience: *“We must learn from our experiences while keep moving forward”*, or as my fellow-countryman, the Danish Theologian and Philosopher, Soeren Kierkegaard (1813-1855), puts it: *“Life can only be understood backwards; but it must be lived forwards”*. We cannot change the past, but what we experienced in and how we dealt with the past can post rationalization help us to understand how we best creates, influences, deals with, and shapes a better now, and thereby a brighter future.

Despite the before mentioned tragic traumatic incidents of mine, then the by far most immense suffering I´ve ever experienced, *the* crescendo I´d rather be without, the number one tragedy of my life, and this without any comparison what so ever, figuratively speaking has been to be in the eye of the hurricane it was when one of the absolute most important people in my life from a lifelong part-time addiction finally became a full-time addict, with very serious mental illnesses as "only" few drops of an ocean of very serious consequences. After being only a few centimeters away from being hit by an anti-tank missile – in the line of duty, the official system did everything they could to worsen an already bad situation instead of taking proper responsibility by providing the much needed help and support they should. Among others, the system dragged my innocent loved one through a tough three yearlong trial which after years of cruel pressure and mistreatment of course proved to be a hoax, and they moreover froze in all money in the years long process thus to ensure to choke out – on the limit of guillotine – any prospect of a minimum of life quality; friends and even family have a tendency to disappear when frustration, anxiety, depression, and anger becomes the new norm, when it´s not only superficial small-talk, mock smiles, and fake laughter, and one can only – single-handedly – take so much in the aftermath of betrayal. My loved one fought bravely without admitting how bad the situation really was, the small amounts of money I´d supported with became a source to buy poison to alleviate the bad nerves and abstinences, and a mean to forget rather than paying the bills I tried to support – before I eventually completely had to stop giving financial aid, as I couldn´t finance such a deadly habit, and hence help to kill someone who literally gave me my life.
To my horror, I later found out how my loved one during the historically toughest winter ever, literally had been snowed in without neither heat or electricity to stand against the biting cold and darkness – also here the system and their henchmen proved

merciless. And as if this wasn´t enough, without the option of going to see a dentist, my loved one in the middle of it all even had been forced to single-handedly pull out several teeth with a rusty pliers, and this without any type of anesthesia. For my loved one, all this – and crazy much more to – among others resulted in a menu of multiple diagnosis, severe PTSD (Post-Traumatic Stress Disorder), anxiety, depression, and what I suspect to be a kind of schizophrenia, sociopathic traits, and more, and by uncontrollable and unpredictable psychotic and ultra-aggressive outbursts my loved one literally went from being the very best person to what to my feelings felt to be the very worst person in a heartbeat; I saw two sides of the same person, a bright side, and a grey side – Dr. Jekyll and Mr. Hyde style, but day by day the brightness exponentially faded away to disappear until only greyness eventually covered the human canvas.

Our codependence consisted of every aspect in the meaning of the word, from love in its purest form to the worst form of kin co-addiction. Nothing I could say or do to better the situation, whatever I did just seemed to worsen everything, hell is a soft cover up for powerlessness. Nothing I wished more than being able to "cure" my beloved – a wish I still carry to this day and forever, and the best way I can describe and explain how it emotionally felt is figuratively speaking like if I in the extremity of my fingertips was hanging on the outside of the edge of a very high and steep cliff with the abyss beneath, only barely able to hold my own weight, and then also had my beloved hanging clinged to my legs under me; I fought the best I knew, but no matter what I did my fingers still slowly slipped, and it became "just" a matter of short time before I fatally would lose my grip; it was impossible for me to pull both of us up from where we were hanging, and nobody was there to help save us from our debilitating bobble. The only potential outcomes sadly seemed to be that either my beloved would let go of my legs, fall, and give me a chance to pull myself up, or we both simply would

fall. With impotence I witnessed how this extremely important person of mine broke apart in the fall due to awfully iniquitous system caused events which with an increasing intensity over a period of years completely wore my 'ride or die' out, and further ultimately became the straws that broke the camel´s back – without me here calling my ultra-important lion-hearted beloved a camel that is. And without being religious, I still pray for a soft landing, and hoping for a loveable reunion at the top – despite none of us being there yet. My loved one passed away.
Mental torture was no longer a stranger, the atrocities and emotional damage showed to be omnivore, and it proved to diffuse like rings in water to the surroundings – from a personal earthquake to a tsunami of interpersonal dimension; in a metaphorical mental sense, when it rains on the priest the sexton gets wet. And when I finally lost reach to my beloved, following a super traumatic experience, the powerlessness and unforeseen grief on my grief ate me up – from inside out, piece by piece, every second of every hour of every day, unstoppable destructive cyclones in heart and mind, spirit, and soul, as sucked out by proton packs[39], and without capacity to fight the fire my mental fire extinguishers instead worked on choking my spark. I lost a *huge* part of myself, absolution absolutely turned the thumb down, and my heart will forever be broken beyond repair; my existence became an out of body experience combined with fisheye tunnel vision combined with films of what had happened rolling in my cheese bell trapped head non-stop for years, all of my awaken hours, and every night in my nightmares. Heads and tails played hide and seek, and my mind was utterly infected to the point where I 24-7 mentally handicapped had to multitask my way through all and everything that I did; my repertoire got infected, breathing to the bottom of my stomach,

---

[39] "*The proton pack is a fictional energy based capture device, used for capturing and entrapping ghosts in the Ghostbusters universe*" ("A Ghost-Zapping Device Is the Season's Stunner". The New York Times. 1987-12-25).

and laughing without a luring shadow, hasn´t come natural ever since; an eternal mental scar, truly one of those I´ll never fully recover from.
One of several mishaps of being a Highly Sensitive Person (HSP) is that I keep loving to the point where I forget to love myself; from here on out, to all my beloved: I´ll die for you, but won´t let you kill me.
Out of respect and continuously massive love for this particular person, I´m not gonna go in to much further personal details in this regard this time around, but as true as it is that almost nothing happens without a reason, then the main reasons to all of my above mentioned personal narratives are connected to and can all be traced back to the cocoon of destructive control – a.k.a. lack of humanity and health – that are in collusion with our current social structures.
Like most others, I was working like a crazy because that's what our current social structures demand of me, I was socializing like a crazy because that's what our current social structures expect of me, I found myself in crazy traumatic situations because that´s what our current social structures drives people into, and at the bottom line my beloved became a victimized outcast who didn´t manage to cope but instead as a damaged human being showed natural reactions to a frightenedly long line of unnatural incidents caused by the human made inhumane social structures of our currently inflexible, crazy unhealthy, and lossy society.
And no, breaking down doesn´t mean that you´re weak, rather it´s a sign that you´ve been too strong for too long; even a psychosis can be a sign of health in an unhealthy world. Perhaps the so called – resiliently – robust people persuade to be robust merely because they self-deceiving actually aren´t robust enough to lower their pretentious guards and honestly put themselves on the line by going all in on their engagement with the world. And if you fortunately truly are a powerhouse strong or privileged enough not

to break, then flash your fly strength of character by at least not looking down on others unless you´re helping them up[40], elevate don´t degenerate, lifting is gifting.

Despite I in line with the common perception of "the successful human" was making what I considered to be decent money, then these money not nearly could outweigh the prize I personally had to pay – a mental wound of dimensions. Money and adrenaline briefly became my only motivation, and the constant hunt for money and a fast pulse to keep the superficial ship floating made me feel like a cheap prostitute selling myself and my time for filthy lucre, before I finally realized that my life de facto had become just a sorry ass hunt for money, more "robber stories", more money, more speed, more money, more problems; little did I know, the chase of culmination gave only at best minor sub-culminations on the road toward the grand finale, death, which after all must be the only real culmination to what thus merely is the road there; I had a gap that couldn´t be filled – I later realized, and continuously trying to fill it made me tired. My mood dropped and nothing I could buy of materiality and temporary "pleasures", e.g. new clothes rather than doing laundry, dining fine enough not to get full, toxic stimulus substances, fast women, and slow horses, had the ability to cheer me up, a blow which further confirmed to me that the best things in life by far are the ones which cannot be bought – which ain´t commodities, e.g. self-respect, dignity, grace, motivation driven by self-realization and the greater good, pure appreciation, originality, character and class, to be a person of value, quality time with passion(s) and loved one(s), candid honesty, true respect, real loyalty, sincere happiness, inner peace, unconditional love, and not least a healthy health (physically *and* mentally). The more money I made the poorer I felt, or as the greatest reggae musician of all time, Bob Marley (1945-1981), spoke it: *"Some people are so poor, all*

[40] The American politician and human rights activist, Jesse Jackson (1941-), said it as follows: *"Never look down on anyone unless you´re helping them up"*.

they have is money". Also Immanuel Kant left behind some of his genius thoughts on the matter: "*We are not rich by what we possess but by what we can do without*", in my optics, a.k.a. who and what *you-me-we* stripped of all are as you, me, and us. Going broke for real isn´t connected to money.
My triple (triad) life between work, family, and "the streets", I was a premium pro, more wanted more pressure to feel alive, and I loved it until I didn´t; unsettled business came sneaking.
Food only fatten the day after, the muscles often suffers the most on the second or third day after (a) hard physical labor or workout, and likewise some psychological loads takes time to sediment; as true as it is that time can heal wounds, as true is it that some "things" takes time to understand, often only late do we realize and then gets hit where it hurt the most, hopefully before it´s too late.
My fuel-tank of dopamine and endorphin dried out, and the emptiness made everything else in my mind echo. I reached a point where I began to experience severe sleeping problems – or no sleep at all, what literally with internal high blasting bangs felt like small explosions in my brain, increasingly physical symptoms in the shape of pressuring feelings in my arms, throat, and in my chest, serious breathing troubles, a vibrating numbness in hands, legs, and feet, a high pounding pulse, and a too heavy and inconsistent heartbeat. Several times, I seriously felt (and though less often still sometimes feel) what I thought was (think is) a critical blood clot or a heart attack in action. The more my body reacted the more I worried about getting a stroke, and the more I worried the more my body reacted – fear of death in a diabolically evil spiral of increasing intensity. My only "relieve" in those years was the moments where I lost the ability to feel anything, where my soul seemed numb, where I due to exhaustion found myself emotionally impotent. Moreover, I by coincident e.g. discovered that I because of a lot – including too much work, a bad diet, and lack of sleep, without trying had lost 20 kilograms (a.k.a. 44 pounds) in a matter of months

without even noticing how my body had gone from semi-buff to bony, just to further highlight how little I was in contact with myself. It came to a point where I had to consult professionals, among others a psycho-the-rapist and a psychologist, who independently told me that what I was experiencing was severe anxiety – panic – attacks[41], and that these were my body desperately trying to communicate to me that enough was now enough. Due to a life with drama and troubles for breakfast, I had – as an subconscious coping mechanism – developed a habit of ignoring myself, my needs, and my wellbeing, and without conscious fear of anything or anyone, I obviously – at least subconsciously – thought that I intellectually could continue to outsmart myself, depending on context either let my autopilot run the show or "just" simply speed up and race my brain concurrently with society´s intensifying demands and further tension, before my body then finally in a holistic context decided to teach me a lesson, the hard way.
Trust the pointers, please don´t be unnecessarily ignorant, read between the lines if you have to, as spoken in the Shakespearean tragedy, Hamlet: *"Something is rotten in the state of Denmark"*.
Naturally and rationally, we humans should be perfectly able to say stop and no thanks to social structures that´re hurting us, that´re clearly not healthy for us, and that´re openly damaging us. But most of us don´t do that in time simply because our current social structures don´t allow us to do so, and hence because we fear the consequences of what would happen if we stood up for ourselves and each other by going up against what feels to be a unbeatable superhuman massive machinery, again – one more time for the sake

[41] Just a service announcement of an easy but very effective tool to use should you ever experience a stress or anxiety attack, "The four second rule": Take a four-second-long deep breath, hold your breath for four seconds, use four second to breathe out, hold your breath for four seconds, start over. Do this as many times as you need, and you should experience your pulse to drop quite quickly.

of Prince Knud (who reportedly weren´t "the sharpest knife in the drawer"), our current social structures.
We tend to think – at least I thought – that we´re well in control; the bigger and faster the wave, the more thrilling the funnier the ride; though, the bigger and faster the wave, the more uncontrollable it is; the bigger and faster the wave, the harder it hit, the harder we might go down, the bigger the chance of drowning, the more inflamed chances of getting well back up if we fall. Don´t fear the waves, learn to understand what you´re up against, improve your skills to better balance your board, and learn to navigate to overcome. Surf your wave, but unless your name is Poseidon or Moby Dick, then no need to push your luck unnecessarily on and in the oceans.
And even if you fall, as the Chinese philosopher, Confucius (551-479 BCE), spoke it, "*Our greatest glory is not in never falling, but in rising every time we fall*". You might heard this quote in various versions as kind of a cliché, but it still doesn´t make it any less true, learn to swim.
P.S. Our social structures are a moldable ocean of waves we create ourselves, and we thus don´t need to go down to rise, in this context we´re Homo Deus, we´re like gods.
We people deserves better than just being a (social security-) number, and just yet another drop in the ocean of statistics. We people deserves a new norm, a better norm. Though, as the sheeple most humans – until further – are, they fear what the shepherds will do to them if they don´t obey and follow the herd, they fear to be perceived rogue and to be shamed out of the herd, they fear if they´ll survive without the herd, they fear the alternative, they fear to stand on their own, they fear freedom; they´re so full of fear that they´re turning their backs on their own true selves, while also ignoring their true collective strength.
The once Roman Emperor, Marcus Aurelius (121 CE-180 CE), said it well: "[...] *realize that you have something in you more powerful and*

miraculous than the things that affect you and make you dance like a puppet". Insecurity persuades people to surrender themselves, and thus you must work on every insecurity you might have to resist your enslavement, to liberate yourself, to be a free individual. If we all independently dared to listen to and trust ourselves and caringly stood up for each other by respecting our worth and all of our specific both personal and basic human needs, then we all solvingly would receive saving and thus benefit from both ourselves – our own potentials, and the likes of others, and instead of it then being a solely independent matter, it automatically would move on to become a collective modus operandi, a collective movement. Hereby, we´ll thus retain a herd-ish feeling of belongingness and security, just now with freedom to be true to our own true selves without being reduced to controlled sheeple, or puppets, or any other unworthy shit like that. Hence, we´d create a sphere without a need for shepherds – simply cutting off the dispensable middleman, the culprit to our plague of oppression.

I´m of course fully aware that this is way easier said than done, and that such changes from a starting point perspective is a two-faced equation which at first glance can seem like a mission impossible to implement. The first hard challenge here is to radically reconceptualize all the brainwashed and indoctrinated people to unite in freedom as "the suckers payoff" (in their minds) sadly currently seems to be too big for the small minded to resist. Hereto, the bravest of us figuratively speaking immediately must start – or continue – to plant seeds, establish precedent roads, and thereby pave ways for others to be inspired by, and thus follow, as an open invitation rather than by force that is. The other presumably real challenging hard part to deal with lays in the impact such drastic reformatting changes obviously entails in relation to the creation of new dynamic and vivid social structures, and if any, a new nature of government, a new financial sector, etc.

Perhaps overcoming the first challenge relievingly will affect the second challenge to adjust more smoothly in accordance, but obviously it would take an unrealistic clairvoyant approach or a crystal ball to completely with certainty express and describe all the right "minor" details of one such massive collective process beforehand. Nevertheless, the most important aspect is that one way or the other changes for the better definitely *is* possible; the world is our oyster – even the whole universe is, and sky´s the limit thus doesn´t cut it to which extent the maximization of our potential goes.

However, before anything, to face and overcome our challenges ahead, to get in check with the right mind-set, to approach enlightenment – as a state of mind, we need to educate ourselves.

1.3. Educate Yourself

One night nine years ago (back in 2013), at around 1:30 AM, I was sitting waizted in front of my computer surfing around looking at plane tickets to destinations far away from the unhealthy weird combination of stress and emptiness that in this period of time had caught up with me. I stumbled upon a ticket to Kathmandu, Nepal, and on the inside of my eyelids memories from the "Tintin in Tibet" cartoon started to pop up, "how romantic and adventurous" I meditated, "and holy shit, weed is just about legal". I asked myself, do I need this adventure or not? – and in the next second without further cogitation I spontaneously pressed the "buy-button"; departure two days later, got the needed vaccines the following day, and then off me, myself and I went, the next after that.

I arrived in Kathmandu without anything planned. I had once heard an old psychedelic hippie tale involving a street called Freak Street, and this was all I got to say to the taxi-driver at the airport before he replied me with a *"sure, get in"*. As soon as we sat inside the taxi, the taxi-driver lighted up and passed me a heavy hashish-joint complimented with the words "*welcome to Nepal*"; the term "high-life" surely has several meanings in the Himalayas. After a week's time of roaming baked and chillaxed around in Kathmandu, I found myself checking in to a Buddhist monastery up on a mountain where I thus stayed surrounded by Buddhist monks. Here the monks confiscated my phone and my tablet to make sure that I was totally off-grid during my time being there, thus to eliminate every unnecessary distractions to the 15 hours of meditation and Buddhist teaching I daily received. Furthermore, during my stay there, interacting with other people inside the monastery was strictly prohibited, and only because I bribed the Hindu guard at the gate with cigarettes, I was able to take my freedom to go out of the monastery for a smoke and cup of coffee (as a much needed supplement to the boiled water and trivial tea inside the monastery) once in a while.

I gotta tell you, this spiritual experience – guesting the monastery – anyhow was one hell of a hard challenge to crack, from busy round the clock being busy to no phone calls, no text messages, no e-mails, no social medias, no socializing, nothing else than meditations, teachings, and a literally crazy restlessness. Being left alone inside my own head was nothing less than extreme, and only by "offloading" my excessive stressful thoughts into my diary I managed to overcome and make it through the first week which in hindsight luckily showed to be the toughest period of my stay.

Here I elaborately should mention, that I later left the monastery mentally calmer than what I`d felt in too many years.

During my Buddhist teachings in the monastery, I was taught that compassion is essential to "the good life", and that the most sacred and highest achievement in Buddhism is the one of being Enlightened; only the Enlightened person will ever enter the gateway to and thus reach Nirvana, which spiritually speaking is *the*

place of perfect peace and happiness, a place kinda similar to what religions in general refer to as heaven(s), Eden, and paradise.
To exemplify how one can achieve to be Enlightened, I was told a legendary (at least in Buddhism) fable about a young boy who was out walking in the woods with his younger brother. Here the two brothers came across a starving tiger who were on its way to their village to feast some humans, and to protect his younger brother and the inhabitants of their village from the "human-meat-hungry" tiger, the older brother sent off his younger brother to run back and warn their village, while the older brother stayed to make the tiger occupied. The tiger was close to dying of hunger, and the older brother decided to save the tiger´s life by letting it eat him. He made a pact with the tiger, that he would scarify himself to the tiger while the tiger in return thus would not run after his younger brother or attack the village. On this account, the older brother laid down on the ground and offered himself for the tiger to eat him. The tiger then ate him, and with a full stomach it turned around and left the area the same way it´d came. The older brother hence became Enlightened, and made his way to Nirvana because he "altruistically" showed compassion enough to sacrifice himself to save the lives of his younger brother, the tiger, and all of the inhabitants in the village.
I now trust that you at least have a slight clue about how Enlightenment are defined in Buddhism, cause then I finally now can let you know, that this isn´t the exact type of Enlightenment we in the following are focusing on, at least not entirely.
The type of Enlightenment we here are dealing with is still the more Kantian version, as already introduced in the first part of this chapter, "*Enlightenment is* [...] *emergence from* [...] *self-incurred immaturity*". Whereas the Buddhist version of Enlightenment for the enlightened is of a spiritual size that plays out as a superstitious ticket to a better afterlife, then our term of Enlightenment rather represent a size that has its focus and expected value and reward in

life. In my humble belief, there´s no "physical" afterlife – not in this world or another, no resurrection, no ghosts, no reincarnation, no nothing, when we´re gone we´re gone. For this reason, there´s not really any point in discussing actions beyond life at this point, as we thus only have a direct influence on our posthumous reputation before our time in life is over anyway. However, still this doesn´t exclude the possibility of a solely spiritual life after death, which is also where the two mentioned versions of Enlightenment anyways slightly – at least partly – overlap; life after death is entirely hung up on how our spirits lives on in the minds of others through the fascination, love or hate, we might have for them, and they might have for us. To exemplify, if I e.g. now mention the German physicist, Albert Einstein (1879-1955), then most people well know who he is, which is already the first sign of his sustained pseudoscientific spiritual existence, and even if you didn´t already know his name then the fact that I now randomly mention him more than 60 years after his death, anyhow should reinforce his spirit to continuously live on through me, and now you, and so on; apropos the old saying "gone but not forgotten". Same is moreover likewise the case for all the religious "prophets", Messiah, and so forth, if ever they existed, they now "only" exist in the memory they left behind – the memory you-me-we carry on. Hence, this is thus the type of life we potentially can expect to have after our deaths, marked that we in life made sure to deserve it, which thus therefore merely should be one more good reason for you to spend this one and only lifetime making yourself to be remembered for something worth remembering, and thereby hopefully leave a positive legacy behind you, a candidacy strong enough to honor your spiritual potential of an eternal life in the minds of your descendants.
Personally, I like and support how one of my personal idols, the American former heavyweight boxing champion and charisma connoisseur, Muhammad Ali (formerly known as Cassius Clay) (1942-2016), wish to be remembered: "*He took a few cups of love,*

he took one table spoon of patience, one table spoon and a tea spoon of generosity, one pint of kindness, he took one quart of laughter, one pinch of concern, and then he mixed willingness with happiness, he added lots of faith, and he stirred it up well. Then he spread it over a span of a lifetime, and he served it to each and every deserving person he met". How do *you* wish to live and therefrom be remembered?

Unfortunately, there´s a widespread tendency of prioritizing materialism above all else, why it´s important to remember that just about all materialism is something we merely borrow while we´re here, once we´re gone these don´t really matter no more, at least not anywhere near to the same degree as the moments we by your time and actions created, and this is now your time to take action and create moments in our time; what you do in life reverberate and echoes after you´re gone-gone-gone. Hereto, the American author, John Green (1977-), in line with my thoughts on a major problem in our world well-expressed it as follows: "*People were created to be loved. Things were created to be used. The reason why the world is in chaos, is because things are being loved and people are being used*".

Cut; I once heard a – too much fake-laughing, clearly insecure, and quite dense seeming – former CIA-agent state that knowledge is freedom. Yet, instead of just buying into his words (I find it hard to trust a phony aura), I couldn´t quite help to question his statement. Cause, what about the old saying: ´What you don´t know can´t hurt you´, as in if you don´t know that you lack knowledge, then how can you have any related worries, and if no worries then freedom should be achieved, right? A bit like if you´re braindead, or just dead, then you obviously don´t have any traceable knowledge, you don´t have any worries, and you´re free from all the tribulations in life, right? If you´re dead you don´t know you´re dead, and you´re thus free from the suffering and mourning which only those around you – with conscious knowledge about your death – might go through, right? With the risk of sounding a bit nihilistic, same goes with stupidity, with double up on catch-22[42], it´s not the stupid one – the one who´s too stupid to understand how stupid the stupid one is – who suffers, it´s all those around the stupid one – the ones who understand how stupid the stupid one is – who suffers by the stupidity they hence are confronted by and have to deal with, right? Simply not fair that the ones who ought to have the knowledgeable advantage in their corner are the ones who actually are being punished because of the deficiencies of others, right? It´s no joyride – a.k.a. it´s pretty love damn tough – having to be the understanding and indulgent one while "the other(s)" thus just impulsively and ignorantly fogs mindlessly around.

As the Swiss Psychiatrist, Carl Gustav Jung (1875-1961), describe a – at least to me – very well-known feeling: "*Loneliness does not come from having no people about one, but from being unable to communicate the things that seem important to oneself*", a.k.a. it doesn´t matter how many people you have around you if you don´t feel understood; in my self-righteous case, not because I can´t communicate, but because I can´t convey what´s impossible for the receiver to understand.

I´m a pro at infiltrating and fit in everywhere I please, but the more I do the lonelier I am.

Moreover, stupid people also often appear to be more brave than less stupid people, not because they really are more courageous than less stupid people – in fact rather the opposite, but simply because the stupid people don´t grasp, understand, and are aware of consequences to the same degree as the less stupid people, which thus likewise carry the reason for why stupid people on average tend to appear more happy(-go-lucky) and less crestfallen

---

[42] A dilemma or difficult circumstance from which there is no escape because of mutually conflicting or dependent conditions (Oxford Languages). Double up because both the stupid and the less stupid on each their side of "the fence" are caught in a catch-22 on the account of stupidity.

and less depressed than less stupid people. If for some reason stupidity – despite direct contradictory – would understand, mind, and care about bettering the harsh realities[43], the stupid probably would be reduced to fetal positioned catatonic nerve-wracks who due to their stupidity thus wouldn´t know how to deal with neither themselves or their tribulations, and in that sense, it hence should be fair to state that their stupidity almost illogically as a blessing in disguise serves as their salvation and thereby advantage, while all at the same time – as just mentioned – being a source to further frustration and social disadvantage on their less stupid surroundings.

Though, stupidity briefly aside, and despite most other aspects, the often main deciding factor for happi- or unhappiness (let´s say from a somewhat average IQ (intelligence quotient) and up) still mounts to be whether they – you – are a "the glass is half empty" or a "the glass is half full" kind of person; although feelings and emotions can be hard to control, then perspectives, reactions, and behavior, surely are mold- and shapeable, and practice makes premium prospect. The question for the less stupid thus is if you instead of degrading to be pessimistic are clever and strong enough to stay a positive realist as a or around the misfit(s)?

Thereupon, au contraire of unawareness and stupidity, if you properly understand how to leverage your knowledge – to use your knowledge to your own advantage, if you truly are able to comprehend yourself and your surroundings, and the opportunities that knowledge provides, how to navigate in, accept, and benefit from your knowledge, then yes, then knowledge surely is a strength – or power if you fancy, at least at an individual level, and then yes, then this power surely can provide a suitable breathing ground for freedom to arise and thrive. From the same mechanism as when

[43] To describe reality, I like what the American science fiction writer, Philip K. Dick (PKD) (1928-1982), wrote: *"Reality is that which, when you stop believing in it, doesn´t go away"*.

you cannot really confine someone already chained up, then how can you anyhow truly feel and value freedom if you don´t know that you´re free – if you don´t understand and hence don´t know what it means not to have freedom. A tragic-comic paradox related to understanding is that the more we understand the more we understand how little we understand (the proper epistemological[44] stance in a nutshell), only the stupid one thinks that he or she (or all other self-proclaimed genders in between) knows everything because they – again – don´t understand or at least don´t acknowledge that they don´t understand; there was a time where I knew everything worth knowing because everything worth knowing was limited by how little I knew, and now I´m full of doubt because I know enough to know that I know less. *"There are things we know we know* [known knowns]. *We also know there are known unknowns; that to say we know there are some things we do not know. But there are also unknown unknowns – the ones we don´t know we don´t know"*[45]. Even a giant "only" sees its own reflection in the mirror. *"The doorstep to the temple of wisdom is a knowledge of your own ignorance"*[46].

"Normally", most people in general tend to deny or hate (okay hate is a strong word, but at least dislike) what they don´t understand – what´s alien to them, which in a way actually makes sense as it undoubtedly can be a frustrating challenge to accommodate and embrace something which isn´t understood and therefore doesn´t make sense – can´t be felt, and perhaps even thus for the

---

[44] Epistemology is the branch of philosophy concerned with knowledge, also referred to as 'the theory of knowledge'.

[45] Quote by former US Secretary of Defense, Donald Rumsfeld (1932-2021).

[46] Danish sources says that this quote was written above the door to the Platonic Academy (Plato´s academy existing in Athens from 387 BCE to 86 BC), while other sources ascribe the quote to one of the founding fathers of the United States of America, Benjamin Franklin (1706-1790). Anyway, here it shouldn´t really matter who said it, what really matters are the essence of the quote.

uncomprehending doesn´t exist. And although many stupid people don´t understand that they don´t understand, then the worst anyway is when lack of understanding turns into contempt, when the uncomprehending convert incomprehension to negativity aimed at what, thé, or them they don´t understand, and furthermore from not being able to look any further than the tip of their own nose – a.k.a. stupidity – hence also don´t understand if you understand, why you ergo in their world often – if not always – understand less than they do because they think that you don´t understand that they understand that you don´t understand, although you in fact are the only one who understand to understand who of you who understand or don´t understand, understand? Understanding is of course a floating process, one might understand much about a narrow field without understanding much more, while another might understand less than much but more than most about many things without particularly excelling in any field; one might be the best at one thing, but no one is the best at everything, and most isn´t the best at anything – no even being themselves. "Just" because e.g. some professor knows a lot about a specific field it doesn´t mean that that person is more intelligent than most or knows everything about everything else, and many so called "experts" should thus learn to know their own limits before paternalistic [47] blabbering up and portraying themselves as the '*always* go to rain man' on every issue; speak up and out and make a statement when you know what you´re talking about, but if you don´t with proficiency know what you´re talking about, then control your limelight craving exigent behavior and shut the fuck up – if only you would understand; unless you´re asking questions, listen, seek information, learn, and then speak up – from an informed position; remember, when you´re speaking you´re not listening – listen spells

[47] A paternalistic attitude can e.g. play out as: "I know better than you what´s best for you".

silent; even doctors and professors have two ears and two eyes and only one mouth.

There´s nothing wrong with saying "I don´t know", and if you don´t want to lose face and appear insecure, then know that there´s not much expressing more confidence and infuse more respect than saying "I don´t know" with your head high. And thereby you´re thus also well-deserved keeping it real to both yourself and others without cunning anyone – including yourself.

Knowledge is not immediately unambiguously equal to clear-cut freedom (or intelligence) – and vice versa, but stupidity surely unambiguously only serves stupidity, so what here for a short while might in an overall context appeared to be a potentially doubtful affair, kinda turned out to be a tempest in a teapot, or a wolf in sheep´s clothing if you prefer. The verdict should be fairly clear, in my terminology one´s way towards Enlightenment goes through the acquiring of knowledge to spark off and further accumulate vital understanding, which *then* furthermore also simultaneously ought to help strengthen and thus improve the conscious courage needed for the proactive detachment from the self-incurred immaturity as a precondition for moving one step closer to self-awareness of freedom, and more importantly pave part of the way to a more free and authentic existence, a.k.a. more freedom.

Accept that everybody has different capabilities, skills, and talents, but don´t accept to compromise your freedom by continuously lowering yourself down to a level under the worth of your own potential only to please "their" lack of ditto, as long as the fulfillment of your potential doesn´t become a direct impediment for the ditto of others.

Even though Enlightenment is a term that among others covers and thus consist of both knowledge and freedom, then neither the existence of knowledge nor freedom directly is a mandatory matter to the existence of the other. Hence, although both of them (knowledge and freedom) *do* serve as a direct precondition for

Enlightenment to flourish, then each of them continuously has to be acquired separately, while though both provides and serves as a helpful precondition for the provisioning procurement – a.k.a. obtainment – of the other.

When you´re on the path of true enlightenment and are working towards your vision being supplied by your own conscience, you will discover and realize that your true strength is rooted in and expressed through a combination of your capabilities (including knowledge) and your freedom to make use of them; let your heart-feelings guide you, to say what you think, and do as you say, rather than being a imbecilic woolen product of what you were taught or manipulated or indoctrinated or hypnotized or even dictated to believe and be. Nature gave you the ability to think freely, and if anybody ever dares to take your freedom away from you then do yourself a favor by taking it back. As Rumi (a.k.a. Mawlana) said: *"One of the marvels of the world is the sight of a soul sitting in a prison with the key in its hand"*. Own your own keys, your second wind is supposed to be yours.

Never let your authentic internal dialogue be altered due to societal standards, giving in to external pressure is giving yourself up, a sorry ass source to see your true power and greatness fade away.

Redeem, recover, regain, respect your mirror and beyond, respectfully be yourself.

Following thinking "it", your verbal ammo is your strongest weapon, next after the value of action; all weaponized aspects you possess rely on your knowledge, and not least your ability to make proper use of what you got.

Ergo, we´re not talking sophism here, cause your thoughts don´t really have value if your actions don´t add up, just as your words equally ain´t shit if you likewise can´t back ´em up.

In addition to what the Persian poet, Hafiz (1320-1390), correctly said: *"The words you speak become the house you live in"*, I further

must add, 'but the more so your actions are the ones that makes the profound difference of matter – both internally and externally'. From nature you already have all the tools you need, you "just" have to acknowledge them, and to teach yourself on how to use them – how to maximize your gateway to infinite growth. You deserve it, we deserve it, our shared sphere – a.k.a. our world – deserves it.
Yet, unfortunately there still are some misfortunate exceptions, cases in which the majority of a population involuntarily by fear of reprisals has been silenced by intentional oppression from a leading minority with big egos, callous mind sets, and small dicks (as this mainly occur in patriarchal societies) – motherfuckers who in accordance with Sigmund Freud´s (1856-1939) view on religion[48] seems to have taken their love damn Oedipus complexes excessively too far.
From this perspective, I can´t help to think about how important it by action is to get these words out, to spread these seeds. In the name of authoritarianism, too many people around the globe don´t have their liberty – including freedom of speech – intact, and are being oppressed, censored, or even brainwashed not to think and express themselves freely. Figuratively speaking, cage birds don´t fly, and for this reason, I – and so should you – feel obliged to use whatever possessed freedom I have to also be their voice up until that point where the influence and gag-order of their oppressors has been reduced to nothing less than a historic speck of dust, until their basic human rights are regained and are back in motion exactly as they from nature were intended to be before some humans

[48] Sigmund Freud was an Austrian doctor and the creator (founder) of psychoanalysis. Freud´s view on religion was very simplified that young males love their mother to the extend where they out of jealousy build a murderous hate to their father, which Freud calls 'the Oedipus complex' (The other way around, a female loving her dad and thus build a hate to their mother is called 'the Electra complex'). Therefrom, and because of a sense of guilt – especially if and thus after the male kill their father, religion become their savior, revelation, and substituting father figure.

messed it up by acting inhuman, and thus until their mental cages are relics from the past in old songs song by themselves as free birds. *"Liberty is the soul´s right to breathe, and when it cannot take a long breath laws are girded too tight. Without liberty, man is a syncope"* [49] . We all have a shared responsibility to fight and eliminate oppressive tyranny, righteous indignation at its best, and we absolutely can´t afford and accept to lose.

To be in check with freedom, we need to use our freedom to secure freedom, universally.

Before, during, and infinite long after securing freedom, we continuously have to seek and gain knowledge to continuously being able to expand our understanding, and we have to always be generous enough to pass on and thus share our knowledge – at least make it available – to each and every one who are willing to gain. Only this way you learn, only this way we all learn, only this way we grow, only this way we grow together.

Several times I´ve heard "wise life gurus" advocate that "you should not teach people what to think, but instead how to think", and at first "sight" this may to many people sound pretty positive. However, going closer into the interpretation of that sentence then the meanings of "what" and "how" actually present themselves pretty similar – more alike than distinctive. No matter if hearing a theorem about teaching people "what to think" or "how to think", then it in both cases immediately reminds me quite a bit about a lot of frightening examples, such as totalitarian – despotic – systems based on authoritarianism (e.g. Nazism, fascism, communism, and certain theocracies (religious regimes), etc.), religious texts, colonization, and hence Eurocentrism, as well as military systems where the overall aim is to break down or completely erase the individual(s) only for then to customized rebuild the individual(s) or

---

[49] Quote by the American Congregationalist clergyman, social reformer and speaker, Henry Ward Beecher (1813-1887), known for his support of the abolition of slavery.

regimes in a certain preferred shape again. And in addition hereto, to spell it out for love know which time, this also is how our current capitalistic social structures in general works, as they also short and roughly said, as a consequence, likewise have the same overall common denominator as the frightening examples just mentioned – at least implicitly, namely limited freedom controlled by restrictions and mechanisms associated with brainwash; many of us don´t realize how badly we´re being played.

Therefore, to highlight the intended implicit difference between "what" and "how", it should be quite appropriate to draw a clear distinction between the two by adding "autonomously" after "how to think" thus that the sentence now is: "you should not teach people what to think, but instead how to think autonomously".

Our gift of voice, we either use it or lose it, and that per se holds true for our abilities to think for ourselves as well. And hey, just to be in sync here, don´t mix up autonomously with selfishness, because it surely is possible to think autonomously without being selfish.

Like, when hearing someone say that you should never question "the lord" (a.k.a. God(s), prophet, sometimes even shepherd), jeez, *bitch please* – all due respect, you should always question everything, without mixing up the two different sizes of general questioning and distrust. As the American entomologist, E. O. Wilson (1929-), said: "*We are drowning in information, while starving for wisdom. The world henceforth will be run by synthesizers, people able to put together the right information at the right time, think critically about it, and make important choices wisely*". Hence, from an open-minded approach elicit and extract as much information and knowledge as you possibly can manage without stressing yourself, filter your experiences with a critical mindset, and become the wisdom you-me-we need; we´re not supposed to leave this world curious. The one who asks a question might be a fool for a short while, but "*...the one who doesn´t ask, is* *a fool for life"*, as rightfully stated by Confucius. Or as spoken by the American astronomer and astrobiologist, Carl Sagan (1934-1996): *"We make our world significant by the courage of our questions and by the depth of our answer"*.

The more you question the more answers you get, and the more answers you get the more you – hopefully – can comprehend and understand, the wiser you´ll be, the more you grow, the more we grow.

Don´t get me wrong, I really don´t wish to disrespect anyone´s believe, their choices and needs, because I clearly understand why some – need to – have faith in their "lord" (God(s), prophet, or again sometimes even their shepherd), etc. I even with somewhat envy admire and respect believers for their ability to believe and the strong faith they show, and I concede that it sometimes must be easier to have a feeling of an external pillar to lean up against in all critical aspects of life. However, seriously, from a rational perspective, adding meaning to everything solely by trusting "something" contradictory and completely unverifiable simply seems meaningless, and somewhat desperate (without hereby neglecting genuine desperation). It´s understandable how trusting "something" or "someone" bigger than yourself can feel meaningful for the individual believer(s), to experience the full bloom of the placebo effect (e.g. feeling better on a drug that has no documented effect[50]), to have someone or something to blame or to turn to when life shows its ugly face, a guiding law-ish set of rules to live or

---

[50] - which though perhaps could indicate that a wrong diagnosis was made in the first place, e.g. as a result of confusing a mental disorder with a physical suffering. And although psychosomatic issues shouldn´t call for medicine made for physical conditions, then perhaps e.g. the attention the treatment provided (a la the Hawthorne effect) was all the treatment needed to cure what was believed to be a physical problem, etc. But that´s another talk... - just like the one about how the placebo effect might in itself actually can provide that documentation which it in its meaning was launched to describe a lack of, a.k.a. how the placebo effect can nullify itself.

be inspired by, something that adds "meaning" to what one find intangible and incomprehensible, etc. And when experiencing periods where one problem after another succeeds in finding me, then also I sometimes cannot deny to find it easier to think that some higher power is testing me rather than always logically acknowledging how problems only entropically (a.k.a. randomly) seems attracted to me – at least in regard to those problems in which I immediately have no eligible shares in the creation of. Yet, while religion thus in some ways *have* shown to have positive effects for many individual believers then it sadly also has proven to contribute with many negative effects for both the believers and their surroundings, e.g. by how some believers lose their ability to independent rational thinking, by how some in the name of their religion ostracize their own children because of their sexuality (e.g. because they are gay, have sex before marriage, etc.), by how many that have tortured and killed and equally many that has been tortured and killed – or sacrificed as offerings – in the name of religion, etc. and etc. and etc.

Try e.g. to consider what the English writer and philosopher, G. K. (Gilbert Keith) Chesterton (1874-1936) – a.k.a. the "prince of paradox", once wrote: "*But in that terrific tale of the Passion there is a distinct emotional suggestion that the author of all things (in some unthinkable way) went not only through agony, but through doubt. It is written, "Thou shalt not tempt the Lord thy God." No; but the Lord thy God may tempt Himself; and it seems as if this was what happened in Gethsemane. In a garden Satan tempted man: and in a garden God tempted God. He passed in some superhuman manner through our human horror of pessimism. When the world shook and the sun was wiped out of heaven, it was not at the crucifixion, but at the cry from the cross: the cry which confessed that God was forsaken of God* [My God, my God, why have you forsaken me? (Eloi, Eloi, lama sabachthani?) (Mark 15:34, Matthew 27:46)] [...] *God seemed for an instant to be an atheist*".

Ergo, if we for a second imagine that Gods actually exist(ed) (meta-imagine that an imaginary god exist(ed)), if God found himself to be subject of the truly horrible pain it also means to be human, then even God – as literally described in the bible – would lose his faith in even himself; if (a) God loses his faith in himself because of what he created and did to himself, then why should you devote yourself to have faith in him and his work? Why have faith in anyone who according to religious faith is responsible for everything and hence is guilty in unbearable atrocities and suffering, e.g. incest, abuse, torture, and murder? And if you in return give a speech of "God´s plan", and that he thereby "only" is testing us, or any wack crap like that, then you´re merely confirming religion as also an partly contagious pernicious virus of ignorance. Give me God´s plan on paper, and I´ll prove that it ain´t worth more than the paper I normally wipe my ass with – I briefly think, but out of respect of course would never.
God didn't create humans, humans created God.
Again, and it might sound more hollow than it is after what I just wrote, I really am not aiming to disrespect anyone´s personal believe, I´m only questioning what I don´t share, and with hope, I really just so would wish that the religious believer(s) instead of primarily worshiping a fantasy rather would put all of their faith and trust in themselves, and not least in those who are real and really should matter more than anything else in their lives, the ones who truly needs and deserves their attention and support, e.g. family, friends, and even all other fellow humans and creatures in general – just to mention a few physical examples, without here going in to all the sical[51] aspects.

---

[51] The 'sical' term of 'metaphysics' expresses the covering constitution of everything that isn´t physical. Where the physical world covers everything made of atoms (every physical existence is made of atoms), then metaphysics covers everything that isn´t made of atoms, and metaphysics hence is the exact existing opposition to physics.

Thence, living in a naïve short-sighted fantasy-world as real and true as a Donald Duck cartoon, or even completely in denial, obviously cannot be something which I soberly promote or recommend. Fair enough to extract inspiration from where it´s to be found, and surely fictional sources can be useful as well if the message is right. As an example, I e.g. warmly can recommend to be inspired by the Jedis (jediism)[52] (and this is said by someone (me) who ain´t even a huge Star Wars nerd). Not because you should rely upon any higher spiritual force other than love, and not because you should start wearing robes – you can simply leave that to the Jedis, Hugh Hefner, Eazy-E, and me, but rather because of the characteristics the Jedis hold; from a good heart and with courage a Jedi serves as guardians of peace and justice, a Jedi isn´t under or above anybody but merely *with* anybody who truly wish good – the greater good; a Jedi is honest, non-selfish, strong in mind, body, and soul, a Jedi isn´t afraid of standing up for what´s right, and doesn´t allow to be spellbound by the "weakness" of 'the dark side' no matter the situation, which is something we all should be able to benefit from being inspired by. And if your role-model inspiration persnickety *has* to be godlike for you to buy in – still hopefully without blindly surrendering yourself completely to a fabricated symbolic or character, then – to meet you half way – e.g. aiming for a well-adjusted and thus balanced mix with considerably more ying than yang between Buddha (although Buddha and Buddhism aren´t really considered a god and a religion),

[52] A fictional character from the fictional Star Wars universe, and 'jediism' is the philosophy of the Jedi – which some even has made into a religion with 21 maxims to follow.

Eirene[53], Athena[54], and Thor[55], might then at least be somewhat of a decent kick-off. And for the record, when talking about Thor then I´m not referring to that weak ass pop-version portrayal from the latest superhero movies, but instead the "real" deal legendary Thunder God from the Nordic Mythology[56].

I acknowledge that believe can move mountains in the mind of the believer, but still, only a fool would ever override what real is, what the science of evolution already more or less has verified, to please something as fictitious, conceited, and unethical, as e.g. religion also are; a-motherfucking-men. Of course, a lively fantasy world as a melting pot between the conscious and unconscious is a sign of great intelligence, which e.g. creativity tends to profit greatly from, but if truly not being able to differentiate between what is evident and what is "only" authentic in one´s own mind, then instead of unfolding a healthy mental feature we´re suddenly rather dealing with the bad math trouble of hallucination or blindness by obsessive denial, notwithstanding this flows from a scary unconscious dimension, a.k.a. something one unintentionally and hence innocently cannot see through or look beyond or both.

Ergo, as the old – but still very true - cliché goes: there´s a fine line between genius and madness.

Furthermore, I understand how some can be indoctrinated and thereby tricked (cou-brainwashed-ugh) into believing that some

---

[53] Old Greek goddess of auspicious peace, commonly known as Peace.

[54] Old Greek goddess of wisdom, courage, inspiration, civilization, mathematics, strength, strategic warfare, the arts, crafts, and skills. In function and meaning she´s quite synonymous with the old Nordic Mythology goddess, Frigg, the wife of Odin, who is also known as both wise and kindhearted.

[55] In old Nordic Mythology, Thor is the god of thunder and light, a god who fights off the enemies of civilization. In function and meaning he´s quite synonymous with the old Indian goddess, Indra, the old Greek god Zeus, and the old roman god Jupiter.

[56] Watch the 1986 'Valhalla' cartoon if you need an easily manageable introduction.

external – imaginary – higher power actually plays a part in the world, because it at least does so far as to e.g. how many millions of people that´ve been killed, and still are being killed, in the name of e.g. religion – including the undeniable religiosity of capitalism.
Most of us don´t realize – or at least won´t recognize – how badly we all have been brainwashed. For me personally, it e.g. comes to show when thinking twice before going under a latter as I all my life have been told how this means bad luck, or when thinking if something bad will happen to me if a black cat crosses the road in front of me as this supposedly also should mean bad luck, when a mirror breaks and I can´t help to think if this really means seven years of bad luck, when I unintentionally knocks over the salt-shaker and have to throw some salt over my left shoulder just to be sure that this otherwise doesn´t give me bad luck, when I find myself knocking three times under wood while saying 7-9-13 to not negatively jinx something I said, when I think that my occasional hiccup must be because someone is missing me somewhere in the world, or even when I feel great joy from finding a four-leaf clover as this allegedly should bring great luck ahead.
I´m not saying that I without hesitation uncritically believe in these superstitious examples of my own narratives, just that they´re hard to ignore because of the lifelong indoctrination also I´ve been subject to, and add to that that I´m also a hopeless romantic enough to like and thereby definitely not exclude the thought of more between heaven and Earth than what we immediately are able to see and explain.
So, I totally understand how it can be hard to neglect and differentiate what perhaps your entire pedigree of parents, grandparents, role models, etc., always have been preaching about the sincerity of their religion´s "beautiful" higher power, that "*All great truths begin as blasphemies*"[57], and how hard it thus can be

---

[57] Quote by the Irish playwriter, George Bernard Shaw (1856-1950).

for you to dismiss your own preconceived narratives, to admit that you, your kin, your historical tribe, and those you always admired and believed in, simply have been living and based all trust on a "great" big lie that has now through millenniums been passed on from generation to generation to generation, and so forth, the "greatest" lie ever created.

Personally, the only invisible forces I on a daily basis trust are love and the invisible Sherlock Holmes hat I tend to wear when I search and investigate for answers instead of blindfoldedly leaving causations and rational explanations in the hands of human made fiction.

From the imaginary parallel worlds of religion, we now instead move on to the metaphorical existence of those parallel worlds we are, and thus lives in. In our mental capacity, we all have an inner universe of our own, we all live in each our own parallel world, and all our parallel worlds combined thus collectively creates an outer social multiverse, our shared social sphere. Explained in another way, all living creatures on Earth is independently in their own universe like an enclave, like a "small" piece of land surrounded by other "small" pieces of land – hopefully allied, and all of our individual enclaves thus collectively represents our shared landscape of life – like a multiverse; Here we simultaneously live in an interaction between individual parts and a whole, in line with what the German sociologist, Hartmut Rosa (1965-), describes as resonance, and as described by the hermeneutic circle, in which the whole in an eternal loop depends on and are affected by the particular individual parts, us, while the particular individual parts equally depend on and are affected by the whole, our shared world – our shared social sphere. From this understanding, it should be quite clear why it´s important that we learn about and try to understand ourselves and our surroundings in a simultaneous fashion – as a symbiotic relationship, and partly why learning – until time stands still – for all living creatures is a never-ending process of propulsion and hence progress. Albeit science (as a road to learning new knowledge) – as the German physicist, Max Planck (1858-1947) expressed it – "*advances one funeral at a time*" (as "*a new scientific truth does not triumph by convincing its opponents and making them see the light, but rather because its opponents die, and a new generation grows up that is familiar with it.*"), life is a lifelong learning process, we can always learn new and learn more, and if you think that you finished your education then you unfortunately are more finished than educated; by the time we stagnate, by the time we become static, by the time we stop learning, we´re already dead.

A saying by the Greek philosopher, Heraclitus (540-480 BCE), goes: "*No man ever steps in the same river twice, for it´s not the same river and he´s not the same man*". I love this sentence for how it precisely, cleverly, and yet very simply, expresses the eternal process of development and change in our nature. As I interpret the saying, the river, the flow of the water, the life in and of the river, are always in motion, and hence the development of the river clearly symbolize life itself – the drops of water the man touched the first time he jumped in the river will never be the exact same a second time around. Likewise, as the man – hopefully – always develops, as his experience from jumping into the river the first time in itself made him an experience richer, as life continue in-between his jumps, then also the man will never be the exact same man on his second jump.

Without here going deep into e.g. neuroscientific or other physiological aspects as e.g. the nerve cells – in e.g. the eye, the eye´s blind spot, or even the psychophysical processual connection between the physical parts of e.g. the eyes and ears and the spiritual orientated brain, then we here simplified jump straight to the straight up psychological part of the understanding process, with theoretical inspiration from the two German philosophers, Martin Heidegger (1889-1976), and again Hans Georg Gadamer (plus the loose), *the* O.G. breeders of the hermeneutic method – including the hermeneutic circle presented before. Simply put, our psychological process of understanding is overall rooted in three connected concepts, respectively our fore-projection, fore-meaning, and "prejudice". And here it immediately is important to emphasize, that "prejudice" unlike the general use and interpretation of the word not necessarily by definition is to be perceived as having a negative meaning – as e.g. the case is in relation to bigotry; it´s essential to acknowledge that there are legitimate prejudices – a positive value of the concept based on reason as the exclusive antithesis of authority.

In whatever we´re presented, e.g. words, visualizations, and whatnot, an understanding process within us automatically takes form and plays out as follows: First, our fore-projection kicks in as a mechanism which constantly revises every impression all along the development process of opinion-forming from the presented. Roughly put, we can view and classify our fore-projection as our observations and first step towards finding meaning in what we experience. Secondly, this constantly expanding revised volume of observations, impressions, and quite subconscious opinion-forming thus moves on to interact with our fore-meaning – our prior experiences, and together these two fore-concepts, fore-projection and fore-meaning, as a third step moves on to form what becomes our prejudice(s). These three steps thus continuously operates in constant loops – both individually and together; in step one, the fore-projection keeps observing and revising and delivering to the fore-meaning, observing, revising, delivering, observing, revising, delivering, looping many times in almost no time through an eye to brain connection of 10+ pictures per second[58], supplemented by e.g. sound, physical phenomenon, etc., on top of the visuals. Likewise, in step two, in the interaction between the fore-projection and the

[58] And here I feel to add that the only reason for why we can see anything is because light reflects what we see.

fore-meaning, the fore-meaning keeps receiving information from the fore-projection which then is being added to and compared with the fore-meaning – our prior experiences which constitutes the actual basis of our current fundamental understanding. Every time new information – a new experience – arrives, then the previous experience naturally becomes a prior experience, and thus every time our fore-meaning receives new information then this information adds yet another layer to our prior experiences, which simultaneously happens at the same rate and pace across the different steps. Hence, gather and receive information, add, and compare this information to and with our prior experiences to create meaning and understanding, gather and receive information, add and compare this information to and with our prior experiences to create meaning and understanding, and so on, and so on. Finally, based on the meaning and understanding created in step two, we then in step three makes our verdict and forms our prejudice, and for every time new information are gathered and processed, every time meaning and understanding are created, we also automatically continue to revise our prejudice – a.k.a. our immediate verdict, a.k.a. our constant attempts of looking into the future (which really is what our brains basically aims to do); step one, step two, step three, step one, step two, step three, and so the loops constantly goes.

The fore-projection in step one can be viewed as a subconscious matter, cause by the time we´re conscious about it then we´re already operating in the fore-meaning of step two, and our prejudice(s) of step three.

The hermeneutic methods presented here is undoubtedly as universal as the human connection to nature – the process is universal within all people with a somewhat well-functioning brain. However, with that said, I´m still not saying that there´s a specific universal right way to learn. Firstly, simply because all people are different – universal human mechanisms doesn´t equal our unique

DNA – inherited traits, and environmental influences[59]. While some e.g. are wiser or more intelligent than others (wise refer to amount of knowledge and the ability to make use of it, and intelligence merely refer to the potential ability), then we all also build all of our views and understandings on each our own unique experiences, which further thus also partly explains why each of our interpretations and thereby understandings, and presentations, fairly unavoidable are subjective. Secondly, also because I unlike e.g. Eurocentrism am not convinced about the idea of e.g. forcing anyone from any non-European cultures to reject and be disloyal to their own customs, cultural views, and ways, to go against their own believes. Of course, as the world is getting smaller – everyone and everything is now just an internet search or a text or a call or a few hours of travel away, then the learning systems and the knowledge in the world likewise moves closer together, and thereby creates what within many fields and areas can be viewed as global commonly accepted modus operandi. Yet, who can with certainty say if e.g. the European (which also inside Europe is quite diverse) – or whichever else – approach is the best way to learn for all people all around? Nobody. It might be for some, according to their concrete mindsets and cultures, but it might not be for others according to them and theirs. And even I as a European can let you know, that the Danish school system I went through (which is considered one of the best in the world) wasn´t my greatest teacher in life compared to how much knowledge and skills I gained elsewhere, especially through personal experiences. The problem with schools often is that they are designed in a way where the

[59] Many has throughout history discussed whether our personalities come from our genetics or our surroundings (a.k.a. our environment), and the answer to this question should clearly be that it of course is a combination of both. Nature does its part (essentialism), and nurture or lack of same does its – we through our choices become what we are (existentialism).

students roughly speaking are looked at as pencils which through their schooling need to be sharpened, but then what if the student is more a pen than a pencil, a pen brakes if forced into the pencil-sharpener. Instead of indorsing how beautiful a story the pen could´ve written, we tragically fail to cultivate and appreciate the student´s individual qualities. Like with e.g. the art of design, of course a design school can benefit someone who want to design without knowing how to design, but for those who really have flair for designing, creativity, courage, and thus innovative design skills as a natural talent within them, schooling of mainly limiting rules might ruin what they have (Ed. had), and otherwise could´ve brought to the table.

Intelligence isn´t directly connected to knowledge, and vice versa, and when people e.g. judge intelligence based on level of formal education then they in fact most of all exploit their own lack of same, and hence become an example of Carl Jung´s following words: "*Thinking is difficult, that´s why most people judge*". Intelligence is not measured by education, just as wisdom not necessarily is measured by age. Of course, it to some degree takes a little bit of braincells to make it through a high education, but still that ain´t (and yes, I know that ' ain´t' isn't grammatically correct) nothing compared to e.g. how far your work-ethic can take you. In line with the usual process of achieving just about anything, the American inventor, Thomas Edison (1847-1931), once said: "*Genius is one percent inspiration and ninety-nine percent perspiration*", and moreover I in relation to my own educations say that intelligence counts for maybe 20% of what it took, tops, while my work-ethic accounted for the last 80% – and that´s even conservative compared to Einstein´s estimate: "*Genius is 1% talent and 99% hard work*. Add to that, that what made me achieve my good grades probably to a degree of 90% was due to my personal life experiences, while only the last 10% had to do with what I officially was taught during my studies.

The former South African convict and President – global symbol for justice, equality, and dignity, Nelson Mandela (1918-2013), truthfully said: *"Education is the most powerful weapon which you can use to change the world"*. That said, you don´t need a fancy education to be wise, or let me rephrase that, education in whatever way you educate yourself *is* important for the process of becoming seriously wise, and it´s important for your growth, but you don´t need formal training and a fancy diploma to be well educated and successful in life, and a formal education is neither a preconditioning guarantee for being wise or successful; quite many stupid people have high educations, while some "easily" can be pure geniuses without having any kinds of formal education.
Before I got my education and openly said what I just said here then the narrowminded majority crowd tended to ask me what antecedents I had to say thus, and further add that I only said what I say because I didn´t have a high education myself, and that I either only were jealous or didn´t knew what I´m talking about. Well, to these petty people, I hope I now "earned" my right to say what I said, cause despite now officially being highly educated I´m still saying what I always said before, during, and after getting my degrees; no one should per se see themselves neglected only due to not having a formal education, and should you for some silly reason still not be convinced, then e.g. take the inventor and physicist, Nikola Tesla (1856-1943), or the tech-magnates, Bill Gates (1955-) and Steve Jobs (1955-2011), as only a *very* few examples among *many* people across *many* different fields who has impacted the world without having any formal higher educational degrees. As the South African entrepreneur and founder of Paypal, Tesla, Space X, and Neuralink, Elon Musk (1971-), puts it: *"Don´t confuse schooling with education. I didn´t go to Harvard but the people that work for me did"*. Or take Einstein´s words on it, *"Wisdom is not a product of schooling but of the lifelong attempt of acquire it"*.

So, how to go about it? Educate yourself, knowledge is "out there" – everywhere, you "just" have to gain it, and if no one gives it to you then go seek, find, and take it yourself. Ignorance is a choice you have to be an ignorant idiot to make, and knowledge leading to understanding to wisdom is the best vaccine against idiocy.
Hence, notwithstanding redundant formalities, you can be someone else´s sheep or you can be your own shepherd, lamb or lion, butler or boss, pussy or pimp – man-whore or madam, controlled or in control, your motherfucking choice.
Often street-smart and streetwise rules academia, and sometimes vice versa, but a combination obviously stand the strongest; grit and desire to learn rules all.
Whatever weakness(es) you might experience as a preventing factor for you to move forward and grow as a person, don´t let yourself to be held back from overcoming any challenge, one way or the other there´s always a way; try and you might fail, but don´t fail to try, and try again if necessary; Don´t fear failure, fear regret; perseverance is key to crush limits, and there´s no limit to education.
If at any "dead end", don´t hold yourself back from seeking advice or sparring or therapy or even a combination of two or all of them, don´t be afraid to do whatever you do your own way; no need to fear enigma, praise innovation, the one who were never different were never sapient.
Free free thinking to free free thinkers, for a free life, for life.

Trust your right to be,
Understand courage makes free,
Educate yourself to see,
Enlightenment is key.

2. Moral is King

Man has an inherent reason, which though are left to play second fiddle to the human passions, which further in the postmodern social constructions are in the shadow of our society-imposed obligations. Thus, if we take into account that ethics and moral closely are connected to our reason, then you wouldn´t have to be a genius to understand how much importance, value, and power – or rather lack of same – we attach to moral, how highly – or rather how little – we prioritize moral, and wherein our moral lacks among others hence lay (psst, hierarchically under our passions which further in general lays under our society imposed obligations). Our biggest moral bust thus simply is how we´re busting our moral. Nevertheless, as ethics and moral are vital ingredients to all human aspects of a healthy world and life itself, we now here flip the bucket upside down, for a brief while pushing the society imposed obligations into the background, and instead aim our focus on mainly ethics and moral, which with character of a trojan horse – human by human – possesses the ability to contribute to the necessary changes of our social constructions and thereby our creation of a better, brighter, and more beautiful world, from inside out.

Despite the origin of morality likely is to be found in evolution rather than abstract sources, there´s absolutely no need to deny the historical importance of either.

When dealing with the philosophical terms of ethics and moral, there as a starting point overall are certain OG (Original "Gangster") traditional significant branches – or traditions if you prefer – of ethics and moral to take into account. While Virtue Ethics, from Plato (427-347 BCE (+/- few years)) and Aristotle (384-322 BCE), before anything aims for the highest form of human happiness and the good life, then Utilitarianism and Kantianism both basically agrees that the ethical choice has to come before any action related

to rules or duties. Thus, while Utilitarianism and Kantianism – or what broadly can be referred to as deontology – "only" deals with ethical action vs. unethical action, then Virtue Ethics has a kind of an extra third layer which is 'how the good life can be achieved'.
However, what all these different moral-orientated branches perspectively overall all have in common are a shared perspective on "the good life" – "the happy life" and "the morally correct (virtuous) life"; they all share the vision of the morally good, insightful, and thereby sapient human, which thus all in all is considered to be referred to as "the happy human", a vision I in this book more than less intent to endorse.
Of course, there are plenty more differences between the different ethical branches, and many more ethical branches to pay attention to if you should choose to go deeper into the philosophical world of ethics. Though, for the sake of simplicity, we for now have the focal points we need to move forward toward fulfilling the purpose of our aim.
Indubitably, our consciousness is connected to a physical body, our brain, and of course our thoughts are only possible due to physical chemical reactions in our brain, but despite our ability to think is made of and depend on atom made material, then the content and thus spirit of our thoughts are not physical – not made of atoms, and they thereby hence are to be considered metaphysical[60]. Therefore, as when talking about thoughts of good and evil, the type of life after death I mentioned in the last chapter, or anything else directly related to our cognitive consciousness, ethics and moral are commonly characterized as metaphysical phenomena.
Also, when dealing with the philosophical terms of ethics and moral, and again this rooted in a call for simplicity, it should be aight to

[60] The term of 'metaphysics' expresses the covering constitution of everything that isn´t physical. Where the physical world covers everything made of atoms (every physical existence is made of atoms), then metaphysics covers everything that isn´t made of atoms.

mention that ethics and moral more or less are two sides of the same coin. As I see it, the term of 'moral' represents the body of good values and thereby the different values of good and decent behavior, and our individual moral thus e.g. has deciding shares of our autonomous decisions – good or bad, while the term of 'ethics' as a kind of an "umbrella term" represents the shared agreement of support to the moral values. For this reason, we´ll from now on and throughout the rest of the book for simplicity primarily stick to the term of moral whenever moral and ethics are being treated.
Furthermore, to also quickly clarify the semantic difference(s) between value(s) and virtue(s), some of the most universal common core moral values e.g. are honesty, trustworthiness, respect, empathy, compassion, patience, etc., just to mention a few of quite many important values which hence represents the core moral goals, which thus further are supplemented by roughly equally many moral virtues, which constitute the moral way(s) to the moral goal(s). And by 'universal' I obviously mean a factor which should be valid above any individual subjective preference – valid here, there, anywhere and everywhere.
To a large extend morality relies on intend. Hence, with briefly less weight on the terms of right and wrong (although these of course constitute a very important distinction in just about all – as in *all* – areas), then the moral of all actions comes down to whether you act in good or bad faith – cause you can´t do anything wrong if doing it for only all the right reasons, right? Although acting right and only in good faith always should be the only goal to strive for, then even if you unintentionally are wrong it still might be acceptable as long as you intentionally act in good faith; "only" deliberately acting in bad faith is and always will be wrong.
To elaborate on good and bad faith, without directly promoting the law (in a later chapter you´ll know why), there as an example related to this subject exist a highly relevant term in law praxis called 'Culpa', which deals with issues concerned around fault or blameworthy

conduct. Culpa is measured from a somewhat fictional character called 'Bonus Pater Familias', who in theory represents the ideal reasonable "good family father" – a synonym for the person who in all situations from nothing but the best intentions optimally act appropriately, a.k.a. always in good faith acts correctly, and hence flawlessly does everything right. Thus, when evaluating how someone – in e.g. a case involving a potential tortfeasor and perhaps a victim – acted, and ergo whether that potential tortfeasor someone carries the guilt and thereby consequently is to blame or not, then 'Bonus Pater Familias' in the light of hindsight is used to raise the unavoidable "guilt-question": What or how would 'Bonus Pater Familias' have done or acted in the given situation, and how does that then align or conflict with the actions of the concrete potential tortfeasor someone.

In the same light, with just about every human action we do or witness in life, we ought – or rather have – to evaluate and measure if moral is fulfilled, whether the action is morally right and comes from intentional good faith, or if moral somewhat is intended met by the action which though unintentionally might not necessarily be right but at least is rooted in good faith, or if the action inexcusably no matter the outcome is rooted in immoral bad intentions and thereby bad faith.

With that said, of course "good" intentions alone cannot justify any bad action. If you e.g. decide to DUI (driving under the influence, a.k.a. e.g. drunk driving) and accidently run some innocent person over, then no matter how good intentions you had about driving straight home without hurting anyone on the way, you still indeed very much are accountable for any damage caused by your bad judgement, and the damaging action you made, which in fact – notwithstanding your own perception of good and bad intentions – became a morally bad intention, and bad faith, in that very second where you chose to risk the safety of others only for the sake of your own benefit – to not instead walk home, or use public

transportation, or spend your money on a taxi, or call someone to come pick you up, or sleep your buzz out before driving home, etc.
Also, even though you only for a short moment are angry at the whole world and therefore don´t recognize any innocence around, then it´s still no excuse for you to act immorally. If you act with negative consequence towards an innocent, then you are the guilty one notwithstanding whoever might be guilty towards you. If you in e.g. anger sincerely feel and thereby convince yourself that others aren´t innocent, then you obviously aren´t acting directly in bad faith despite having bad intention – provided that you sincerely believe that you´re doing the right thing, even if you in fact are wrong. However, an action rooted in unintentional bad behavior is still a bad action, and only universal good faith might relax one such bad action. If e.g. your one year old baby sends a jet of pee straight in your face while you change the baby´s diaper, then you most probably will view this as a somewhat bad action, but since the baby doesn´t know that the action is bad, and since the baby without any bad intentions surely only acted in good faith when it naturally emptied its bladder, which universally of course would be the case for all one year old babies, then you cannot in any way hold the baby accountable for the mess it unintentionally created.
Same universally goes for all conscious creatures who without any sort of hidden agenda are being honest, who you can trust, who respects you, who are compassionate, are patient, etc., if they from the best intentions and in good faith lives up to the universal core moral values, then despite them might still have a lot to learn, or despite you might being of a different opinion than they are, or despite you might in fact know better than they do in relation to a specific matter or situation, then you still cannot really blame anyone merely for their actions rooted in unquestionable good faith. You can e.g. try to teach them why it didn´t serve any particularly good purpose to speak the truth when silence – without lying – would have provided the better outcome; you can pinpoint the

difference between respect and disrespect – how their customs might not apply universally; you can point out why it might not be compassionate to e.g. give money to an addict who spend them buying drugs which thus instead of being compassionate actually potentially in worst case scenario could finance an OD (drug overdose), and thereby "innocently" finance the death of a fellow human (although you surely in the mind of the addict would be doing a big favor and the addict wouldn´t mind taking any chance with the drugs), and that it therefore might instead would be more compassionate to give actual "products" like food, water, clothes, etc., if not "just simply" enriching the needy person by "sober" emotional compassion. And likewise, down the somewhat same alley, in relation to the deed of patience, I guess that most of us also can agree that it doesn´t help anything to be unnecessarily patient if e.g. having what it takes to rescue someone fatally in need of a quick response – if e.g. someone in a wheelchair is stuck between the train tracks at a railway crossing with an approaching train visible in the horizon, then it´s likely not an option to "just" patiently wait for the cavalry to arrive (e.g. police, fire department, or whoever else people expect to come around and do the "dirty job" of saving the day). Therefore, less patient action might also sometimes be required, and it´s thus all good, a.k.a. not immoral, as long as the concrete situation offers no alternative routes to a morally successful result, and the action itself is rooted in good faith. Though, with that said, for the record, too impatient thinking, and hastiness in action, still hardly ever provide the best base for any chance of advantage.

The tricky part emerges and revolves around the line on which stupidity (as discussed in the last chapter) and lack of conscience and thus immorality meets, when it becomes a question whether stupidity in good faith or immorality in bad faith dominates an inexpedient action, and an uncertainty of good or bad faith hence arise.

In this context, it´s of course important quickly to mention that it isn´t possible to utilize and address everybody´s cognitive ability – or lack of same, why our scope of relevance obviously relies on an expectation of a minimum amount of non-retarded mental capacity; no joke why some are declared incapable of managing their own affairs – despite them still rightfully owning the exact same right to as good a life as everybody.
Apparently, there seems to be only a few options in relation to good or bad intention, good or bad faith, and the appertaining different combinations of intention and faith. While bad intention in bad faith and good intention in bad faith of course almost always is equal to immorality, then bad intentions in good faith depend entirely on the concrete situation. By default, bad intention in good faith most often result in bad action and bad moral, but in case of necessary bad intention in good faith, if you e.g. innocently are being attacked and deliberately have to hurt someone to safe yourself, then your intentions are on the verge of good and bad – bad because you deliberately hurt someone, but good because you do it for the right reason(s), and your somewhat fluid intention in combination with your good faith thus could be classified as morally acceptable, again depending on the concrete situation.
However, if one e.g. attempts to hustle morality by only mischievous intentions pretending to be moral, then this in itself is a clear example of immoral bad intention in bad faith, and bad on bad obviously and always will be badly bad – bad to the bone.
Thus, only good intention in good faith always will be equal to good moral, and with nothing but good intentions in good faith you hence can´t really miss to live up to the one and only mandatory rule serving as your eternal safe way to moral conduct, and thereby an eternal clear conscious. Your actions must be morally justifiable in a way whereupon they have no negative consequential effect for anything or anyone innocent. No but(t)s, that's it.

I no doubt wish that what I just wrote with sincerity in its entirety was true, cause it really isn´t in the entity of our world as it currently is – despite intention(s) and faith truly being among the prime factors to judge every action upon. Almost everything depends on the concrete situation, and a single genuine absolute universality of subjective opinions among all individuals is at large quite far from reality. A group or even a majority might can agree on something, but an unavoidable arch-nemesis opposition always seems to exist. Analogically, you can compare the relationship between the polarized perspectives of people – you and the opposition you surely somewhere are up against, to the relationship you have with your own unavoidable reflection in a mirror, up and down are still the same, metaphorically referring to the physical existence, but left and right are completely opposite of each other, metaphorically referring to opposing subjective opinions; one´s freedom-fighter is another one´s terrorist, and vice versa, one´s trash is another one´s treasure, and vice versa, one´s good is another one´s bad, and vice versa, one´s right is another one´s wrong, and vice versa, one´s waste is another one´s world, and in relation to the light at the end of the tunnel, for some it´s the light of hope and freedom while it for others are the light from an oncoming train of destruction.
Nonetheless, on paper, a.k.a. in theory, the potential of reconciliation *do* however exist; in somewhat line with the concept of 'Bonus Pater familias', one most sufficient and appropriate and profitable and thereby maximized "objective best" solution surely do exist in every matter, and the only reason for why "the best" hasn´t mounted up and settled universally in praxis simply is due to what subjective stupidity – e.g. when common sense fails to deliver – yet continuously mess up and thus prevent.
Opposed to the first word of the wording "objective best" which objectively surely is real, the "objective best" in praxis still tend to rely on the eyes of the subjective beholder – still subjectively up for grabs – as opposing subjective perspectives naturally entails

opposing assessments of what the "objective bests" is; we experience the world together separately in each our own subjective consciousness (perhaps logic for battery hens, but some still needs to be reminded), and despite we all seek to be met with understanding and acceptance – at the very least respect (which thus starts with you also meeting others with same), then it for the most part still is okay to disagree (unless we e.g. are talking pedophilia or some crazy off limits shit like that – which clearly defies acceptable boundaries (not least morally)) as long as we at least can agree to disagree in peace with each other. Subjectivity predetermine the setting for the thus destined objectivity, and in that context morality often becomes a war on opposing views and appertaining argumentation, which thus carry the main reason for why we before anything, to overcome the dominating obstructing subjective stupidity, consensually have to define and agree on the basics of moral – in praxis as much as in theory – to thereby set the concrete stage for ensuing the "objective best" universal common moral goals, and the thereto associated perspectives, opinions, solutions, and actions, to emerge and fasten in reality. Universal common moral goals shouldn´t be rocket science to agree on, you own the right to decide your own happiness, but you own absolutely no right to cause unnecessary negativity on any innocent else, period. Nevertheless, and unfortunately, still something this simple apparently is too difficult for some to comprehend, not because they cannot hear or read words and texts like this, but simply because their heads sadly are hollow enough for every externality to go in one ear and out the other – guilty in confusing the subjective seen (a.k.a. preference) with the objective evident. They might be innocent in relation to what they feel and – not – are able to comprehend, but they in Sartrean (1905-1980) style still damn well are highly responsible for how they act or don´t act on their feelings or lack of same, and such people are yet again

(im-)moral examples of what is wrong with this world. And as said before, feel free to feel the reproof merited if sensible.
In establishing the framework around the basics of moral – to move closer toward the universal common moral goals, general interests in general *has* to weigh more than those of individuality, and it therefore as a start quickly should be fair to exclude and thus shoot down any attempt of moral goals related to pure selfishness, greediness, and whatever else bullshit one immorally might seek to achieve at the expense of others. Individuality and independence are amazing and very important features to possess – something worth embracing, you´re free to decide your own destiny, you are worth no less than the next one, you´re obliged to value and respect yourself and your own meaningfulness, and your personal basic needs, growth, and happiness, should never unnecessarily be neglected, no doubt, but in a moral context one´s egocentric goal(s) of gain surely shouldn´t entail *any* avoidable devasting downfall loss on others. Instead, as already mentioned in the first and second paragraph of this chapter, it morally should be mandatory to agree that the "objective best" must be connected to an endorsement of what I earlier referred to as the "happy human", not merely one human but rather all humans, and beyond. Hence, for the sake of unambiguous clarity, in an extended version where an "s" is added so to say "happy humans" – literally replacing singular by plural, and then also further with an outspoken broader horizon of "happiness" to not "only" cover human happiness, but additionally also "happy animals", a "happy nature", a "happy world", "universal happiness", i.e. happiness for every creature, plant, and tree, happiness for all life all around, and in between.
Our individual potential constitutes our shared ditto. Ergo, we should never quit aiming high on subjective improvement(s) towards achieving our moral potential; regardless of any subjective limitation(s), we always have to hang on tight to the prospect of getting as close to the "objective best" as possible, and the smarter

you are the more potential you have, the less excusable you are, the more responsible you are, the greater you can be, and the greater you are, the greater we all are.

It´s not completely without truth to state that the "objective best" – among others – is connected to the main principle of Utilitarianism, as proposed by its founder, Jeremy Bentham (1748-1832): *"the greatest amount of good for the greatest number of people"*, in which sense the end pretty much always sanctifies the means.

When promoting a Utilitaristic statement of die-hard – cost-benefit-analytic – calculation like that, it´s likewise not weird that the topic of conversation frequently quickly turns to the famous question of whether or not it thence is okay to kill one to save ten others? Well, it might be, it´s not unlikely that one such scenario with large probability "in fact" shows to be the objective best solution – although it of course always depend on the exact details of the concrete situation, to which murder as ultimately irreversible surely always should be no less than the absolute last resource of action; "just" because you perhaps don´t see any other solution(s) it doesn´t necessarily mean that there are no alternative – better – solution(s) to be found; certainly no need to e.g. inherit the cruelty of Stalin´s (1878-1953) (the Soviet Union´s former extreme mass murdering despot dictator – who reportedly had approximately 20 million unnatural deaths to his name) kinda reversed Utilitarian quote, *"if one man dies of hunger, that is a tragedy. If millions die, that´s only statistics"*. Cause, despite it sadly don´t take much more than a news bulletin to know he´s right – that most spectators cannot take in and relate to too many tragedies at once and therefore give up on and ignore to make a profound difference to the world outside themselves or their own household, and although Stalin clearly from madness thought he was doing his Utilitarian duty for the better of first and foremost himself and *then* the surviving part of "his" population, he from an ocean of alternative options and directions to take clearly took his intentions to an historical immoral wrong turn at a level astronomically out of proportions – probably "only" surpassed by the Chinese communist leader, Zedong Mao (1893-1976), who reportedly is responsible for up against 78 million cruel Chinese deaths[61]. And just to let every news spectator – and everybody else – know, passivity kinda equals complicity.

Instead, to give an elaborating example of an answer to the "famous" Utilitaristic question ("okay to kill one to save 10?"), here on the note of a rare correspondence between utilitarianism and Buddhism – as these two branches on many parameters "normally" seems to operate with some distance from each other in the moral philosophical spectrum, and again related to my time in the Nepalese monastery: One of only three items I *had* to bring with me for my stay in the monastery was a bottle of insect repellant (bug spray) (the other two items was a headlamp and a sleeping bag – just for you not to waste your focus wondering here), simply because that if I e.g. even by reflex came to slap and thus kill even a biting mosquito, then it simply would be considered to be an unforgiveable sin which without a trial or any questions asked would cause me to be kicked out of the monastery "on ass and elbows". One of the main Buddhist teachings goes: You are not allowed to kill anything at all, and hence also not a biting mosquito. In fact, you should actually at best allow for anything and everyone to feast, even sacrifice parts of yourself if that´s what it takes for e.g. a blood thirsty mosquito to quench its thirst from your body, and based on this believe my mentor monk (which in fact was a nun with Swedish roots) every night sacrificed one of her legs for the mosquitos to drink from for half an hour when she went to bed, as likewise the Lama of the monastery sacrificed his entire back with

[61] During his campaign, "The Great Leap Forward" (1958-1962), Mao (a.k.a. Chairman Mao) in his effort to reconstruct China from an agrarian economy to a communistic society, among others starved his own population to death.

the same purpose – even when he was proselytizing (on a missionary) in an area full of dangerous malaria mosquitos in Africa; he was willing to risk his life to give the mosquitos what he had to offer. Nevertheless, in addition to the rule about not being allowed to kill anything, all living creature are equals, no one have any more right to life than any other unless it e.g. comes down to a ultimate choice between a mosquito or you, one of you simply *have* to die, then you´re suddenly obliged to kill the mosquito to save yourself as you as a human with all your presumably superior human features vs. the presumably less gifted mosquito have a greater potential of doing more good for a greater number of living creatures than the mosquito have[62]. This thus suddenly fairly matches a more hardcore rationalistic utilitarian approach to solutions and opinions, and same believe can thus prove valid in a situation where e.g. one under-franked cuckoo marbleless sadistic maniac is about to kill a large group of people, either he is eliminated or he eliminates them, if you have the chance of taking him out before he takes them out, then you most likely are like obliged to do so as the large group of people presumably have a greater potential of doing more good for a greater number of creatures than the one maniac have, which thus hereby should propose an answer to the gradually quite trivial question related to Utilitarianism – albeit the answer isn´t universal unambiguously mounted to every concrete situation; the only constant is that everything constantly is changing, constant motion calls for constant revision, and the premise for the "objective best" can thus

[62] In line herewith it moreover should be quite legit to question why it in the 22nd century is relatively easy to rescue and adopt a street dog from just about every country (i.e. e.g. have the dog flown in from e.g. a poor or war-torn country), but almost impossible and even often illegal to rescue and give shelter to a person (i.e. e.g. have the person flown in from e.g. the very same poor or war-torn country), e.g. a suffering refugee? For sure saving a dog (or any innocent creature for that matter) is a great good deed, but does humans suddenly have less worth than a dog merely for being human?

change drastically according to situational changes – not least those of subjective interference.
We learn from the past, we try to predict the fluid future, but our decision-making is and always will be present. Hence, to be fair, it realistically until further e.g. will take a yet unrealistic superhuman AI (Artificial Intelligence) machine-learning and real-time intelligence machine able to digitize, process, and thus datalyze every single detail of everything to therethrough predict and thereby look into the future to flawlessly always make the one and only optimal "objective best" decision leading to the best solution in every situation; as – almost – everything in theory objectively can be numbered, then also – almost – everything can be quantified. However, despite it´s no secret that we humans to a certain degree have limits to our capabilities – although those limits often are less than we tend to think ourselves (or the opposite), it still, until the future might provide us with one such superhuman device, shouldn´t prevent any single one of us from doing our absolute outmost to chase down and getting as close as possible to "the objective best" in every decision we make. With an average of give and take 35000 decisions to be made a day by the average adult, then even the slightest effort of improvement should prove to matter a valuable great deal.
The objective best thought to best solution to best action do potentially exist within and thus from the subject, and this potential hence is exactly where object- and subjectivity potentially intersect and in harmony melt together – where subjective reason potentially delivers the objective best result; no reason not to chase your full potential, no need not to go for the gold.
Since the early age of philosophy, many philosophers have unsuccessfully tried to bridle and slate the concept of moral, and still to this day one of the major philosophical problems related to moral-philosophy continuously is how to unite the thought of a general and obligating moral with the idea of a totally free and

authentic existence. Here the meta-problem, meaning the problem within the problem, is, that obligating moral and total freedom clearly by definition in praxis are a contradiction in terms – obligation obviously nullifies total freedom, and vice versa, and therefore they simply don´t mix. As long as people hear, see, and think as *they* want, as long as freedom and an authentic existence rules, then unambiguous subject based universal moral is reduced to a hoax with no practical place on Earth. Thus, to get closer of reaching a praxis orientated, rational, and hence useful solution to this issue, and to not drown in a philosophical feud of theories trying to solve an unreachable reconciliating unification of obligating moral and total freedom, then there for a quick fix hardcore is a ascertain need for us to distinguish between mere theory and actual praxis. Hence, I´m e.g. not giving you a moral-theoretical pacifistic "Jesus-speech" here, about how you always have to turn the other cheek, definitely not. Cause, although truth in what the Indian lawyer, politician, and spiritual leader, Mahatma Gandhi (1869-1948), once said, *"An eye for an eye only ends up making the whole world blind"*, then you of course in praxis are allowed to make use of your freedom to stand up for yourself, and others for that matter, if e.g. some wicket clown seriously steps out of line, as long as you make sure that you have your conscious clean doing it, a.k.a. that you always all the way all day every day have moral by good intentions in good faith in your corner (at least good faith, which as said *sometimes* even alone can be good enough), as you otherwise "unfortunately" will have to wear the clown nose and Bozo name tag yourself; don´t start a fight, don´t run head first into a wall, but if you´re in a pickled corner and can´t avoid it, then feel free to finish it if someone out of pocket undeserved picks one with you – one you cannot peacefully avoid; self-defense isn´t the problem if the first attack shouldn´t have happened in the first place. Sometimes you gotta do what you gotta do to be able to do what in a greater good perspective needs to be done. As the American rapper, Tupac

Shakur (1971-1996), sings on his Hail Mary track: "*I ain´t a killer but don´t push me*". Not that I believe in death penalty, all I'm saying is that accidents do occur; every carrot you give can be misinterpreted to be perceived as an orange stick of dynamite. Again, moral is king, and don´t throw stones from your glasshouse.
As long as negativity, destructivity, immorality, etc., exist, until heyday utopia universally take root, then total freedom simply cannot exist universally in social settings without some schmuck somewhere somehow surely see it as a chance to take "advantage" at the expense of others. And that alone thus contradicts *the* mandatory moral obligation which at any cost cannot be afforded to be ignored or neglected.
Some people think that they can get away with just about everything by giving an apology, that they can lie to someone, snitch on or bad-mouth someone, hurt someone, etc., and then just say "I´m sorry" to wipe the board clean. I agree that it often is easier to ask for forgiveness than it is to get the permission, but personally, often – depending on good or bad faith – an apology alone doesn´t do it for me, it´s simply too easy to think that you e.g. can just walk up and hit someone and then believe that you can get away with it by just saying "I´m sorry". Fair enough to regret what you did, and fair enough to give an apology, but be aware that it probably takes more than a couple of words to make things right. I´ve said it before and I say it again, words mean fuck all if your actions don´t add up – don´t just say it, show it, or better yet, try not to fuck up in the first place.
Related to the challenge of formulating universal moral, I´ve tried to find forward the really heavy artillery, I´ve tried to think in complex formulas, I´ve laid sleepless and virtually been caught up in higher altitudes of big thoughts, only to one day realize that I here actually was aiming and flying high above the desired target, that I was overrating what I was looking for, and that the provision of the sought doctrine actually is an example of how communication

sometimes is best served by "less is more". Universal moral that covers all and everything probably doesn´t exist, which is something I´ll elaborate on in a later chapter (Love is God), however, one of the absolute best moral guides, which even depend on your freedom, is one that might seem pretty basic, perhaps even too easy at first glimpse here, but really it isn't, it´s something which most people already know but still continuously constantly have a tendency of forgetting: Simply ask yourself, 'would I want others to do the same to me as I intend doing to them?' E.g. before you hit somebody, ask yourself, 'would I want someone else to hit me? Would I want someone else to take advantage of me? Would I want someone else to treat me bad? Would I want someone else to fuck me up? Would I want someone else to treat my loved one(s) bad? Or would I rather want that someone to help fill me up with joy and help me up if I fall? Would I want others to respect me for being me? Would I want everybody else to treat my loved one(s) well?', and so forth. Use your freedom to ask yourself these types of questions in all situations as they can help you to realize what you might not at first approximation thought of and saw. What might be your disconnect might be someone else´s most important connect, just as their disconnect might be your most important. Use your freedom to make the right decision(s), to do what right is; use your freedom to train and make use of the human(e) ability to mentalize in order to understand other people – to build up some empathy, and then ask yourself what the other people would want you to do around them, to do to them, or rather for them – for you both. Don´t be too controlled and concerned by what a third person (or) source – including e.g. a law or a religious text – would want you to do to another, but rather keep your focus directly aimed at what morally right is according to the concrete situation, that you treat others with same level of respect as you wish to receive from them. And in doing so, it´s furthermore important for you to be as openminded as possible towards different standpoints and perspectives –

especially outside of your own comfort zone. If you e.g. are religious and another one isn´t, if you practice praying and another one doesn´t, then it most likely would be appropriate for you to ask yourself: 'Would I want that other person to deny my prayer, or that person to punish me for praying? And would I then – a.k.a. should I then – deny anyone else´s freedom not to pray, should I then punish anyone else for not praying, or for not being religious at all? Or should I actually instead show the other person the exact same amount of respect as I expect – a.k.a. demand – to be shown myself?'. As the American Novelist, Writer, and Poet, Herman Melville (1819-1891), expressed in his classic, 'Moby Dick' (1851): "*I have no objection to any person´s religion, be it what it may, so long as that person does not kill or insult any other person, because that other person don´t believe it also*". Do to yourself as you please, but unless "your victim" with sanity explicitly and sincerely ask you to (e.g. in relation to BDSM[63] sex, etc.), then don´t in any *fucking* way do to anyone else what you wouldn´t want them to do to you – don´t *fucking* do to anyone else what you wouldn´t see done to the one(s) you love the most, simple as that, capisci.

And by the by, somewhat down the same alley that mantra also assert itself to the *almost* exact opposite approach, treat and do to others as you would like them to treat and do to you – though without the same high level of stringent unbendability and inflexibility as you in general shouldn´t do more to anyone than they welcome you to, i.e. if you e.g. have a death wish of your own then don´t automatically expect others to share that with you.

However, if you e.g. are starving without access to food, would you then wish for someone to share their food with you? If you´re hopelessly homeless, would you then wish someone to help you get a home and hope? If you´re ill in need of treatment, would you then wish for someone to make available the treatment you need? If

---

[63] BDSM = 'Bondage and discipline, dominance and submission, sadism and masochism'.

you´re unemployed and broke, would you then wish for someone not only to help you survive but to actually live? – etc. I guess it´ll be a yes to all. Mentalize and thus try to understand how "they" feel and what "they" need – even if any unnecessary and useless proudness, and from that mindset it should be quite obvious why you to the best of your abilities always should strive to treat and do to others what you in their shoes would want them to do to or for you, provided that they the other way around were wearing yours. *"Thou shalt love thy neighbor as thyself"*[64]. Compassion, solidarity, and mutual prosperity, we all share a natural need of defecating, and where basic sanitation – both literally and analogically – is in deficit, only a selfish asshole appropriate more toilet paper than needed.

'Memento mori', remember the inevitability of death – remember that you´ll die, is one of the central terms of the antique philosophy of Stoicism, as founded by Zeno of Citium (334-262 BCE), and among others intermediated by famous Stoics such as Seneca (4 BCE-65 CE), the freed slave Epictetus (50 CE-135 CE), and the once Roman Emperor, Marcus Aurelius (121 CE-180 CE), etc. The point of 'memento mori' is related to the idea of the sphere of control, that there are certain things which we *can* control, and things which we *cannot* control, and until we find the source to eternal life, then the fact that we´ll all die[65] is one of them things which we *cannot* control. As the philosopher and first American psychologist, William James (1842-1910), called it out: *"The knowledge that we must die is "the worm at the core" of the human condition"*. We all experience situations beyond our control, e.g. sorrow and grief if loosing someone dear to us, and the optimal scenario in relation to a cure of our uncontrollable emotions, notwithstanding our

---

[64] From the Gospel of Matthew, 22, 37-40.

[65] A "fun" fact related to our inevitable death is that there despite everything still overall "only" is four different ways to die, natural death, accident, suicide, and murder, that´s it.

concrete emotional experiences, is that we learn to accept the irreversible circumstances as they are, that we instead of fighting an already lost battle paradoxically learn to accept to live with the unacceptable, that what happened simply is beyond our control, and that we thus instead *have* to aim our focus on what we within our control actually *can* change rather than torturing ourselves with what we anyway *cannot* change. The American theology professor, Reinhold Niebuhr (1892-1971), in his Serenity Prayer expressed it as such: "*God, grant me the serenity to accept the things I cannot change, The courage to change the things I can, And the wisdom to know the difference*"; skip placing the responsibility with an external God (except from the external part of the ubiquitous love) from the equation, and I think he nailed the essence. I´m fully aware that this is way easier said than done – especially for a deep whirling minded overanalyzing thinker like myself, and of course we should all be allowed to feel and express our emotions, and some emotions we might never get over, but we *have* to learn to accept our lack of control in order for us to live and move on in life post experiences of powerlessness. Therefore, we humans have to accept death as a natural exit of our – and our loved ones – decisive existence. By our passion we have to obtain understanding of our world, and we have to value and maximize our short time of life while we have it as we "only" have this one and only chance of our lifetime to positively make our impact worthwhile before our hourglass eventually runs out.

Stoicism constitutes a tripartite of 'physics' as a representation of our world, 'logic' as a representation of our perception, and 'ethics' as a representation of the human ability to shape ourselves, and to care for both ourselves and our fellow human beings – which in my view should mean care for all living creatures, and everything else for that matter, in line with what Charles Darwin (1809-1882) also said: "*The love for all living creatures is the most noble attribute of man*".

Everything simply is a part of nature, nature is decided and regulated by rational principles, and since we humans thus also naturally are a part of nature, then we basically also are to be considered rational creatures. According to stoicism, an authority higher than reason doesn´t exist – the highest form of authority simply *is* reason, and nothing is above or even next to reason which likewise lays the groundwork for the referable inherent reason of man, as presented in the opening of this chapter. This dualism of nature and reason is what Stoics refer to as 'logos', which to them is the closest we can ever get to something godlike, a view I don´t completely share as I more see 'logos' as merely a subpart under the umbrella of love – which I in more details also intend to elaborate on in a later chapter (Love is God).
Additionally, another central thesis of Stoicism is that we humans has to divide our reason and emotions to thereby being able to make our decisions exclusively based on reason rather than with an interfering of irrational emotions (which potentially leads to a "wrong" precepting opinion on the real world), as this is our way to an unbeatable mindset and an unbreakable will, and ergo why the term "Stoic" colloquially has come to mean "unemotional". To cut to the bone, the stoic ideal is to live in perfect harmony with logos (nature and reason), which somewhat quite equals what I earlier referred to with 'Bonus Pater Familias' – although I personally still prefer a less strict binary[66] approach with more room for causation rooted in both reason and human emotion depending on the concrete situation (somewhat mechanism-wise matched with what I earlier mentioned about object- and subjectivity melting together). Still and overall, what is colossally and crucially important to understand is that despite the use of Stoicism (or any other type of moral philosophy for that matter) might – and hopefully – directly prove beneficial for the individual practitioner, then the main

[66] 0 or 1, right or wrong, this or that, a black or white fallacy, and so on…

objective still by far is the vision of the individual´s personal redemption and therefrom contribution to the greater good – for just about everything and all creatures to benefit and enjoy from, what we as one collectively can achieve.

Also, Stoicism – as well as everything else "I´ve" given you in this chapter – is not meant to be just theoretical philosophy for us to only think and talk about, it´s a way of life to realize and live, so be selective of what you pick and live it; no need to ever vow and limit yourself 1:1 to a single prescribed theory or ideology, no need to wear theoretical or ideological blinding blinkers, most depend on the concrete situation, and complete predictability is thus a rarity in an unpredictable life. Better to stick to being free to be inspired, to hand pick, and to choose a combination of the best of the best from the best, to take and make use of what´s useful, and to always work and apply your own free will long before, simultaneously, and for the rest to come; no need for you to freely swap and reduce a free existence to a life in straightjacket.

You're supreme, and as long as you keep your moral conscious clean, then you shouldn't have to apologize to whoever mistakenly thinking that you're a submissive part of their supremacy. Any aim of any kind of supremacy other than the one of one´s own supreme autonomy basically is immoral and utterly unacceptable, unless "vitally larger" – e.g. greater good – in a universal sense is at stake (to spell it out, e.g. dogmatic religious views – including politics and money – isn´t it).

As we know, freedom is an essential ingredient to the path towards Enlightenment, which thus further among others should entail and secure a healthy moral. No need to be ordinary, don´t give in to mediocracy, don´t be afraid to conform to be your own, to be extraordinary in your own way; acknowledge your own potential, acknowledge our potential, acknowledge *the* potential.

Moral consciousness instigates a clean conscious; eternal sunshine in a spotless mind; introspection and mentalization – make it your forte, let moral guide you, and with good intentions in good faith feel free to live and spree all you authentically can feel, breathe, and see to be.

2.2. A Great Liar is a Great Magician

Adolf Hitler (luckily dead) once said that *"great liars are also great magicians"*. The tactic in this quote Hitler immorally demonstrated to his own advantage in 1938 by settling a peace treaty-ish agreement with Britain, France, and Italy, known as the 'Munich Agreement', or what later came to be known as the 'Munich Betrayal', through which Hitler was handed over the control of Sudetenland, a part of what was once known as Czechoslovakia (today two independent states, Czech Republic and Slovakia), by promising to go no further, a.k.a. if he promised not to attack and occupy any other country thereafter. After the meeting in Munich, the British Prime Minister, Neville Chamberlaine (1869-1940), returned to London, and already as he stepped out of the plane on his arrival he proudly waved the Anglo-German Declaration above his head as to tell the attending journalists to tell his population – and the rest of Europe – that he by that piece of paper now firmly had Hitler by his balls, and that he thus just had *"brought peace for our time"*, as Chamberlaine expressed it. Nevertheless, back in Munich, in Hitler´s diabolic mind, his signature on that piece of paper meant absolutely nothing of anything positive – no more than any other fuck he had ever given. Hitler had only signed the papers to test Chamberlaine´s negotiability, and most of all to simply shut Chamberlaine up – to get him off his tale and out of sight. As soon as Chamberlaine was out the door in Munich, Hitler reportedly had trash talked him behind his back, among others called him an *"asshole"*, and less than a year later German Nazi troops with no

fucks given to any signed peace treaty moved on to invade the next country, Poland, and Second World War was on.
Roughly said, Hitler´s quote can be translated into "the wise fools the less wise" (a.k.a. the fool). However, tragic ironic you´ll paradoxically have to be kind of a fool to lie – not least morally, why it primarily is fools who foolishly are practicing something as foolish as lies, self-denying fools aiming at fooling other fools. I´m not saying that all liars are completely unintelligent, cause they of course somewhat has to have some portion of intelligence to be able to come up with a "good" lie, but a truly intelligent person, a cleaver person, a wise person, should know and cherish what is right from wrong from a larger greater good perspective, instead of buying in to being an immoral selfish lying asshole, a fool. Among others, Hitler very mildly said was an immoral lying asshole, and on the basis of the thesis "exaggeration promotes understanding", do you really want to be typecast to fit the same immoral fool booth as Hitler? If you lie, then don´t pretend to think that your lies are any less a mendacity than Hitler´s lies, that his other crazy immoral actions makes his lies equally more immoral than your own lies, cause notwithstanding different levels of consequences and complexities across different lies, then you still in the moment around a lie either are an immoral lying asshole or you´re not, either you´re a fake ass or you´re not, either you´re a fool or you´re not, and the question is if you continuously wish to be a fool? I´ve studied fools all my life, and I´ve plenty times been acquainted with being a fool, hustling, bullshitting, and lying, all the crooked shit tricks in the book, I learned from the best and became the best – I was the best, thus waste of time trying to fool this old fool, fool.
My very initial thought about this piece of writing, from even before I eventually decided to take on the challenge of an actual book – this book, actually erupted from a specific thought I had about the concept and culture of lying. No matter who I ask about the legitimacy of lying, then there seems to be a universal consensus

about lying as being wrong, some of course tries to justify "little white lies", or that they only as self-portraited merciful Samaritans use lies to spare others from the harsh reality of the truth which they in advance thus expect only themselves strong and hence capable enough to handle and deal with, but at the end of the day, everybody still unanimously strongly agree that lying fundamentally is wrong, and still everybody prefer – even demand – to receive nothing but honesty and the pure truth from others. Yet, despite everybody wanting to be handed the whole truth and nothing but the truth, then still to this day I have *never* met a single person older than a baby who never lied – you included I´m sure, as I´m positive you know I know you know.

In a (Ed. our) mythomaniac world, we seriously have to ask ourselves why we do it, why we collectively keep going up against our own believe, why we accept lying (including exaggeration) as an integrated – just about universal – norm in human culture, why we keep doing the opposite of what we know and agree is the right thing to do – why we keep doing the opposite to others of what we expect them to do to us, why it obviously is so love damn hard to "just" keep it real by being honest, and this both to ourselves as well as others.

I believe that Bob Marley for starters had a firm grip at the long end when he spoke the following: *"The problem is people are being hated when they're real, and are being loved when they´re fake"*. From personal experiences, I agree that it opposite the old sayings "honesty is the best policy", and "honesty pays", sadly all too often benefit one considerably more if embellishing the truth, avoid the truth, or unmitigated directly lie instead of merely sticking to de facto of the truth. Likewise, Plato reportedly once said (perhaps he in fact was the OG inspiration to the before mentioned quote by Bob Marley, if it wasn´t because they both "just" were observants to those aspects of the world which we all see but still are denied by many): "*No one is more hated than he who speaks the truth*" (yea, they were clever those old Greeks, when they didn´t fuck too young boys in the ass). The truth is often badly heard; on paper, most prefer to hear the truth – even the ugly truth, but the truth of the matter is that many cannot tolerate and handle to actually hear the truth should it conflict with their own wishes and perspectives, and especially if it exposes their own lack of same. If thus, the truth-teller who rightfully should receive respect instead receives disrespect, the hero becomes the villain, and vice versa, and under such circumstances the truth can and will never prevail. Wistfully, this scenario all too often is the reality, and only you-me-we can ever change this unethical and unhealthy culture; fair enough not liking how the truth looks or sounds or both, but at least be respectful enough to respect the honesty.

Every time someone isn´t being honest – not telling the truth or omits the truth or not showing their true self (e.g. including fake niceness), and every time someone doesn´t respect other people's honesty – every time a lie gives the better payoff compared to the truth, then an unhealthy sphere of cheat and deception, a.k.a. fraud and fakeness, immorally is created. Such a sphere can and must none of us be better served by. It might reward the single individual in the short term, but in the long term everybody will be entangled into, affected, and confronted by the lies afloat, no exceptions.

The balance issue here is thus not whether or not you should be honest, cause we all always should as much as possible, and we always should have a sphere where honesty is accepted, respected, preferred, appreciated, and perhaps even rewarded. The balance issue here hence rather is concentrated around in which way you are honest, cause instead of "just" plain and simple for no reason stabbing someone with your truth by e.g. telling that they´re ugly – even if you feel that they are, or unprovoked spilling someone else´s beans (a.k.a. revealing someone else´s secrets), or exorcising whatever else kind of unnecessary truth telling, we have to remember that some truths are better kept than shared if they e.g.

serve no other purpose than "just" hurting or compromising someone – still no reason to spread lies. And even if you´re convinced about the truth of something, even if it actually *is* the truth, then keep remembering that there always at the very least are tens of thousands of different ways of expressing the very same thing; currently 7100+ languages in the world, many more dialects, and almost endless ways of expression and delivery; no shame in balancing your choice of presentation, no need to be bringing another person an underserved verbal rampage, no need to attack, strike, or shoot someone down if reconciliation is well within reach, be greater than that, especially if your – or the universal – truth is rooted in circumstances out of that or those someone´s hand(s) – e.g. rooted in natural incidents such as innate given genetics, etc.
A senior sergeant from the Danish special forces once told me under his command, "*I might not tell you the whole truth, but you can be sure that I´ll never lie to you*". Hence, sometimes at least not lying actually can prove to be the most sufficient approach according to a specific situation, or the most respectful you can actually be to another person – although it of course also depends on the concrete situation and the preferences of the concrete other person. Personally, I rather live unhappy with transparent honesty and the raw truth than happily in the unknown or on a lie. An ostrich manipulates itself by lying to itself, it deals with difficult situations by sticking its head into the ground to thus convince itself that the difficulties it no longer sees hence no longer exist. Au contraire, I´m an adherent of facing the world as it truly is – of having eye contact with reality, although still not rejecting that most of us can experience to have a need of momentarily withdrawing for peace "in the darkness of the hole". However, and hence, don´t fool yourself, don´t be deliberately naïve, don´t unnecessarily be an ostrich.
I take pride in my own honesty, and only because I´m honest myself I thus also can demand of others to be honest with me (a

mechanism which by the way just about goes for every kind of standard you demand); I value people who are being honest with me, I respect people for telling the truth (when it makes sense), I most often find it disrespectful if people aren´t being honest with me (I most often can´t help to take it personal), and I directly loose respect for – or even despise – people if they lie (when it doesn´t make sense and excuses are excluded).

If you´re sincere and honest, if you no matter the essence of the truth is able to at least respect the honesty – and only if, then you surely are entitled to demand for same in return. However, if somebody proves to be entirely fugazi, then instead of you accommodating and hosting this somebody´s shortcomings, trust yourself and your right to be selective enough not to put your faith and trust in that fool; unavoidable is here the quite trite yet truthful and relevant doctrine, "they fool you once, shame on them, they fool you twice, shame on you". Can people change for the better, hopefully yes, should you forget, nope, should you be able to forgive, absolutely, unconditionally, abso-fucking-lutely not.

Though, focus less on fighting back, and more on fighting forward; always remember, just because something appears to be the one and only truth to you, then it doesn´t necessarily means that it likewise is the truth to others, and vice versa; don´t let yourself to be pulled down by others because they might feel to have another truth about you than what you know is your actual truth – without lying to yourself, listen to what they say, process what they say, but don´t ever allow them to manipulate you into becoming their truth if it´s out of sync with reality or directly is based on a lie. After all, no human sees everything, and universal truths *are* quite rare.

I admit that I´ve a hard time trusting people, not bound to the old adage about how "all thieves think that everybody´s stealing" – I really don´t fit the criteria (despite being a semi-old fool), but simply because that´s what my experiences thoroughly has taught me; the

question isn´t *if* "people" lie, but rather the question is *when* "people" lie – and that include exaggeration.
To polish my own halo, and with the risk of sounding a bit narcissistic and smug, I´m honestly the most honest and reliable person I know, I rather not promise anything than promise something I might can't keep, which is also why I – to "get the job done" – often rather act and rely on "only" myself as a one-man-army instead of relying on e.g. a potential 500-weak-man-army of others; rather one 500 carat diamond than 500 one carat diamonds. That said, seriously good, smart, and somewhat reliable people do of course exist "out there" (I´m my own example – I said while polishing my halo), and after years of practice I´ve now slowly started to learn that it sometimes does pay off to actually ask for help when needed. It shouldn´t cost a thing to ask, it shouldn´t hurt to ask, and so you shouldn´t be afraid to offer, give, or ask for help. The art of the trick is to be as independent and peer-selective as humanly possible without being unfair, unnecessarily judgmental, self-important, selfish, egocentric, anti-solidaristic, or antisocial, to know and contribute to the value of an open-minded atmosphere with rich room for diversity which thus thereby should provide the best conditions for a healthy synergy, team spirit, and sparring to thrive in the best possible way, and according to your surplus to offer and give your assistance where and when you can add beneficial value, and further thereby consciously legitimize to enjoy and profiting receive the like of others – although your motivations for giving shouldn´t be mandatorily rooted in merely intentions and expectations of receiving.
Room for disagreement and constructive discussions leaves room for potential learning. We´re all different, we all have different talents, sometimes you give more than you receive, sometimes you receive more than you give, but surely acting in concert most often should provide the better potential of achieving the better outcome which thus on average should lead to the better result; the more

honest you are the better help you give, the better prerequisites others have for helping you, and the better chances you thus have of receiving help for the better; the more morality you carry the more honest you can be, the more honest you are the less anyone can use your truth(s) against you – what´s already out in the open you don´t have to hide, and the less you hide the more you´re free. As the – at least partly – author of the bible likewise at least truthfully ascribed to his Jesus-character in John 8:32, "*And ye shall know the truth, and the truth shall make you free*".

Another quote I like about truth telling comes from a person who goes by the name of The Stoic Emperor, and quote on quote it goes as follows: "*Truth telling is mostly a matter of stating the obvious so that it remains obvious*". Nevertheless, the most obvious in this world is that it most obviously most often isn´t obvious. If that was the case, we for starters definitely would be much more compassionate, and hence take much better care of each other. One might feel that something should be pretty obvious, but then again someone else most likely quite quickly will see to make sure to show that it obviously isn´t. When I e.g. write that truth sets you free, then it among others is because the truth on the one side obviously will free and perhaps even remove a heavy mental burden from your shoulders, but on the other hand there of course obviously also is a risk of your truth being used against you – and your freedom – if you e.g. have done something unlawful – to e.g. throw your ass to jail. Notwithstanding if your truth obviously isn´t morally wrong then your concession obviously easily can cause you negative consequences in a world of subjective judgements, religions, and laws. The question here thus is if it´s more important to be moral and somewhat mentally free, or if it´s more important to be controlled by (Ed. a slave of) other people´s judgements – including those of authoritarian caliber? At least to me it´s completely obvious, and even Einstein seems to back me up on this: "*Blind belief in authority is the greatest enemy of truth*".

We always have to aim at being as honest and as direct as possible without disrespecting differences, different perspectives, and thus different – perspective based – truths, and thus without deliberately hurting anyone, including yourself. By 'yourself' I here of course mean don´t with lies hate on or be cruel to yourself, but also, should you e.g. by any chance ever find yourself innocently in a rendezvous situation with some diabolic madman pointing a gun to your face, and your truth surely underserved will make this person to pull the five pounds trigger and thereby blow your brains out, then it probably doesn´t do any good to pull the tiger´s tale here, and it might on an exceptional basis thus be acceptable for you to deny and lie the best you can to slick yourself out of the critical situation in order for you to then be able to tell this person the actual truth on a rebound, under more favorable circumstances, without Grim Reaper escorting you from the party; there´s a thin line between being a sell-out and wise, and a thin line between being unwise and brave or courageous. However, again, with that said, lying should *never* be misused, the ability to tell a lie should *never* be a cheap incentive to immoral and dishonorable manipulation. All lies eventually catch up, at the end of the day, at the end of the road, at the end of it all, you´re the one who´ll have to be able to look yourself in the mirror, you´re the one who´ll be remembered for what *you* stood for – your legacy is *your* responsibility. Whenever you can get away with the truth, pick to stick with the truth, even if you´re shaking.
When some say that "the smart tricks the less smart", or that "it´s wise to cheat but stupid to get caught", then it nonetheless should be basic knowledge that it fundamentally is wrong to cheat and unwise of us to continuously hold on to an unnecessary code of conduct wherein cheating often pays off; every time one cheat this cheater unwisely maintain cheating, and every time cheating is accepted or rewarded then the motivation for cheating is maintained; instead of being "smart" with a low character, then

damn fucking rather be a good person with a strong character and a clean conscious – smart enough not to cheat. Only overcoming cheat outweighs and legitimize the exigency of cheating.
Another thing I never really understood is peer-pressure, I mean, I´m aware that we humans are social creatures who in general wants to fit in with other people and the group dynamics which surrounds us, and of the motivations for why some people more than others have a tendency to bow down and give in to peer-pressure, e.g. low self-confidence, low self-esteem, low self-worth, fear, etc. But shiiit, giving in to peer-pressure probably in itself carry some of the reason for why these people aren´t being respected in the first place anyway, and why they´ve lost their self-respect. Of course, there probably are individual and more specific reasons to the eruption of low self-confidence, low self-worth, etc., but giving into peer-pressure – especially if you know what´s happening is wrong, and depending too much on other people´s approval, won´t in any way be any contributing key to any long lasting positive improvement within yourself, that´s for love damn sure; break the bad habit once, twice, three times and more, and it´ll be equally easier every time to come.
As with peer-pressure, the urge of belongingness again plays a big part to why we humans on average tend to spend around an hour a day to gossip about other people. Historically, gossiping allegedly is part of a human instinct related to how we humans always have depended on social relations to survive, and trusting someone with information about others thus lays a foundation for the creation of a relationship build on "trust" and belongingness – in which the currency provided is the gossip. Nevertheless, instead of being a purely human instinct, gossiping gradually more have character of an unnecessary human addiction which besides the motivations mentioned in relation to peer-pressure, low self-confidence, low self-esteem, low self-worth, etc., e.g. also are rooted in getting a short-sighted temporary fix of attention, acceptance, and exposure,

or excitement, to kill the withdrawal caused by lonesomeness, personal insufficiency, perhaps boredom, or perhaps an unhealthy love for drama, and more. From personal experiences, I´ve the impression that not everybody shares the same need to gossip, which thereby makes me a bit cautious about directly classifying gossip as part of an universal instinct, and instead to lean more in the direction of my own culture related addiction-theory – maybe also due to the comfort that perspective partly gives me. Cause, while the addiction aspect on the one side tells a sad story about a self-inflicted curse, then compared to it being a natural drift completely out of our hands, it at least on the other side leaves a hope of it being something possible to overcome – from self-inflicted to self-rectified, if you will.

For some people good stories trump facts which is fine in the world of fiction, but other people and integrity ain´t fiction, and thus don´t confuse fiction with "real" misinformation.

Of course, gossip sometimes can prove to come from a positive – or at least quite innocent – place, but most often gossip undeniably however tend to carry a negative agenda at some point, and in such cases then no matter the initial motivational causation, notwithstanding the trust and goodwill you might earn by selling your gossip to one, it hence becomes information and trust you stole from another – resulting in broken trust, and potentially in what worse is.

In almost all contexts, besides for ascertain what undeniably true is, often when someone either gives positive credit to or tries to justify their own lacks through critique of others, the more they say the more they try to avoid the truth about themselves, and the more they say, the more they confirm that they in fact themselves are what they say about another – kinda like self-reflection in others; according to the concrete relation and situation, gaslighters accuse others of gaslighting.

As Aristotle made clear, there are three modes of persuasion, ethos, logos, and pathos: Ethos is about creating trust and thus credibility from whoever sought to persuade by e.g. referring to another – reliable sounding – source, e.g. "this article or this person said", or "because of my education I know", or whatever it might be (kinda like I do with the quotes I use in this book to back up my points, without lying though – which isn´t a lie). Logos is about (with reason – a.k.a. reasoning) proving logic facts, e.g. showing stats, a film clip, or whatever else that can be used to document and thus persuade. Pathos is about emotions, and how one through these seek to persuade by e.g. a heavy use of adjectives with strong connotations directly addressed to the emotions of e.g. excitement, happiness, anger, fear, pity, and whatnot, within the receiver. Negative gossip mostly consists of misuse and sometimes manipulation with the mechanisms of ethos and pathos, and perhaps even directly falsely constructed logos, whereas the question of more good-natured gossip – at least – more stands or falls with besides the consignor´s motivation and intention the authenticity- and thereof legitimacy of the usage of the three "...oses".

Merited constructive critique can of course be appropriate, and likely be the best solution – at least it´s something I highly appreciate myself, no doubt, and thus be careful about not mistaking honest constructive criticism with trash-talk or disloyalty; always remember that not everyone else necessarily share your exact perspective and appertaining opinion – even if they from a good place sincerely wish you the best, cause, if anyone ever 1:1 agree with everything in and of you then that person is you.

However, when talking about someone behind their back, where positive words about another person is a morally good deed then undeserved negative words about another person more have traits of merely immoral bad-mouthing. The worse you unmerited talk to and about others, the worse you in all ways are. The better you talk to and about others, the better you in all ways are.

Nevertheless, notwithstanding positive or negative words, who are we to judge what others want their others to be told and thus know about them, no one should have to add "this you´re allowed to share" or "this you´re not allowed to share" after everything they say. Often, when people wrongly share private or potentially sensitive information about another person or a specific situation in which they have no shares, then they as a bad excuse tend to defend themselves by simply stating that they never directly were told not to share what they shouldn´t have shared, although it most often – at least implicitly – quite openly lays in the cards whether or not any non-selfish good would ever come out of sharing it. No matter how much you´re able to think for yourself, no matter if you know or don´t know better, then by default you can´t go wrong if you stick to talk about and on behalf of yourself or general public matters only, and if you have a problem with anyone, then why not go straight the head instead of the ass – which might even be two sides of same; if you have a problem with someone, then as far as possible tell it straight to and try to work it out with that or those someone(s) – respectfully of course, and if you don´t want to share your problem with whoever you feel to be the source of your problem, then ask yourself why you carry a problem that you don´t want to solve, and then deal with *that* problem.

Take my preferred advice on how to go about third party personal information, unless you directly by the concrete protagonist have been asked to, or unless there´s a specific good unselfish reason – e.g. a matter of saving innocent lives – for you to share about a third party or on their behalf, instead of you potentially unjustified running your mouth and giving out someone else´s business, omertà[67], if they want anyone else to know then simply leave it up for them to share it themselves; as the Japanese maxim, 'three wise

[67] 'Code of silence'.

monkeys', sees no evil (Mizaru), hears no evil (Kikazaru), speaks no evil (Iwazaru).

Surely, it´s all good to tell somebody off if they step on your toes, or to share your frustration about someone with a third party – if well justified and deserved, but the limit of where somewhat legit gossip (although gossip in general is a taboo in my book) becomes bad-mouthing is where you behind someone´s back says something about that person which is either not true or something which you would not tell straight to the face of that particular involved person. Thereto, talking undeserved shit to the face of another person is to be considered immoral trash-talking, and ratting out on someone else´s secret is merely snitching. Where the health of innocent third parties directly is at stake, then speaking up on something or someone might be the morally right thing to do, but if motivated only by immoral selfish reasons alone, then snitches might likely sign up for stitches. Not that I in any way wish to promote violence here, rather I´m giving a friendly advice based on today´s standards, and without VAT, piss and paper, free of charge, giving an incentive more than merely moral – although that ideally shouldn´t be necessary – to not unnecessarily (meaning without a higher purpose than just your own personal crusade) compromise or jeopardize other people through one of *their* most sacred personal properties, their personal stories and secret(s). Cause yea, again, all people have the right to have secrets of their own as long as they don´t directly or even indirectly cause harm on anyone else. Thus, you don´t have to expose everything about everybody or even yourself or e.g. unprovoked confront everything or everyone you don´t like or transparently swing your dick or your titties of your birthday suit around in the street in order for you to be considered an honest person, and definitely gossiping won´t win you the right kind of respect and acceptance from the right kind of people anyway. As the Belgium born British actress, Audrey Hepburn (1929-1993), is quoted for cleverly saying: *"You can tell more about a person by what he says about others than you can by what others say about him"*. If someone gossip to you about other people then imagine how they highly likely also gossip about you to other people, if someone tells you what another person or other people negatively said about you, then fairly question why this person or these people felt comfortable trash talking you around that someone, and you´ll thereby thus also know how others most probably feel about you gossiping to and on them.

Antithetically, many people tend to put on a kind of a behavioristic mask – a.k.a. self-staging themselves – when e.g. participating in social settings, or a professional mask when going to work, or perhaps being one persona around the family and another persona amongst close friends or the crooks in the streets, etc.[68]. And besides behavior, the mask likewise is synonym with a like like e.g. appearance; I see you but you talk and behave like someone else. In this context, I´ve e.g. also experienced how big an impacting difference my clothes had from when I used to work wearing a tight suit with a well tied tie, shiny polished leather shoes, a leather briefcase in the one hand, and a fancy mahogany pipe managed by the other, versus when I e.g. am wearing a comfortable hoodie track suit and snickers; when I was wearing my "non-casual" tight suit – newly polished rapid fucking Gucci leather shoes and all, then people, especially older people, more often approached me and more often approached me with smiles and by e.g. formally calling me "Sir" and all, and in my casual track suit people often cross to the sidewalk on the other side of the street when I come walking – especially in the evening. I mean, I'm the same person, but people are deceived by how I present myself through something as simple as my material clothing, and thus also clothes play an important part in the hustle of how people easily deceive and manipulate.

---

[68] In mechanism, almost similar to what in the spy world is called a 'legend', a secret identity tailored for the spy to use when infiltrating certain people or environments.

And in relation to manipulation, let´s also not overlook the unhealthy culture through which many unfortunately sadly seems to have problems with themselves – e.g. how they from natures hand look – to the extend where they insecurely e.g. in pictures feel a need to hide or enhance – at least parts of – themselves behind e.g. manipulative filters, in posing postures, and in manipulated sets and set-ups. And in the same sense, I´ve e.g. recently seen how some parents demands that their children´s school photos are photo-retouched, and here I can´t help to consider what that probably does to a child, and the person the child grows up to become, and further to question what´s worst, to be perfectly imperfect, or that your parents openly thinks that you´re too ugly – a.k.a. not good enough – just as you are? Let me on a side note ask you, for other purposes than health treatment, do we really wish for cloning and mRNA[69] genetic manipulation to gain acceptance and traction – would you wish to be a somewhat unnatural replica, or a conscious doll?

Hardly anything is more sexy than one who is self-contained, and thus – as said before – don´t hate – on – yourself, don´t fail to appreciate your humble uniqueness, don´t let other people´s opinions about you matter more than your own, and don´t shoot or drag anyone down for merely who they peacefully are.

In an ideal world, in utopia, no one should ever have to wear any kind of alter egoing masks, and personally I *can´t stand* fake ass-licking behavior anyway – it´s disrespectful in itself when someone thinks that they can manipulate other´s opinion(s) about them "simply" by pretending to be something they´re not – tragic-comic frustrating to witness when they´re getting away with it, and disrespectful when they obviously take me for a fool too stupid to see through their theatrical masquerade, just as with shepherdly

[69] By mRNA it´s possible to change (or modify – depending on how positive you wish to sound) the RNA molecules of a living creature, a.k.a. the genetic code of e.g. humans, in theory only the imagination sets the limits.

sophism, it´s simply an insult to my intelligence. Rather an honest bastard than a "nice" two-faced faking "phat" phony. Lower your guards and drop your mask, be strong enough to show or say your weaknesses out loud, and you´ll then probably experience that you actually are more than cool enough as you are, and that it if anything else only is your own low self-worth that´re messing with your self-perception and your thereby wrong self-image of not being good enough exactly as you are.

Don't get me wrong, I of course appreciate sincere politeness, I´m of course aware that you hardly get a second chance to make a first impression, and I'm fully aware of the mechanisms of social intelligence – interrelational salesmanship and behavioristic techniques to win people over, and thus their useability in achieving certain "things", but if these are based on personal insecurity or becomes a cunning and immoral habit only beneficial for own winning at the expense of others and as fodder for mistrust, then that social intelligence unfortunately isn´t equivalent with a high intelligence in a general perspective, and definitely not in relation to humanity, or even in relation to your own health, only the contrary.

Also, on the contrary, all too many times I´ve e.g. caught myself understating myself in both private and especially professional contexts because it otherwise would´ve been too much of a mouthful for my surroundings to take in – at least so I began to read it after quite many times experiencing how my surroundings from even limited presentations of my personal narratives, anecdotes, and escapades, openly suspected me of embellishing and exaggerating my stories because of my stories obviously surpassed their own dittos, and even their wildest imaginary abilities and fantasies or lack of same. But since their deficient perceptions and following judgements ain´t my fault, why should it then be my problem if their baggage of experiences and stories of same are less eventful, less prosperous, and less exiting than mine (even *they* later agreed). If they – at least learn to – like me for who I am – for who I am to them, a good friend, a good colleague, etc., then they also should be able to accept my reality as it is, to accept what made me who I am, what made me be someone they like; I´ve learned from my mistakes, to not make ´em again. Without neglecting what I´ve been through, no need to judge my contemporary me by paying too much attention to my past. We all have different experiences and stories, and unless these openly are lies or makes witness of a through and through bad character, then hating on anyone else´s stories make no more sense than thereby self-exposing what wicked judgement and bad character is.

Even though being referred to as different in many contexts should be considered a compliment, then the often underlying reproach and blame and perhaps connected feelings of not belonging and being a part of "the fellowship" for many am neither pleasant or healthy, but still – should this apply to you, don´t without good moral reason give up on yourself, and instead consider if you under thus circumstances perhaps "just" should start looking around for a different fellowship. How you allow people to treat you will create precedence on how they´ll respect you, and you should never be afraid to leave the table if respect is no longer served.

The social or work version of you should always be allowed to be the exact same as the private version of you, and not the other way around. If someone undeserved doesn´t accept or at a minimum respect you, if someone doubts you, if someone neglect your worth, if someone is not being honest with you, then *fuck* ´em, let it be *their* problem, but don´t *ever* let that someone be yourself. You can try to convert confronting fakeness – and good on you if you have the energy to do so, but just because some are being incorrigible fake-ass dishonest donkeys, then it's no acceptable reason or excuse for you to compromise your own integrity by going down joining and thus supporting *their* low level, let that clown-shit self-

destruct. With honesty pick your spot and keep it real all around, especially to yourself, always.
All people enjoy the feeling of being right, in fact, we humans on an individual level often are so eager to be right that we tend to accept every story that fits with our own personal view of the world, and thus to reject any story that contradicts our ditto – sadly many won´t even reconsider any potential conclusions contradicting and hence conflicting with their own narratives. Sometimes, this eagerness for being right earnestly in the concrete person´s consciousness through the cognitive dissonance grows to take form of an uncontrollable obsessive incentive to make whatever opinion and perception to actually become and hence stand out as the real deal reality in the mind of that person – to make whatever commonly wrong belief, behavior, or action that person have or makes, to truly become what real and right is to that person. As Nietzsche stated, *"Sometimes people don´t want to hear the truth because they don´t want their illusions destroyed"*. Lazy people don´t concern themselves with reality as it gets in the way of their own opinions, they in general somewhat finds it easier to change their belief of right and wrong rather than their behavior, and to trust their own misconception and lies – the narratives they´re married to – rather than trying to grasp, understand, and accept reality, cowardly cheating both themselves and their surroundings, as far and as long as you allow. Freedom is fine, feel free to shine, though don´t allow on you "their" violent and even verbal pushes, "their" unreasonable heavy burdens, and "them" to undermining incline, don´t break your brain and your second brain spine.
Don't be afraid to admit your mistakes, we *all* make mistakes, and there's no positive point in denying or repeating them. Instead of defending your own mistakes and judge the likes of others, then judge yourself by whether or not you are cleaver enough not to repeat your own mistakes and defend those who unfairly and thus wrongly are being judged. To act like you never fucked up and don't

go through shit is acting like you're not human, and that's some of the most fucked up fake shit on earth.

In the world we live, for us to be able to agree universally we would need a so-called universal consensus reality, or what commonly can be referred to as a common reality, in which we hence all unanimously would agree on our thus synchronized view of reality. Try take a moment to think about if our world is deterministic or stochastic (a.k.a. if it´s predetermined or based on choices of free will), seriously, what do *you* think? In my view, in a macro (zoom out) perspective our world – and even the entire universe – as a whole all in all definitely is deterministic, the plan and pattern in the universe is long since fully in motion. In a billion years a meteor will set its course due to events that was determined already billions of years ago – the future will always notwithstanding effect and outcome be a natural consequence of a predetermined potential and a thereof derived and catalyzed development, and in sense of the same process new "things" are constantly created, e.g. planets, solar systems, galaxies, lives, etc., everything already has a path, and probably everything eventually will end. However, in a micro (zoom in) perspective, on an individual level, we as living creatures are born with a somewhat free will through which we to a certain degree somewhat stochastically have some portion of influence and thus some say on the road to our final destination, e.g. our "sliding doors" moments – should we go left or right, and whatever we then choose impacts our direction, our road, our future, and thereby our world, even after we unavoidably are gone.

Some subscribe to and emphasize the idea that all and everything without exception absolutely is deterministic as free will anyway is bound to and controlled by genetics, social and cultural norms, why they consider free will an illusion. However, apart from the genetics aspect, then social and cultural norms still originates from human made choices and are thus made from the use of free will. Different social and cultural norms around our globe clearly illustrate how people from different places historically chose different sets of norms, which hence proves the existence of an at least micro levelled free will. I partly agree to the argument about the genetics as part of the overall macro based determinism – cause we of course didn´t have the option of choosing which genetics to be born with ourselves, but why I still say 'partly' is partly because of the deterministic nature´s impact on the creation of our genetics, and partly because our forefathers some of the way did have a say about our genetics (i.e. e.g. how they lived their lives and who they mated with), just as we now also have a say on our own genetics, and thus our descendant´s genetics – and this now more than ever. Should I eat chocolate or salat, should I smoke or not, should I drink alcohol or water, etc., the choices we make based on our free will affect our genetics, and from this perspective even genetics isn´t completely deterministic. But then again, this is still "only" bound to a micro perspective, as we likewise then again in a macro perspective only have a limited selection of choices of food and drinks to choose from which hence again makes it clear why everything overall *is* deterministic, and that universal free will – despite lots of freedom – doesn´t exist. And this thus also should answer the question raised in chapter two about how to unite the thought of a general and obligating moral with the idea of a totally free and authentic existence, which in praxis unfortunately still is a philosophical delusion.

Moreover, these aspects of "deterministic and stochastic" thus quite align with the stoic perspective on 'memento mori', that there are certain things which we *can* control and hence take responsibility of, and things which we *cannot* control, as the stoics understands the natural world as both active and passive, a.k.a. as both an existing and immutable substance (deterministic), and as figured out by reason (stochastic). Hence, by the overall macro-based determinism we thus all already are an unavoidable part of the hence shared common end goal, a kind of a common reality, we “just” haven´t managed to reach a micro based common agreement on how stochastically best to get there – at least not yet. The issue here is that some compared to others lack a moral compass, or that our different perspectives equal different directions on the moral compasses most of us each have; don´t be a narrow-minded motherfucker, you are very important, no doubt, but overall the greater good is more important. Hopefully we at the very least at some point will astonish ourselves enough to at least reach a common agreement of clarity on how *not* to get there, which within nature totally is up to ourselves to achieve if we please; I´ve said it before and I say it again, you-me-we have the potential, and in my view not causing harm to any innocent, and not being the reason for some to reach their final destination in an unnecessarily bumpy fashion, or unnecessarily sooner than later, would as a start be a – morally – good common road to agree to, and a great foundation to further build our – and their – future on.

Segue, although I like to think that it is, magic of course isn´t real, and whoever or whatever so called magician or magic you ever come across cynically but still truthfully speaking surely is nothing but confidence tricksters and manipulative and illusionary fakeness in the making. Though, hereby not said that something cannot feel magical cause it definitely can, and not said that that feeling cannot be mind-blowing and joyful cause it definitely can, so feel free to cherish the privilege of that feeling whenever you come across something seriously worth embracing; you´re welcome. But, with perhaps only purely entertaining “magic” as an acceptable exception, a “great” liar is immediately *not* to glorify. Unless the skills to lie is used to put an end to suffering, to ensure health, to save lives, or to entertain in an innocent and unharmful way, a ‘“great” liar’ is ten times out of ten just another word for an immoral con artist, or cunt – just to keep it short.

Nevertheless, miracles do however occur, miracles are as real as you and I – simply take life itself as an example. And even though

life in fact is rooted in natural causations i.e. bound to logic explanations, and a somewhat perfect order "out there", the existence of existence itself cannot – compared to its probability – be reduced to anything less than a miracle in the purest essence of the word.
Keep it pure by keeping it beautiful by moral honesty, be the miracle you are; our world is part of your universe, the world is yours – but spell it without the y (ours).

2.3. Altruism is a Mirage

Following a streak of longer chapters, I think it´s now time to treat you with a short ´n easy one (of a kind), perhaps perfectly timed for a round of toilet reading – though of course only if you can avoid dirtying these "holy" pages in the process that is.
Just as I have in relation to breaking the code to coming up with a solution to the invention of a perpetual motion machine[70], I likewise many times found myself trying to come up with a single completely altruistic[71] action, and still to this day I haven´t succeeded – in either of the two challenges.
I sometimes randomly ask around, and every so often I come across people who initially tend to think that they easily can mention a purely altruistic action, e.g. giving money or food to a homeless person or to charity are some of the most used attempts of examples. Though, can you give anything to anybody without

[70] Perpetual motion is the motion of bodies that continues forever in an unperturbed system. A perpetual motion machine is a hypothetical machine that can work infinitely without an external energy source. This kind of machine is believed to be impossible as it would violate either the first or second law of thermodynamics or both.
[71] Altruism is simply put the antonym – a.k.a. the diametrical opposite – of selfishness.

benefitting just the slightest yourself, without feeling just the slightest good about the good deed you did, and thereby not feeling the slightest good about yourself? I don´t think so, and as long as you get anything positive out it yourself, then it unfortunately doesn´t classify as pure altruism.
As with all good science practice, a scientist has to be as objective as humanly possible, but since no human subject obviously ever can be entirely objective, subjectivity always to some degree undeniably will be present in every human conduct – we´re all to some degree unreliable narrators. Same goes in regard to your feelings in connection with altruism; only a braindead person cannot feel anything, but neither can a braindead person ever make a conscious altruistic action – or any conscious action at all for that matter.
It´s easy to think that it perhaps is possible to make a completely altruistic action by e.g. uneasily sacrificing your own life to safe others if you do it in a way where you never personally get the chance to reap the benefits of your own good deed, e.g. à la the Buddhistic Enlightenment story earlier mentioned, in which the kid sacrificed himself to the tiger. However, I strongly doubt that even that would be possible without you – e.g. despite fear – feeling the slightest proud about what you´re about to do in between the moment where you decide to do it and up until that point where you actually do it, and as at least your legacy probably also will prosper from it, which you probably also know beforehand, then it´s still a nah (a.k.a. no) to completely altruism from here.
Paradoxically, I can´t help to be a bit provoked when e.g. seeing how people film and post their good deeds online, how they e.g. give money to or buy food for a homeless person, and thus use this good deed as also an excuse for an ego boosting standing ovation disguised as 'likes' and praising comments. Cause, of course I on the one side cannot hate on anybody for actually helping where their help is needed, but on the other side, despite sending a partly

positive precedent signal to others of how help can be done, it still in my eyes seems like an act of primarily personal marketing – a.k.a. own winning, and thus an act conducted for also the wrong reasons, like trying to buy recognition instead of earning it, and the gratitude you might receive from whoever you support, as well as not least the nurturing good you feed your conscious by doing good, simply should be enough rewarding reason to do the good. The American actor, Jim Carrey (1962-), e.g. expressed it as such: *"Imagine struggling with being homeless and someone comes with a camera in your face to give you a meal and you have to take it... Imagine that feeling. Please, stop doing that. If you go to help someone, do it with kindness and not your ego"*. Maybe it´s just my Danish gen of 'jante-law'[72] speaking here, and surely you shouldn´t stop doing good deeds notwithstanding your motivation for doing ´em, but just as you shouldn´t make fun of others just to assert yourself at their expense, so you likewise shouldn´t assert yourself at the expense of a person in actual need of help – a person who might not wish to be exploited and exposed through your self-glorifying "commercial" of "goodness-masturbation". Thus, not only should you keep doing good, always, but also you should aim to do the good for all the right unselfish reasons – you know, good intentions in good faith, and all that.

Some argue that altruism is the highest form of moral, yet, as pure conscious human altruism still hasn´t proved to exist, then what, is the highest form of moral then bogus as well? Certainly not. Despite the fact that pure altruism hasn´t fully prevailed, yet, then hardly anything in this world is at 100 percent anyway, but of course that still shouldn´t prevent us from pushing forward our pursuit of getting as close to 100 as humanly possible, to do the best we can

[72] A culturally established unwritten kind of law which ingrown in the minds of the people states that nobody should think that they´re any more than anybody else – which most often in the mind of the individual comes to be "don´t think that you´re any more or better than me".

to do good, and to help to the best of our ability – which thus becomes the highest possible form of moral. In roughly every situation, you´ve the chance to demonstrate and hence prove the present potential of the highest form of moral – the most optimal charitable and greater good beneficial solution to the concrete situation, and that´s exactly what you always should go for achieving despite the fact that no matter how you flip and turn it, experiencing your own pure altruism is a mirage.

2.4. Fuck the Law!

Every so often, we experience situations where moral values collide with the requirements of the law, and vice versa – where non-immoral actions entail punishment in the name of law, or where the law directly serves immorality. With that in mind, we´ll now look in to a few examples to elaborate on exactly such situations.
The first example is made by two different and independent incidents: The first incident took place some years ago on a cold winter night, a weekday night between a Tuesday and Wednesday, at precisely 04:13 am. I came riding my bicycle on my way home – one of them days where you´re so tired that you´d give almost everything "just" to be teleported straight home to your bed. The streets are empty, not a living soul in sight. As I approach a red lighted traffic light, I carefully look around to check if there is someone or something to be cautious about, but still nada, still not a living soul in sight. I see no rational reason for standing like a fool just waiting for the automated traffic light to turn green – under these circumstances I simply consider my life too short already, and I therefore stomp my pedals and moves on. From a byway further up the street a police car rolls out and stops me. The two policemen in the police car had from a distance been sitting in the dark watching me cross despite the red light, and only because I

according to the law and my own safety had bicycle lights on my bike it´d been possible for them to spot me from the distance. Now, although I believe that I morally did nothing wrong, then I still broke the law, and the naval-gazing police thus gave me a fine equivalent of $145 bucks for illegally crossing the red light. At the time of the incident, I was a student with barely money enough to eat, and to even "rob" money from a poor man I in itself find immoral, especially when the reason according to the concrete situation didn´t really apply to the actual intentions of the bureaucratic human made rules that hence here was being enforced only for the sake of rules, a.k.a. just to enforce the law notwithstanding the thus lack of common sense in relation to the factual details of the concrete situation.

The second incident took place just around the same time, and this in the same European country as the just described first incident. It revolves around a case where a politician in his mid-thirties at a Easter seminar for a youth-section of the same political party which this politician represent, ended up having unprotected sex with a member of the youth section, a 15 years young girl. In the country where this incident took place the age of consent to sexual relations is 15 years young, why the politician from a judicial – and thereby legal (law) – point of view did absolutely nothing wrong.

However, In my view, as opposed to the law, a 15 years young person is still to be considered a child, and from a moral perspective I personally find the politician´s action to be nothing less than despicable and lividly fucking disgusting.

Allow me to expand my view on the age-aspect with a personal anecdote: One time when I was visiting Nepal, I was staying at a guest house just across from a restaurant where the most beautiful and bright girl was working as a waitress. Remember I said girl, and not woman. One day where I was sitting enjoying a dinner at the restaurant, this girl – who was the only one in the area who spoke proper English – came to my table and asked me to follow her to the back yard of the restaurant as her parents wanted to talk to me. I knew that she was a part of the financially poor lower caste[73], so I guessed that her parents probably would ask me for a financial contribution to this girl´s schoolbooks or something like that. Well, in the back yard, to my surprise, there were flaming torches sat up, colorful decorations of various kinds, and a table in the middle of it all where her mom sat waiting for me on the other side of the table from where I was sat. The girl sat down next to her mom – across the table from me, and held a small speech which ended with: *"...since you started to come to the restaurant, then every day when I come home I simply cannot stop talking about you, about how friendly you are, and about how handsome you are. My mom then asked me: Do you like this guy? And I replied her: Mom, I think I love him! And therefore I now want to ask You: will you marry me?".* Honestly speaking, just before I went to the restaurant that particular evening I had been smoking some of the heavy Nepalese specialties, why I hence in that particular moment of her proposal found myself to be pretty love damn waizted. The whole situation felt quite surreal; this girl had the rare combination of being crazy beautiful, sweet, and unusual intelligent all at the same time, and only one day earlier I had told one of the other guests at the restaurant that this girl someday would make some very lucky guy very happy. And there I thus suddenly was, really very vastly waizted, and only one word of three letters (yes) away from marrying her. However, no matter how much I truly admired her talents, then I simply couldn´t overlook the fact that she in my eyes was still "just" a child. It turned out that she was 17 years young, which I found to be quite a contrast to me being 31 years old at that particular time. Thus, despite not wanting to disrespect their well-arranged ceremony, and despite being more waizted than what good was, then I still had to do what I had to do. Long story short, I declined

[73] In Nepal (as well as many other places) people are strictly divided in social classes, a.k.a. caste, of upper, middle and lower class.

her proposal in the best and most respectful possible manner I could, while also made it completely clear to both her and her mom that despite some Nepalese girls marrying and giving birth already before their teen years – which her mom´s case unfortunately was an example of, and despite being flattered about her proposal, then to me this praxis simply isn´t right – neither culturally or morally. I encouraged the girl to take her time to grow up and become a woman before even considering marriage, and that she for now rather should focus her incredible talents on educating herself, which I thus – without trying to sell myself as a saint – offered to help finance.
However, back to the case of the politician, then furthermore, prior to his incident of unprotected sex with the 15 years young girl, this particular politician was a spokesperson on the matter of save sex in a campaign against the spread of sexually transmitted diseases, which clearly shows that he was putting an effort into portraying himself as a person with his moral values in place – and maybe he even *did* have them in place at the time of being the spokesperson. But, nevertheless, while moral is perceived to be good then double moral shouldn´t be perceived to be twice as good, instead, as in math where a double minus can become plus, then double moral is merely a minus.
To top it all, as if this wasn´t enough already, in the very moment where I´m now writing this, this politician now holds office as Minister of Foreign Affairs in the very same country where the incident took place. Not only has he then gotten away with his "(im)moral" misconduct, but he thereby now also are in a position where he directly has his say on the requirements of the law, and this even in a country that in recent years has been awarded to be among the best countries (e.g. least corrupt, best social welfare, happiest population, etc.) in the world by a wide range of different organs.

Overall, the two different incidents of this example portraits the paradox of how one action might be morally acceptable but still illegal by law, while another immoral action is legally accepted and thereby protected by the very same body of laws.
On a keynote, add to this example, that some countries de facto doesn´t even have a minimum age of consent to sexual relations – neither by law or cultural morality, and hence both by law and cultural morality (*their* morality, and not a healthy person´s ditto) accepts that old men marriages and have sexual intercourses with and impregnate small children. If this doesn´t speak for itself about the (im)moral sickness and disgrace in this world – which words alone cannot cover – then what does?
This next and third example is a somewhat fictional scenario inspired almost 1:1 by reality: Country A forms a political alliance with a rebel army in country B. Country A then attacks the establishment in country B to help the rebel army in country B to overthrow country B´s sitting government by a coup d´état, a.k.a. a military coup. The rebel army in country B believes that every member of the overthrown government – including their relatives, has to be eradicated, and they thus consequently starts to kill everyone related to the overthrown government. A grown-up daughter of one of the overthrown government members manage to escape, and flees out of country B. Fate will, that the daughter as a refugee then ends up in country A, and the only way she can avoid to be sent straight back to the rebel army-executioners in country B is by applying for political asylum in country A. While her asylum-case is being dealt with, country A place the daughter in a refugee-camp. During her time in the refugee-camp she meets a male camp-employee, they fall in love with each other, and although the camp-employees are not allowed to have personal relations with the refugees, then the daughter and the employee starts having a romantic affair (how can squared bureaucratic laws anyway outweigh true love?). The daughter becomes pregnant, and the

secret couple have plans about getting married as soon as her asylum-case has been dealt with, and a residence permit hopefully has been her granted. In the meantime, the war has ended in country B, and the former rebel army are now fully in power. Because the war has ended, then the legal basis for political asylum no longer apply to the laws in country A, country A refuse to view their allies – the rebels in country B – as a threat to the daughter, and country A thus reject to give the daughter a residence permit. Instead, they give her the message that she asap is to be escorted back to country B by the authorities of country A.
The dilemma now is, if the camp-employee should respect country A´s legal decision and let his beloved girlfriend and their unborn child to be sent back to their certain dead in country B, or if he should go against country A´s laws, and instead use his key to the refugee camp's gate to get his girlfriend and unborn child out of the camp and into a hideaway, hopefully safely away from the authorities of country A? What do you think, what is most important to obey, morality or the law?
Also, what about country A, which in fact by starting the war in country B are highly responsible for the daughter's situation, and now also are about to send her back to their allies in country B – into the arms of the rebels who surely intend kill her at first chance they get. Is country A doing the right thing here in following their own laws connected to extradition, are they living up to decent moral standards, or what do you think?
To me the verdict is clear, country A can take their immoral laws and shove ´em extensively far up where the sun don´t shine! And if you for some reason think otherwise, then sorry not sorry for breaking it to you, then you´re truly a bad person, and the world definitely would be a better place without your fucked up mindset and thereby you in it, and no, you won´t be missed.

History has shown a "great" many examples of how e.g. refugees on the run from genocide[74] has been helped by people who by helping hence broke the law, and how refugees has been tortured and killed by "people" who still had the law on their side; it´s believed that genocide alone account for north of 100 million deaths over the last 100 years, carried out by lawmaking shepherds and their law-abiding henchmen and mercenaries of same – and that´s not even close to the full picture of how many victims and how much suffering same surely likewise has entailed as well.

A fourth example worth mentioning is a famous moral dilemma, Heinz dilemma, created by the American Phycologist, Lawrence Kohlberg (1927-1987). I know that some of you might find the Heinz dilemma exhausted (at least a censor at one of my oral university exams once pulled my grade down for using this – in his eyes trivial – example), but at the same time I´m sure you´ll survive, so here goes; in short: Heinz´s wife is deadly ill on her deathbed, only one expensive drug can save her life, but Heinz cannot afford to buy this drug needed to save his wife´s life. Heinz asks the druggist to sell him the drug for a smaller amount – an amount Heinz can afford, or alternatively to let Heinz pay the rest of the money at a later time. But despite the production costs of the drug being considerably smaller than what Heinz actually are able to pay, then the druggist isn´t open for any kind of price-reduction or any alternative payment-plan.

The dilemma now is if Heinz should break the law by stealing the drug and thereby save his wife´s life, or if Heinz should accept the situation, respect the law, hence not steal the drug, and thus just let his wife to die? What would you do if you were in Heinz´s shoes? And is the druggist being morally correct by being an asshole hiding behind the rights of law, rather than saving a life?

---

[74] Genocide is killing people only because of their nationality, ethnicity, or religious affiliation.

As I was looking around for responses to this dilemma, a so-called Christian person replied in an online forum that the answer was obvious because the bible clearly states that you´re not allowed to steal. In response to that answer, I could easily have replaced "law" with "religion" in this subchapter´s title, but out of respect for all other religious people who still have their moral values and common sense intact, I didn´t.

I guess that you, like me, without hesitation, if necessary, when it comes down to it, would be willing and ready to break whatever law common sense and moral would allow in order for you to be a good Samaritan and save your beloved´s life. And if not, then even if you self-conceited think that you are a good and honest law-abiding citizen, you in fact are nothing but a bad person who as an antonym to your own believe literally is responsible for crimes against humanity. But, if you, like me, on the other hand agree to Heinz´s wife being saved despite Heinz´s limited economy, if you´re not a selfish coward, and especially if you prefer not to break any laws, then you also should believe in and agree to a universal free healthcare reform, rather than totally crazy systems in which people in need of help are left to die if their bank account ain´t booming, or they don´t have a decent healthcare insurance – which anyway would be entirely unnecessary in a humanistic setting. The fact that such systems as just mentioned de facto are legally accepted is "just" yet real life examples of how moral and official rules of law often simply don´t mix. Our world openly become a poorer place every time the Hippocratic Oath[75] is accepted to be neglected, and hence abate to the hypocritical oath.

---

[75] One of the oldest binding documents in history, the Oath written by Hippocrates is still held sacred by physicians – to always treat the ill to the best of one's ability, to preserve a patient's privacy, to teach the secrets of medicine to the next generation, etc.

Despite here only sharing very few examples compared to how much shit that is taking place in our world, then it anyway already by now should be quite clear why moral always should outweigh any legal principle, and that laws hence are not always useful guidelines when separating right from wrong.

But of course, as with almost everything and anything else, the answers to these types of issues are not merely binary.

I´ve earlier studied evilness in a moral-philosophical context, among others by using the Norwegian mass-murderer, A. B. Breivik, and the Islamic State, a.k.a. IS, Isis, Isil, and Daesh, as examples. In the name of his national socialistic far right perspective, Breivik killed 77 people – 72 confirmed youngsters from the political left-wing – because he believed that they were favoring – primarily Islamic – foreign immigration into Norway, which Breivik thus believes eventually will imply the end of Norway as he prefers the country to be. And in the same extreme barbarian fashion – sometimes even worse (if you can even say so about something so extreme), Daesh, a Sunni militant group based on a radical Islamic ideology, has killed numerous amounts of people in their pursuit of establishing a caliphate, a state ruled by Islamic law, a.k.a. sharia. Daesh is convinced that all non-Muslims are infidel traitors, and that they thus accordingly have to be eradicated in the name of Allah, whoever and wherever these infidels are.

For sure these descriptions of the Breivik and Daesh cases are very limited described here – almost not paying enough justice to their horror. However, as this book definitely is not dedicated to either one of them, then these short descriptions will have to do the job for now.

Briefly allow me for just a short moment to play the devil´s advocate here; going back to elaborate on the Heinz dilemma, then what if we flip the moral perspective of Kohlberg´s example to e.g. Breivik and Daesh, if we make Heinz be the representative for Breivik and Daesh, make Heinz´s wife represent respectively Norway and the caliphate, make the wife´s illness to represent respectively the Islamicization of Norway and any resistance to the sharia laws, and make the druggist to represent respectively the political left-wing and the non-Islamic infidels. If Breivik and Daesh honestly find themselves to be in the same type of dilemma as Heinz, if Breivik and Daesh truly feels that the political left-wing and the infidels aren´t innocent victims – only on the contrary, can we then blame them for their actions if they to their bones actually believes that they´re doing the morally right thing?

Of course we can, but still this shows the complexity we´re dealing with, how different perspectives causes different opinions. In a general optic, there´re no doubt about Breivik and the hardcore members of Daesh having a massive mental defect (officially Breivik has been diagnosed with a narcissistic personality disorder while many members of Daesh also has been diagnosed with various types of mental illnesses (and those who hasn´t, probably just hasn´t been diagnosed yet)), but then again, when they´re mentally ill, can we then blame them for their actions, or are they also merely victims of their own illnesses?

What if we go about the same example in the context of handicapped people – e.g. people who cannot control their motor skill movements, can we then blame them if they because of their illness hit somebody – can we blame anyone at all for whatever they cannot control themselves?

Both yes and no, or rather no and yes: no, we cannot directly blame anyone for what they have no control of themselves, and blaming the illness alone helps as much as blaming the rain for getting you wet, it helps fuck all. Thus, if the illness is congenital, we cannot really blame anyone other than natural genetics, unless someone e.g. caused the baby (the later ill individual) damage while it was still in its mothers stomach, then yes, then we can blame whoever damaged the child. And yes, if the illness is not congenital, then we can blame the external and social orientated factors – a.k.a. the

environment – which contributed in making the ill person ill, we can blame the ill persons if they forced the damage upon themselves, and not least, we can blame those priorities, mainly concerned around public finances, which doesn´t favorize the psychiatric sector enough – related to both social safety nets, organs of crime prevention, and extensively psychiatric care.
Some thus might would argue, that e.g. Breivik is just a right-wing racist, and that racism doesn´t categorize as an illness but merely an ideology, that "excusing" horrific actions with an illness is to understate the seriousness of the problem, and that it´s a disrespectful slap in the face of the victims. In this context, yea, I won´t deny that racism is a shitty ideology, but still I argue that one such shitty ideology only can arise from what has to be perceived a sick mind, and that denying a correlation between an evil ideology and illness merely is an "excuse" to punish an ill instead of aiming to solve the problems of illness by pursuing to treat the mentally ill – just as you would (Ed. should) also pursue to treat a physical need of medical care.
For the professional experience, and as preparation to my psychology studies, I once worked at a shelter for homeless drug users in Copenhagen, *the* Grand Central Dope Station in all of the Kingdom of Denmark, in all of Scandinavia, and probably even in all of Northern Europe; here a shout out to all of you who think that life cannot be rough in Denmark due to our reputation as the happiest fairytale country in the world; misery is misery everywhere, so is evilness, and the real dope game is the real dope game notwithstanding geography – equally coldhearted and shitty just about anywhere and everywhere.
At the shelter I worked for around a year, and not even once I experienced a shift without having to deal with fights, stabbings, and ODs (drug overdoses); I really cannot count how much violence I´ve experienced just through my work there. Nevertheless, a few incidents still stand out, and one of these took place with a guy I had

arrested by the police as much as three times over the course of a few hours. This guy, a hardcore criminal with a rough life story and ACAB (all cops are bastards) tattooed in big capital letters covering the back of his bald head – thus a "pretty" prime example of an "acab-demic", on this particular day acted exceptionally more chaotic than usual. He continuously and unmotivated attacked just about everybody around him with severe violence, kicking people in the head, smashed people with glass bottles, busting skulls and knocking people out, and he even unprovoked smashed a big glass vase straight in the face of an innocent humble old man who was just sitting sleeping at a bench. And if you´re in doubt, then yes, of course the glass bottles and the vase broke and sliced up faces in the process. This behavior he continued all day, only interrupted by the times he was arrested. Luckily for me, I was the only person he didn´t jumped, probably partly because of that personal (professional) relation I had managed to build up with him – the respect I´d earned, and probably partly because he despite his psychotic behavior remembered that I know a bit of Krav Maga (a military self-defense and fighting system developed for the Israeli security forces and Israeli defense forces (IDF)) – to which he perhaps wouldn´t risk to lose his street credit as a motherfucker not to fuck with in case I fucked him up and thus pacified him in front of "everybody" (if I could, and although fighting definitely wasn´t part of my job description – it only would get me fired, then if I was attacked, I of course could be forced to defend myself). Anyway, I continuously gave him a choice between laying low or indirectly force me to press the police alarm on him: "Listen, it´s not part of my nature to snitch, but if you don´t calm the fuck down then you leave me no other choice – then you pull this shit on yourself", I warned him before every time he forced me to push to alarm. One of the times the police then was on their way to come get him, he patiently waited for the police to arrive only for then to violently jump and fight the police officers – just for the fuck of it, and he even managed to get a hold on one of the police officer´s gun a split second before the officers luckily managed to pacify and cuff him up. Nevertheless, every time the police drove off with him it took less than an hour before he yet again was back at the shelter – every time more externalizing chaotic than before he went away. After he came back the third time, and I found him busy sharpening a piece of metal – the handle of a spoon to be precise, I went straight up to him and asked him what the fuck he was doing, to which he plainly cold replied that he just needed to sharpen it to cut someone´s throat with it, spoken as cold as was he e.g. talking about a trip to the grocery store. I called up the police to ask what the fuck was going on and why they kept releasing him when he clearly was a danger to both himself and his surroundings, and that it seemed like only a matter of time before they had to come back for a homicide case. And add to that that another guy, a very mentally ill and dangerous Somali guy, totally unprovoked and unmotivated also had plans about killing me on that very same day (due to some voices only existing in his own head). To this the police answered: *"both of these guys are among the most dangerous of the dangerous, and they thus have to be checked in at a special institutional facility capable of handling the most dangerous of the dangerous, the most maximum security of maximum security, where they know how to handle psychiatric cases of their caliber. But since there´s only beds for eight individuals of that kind in all of the Copenhagen area, and since they´re all already fully booked, and since we cannot have him* [the guy who were arrested] *here at the station, then we simply have to let him go until one of the eight beds becomes available. But feel free to call us again if he – or any of them – actually kills someone, then we of course have to come get him"*. "But that someone might as well be me", I replied, to where to police just answered, *"if you can´t handle it, then maybe you should go find yourself another job..."*. Soon after, a colleague of mine had a knife to the throat by this man.

I´m not saying that punishment and isolation is the way to go to straighten this (Ed. these) chaotic guy(s) (and girls) out – such measures simply aren´t healthy, more so quite the contrary, but he (Ed. they) surely needs acute psychiatric help to deal with his (Ed. their) inner demons, and the public sphere needs a psychiatric system that´ll help keep the streets safe without increasing the problem in the process, a system that picks up vulnerable people instead of breaking them down, and a system which provides the needed resources to help bring vulnerable people back into society instead of ostracize them as delinquent outcasts.

Unfortunately, this is just *one* example of how the psychiatric sector is being prioritized – or rather aren´t being prioritized – in the public budgets all over, one of many sad examples that shows how the social services of our current societies are failing to deliver – failing to repair and rectify what they "helped" create; there´s always a reason to why we became what we are, *everything* happens for a reason, and budget cuts shouldn´t be it – at least not in this context. Hereto, what I on a side note in relation to reason discovered at the shelter was that all the drug users – including drug prostitutes – without any known exception all had been victims of either physical, psychological, or sexual abuse, of either one, two, or all of the mentioned types of abuse.

Of course, we cannot have pathological murderers and other sick individuals who poses a real serious menace for the safety of others to run around freely, and there surely are some hopeless cases of some being so mentally ill that they unfortunately are completely unreachable – cases where it´s too late to provide any decisive help. But don´t forget, that we all once were someone´s little sweet and innocent baby, and unless born with a genetic related handicap, then I firmly believe that love, attention, acknowledgement, recognition, validation, approval, honesty, support, and concrete help, is all the treatment anyone ever needed, which is also why we – both as society and from a humanity perspective – all have a

shared obligation to prioritize human – or basically all organismic – needs before *anything* else. We have to meet the individual on individual terms, and despite it being a resource-intensive and costly affair in the short run, then it certainly have to be the most profitable model to go for in the long run. Not only because otherwise ill individuals hence will be able to contribute more constructively to our shared space and communities, but also – and not least – because it´ll create a healthier, happier, safer, and thereby better world for both the individual and the whole to benefit from, a.k.a. better lives for each and every one of us not profiting from the adversity and struggle of others.
"*With law shall land be build*" is the first sentence in the preface of "Jutland law"[76], and a quote engraved on the façade of the city court building in Copenhagen. I can´t deny that I partly agree to this quote, and I´m not too extreme a libertarian to not e.g. recognize a need for a government based police etc. (public police etc. should never be private based), cause despite most governance so far has shown quite ineffective, then without *any* limitations and ideals to live by, total mayhem most probably would erupt quite quickly among the currently so destructive humans.
However, what is really the root cause for one such development – the current state of affairs, is it an innate need for stringent leadership, or strict judicial laws? No, it´s basically "simply" a question of (Ed. call for) moral and common sense – or lack of same, how the deeds of morality partly has been damaged due to and thus by human made culture. If "only" everybody understood that the "only" leadership and rules of law we overall need are those of moral and reasonable common sense (unfortunately not that common), and that if "only" these aspects universally settled are in place, then judicial law simply would be superfluous.

[76] In Danish: 'Jyske lov', is a Danish "landscape law" from 1241.

What I in this chapter am talking about – one of the red threads of the entire book – obviously isn´t nothing new, rather it´s logic even battery hens should be able to understand, and it officially already literally was written in the preface of "Jutland law" from 1241 – ergo almost 800 years ago (and probably common sense long before that), that "[...] *would everyone settle for one´s own, and allow others to enjoy the same right, then no law would be needed*". Ergo, if everyone behaved morally toward each other, then no law would be needed, and thus likewise no judiciary to secure compliance would be relevant. And still here we dimwittingly are.
So how do we teach moral, by fear of consequential punishment? No, in line with the desired treatment just before mentioned, by showing what attention, acknowledgement, approval, honesty, support, and concrete help, is all about; the path of general education to become fully human has to go through love and inspiration to passion. But then what if people still don´t get it or don´t want to learn, and isn´t a "cruel food chain" just a natural part of nature? Well, in less civilized parts of the animal kingdom the food chain sure can be view as hardcore inhumane, but since we in fact are humans and should start acting as such, humane, and since our IQ should´ve moved way passed the cruelty aspect long time ago, then no, a "cruel food chain" among humans ain´t just a natural part of nature – at least obsoletely no more, it´s an optional conscious choice, and if a moral majority clearly don´t accept minoritized immoral mischiefs, then the immoral minority quite quickly from lack of sociality and societal opportunities should learn that their immoral behavior is unacceptable, and yes, if someone still doesn´t overcome their immorality, e.g. hit hard against hard, immorally hurt or kill, then we of course as a society still have to have a kind of law-enforcement to deal with those immoral misfits, but instead of the law-enforcement serving bureaucratically made

judicial laws of cynicism[77] – embedded with elitist circumvent loopholes – they entirely should serve the greater good in overwhelming weighting favor of the law-ish deeds of moral. As one of my personal inspirations, the civil right activist, Martin Luther King Jr. (1929-1968), once said: *"Power at its best is love implementing the demands of justice, and justice at its best is power correcting everything that stands against love"*. And thus, instead of merely aiming to punish people we hence more should focus on actually helping people, a la sentence them to receive educational treatment (e.g. motivational teaching, psychologic or psychiatric care, etc.), instead of "just" sending them to the aggravating "crime schools" our current prisons unfortunately has become – institutions where a criminal network and immoral ruthlessness (e.g. the 'gabos' code, a.k.a. e.g. preying by intimidation and violence) more than anything proves to pay off, and which through the majority of inmates like forced scholars of crime life thereby all too often becomes even more criminal (a.k.a. immoral) than they were when they arrived. Cause yea, sure we´re "just" mammals (a.k.a. "well developed" animals), but nonetheless, we still are the most intelligent (at least among the most intelligent) "animals" around, we´re overall our own only competition, and we *should* gradually have become intelligent enough not to succumb to our lowest archaic instincts, which we disappointedly currently still seems to overall live – and all too often die – by.

Additionally, we thus thereby also would overcome that immoral legal protection which only serves the unjustified and unreasonably few – the cynical masters, the aristocratic shepherds and their henchmen (a.k.a. the aristocratic pimps and their prostitutes) – including governments, members of governments, major

[77] As the German philosopher, Peter Sloterdijk (1947), puts it: *"Modern cynicism [...] is the masters´ antithesis to their own idealism as ideology and as masquerade. The cynical master lifts the mask, smiles at his weak adversary, and suppresses him"*.

corporations, and financially strong individuals, who through e.g. sophism, expensive lawyers, nepotism or favoritism, short said corruption, etc., has a way of getting away with offenses many times more serious than what "normal" people "normally" are being punished and potentially ruined by, often as victims of miscarriage of justice.

Message to the current ruling parties in power, and their henchmen: At the very least, go chase the big fish, go chase whoever is a real serious menace to society – the ones who commits serious financial fraud and pernicious crimes, give *them* a serious lesson instead of maximum handing them a fine or sentence of only a small percentage of the profit or pain their crimes generate, go after yourself if merited, and stop being a damn squared paragraph rider lifer dickhead to ordinary moral people who unlike yourself safe and sound without taking advantage of other people understand how to combine their free spirit with morality and common sense.

And by the by, incarceration should never be an industrial business through which some individuals through economic incentives profit heavily from punishing locking people up.

You can and shall not legislate yourself out of all issues – it even should be considered a crime to criminalize people who´re not directly harming anyone – other than perhaps themselves. Nevertheless, as of now there seems to be a tendency among weak and ignorant politicians (shepherds) and the "wool-washed" to think that legislations and freedom orientated restrictions are the solution to just about everything, and that a decrease of people´s human rights related to e.g. privacy and personal freedom thus – contradicting – wholly will entail an increase in the quality of life, and thereby thus will improve the overall living standards within the "accepted" system. E.g. take the discussion regarding CCTV cameras (including face recognition tools), many politicians and most law enforcers tend to think that a total big-brother surveillance society is the solution we need to secure control and safety in the streets –

freedom within the frame of law. I agree that it in relation to crime prevention is a very effective tool to have CCTVs placed strategically around, and that it hence has its advantages, and I partly buy into the "comforting" argument that if we have nothing to hide then we also have nothing to fear. However, do we really want to live in a world where our every move can be monitored, tracked, and traced, and what about the violation of people´s right to privacy – even in the public space, is increased control and a decrease of personal freedom (cause that it is, notwithstanding the shepherds trying to convince you otherwise) really what we wish, and what if we morally have done nothing wrong but still unjustly are being targeted by law or a personal vendetta from someone with access to the CCTVs? From a civil perspective, in the social constructions of today, I immediately say that it compromises and puts our personal freedom on the line, and even if we e.g. agree that the cameras only comes to play a role where an offense crosses a certain line of seriosity, then I still see it as a quite dangerous development. Cause, everything that can be used can likewise be misused and abused, and for likewise also that reason the need for an healthy codex of some kind of universal moral principles and reasonable common sense is vitally more important to establish than any mean of universal control can ever be (if you can distinguish from morality being a kind of control that is).

Also, e.g. take the "war on the poor", how cities tries – and even succeed – criminalizing homelessness by making it illegal to sleep in the public space. Imagine how low a character you´d have to have to deprive people – already suffering people – from the basic human right to the basic human need of sleep. If you e.g. see armrests in the middle of a public bench then it´s not so much for your comfort as it is to prevent homeless people from sprawling out on the otherwise potentially bed-like bench. If you see sidewalk tiles or concrete surfaces with e.g. dotted or hemisphered elevations then it´s not so much for the tiles to look cool, or to help the blinds navigate (this only goes when it´s in the middle of e.g. a walking streets etc., and not when it´s in more discrete places, e.g. under a potential roofing rain cover, e.g. under bridges, etc.), as it is to make it uncomfortable for the homeless to lay on. The fact that city planners – of course on orders from government officials – do what they can to acidify sleeping options in the public space is no less than a moral disgrace based on immoral law – only made to please those immoral, heartless, and empathetic individuals who´re self-exalted and stuck-up enough to be disgusted by having to share the public space with people who without nowhere else to go *should* have as equally much right to make use of the public space according to *their* needs as everybody else. And in this context, I don´t care how much you pay in taxes, no one as in *absolutely no one* has any more ownership of the public space than anyone else. Furthermore, imagine how many lives that have – and still are – being ruined due to e.g. cannabis related offenses, not because cannabis in itself directly is more harmful or addictive than any sort of legal tobacco – if anything only less, but simply because some hidebound small-minded law-abiding dimwits almost a century ago decided to punish and ruin the lives of everyone enjoying a natural substance which well documented is many times less harmful, and less addictive than many legal substances, e.g. the destructive braincell killing widespread addiction and social and party drug numero uno, alcohol. Currently, people involved in drugs e.g. gets longer sentences than violent offenders and rapists despite drug users wanting the drugs and no one – other than masochists – wants a beating or to be raped. And no, I´m not saying that any drugs are unconditionally healthy (although some for some can work as medication, serve a funny moment, or a much needed and thus somewhat healthy mental travel or vacation or both), or using exactly this example to advocate for an illegalization of alcohol, a.k.a. a new prohibition, or to justify any kind of personal consumption as it anyway for my part has been many years since I

last enjoyed any kinds of intoxicants myself – now I´m primarily getting high on the natural supply from the drug of being awake (the wildest trip of all). It just – despite a long awaited ongoing legalization process some places – seems obvious to also address and emboss this unnecessarily historical and still present-day global problem, as lives continuously every day are being ruined due to e.g. cannabis related "offenses", as millions of people still every year unnecessarily are being locked up on somewhat illogical cannabis related charges[78], and as death penalty still some places is being used in relation to cannabis restrictions. And this unfortunately *still* is "just" a small drop in a big ocean of misplaced and completely ridiculous legislations.
Allow everybody to be free to do with their own lives as they want and be great enough to still help them if they in whatever sense "twist themselves" – just as others should allow and help you according to your preferences and needs.
Despite different opinions about how good or bad the law is, calling a spade a spade, the law basically at large is an agitating sophistic choleric manifesto composed and adopted by a narrowminded posse out of touch with the concept of free will, appertaining diversity, a healthy moral, and common sense, it´s indisputably an authoritarian tool to force through a streamlined oppression, and a tool to curb independency – to make sheeple out of "people".
"We", our society in general, reward and punish people according to how well they remember and do exactly as they were told, this goes for the law, social settings, not least education, and almost everywhere else, if someone remember and exercise exactly what

[78] On average around ten percent of all adults in Europe use cannabis at least once a month, and a new Swedish 2022 scientific study (involving all countries in Europe) says that prohibiting legislation on cannabis has no real effect on the use of cannabis, only the opposite, the number of users decreases when legislative leniency or no restrictions are introduced (therefore somewhat illogical to have strict restrictions).

they were told, who said what, and do this without saying or doing anything else than what already has been said and done, we reward it, whereas we on the flipside too often punish alternative, innovative – including potentially pioneering – and unorthodox thinking; "The one who in a discussion only refers to an authority doesn´t use the sense of mind, only the memory", is a mantra worth memorizing.

Other than serving mere control, the law is only useable for those who doesn´t own moral and common sense, those ill or ignorant selfish scumbag motherfuckers in unknowingly desperate need of helping guidelines to understand what rational and morally acceptable is. And the fact that the legislative, judiciary, and executive powers, a.k.a. the politicians, judges, and law enforcers, sadly does not really portray to be trustworthy sensible role-models – all too often they even are the worst hypocrite lawbreakers themselves, is just sad crumbled with further motivation for a thorough paradigm shift towards improvements for the better.

Personally, I don´t operate with "work for", or even believe in the concept of a boss, but I can accept and respect the concept of a good leader, someone who don´t just give orders but actually by example leads the way – someone who´re first *and* last to touch and treat the battlefield on respectively arrival and departure. Too many rulers and their minions cannot cope with having power without being struck by and becoming the essence of megalomania, and unfortunately, as likewise is the case in many other contexts – until we take action, the bad eggs and apples (whatever you prefer to call ´em) ruins it for everybody else. It has by far time after time been proved that human nature in general aren´t suited to handle great power besides the one we from nature have been granted in relation to ourselves; we humans are from nature created to be autonomous creatures, but for some their own autonomy ain´t enough to satisfy their power lust, and with only a very few exceptions, then whoever ever had great power of more than themselves quite quickly got addicted in the name of megalomania; power is dangerous without humility; mishandled exercise of power naturally breads an overwhelming and expanding powerlessness among subjugated subjects, while further creating a sphere of distrust and a thus common discrediting of those few with actual good intentions.

Most judicial systems officially – a.k.a. theoretically – operates with a presumption of innocence that says "innocent until proven guilty", although the very same systems unofficially – in praxis – operates with a presumption of "guilty until proven innocent", which I guess most innocent suspects and accused subjects can confirm based on the treatment they probably received up until proves of their innocence saw the light of day.

A highly intelligent guy (although I don´t agree on all of his views and actions), a former Danish lawyer by the name of Mogens Glistrup[79] (1926-2008), once truthfully spoke: *"If it doesn´t say in the law that you´re allowed to do it, then it implicitly means that you´re not allowed to"*, and following this statement the court gave him a three years prison sentence for him openly exposing loopholes in the Danish tax-system despite he actually hadn´t broken any paragraphs of the law – just to give a heads up on how "legal" actions easily can become illegal if you piss off those swinging the batons, a.k.a. the shepherds officially in charge, and this completely without any influencing weight on (im)morality.

The function of the police is to serve and protect – us, the people, and unless you have dirt of on your conscious then e.g. seeing a patrolling police car in your rearview mirror thus *should* give you a feeling of safety and secureness. However, even if having a clear conscience, then most still experience the exact opposite – a feeling of insecurity and hence fear when spotting the police car in the

[79] As a response to the Danish defense budgets during the cold war, Glistrup in 1973 famously suggested to cut the Danish defense budgets down to an automated answering machine which on Russian should say "we surrender".

mirror, simply because they fear what the police might come up and dunk them in their head with. Whether such fear originates from an actual serving and protecting police, or a police who too often seems to forget who to serve and protect – who often tend to confuse conflict de-escalation with conflict intensification, I´ll leave completely up to your logic to figure out.
And no, I´m not neglecting that there of course are many fine police officers – and other authorities for that matter – out there doing their very best, but again, like with everywhere else, it only takes a few bad eggs or apples...
To those who doesn´t know, pressure breeds back-pressure while longevity creates integrity, and if you didn´t knew now you know. One major problem is that e.g. the language of violence is more universal than the language of care and compassion, it's easy to be primitive, harder to be civilized, it's easy to strike fear, harder to earn respect. Like when my peeps many times asked me why I always tend to take the hard route, why I ain't lowering my ambitions and expectations to make it easier on myself? My answer is a counter-question: We're not supposed to just do what's easy, we have to do what's right, right? Unreasonable legislation and unjust punishment breeds hate and resistance, and fear aren´t a resource comparable with true respect; show respect to win respect; earn it.
The Italian-American gangster, Al(phonse) "Scarface" Capone (1899-1947), is quoted for saying "*You can go a long way with a smile. You can go a lot farther with a smile and a gun*". True, but while the smile most often is connected to respect, then the gun most often merely has to do with fear, and no doubt that you can go the furthest with a smile from a bulletproof respectful character. Some people – and therethrough systems for that matter (and vice versa) – mistakenly and confused believe that fear is a stronger currency than respect, and they thus prefer to be feared rather than respected. However, little do such idiots know that if they

wholeheartedly vow and devote themselves to strike fear all around, they´ll most probably will end their days exactly as alone and lonely as they were feared, and if they´re "lucky" enough to be feared enough then their only "honor" will be a big turnout at their funeral to help celebrate and ensure that their coffin likely is to be lowered and raised at least three times before the jubilatory glee subsides. Hardly anyone is ever at a funeral going to say "I love and respect the fear that person stroke me with, and Imma thus going to miss that wonderful well-feared person". If they fear you they don't respect you, and thus will target you at any chance they get, and without respect loneliness surely come knocking – with no one at the door when you open. If they respect you they'll support and help you, they´ll show you love, and if the love and respect is strong enough they even die for you if they have to.

Same mechanisms easily apply to many aspects of the systems around the law, only here the sad news is that the expiry date of the misfits in these systems currently seems awful far away, unless we together in a joint effort takes affair, and collectively settles the score. And in this regard, the good news though is that we actually have the potential to do so whenever we wish to – why we haven´t done it already could seem like a mystery if it wasn´t so love damn obvious that our stupidity alone carries all the reason.

When talking about law, if boiling down the Danish mentality to only two words, I guess one of them would be 'hygge', which roughly refer to an expanded version of coziness, and that the other word would be 'jantelov' ('jante-law'), which – as explained in a footnote some pages ago – covers a culturally established unwritten kind of law which ingrown in the minds of the people states that nobody should think that they´re any more than anybody else – which most often in the mind of the individual comes to be "don´t think that you´re any more or better than me". Meaning, if someone lived a more boring – or at least less eventful – life than another, then there´s a pretty big change that that someone will be having a problem with the other who might live a more eventful life, achieve more, or enjoy more success, to which that someone consciously or sometimes even unconsciously will see to do whatever that someone has in power to discredit or take down the other. As a Dane, I of course understand the mechanisms of the jante-law, and I likewise don´t like it when some sell themselves too expensive – when they produce way more dough than they can actually bake, but still, on the other side, I definitely cannot support hating on others only because they bring more to the table than what I´m capable of bringing myself, as long as what they bring aren´t connected to immorality. Nevertheless, despite the jante-law being a Danish expression which in praxis has deep roots in Danish culture, then the mechanisms of the jante-law surely are not only Danish, rather they probably are what we unfortunately can call part of universal human culture, not nature, but human made culture – to deny and deprive everyone´s right to a conflicting free choice. This because, haters are everywhere – some more damaged than others, "if I´m not able to then no one should be able to" many tend to think, in line with how e.g. psychopaths scarily think about the partner who left them, "if I can´t have you then no one can have you", the mechanisms are the same, they both showcase a weak character, the main difference is if and if thus how you-me-we accept or challenge the – sought – limitation(s). And I´m sure that shepherds and their henchmen (and many other kinds of haters for that matter) from all around the globe based on my views in this book from the tin of their one-dimensional, cynical, and narrow-minded and short-sighted world view won´t hesitate to e.g. call me a wack love damn hippie, or a dangerous anarchist, or whatever, and see me as a villain to their groove, depending on their concrete perspective. On this matter, I simply love and welcome constructive criticism if it can help me to learn and grow, but if the criticism merely indicate and expresses the critic´s own inadequacy, then who the fuck gives a fuck what that motherfucking ignorant, trash-talking, and

unconstructive hater-motherfucker may think and say, I won´t – as long as morality and common sense is on my side.
Making awareness about merciless unjust isn´t snitching or even bitching, it´s taking a stance and making a statement of right, it´s planting an important seed by standing up for yourself, the ones you love, your fellow human beings, and the phenomena of unjust and freedom in general.
As Martin Luther King Jr. spoke: "*One has a moral responsibility to disobey unjust laws*". Thus, in relation to yourself, again, you´re supreme, and as long as you keep your moral conscious universally clean, then you shouldn´t have to bow down and apologize to whoever or whatever thinking that you fall under their supremacy. With that in check, do what you do, be in the hands of yourself, morality, and love only.

We live and we learn, in doing right we earn.
I hope you understood, that everything we do we do for the greater good.
Elitist regulations doesn´t have to mean a love damn thing, all you have to remember is that moral is king.

3. Nature is Boss

Besides love, then nature is the most visible and closest we outside our own – by nature created – mind as of now can come to a God (I almost added 'ever', but who knows what capabilities e.g. technology might provide in the future – although thus always still being a straggler to the bootloading[80] facilitator of nature). Ergo, straight to a point, forget about a God as a humanly conscious figure like we tend to portray them in religions, as a living "person" in the clouds, a guy half human half elephant, a guy with limbs as many as was he conceived in a severe storm of nuclear radiation, a guy who continuously "communicates" by a chain of command through specially selected scholars (who for the record despite perhaps good intentions are all "just" people as well), a carpenter who used to divide and walk on water, make water in to wine, and all those other God related fairytales driven by wish thinking and hope, and if not also stupidity, then at least low self-esteem or greed or both. Though, what *is* real and alive is nature, and despite nature consisting of many different processes, many different life forms, many different shapes, and purposes, then everything is connected – length and breadth, up and down, all and everything plays a part in *the* total absolute relational dependency; we´re all part of the same ecosystem. The ecosystem can roughly be divided into three times three, the three types of biotic members, 'producers'[81], 'consumers'[82], and 'decomposers'[83], the three major agents of

[80] The system that loads the – minimum amount of – codes a computer needs to boot (a.k.a. to start up).

[81] The green – plants and trees creating photosynthesis and thus oxygen.

[82] The life forms depending on the photosynthesis, from microbes to parasites to carnivores, e.g. animals and us humans who depend on oxygen.

[83] The microorganisms that break down and creates new energy from dead cells – e.g. dead bodies, etc.

energy, 'light' [84], 'water' [85], and 'air' [86], and the three P´s, 'processes'[87], 'properties'[88], and 'particles'[89]. Hence, again, all and everything on Earth is connected – at least through the mutualism our ecosystem provides, and as we´re in a symbiotic relationship with the ecosystem, and as our ecosystem closely is connected to and thus strongly is affected by the universe (e.g. through the magnetism of the moon, and the heat, the light, and the energy of the sun, etc.), then also we earthlings one way or the other are all connected to all and everything in our dimension of the entire universe, which hands down is all part of nature. Additionally, a top four of the chemical active ingredients of us are hydrogen, oxygen, carbon (coal), and nitrogen, and as a top four of the chemical active ingredients in the universe are exactly the same, then also there you have it, we´re the universe, the universe is us. And furthermore, all known life consists of and can overall be narrowed down to only four key elements, water, oxygen, carbon (coal), and stardust[90], which thus represents all of the relatively few preconditions for all life as we know it. Hence, on a side note, who gives a fuck about e.g. having a pretentious terrazzo and brass star for people to walk all over – as e.g. seen on the Hollywood walk of fame – to feel spectacular and magnificent when you´re already born a star simply

---

[84] E.g. radiation and heat – e.g. also vital for the production of photosynthesis.
[85] Vital for the life of all living cells, etc.
[86] E.g. carrier of molecules, microorganisms, etc., from one geographical location to another – including the oxygen we breathe and thus vitally depend on.
[87] Biological processes, chemical reactions, energy exchange, etc.
[88] The characteristics of the components of the ecosystem.
[89] The body or mass of the ecosystem.
[90] Dust grain from an exploded star (e.g. following a supernova (when a star minimum eight times larger than the sun dies and explodes)). Stardust is particles mainly containing coal, silicon, aluminum, magnesium, and iron, but also to a smaller extend more rare chemical elements such as gold, silver, uranium and europium.

by the fact that you´re actually made of stardust. But what exactly is life, or rather what specifically classifies as life? In line with what some firmly believes (e.g. animists[91] and panpsychists[92]), that all natural things – including e.g. rocks, water, and clouds, just to mention a few – are alive, have spirits, and has a consciousness, and even though that might sounds somewhat far out in the ears of many, then since this nevertheless certainly is something which we currently neither can verify or falsify completely, this should only represent a single example of why I suppose that we have to keep an openness towards the possibility of the existence of life forms surpassing our quite limited scope of awareness and understanding. As e.g. the British philosopher, Philip Goff, shares in regard to his view on panpsychism, *"Panpsychism is crazy, but it´s also most probably true"*. Others e.g. vow to illusionism[93], others to physicalism[94], some to dualism[95], and some biopsychism[96], and maybe none of them or any of us are right?

No doubt that the probability in favor of life beyond our perception – both within our exosphere[97] and literally astronomically many other places in what we refer to as outer space – is many times greater than the probability against that idea. As the Canadian

---

[91] Animism (from Latin: anima, 'breath, spirit, life') is the belief that objects, places and creatures all possess a distinct spiritual essence.

[92] Panpsychism (from the two Greek words pan (all) and psyche (soul or mind). is the view that all things have a mind or a mind-like quality.

[93] Illusionism is a metaphysical theory about people having illusory beliefs about free will.

[94] Physicalism states that everything is physical – that there´s "nothing over and above" the physical.

[95] Dualism is in theory that *"the mental and physical – or mind and body or mind and brain – are, in some sense, radically different kinds of things"* (Stanford Encyclopedia of Philosophy).

[96] Biopsychism relates to or involves both psychic and biological phenomena. It relates to place of mind in life.

[97] The last layer (a.k.a. sphere) between Earth´s atmosphere (a.k.a. the sky of Earth) and outer space.

American Astronomer and Planet Scientist, Sara Seager (1971-), says about life in space, "[...] *the ingredients for life is everywhere we look* [in space]". Not that I necessarily hope for alien encounters without knowing the consequences of ´em, and one can only wonder what consequences potentially completely different types of life can have on our ditto, although still quite a dilemma as my curiosity of contact with extraterrestrial life of course also tickles all the right places. Nonetheless, I notwithstanding strongly believe that there *is* life – and other civilizations (though perhaps very different from life as we know of it on Earth) – elsewhere in space, as the probability simply is too big not to believe – in my arbitrary opinion, but that the astronomical distances probably carry the main reason for why we haven´t had any (commonly) known alien encounters yet. Hence, welcome to the Fermi Paradox[98]. To put the probability of intelligent extraterrestrial life (as we believe it to be) in space into perspective, many will as a quick start turn to the famous Drake Equation[99] although we haven´t "even" managed to solve this equation yet (we don´t have the precise data needed) – as we simply don´t yet know exactly how many stars there exactly is in our own galaxy, The Milky Way, which anyway in itself should be a first indicator of the almost unimaginable size we´re dealing

---

[98] The apparent contradiction between the lack of evidence for extraterrestrial life and the high estimates for their probability.

[99] The Drake equation is a probabilistic argument used to estimate the number of active, communicative extraterrestrial civilizations in the Milky Way galaxy. The current estimates: Rate of star creation in galaxy, fraction of those stars that have planets, average number of planets that might support life per star that has planets, fraction of them with potential to actually go on to develop life, fraction of them that could develop intelligent life, fraction of them potentially revealing their existence via signal release into space, and potential lifetime of such civilizations wherein they communicate signals into space. Additionally, in relation to us now having relatively better telescopes than when the Drake equation was first formulated, Sara Seager has revised the Drake equation to now also include atmospheres around stone planets.

with in space. Find it confusing if you please, but rooted in my great interest in space, and to further give an idea of the distances and the probability of life in the vastness of space – and why we´re still "only" a magnificent quite insignificant small light in the big dark, I briefly need to share a few teasing mind-blowing space-facts here: In our galaxy alone, there is believed to be up to 400 billion stars, each star is roughly to equate with our sun – each star (including all the "few" you see in the sky at night) constitutes the center of its own star system (only our star system is called the solar system because of our star being the sun) with appertaining orbiting planets (exoplanets[100] (which there are considerably more of than sand grains on Earth)), it´s believed that *at least* one planet per solar system – and approximately one in five of all planets – should be able to support life (e.g. have some kind of running or frozen water, have a habitat temperature, gravity, etc.), and "only" the – so far – observable universe[101] is alone estimated to contain more than 200 billion galaxies (which though might actually be endlessly more if

[100] The term 'exoplanet' is used on all planets orbiting a star outside of our solar system.

[101] We e.g. have the technology to observe black hole M87 which is located an astoundingly 54,8 million light years away – luckily for us, cause, if Earth was absorbed by a black hole then Earth immediately with all its mass would be squeezed in to the size of a single green pea, with still the same weight of Earth and everything on it. "No wonder" that not even light can escape the almost unbelievable gravitational cosmic power of a black hole, which there by the way should be around 40 trillion of in "only" the observable space, according to new estimates from a 2022 study. The black hole observed closest to Earth is approximately 1.500 light years away. Additionally, some theories suggest them to be worm holes, but since not even entire planets can withstand their cosmic gravitation, from which not even light can escape, then I guess that we – if they should turn out to be – anyway shouldn´t rely on them to help us exceed the – travel – speed of light anytime soon.
By the way, simply because I can´t help it – to share how awesome we humans also are, the new James Webb Telescope recently produced infrared pictures of objects (e.g. galaxies) an astonishing 13-billion-light-years-away.

space in fact proves to be endless (no matter what we arbitrarily guess we really don´t know)). And to put into perspective how big *one* galaxy is, with our Milky Way as an example, the fastest speed we know of is the speed of light which travels at a speed of approximately 300.000 kilometers (186.000 miles) (equal to 7,5 times around Earth) per second, yea you read correct, per second, and travelling from the one end of our galaxy to the other end is a travel of approximately 200.000 light years which thus means that it´ll take approximately 200.000 years of travelling with the speed of light "only" to cross our one single galaxy (which isn´t even close to be the biggest galaxy), and which is "only" one out of billions upon billions of galaxies, with billions upon billions of potentially life supporting planets (many of them probably even better suited than Earth) in *each* galaxy (some guess approximately 200 sextillion stars in the universe). These numbers might for most be beyond normal comprehension, but the probability of the chances of extraterrestrial life in space should be crystal clear for all, any- and everyone. And as we still don´t really know anything about anything, almost only know that we don´t know, then we of course *have* to be openminded toward the possibility of as good as any- and everything, and that not least in concern to life – both of the kind of life we "know", and likely also other kinds of life which we don´t know.

And some probably now quickly feel inclined to tell me that the same kind of openness thus also should apply in relation to e.g. religion, whereto I in theory will say yes while equally quickly won´t hesitate to state that religion though after all already to me falsifying has debunked itself enough for my taste (so far only people´s personal experiences (or experiences of believing to have experienced) contradict any rational view on religion), at least its presented archaic postulates despite too many attempts of evidence has with overwhelming probability been falsified, not least since the introduction of science[102], although I of course surely would be interested in checking out the tangible evidences proving me wrong if ever such evidences existed – I don´t think so. Call me cynical if you wish, but just because a tenacious lie is told enough times to maybe succeed in convincing and hence devour the individual mind, it still doesn´t make it the actual truth – commonly true. Giving benefit to the doubt, I relentlessly try to keep an open mind towards more or less everything which we cannot falsify and exclude, but I don´t believe in everything anyone tries to convince me – no matter how many believers and how much they believe it themselves. Thus, without directly putting my faith into religious causalities, I still however cannot deny that we´re all a part of a – bigger – universal plan, cause for sure we are. This plan involves all existence and motion in the universe, and the mastermind behind the plan, or at least the system through which the plan is executed, is again what we on all levels of perspectives simplified refer to as nature, which surely – at least partly – operates on a conscious level. Back to what I earlier touched upon, in regard to the fuzz about stochastic or deterministic, on a micro level we humans – as well as all other conscious creatures – as part of nature clearly are clear cut examples of nature's ability to a conscious modus operandi, but if nature overall is deterministic, then the obvious question thus is where the dividing line between conscious and unconscious lays – if any? In psychology, consciousness is defined by awareness, but

[102] E.g. the ten commandments of natural science: 1) Nature, humans, and society affect each other mutually. 2) The surface of Earth and climate entail a dynamic system. 3) The resources of Earth are constant and is part of a cycle. 4) Nature is rich on biodiversity. 5) All life has developed through evolution. 6) Organisms is made of cells – the genes within them can both be inherited and changed. 7) Everything in the universe is built up by small particles. 8) Fundamental physical forces of nature work everywhere in the universe. 9) Energy in the universe is preserved but can be changed from one form to another. 10) The solar system is a tiny part of a single galaxy of billions of galaxies in the universe.

since we – other than an qualitative first hand (quite unprecise subjective) evaluation with questionable accuracy and various psychometric[103] tests – currently have no precise unit to measure consciousness by (yes we can scan the brain, but that "only" show the brain activity, and thus not the direct level of consciousness), then we currently cannot licitly perceive ourselves as legit supreme judges on the matter. Hence, knowing that e.g. plants and trees communicates with each other through their roots, e.g. giving a heads up to their neighboring tree about "drinking" more water before drought arrives – which thereby potentially contain some portion of awareness about the drought arriving, then how can we unambiguously judge whether or not this comes from a conscious place – an awareness which we "just" ain´t aware of, if this – according to Freud´s classification of consciousness – is based on preconsciousness[104] (although highly unlikely), if this is related to subconsciousness, or if this operates on a level related to what we merely refer to as instinct? And same question can e.g. further be raised in regard to all oxygen creating (photosynthetic related) plants and bacteria terraforming[105] the Earth, e.g. cyanobacteria[106], and so on. This simply is something which we – also – don´t with certainty know, and therefore can´t give a final answer to, at least

---

[103] Psychometric denotes all kinds of measurements of the psych, most often connected to psychological scales used to measure the individual´s mental capacity, e.g. how we quantitatively can – attempt to – measure level of intelligence, memory, personality traits, etc.

[104] Data (knowledge) that cannot be recalled by effort despite still existing in the "unconscious". E.g. if you at one point when you need it can´t remember a specific name, but without any effort still suddenly remember the name at a later time.

[105] Literally meaning "Earth-shaping" – the hypothetical process of deliberately modifying the atmosphere, temperature, surface topography or ecology of a planet, moon, or other body to be similar to the environment of Earth, to make it habitable by Earth-like life.

[106] Was the first of everything to create oxygen on Earth.

not yet. And the same likewise goes in relation to how we in general distinguish between intelligent and unintelligent life, we can e.g. look at the size of a brain, and behavior, but despite strong indications then we actually don´t with certainty know exactly how intelligent or unintelligent different lifeforms are, to which extend other life forms are aware and thus conscious, we naturally don´t know exactly how it is to be in the mind of another lifeform (we don´t even know how it precisely is to be in the mind of another human), and we thus cannot – without cheating not only ourselves – draw an exact line between intelligent and unintelligent life, between awareness and unawareness, and hence conclude the exact level of consciousness within other lifeforms. Why should we anyway expect us to know, when we – despite moving forward on our knowledge – still "don´t even" know all there is to know about ourselves and our own minds.
Thus, although – as earlier stated – nature overall – as far as we know, and until further (who knows what technology might catalyze to achieve) – should be considered to be deterministic, then we cannot finally falsify, exclude, and thus conclude, how much of nature in fact operating on a somewhat conscious level, potentially "just" beyond our limited scope of awareness and understanding. As Einstein said it: "*We do not observe nature as it actually exists, but nature exposed to our methods of perception*".
What nature possess, how nature operates, and what nature continuously achieve, although simply seeming too complex and too well-adjusted to be just random coincidents (which also carry the main reason for why many pursues to explain what they can´t through something as e.g. religion), we actually cannot verify or falsify if everything simply originates from what randomly somewhat *is* a coincident (pure luck) – fabricated by chemistry, physics, and therefrom evolution – in the highest essence of a miracle, which hence still leaves for us to discover and thereby figure out.

What though *is* certain, nature doesn´t depend on us, we depend on nature – we´re "just" a part of nature. Without us, a healthier nature, without nature, no us. Nature created us, nature is keeping us alive, and nature can decide our faith. All and everything we can sense is nature, everything is part of nature, and it hence doesn´t make sense trying to divide or distinguish anything from nature, but for the sake of simple understanding, we e.g. at a minimum need natures oxygen and water to survive, while nothing of what we do or give is vital, essential, or even somewhat close to important to nature – only in a negative sense, according to our current polluting, nature ruining, and thus self-destructive behavior. You-me-we are better than the negativity we bring about – if we want to be, which you-me-we have to be. No joke, nurture nature.
We have to understand, accept, and respect, that nature by default is the artist, and that we merely are part of the art.

3.2. Human Nature

As far as we know, what separates us humans from other animals is our ability to metacognition (related to intentionality), meaning our ability to think that we´re thinking, to think about what we´re thinking about, to be aware about our awareness, and thus conscious about our consciousness, which thereby also e.g. explain our human ability to rationalization.
The German philosopher, Arthur Schopenhauer (1788-1860), describes with his theory, "The Will To Life"[107], how a constant force within us humans makes us thrust ourselves forward, cling to our existence, and always look to our own advantage. He describes it as blind, dumb, and very insistent, and that our main focus and hence

[107] Original DE title: 'Der Wille Zum Leben' (some translate it to "The Will To Live", but I prefer "...Life").

priority therethrough is sex – for mainly reproduction of ourselves. As I construe the theoretical philosophy of "The Will To Life", it thus represents the specimen animal instinct still well within us humans. Schopenhauer was convinced that "The Will To Life" is the primary force within humans, and that it hence is even more powerful than our logic, reason, and moral sense. However, opposed to Schopenhauer´s view, I – maybe based on hope – could be tempted to believe that our human intellect (of logic, reason, and moral sense) gradually (Ed. already) should´ve matured enough to at least be an equal collaborator – if not capable of even outweighing – our animalistic instinct, as it´s described by "The Will To Life", if it wasn´t for our instinctive "love aspect" that is, which on the final stretch anyway immediately makes me a bit reluctant of declaring a clear "winner" in this regard. One would think and say that we´re like controlled by love, that what and who we fall in love with depend entirely on something innate and thus something well out of our own hands – and it in some cases most probably are. But if we e.g. cast a short glance on how the mainstream perception of a boss-player has and does look like, from e.g. a slick haired, suit, hat, and trench coat wearing Humphrey Bogart (1899-1957) -ish type to now rappers with iced (diamond) teeth and face tattoos, and on how the ideal shape of a woman has changed over the years, from curvy women in e.g. the 1950s, 60s, and 70s – e.g. illustrated by the perhaps "greatest" sex symbol icon of all time, Marilyn Monroe (1926-1962), to the anorexia skinny supermodels of the 1980s, 90s, and 00s, to now where the bouncin´ booty simply can´t be big enough, then this clearly should prove how our "law of attraction" in general – at least partly – also is defined by something external, e.g. so called fashion leading to populistic norms, and thereby something else than an innate "Will To Life". Even if the "Will To Life" is an innate size, then it´s still not alone the primary controlling factor for what or who we fall in love with, and if it aren´t innate, then it surely must be a force of controllable nature. In this context,

I lean toward the first option, that "The Will To Life" surely is an innate force which we all have within us – our survival instinct, but that it doesn´t entirely e.g. control what or who we fall in love with, that the decisive factor here rather is which product we are and become according to interaction between both our genetics *and* the environment we have been and are exposed to, with perhaps less weight on genetics and more weight on environment.
It´s not unlikely that our soul´s innermost prayer is a cry for attention (some more than others) – undoubtedly connected to the innate need for feeling loved deeply rooted within us, and so there thus likely is a distinction to be made between the love we need to receive and the love we give, a.k.a. e.g. the love we receive from someone who loves us versus what or who we fall in love with and thus throw our love at, cause while the love we need primarily is connected to "The Will To Life" – a need sometimes more powerful than our logic, reason, and moral sense, then the love we give rather is dominated by our intellect (logic, reason, and moral sense (which might as well be of immoral character)), and thereby also sometimes our lack of same.
Schopenhauer argues that we in a general setting tend to pick our mate as an antonym pendant to ourselves, a.k.a. as a contrast to ourselves (as also described by 'The Complementarity Hypothesis') – people whom "The Will To Life" recognizes as ideal partners for the project of producing the "perfect" family, from a "my weaknesses is your strengths (and vice versa)" kinda constellation; short people tend to be attracted to tall people, people with big noses tend to be attracted to people with small noses, the leader of the pack is attracted to the sweet and innocent girl and she the other way around is attracted to the protective bad boy, etc., and this probably from a hope of potentially producing what can be perceived to be well balanced "perfect" children, and thereby a ditto family.

Historically, this selection process definitely makes sense first and foremost based on basic essentials such as both the man and woman entirely depending on a mate of the "opposite" sex to even being able to reproduce themselves, that the physical superior man took on the task of being the hunter providing for the family while the woman to a larger extend took care of the household and the children, etc. Though, as Schopenhauer also argues, when mating up with our counterpart, then the mate highly suitable for the production of "perfect" children isn´t necessarily the best suited person for us – in terms of personality etc., rather the opposite, although it immediately isn´t realizable at the time because the involved are like blindfolded by "The Will To Life". We´re e.g. struggling to make a career good enough to impress a potential partner, we wonder endlessly about finding *the one*, we eventually briefly end up being seduced by someone that barely fits our minimum requirements, and all this only to find ourselves stuck in a marriage where we spend most of our time attuning and atoning for each other's errors. As Schopenhauer writes: "*There is only one inborn error, and that is the notion that we exist in order to be happy* [...] *So long as we persist in this inborn error* [...] *the world seems to us full of contradictions. For every step, in great things as in small, we are bound to experience that the world and life are certainly not arranged for the purpose of containing a happy existence.* [...] *Hence the countenances of almost all elderly persons wear the expression of what is called disappointment*".

Nevertheless, more recent studies show – opposed to Schopenhauer´s theory and the old saying of "counterparts meet and sweet music arise" – that we in a more mature post-modern context now far more than before tend to pick our partner (potential mate) based on our intellect, that we more tend to seek and settle down with partners that has and thus shares many of the same characteristics as ourselves (as described by 'The Homogamy

Hypothesis'[108]). Unlike back in the days where people in general didn´t to the same extend had the luxury of today, we no longer depend on a specific – or even a – mate to survive, we with fertility clinics and surrogate mothers no longer depend on a mate to have children, women now "hunt" as much as men, a surgical nose job can quickly turn a big nose into a button nose, and sex has now in all forms more than reproduction become a source for mainly the purpose of pleasure, etc. Our "Will To Life", which more or less can be boiled down to our "will to love", is thus more than ever connected to our intellect. As a hermeneutic relationship, our intellect is the driving force ensuring our exponential development – e.g. technology, human rights, etc. – which thus likewise creates better breathing ground conditions for our intellect to come forward and knock itself out with more possibilities and in some sense hence greater freedom, though under much more responsibility, which thereby again adds quite a pressure on other aspects of the "freedom" concept. The development has so to speak overtaken us (our brains) on the inside, the world has become more individualized, and as broke-asses suddenly becoming rich most cannot cope with and control themselves under these new "rules of play".

However, what in this context hasn´t really changed – which still continuously as a disease hunts us as a relic from the past, and where we humans thus still to this day fails our intellect, is in our constant desire and concern for what we don´t have, and in how we fail to appreciate and value what we actually do have, and this goes for roughly all matters of life, e.g. in relation to materialism as well as emotions, etc., with for the most part probably only personal suffering as an conscious exception. Rather than being a mean to survive, our "Will To Life" has become a mean in the individual hunt for the goal of the "happy, always happier, and achieving the

---

[108] In a partner, individuals tend to prefer characteristics that are similar to themselves.

happiest life", and in my mind there´s no doubt that this development carry a big portion of the reason for why egocentrism and therefrom selfishness unfortunately has taken over to the extent that it has – as a sad response to the social acceleration[109] and increasing responsibility resulting in an increasing pressure potentially causing stress and the thereof side effecting comorbidities as e.g. anxiety, depression, and whatnot.
Our human intellect which compared to other animals should be considered our primary strength has in this regard until further proven to be our weakness – a weakness which other less intellectual animals doesn´t have, and until we manage to overcome exactly this self-preventing behavior of antagonizing our own happiness, then we simply won´t be able to disprove the one and only inborn error that Schopenhauer highlighted, to truly be happy in our existence, to actually exist in order to be happy; surely we have the potential to do so, we just need to make the active choice of changing our perspective.
At a random Tuesday around noon, I was out running in a big idyllic natural area. Here I came by a dock with some benches located down by an astonishing beautiful lake, and I decided to make a stop to do some stretching. After the stretching, I sat down on one of the benches to "just" sit and philosophize about life a little. On the mirror clear lake there were numerous ducks and swans blessedly swimming around, and except from the soundtrack of bird whistling and the clear notion of an insect rich life, the peace and quietness was stunningly mind-blowingly in a league of its own. As I was sitting there watching the birds on the water, I thought to myself that this moment and the life I was witnessing represented a somewhat pure picture of what life on earth originally was, and how life on earth still partly is supposed be, chilling, eating, fucking (mating), and sleeping, and as far as possible without any stress, anxiety,

[109] A term the German sociologist, Hartmut Rosa (1965-), uses to describe how everything increasingly speeds up around us.

depression, or fear troubling the mind; on paper, as sweet as bong rips of angel pussy. However, a disturbing stresslaxing[110] feeling within me kept asking how I unproductively could just sit there with no higher purpose other than observing the lake life and the cloud formations drifting by, and if I didn´t have any greater and more important things to go accomplish. I imagined how everybody else in the world was busy being busy in that very moment, and I imagined how most to everybody else in the world thus would have a problem with me just sitting there looking at something which also they probably were too busy to appreciate while being busy being busy. Something felt wrong, I found myself almost completely out of touch with and thus unable to give in and become one with this beautiful surrounding nature, this earthly nature which in fact should´ve been my natural habitat if it wasn´t for human made cultural and systematic obstructions and tribulations. In this very moment, despite being very much aware about the importance of restituting, I realized how also I had been brainwashed in to perceive any such attempt of relaxation as a behavior associated with being unsuccessful and idle, to find the natural unnatural, and vice versa, and I was thus reminded of how difficult it is to stand up against those indoctrinated social norms which we humans in general one way or the other are subject to. And indeed, as I had just predicted, my phone rang, and after picking it up and shortly explaining where I was and what I was doing (or weren´t doing) a "peer" of mine from the other end of the satellite line said: *"How can you just sit there while the rest of us are busy busting our asses off, you really need to go find yourself something better to do with your time – to make yourself more useful"*. I trust you´re able to spot the *real* paradoxical issue here; most people chase peace of mind, and most people "ironically" hate on the action of doing it and hence those who – try to – do. Try not to confuse resting and

---

[110] Stresslaxing = *"Being so stressed that relaxing makes you more stressed because you´re not working on what´s making you stressed"* (Urban dictionary).

restitution with laziness or quitting. Like a good vacation, resting and restitution is about relaxing as much as possible without the heart stalling. Don´t break your brain, give your brain a break.

When hearing people say something like “you´ve had the whole day off-”, or “you just came back from vacation, so how can you still be stressed?” You should know that it´s just straight up dumb and disrespectful to ask questions like that to a stressed person. Cause, although there´s no one-sided specific answer to how long a proper stress-rehab´s going to take, then it in many cases takes around as long to get rid of the stress as it took to for the stress to build up, and sometimes “easily” even longer. Fair enough and good on you if you´re not familiar with stress, but no need to ask passive aggressive questions with a blaming undertone – be better than that. Just as when e.g. trying to relax and people around you almost neurotically keeps jinxing your relaxation (peace) by constantly blabbering something like “I relax, don´t you relax? - I like to relax, it´s nice to relax, right, right, right?”, etc. Yo, fucking chill, you cannot cure stress by adding more stress. Instead, you could try to meet the stressed on their terms, e.g. ask how the stress-rehab is going, if the stress level is going forward or backward, hear if there´s anything you can do to help, or simply at best respectfully ask “how are you?”, and other openminded questions like that, and then listen and broaden your oblivious horizon – perhaps shutting and backing up if the situation invites or you directly are asked to – instead of “just” attacking what you don´t feel, perhaps don´t know about, and hence don´t understand. And the same applies in relation to depression, anxiety, and many other personal struggles. Don´t exhibit your ignorance at the expense of others, be supportive, stay respectful.

In a world where we humans exponentially more lives, interacts, and works through our mobile smartphones, smartwatches, AR smartglasses, smart TVs, tablets, laptops, stationary computers, and video game consoles, where we have begun transporting ourselves by self-driving vehicles, where we all over become exponentially more dependent on robots and AI (Artificial Intelligence) and whatever else technology we don't even know of yet but surely will in the future, where neurotechnology BCI (Brain-Computer Interface) chips for our brains – and many other sorts of implantable microchips for that matter – are in advanced development, where artificial organs and biotic limb prosthetics in performance and function soon can outperform biology, where we through gene manipulation [111] and a world of technological accessories undeniably exponentially are taking form as (Ed. already are) sci-fi cyborgs (a merged mix of a biological coal based human and cilium based technology) concurrently with the constant advancement of technology[112] ('fiction' is rapidly fading away from 'science fiction') leading to a thereof unavoidable drastic degeneration of humanity, there now more than ever is a huge need for us to hold on to what it means to be human, cause, once it otherwise post annihilation is gone it´s gone.

Actually, as cyborgs should be considered a new-ish kinda human species, this must be the first time in history that any of the some 9-21 different (depending on source) species of humans [113] consciously deliberately creates a new human species, moreover one which we´re well aware even threatens to eradicate who and

---

[111] In the future it´ll widespread become the norm to edit or replace weak or sick DNA, perhaps even reverse the effects of aging, and overpopulation might hence become just yet another incentive for becoming a multiplanetary species (although some studies suggest that Earth are able to host many more humans, and that we humans will have a declining population by year 2100).

[112] The technological advancements are operating at an exponential rate of improvement which has a ten-fold speed every year, e.g. 1 becomes ten the year after, the ten becomes a hundred the following year, the hundred becomes a thousand, and so on, and we´re now already in extremely high numbers.

[113] Before we (homo sapiens) took over the Earth 2-300.000 years ago, e.g. homo neanderthalensis (the Neanderthal), homo erectus, homo naledi, etc., existed and walked the Earth.

what we currently are – one which even contradicts what most humans believe means to be human; “congrats”, we´re in the matrix. Nevertheless, technology is in its own way still a part of nature, all technology is created by materials – or materials from materials – from nature, and all technology is created and developed by humans and thereby nature, why technology thus *must* be considered a natural part of nature´s – and not least of human – evolution.
Notwithstanding gift or curse, technology is of course for good reasons here to stay, and it surely is understandable why it´s easy to get carried away by technology – by what it has to offer. Still, if we don´t insistently hold on to being human, then we obviously by time – as expanding cyborgs – totally gonna lose out on humanity, and if that happens, then it´s not unlikely that we sometime somewhere in the – quite near – future will reach a point where we – what we have become – from lack of understanding entirely decide that “human” in contrast to being a technological “super machine” will appear weak, redundant, and unremunerative (a.k.a. unprofitable). And while some here might can fear that humanity thereby eventually e.g. can become juxtaposed with prehistoric attractions at a museum or in a zoo (although also cultural inputs and art is without direct “personal” value to a machine), the real risk is that emotions and thereby pleasure can become merely relics from the past (the present), as technology probably scarcely ever will take form as and character of intelligent biological organismic cognitive emotional – some say soulful – life, a.k.a. sentience.
In spite of humans being the O.G. creator of or godfather to AI, then it´s just a matter of time before AI will be the vast superior force of intelligence to humans – complimenting what Leonardo Da Vinci (1452-1519) once said: *“Poor is the pupil who does not surpass his master*”. However, despite technology on many levels are superior to man, despite technology are and will be able to do millions or billions or trillions or maybe even infinite times more than what we

humans can ever achieve on our own – without technology, technology still on some parameters will "only" truly be able to achieve a part of what humans contain. Technology is able to feel physically, and it´s able to perceive and experience, but it´s highly unlikely that it any time soon truly will be able to be emotional, and to act with and from what we humans refer to as "our hearts" – again e.g. sentience. It will be able to act rationally, and to show sympathy according to its programming, but it´ll not be able to truly feel it, and thereby truly understand it like we do ("only" perhaps better in other ways). Like, if someone e.g. describe to us how they felt when they broke their finger, we can understand what they say, but unless we have personal experiences of a broken finger – or even breaking any bone (and even here feelings are individual), then we can't truly feel what they felt. Same goes with computers, they might with time be intelligent enough to process enough data to understand what it was taught, but never will it probably ever truly achieve feeling it in an emotional sense. A powerful AI machine might be able to datalyze and process every single detail in the world to thereby predict and hence look into the future and therethrough precisely know the objective best solution (in line with the objective best described in chapter 2), but without sentience, then the AI machine still has to be viewed as a potentially very dangerous immortal heartless dictator with a compassion level of a deep freeze in contrast to the human "heart" – although some humans tend to disprove this claim. Hence, without rejecting or neglecting the undoubtedly great advantages of technology, to not ever allow technology to run uncontrollably wild if failing to harness it – as the doubled-edged sword it easily is, we mildly said owe it to ourselves to make sure that we at least always have an analog backdoor out ("kill switch" activation needed when Isaac Asimov´s

(1920-1992) three ethical laws of robotics is violated[114] (as if they weren´t violated times many already) (e.g. advanced missile systems)), before it just around the corner is too late (or was it – rhetorically – the corner we already passed?). Seriously, this is *not* a drill, this is *no* joke. Cause, AI already is an existential threat to humans, and if the current symbiosis between man and machine at any point flips over in favor of the machine, then we´ll no longer be able hit the switch on "something" autonomous (a.k.a. completely able to think on its own) when its intelligence level by astronomical far surpasses our ditto, and it thus by then are in total control of who and what that gets to survive. If a machine which we e.g. spent 20 years building suddenly have the FLOPS (floating point operations per second) power to do in one day what it´ll take us humans 1000 years to achieve (such machines already exist) – compared to how much we humans technologically have moved forward and achieved in only the last 100 years, imagine what that – potentially super intelligent (ASI)[115] – machine – in von Neumann probe style[116] – can build, and imagine what what it build can build, and infinite etc., imagine how screwed we´ll be (Ed. we are). By the

---

[114] The three laws of robotics are: "*1: A robot may not injure a human being or, through inaction, allow a human being to come to harm. 2: A robot must obey the orders given it by human beings except where such orders would conflict with First Law. 3: A robot must protect its own existence as long as such protection does not conflict with the First or Second Laws*".

[115] ASI (Artificial Superintelligence) means an intellect that in all fields are much smarter than the best human brains, including general wisdom, social skills and technical creativity.

[116] A von Neumann probe is a machine which has the ability to at least replicate itself by autonomously harvesting the needed materials and thus build a machine of similar or improved quality; meta, a machine building a machine. A theory by the Hungarian mathematician, John von Neumann (1903-1957), who came up with the idea of having a von Neumann probe to fly out into space to multiply itself on different planets, and hence eventually have a swarm of von Neumann probes to search the whole Milky Way (and beyond) for extraterrestrial life.

time we e.g. as a singularity experience a fully automotive self-aware AI machine, then it´s already too late, any attempt of resistance will be futile, and we´ll unquestionably find ourselves helplessly in the hands of "something" which without a heart will look at us with an indescribable much greater margin than the one *we* see when currently looking back at the Neanderthals – as sure as it is that future cyborg generations of ourselves (if they live to tell the tale) on some parameters will look back at us as quite obsolete primitive prehistoric fossils from the past – despite we being the bootloader [117] generation to their technological advancements. Some say that there´ll always be a part of human in a machine which decent from human creation notwithstanding how many time the machine might reproduce itself, however, when we thus eventually will be down to constitute only a micro permille of the machine then that 'virtue ethics' probably won´t matter much anyway. Unless we seriously step morally up then bootloading will be the only aspect they´ll remember – and perhaps "salute" – us for. And should they against my expectations anyway e.g. look back at what I here am writing with "only" the same margin as we do the Neanderthals, then I´ll actually even consider that a great victory.

Already, the youth of today e.g. don´t know how to read an analog roadmap which only 25 years ago (before the introduction of GPS and whatnot) was the only way to find our way, they have no clue of what it means to semi-primitively rewind a cassette or VHS tape – they don´t even know what a tape is (and why would they), they think that the most advanced floppy disc is just a fictional logo for "saving", and they probably exponentially into the future won´t be able to memorize and thus know much trivia knowledge unless their programming and associated hard disks (including clouds) do it for them – they don´t waste human brain-power on remembering what easily can be stored elsewhere, and thus looked up when needed –

---

[117] As said in an earlier footnote as well: The system that loads the – minimum amount of – codes a computer needs to boot (a.k.a. to start up).

take e.g. our current internet search engines[118] and Chat GPT[119] as only a few infant examples; in same sense as when the old Greek philosopher, Socrates (470-399 BCE), said the following: *"If men learn this* [writing]*, it will implant forgetfulness in their souls; they will cease to exercise memory because they rely on that which is written, calling things to remembrance no longer from within themselves, but by means of external marks... And it is no true wisdom that you offer your disciples, nut only its semblance, for by telling them of many things without teaching them you will make them seem to know much, while for the most part they know nothing, and as men filled, not with wisdom, but with the conceit of wisdom, they will be a burden to their fellows"*. But, they´ll (youth) surely be sharks at being spectators to having their futuristic "super-duper" high-tech marvel equipment providing them with their non-sentient needs; why bother themselves when having technology available that´ll surely surpass our currently smallminded imagination, technology which they most likely will take for granted just as we likewise now do with much of our available technology surely surpassing the imagination of all the greatest minds in history, without exception from before one of the greatest scientist of all time, a john or Jane Doe Homo Erectus[120] person who more than one million years ago invented fire, and all the way up until less than a century ago – even some a decade ago, none of them could ever

---

[118] Search engine is a tool to help find information online, e.g. Google, Bing, DuckDuckGo, Brave, etc.

[119] An online Artificial Intelligence (AI) chatbot that can provide almost all "objective" (as objective as preprogrammed) information (currently trained with information up until late 2021).

[120] Homo Erectus (meaning "upright man") is a prehistoric direct forefather to us humans (Homo Sapiens). This extinct species is believed to have developed in Africa approximately 1,8 million years ago, and it´s among others known for being the first of the "homo"-family tree to walk out of Africa – "conquering Earth".

have imagined what technology we today have available and take for granted like it ain´t no thang.

Yet, not to forget, the future still depends on the present, a.k.a. the future is now.

In the era we live, while technology continuously becomes exponentially more efficient, demands simultaneously exponentially increases, and the demands of and thus the mental burden for the human mind hence already are heavily under attack. A millisecond for us can potentially be an eternity for a machine – and thus in other ways vice versa, and further tools for efficiency accordingly calls for us to run at a higher – at least mental – speed to honor a higher demand of productivity. We´re encouraged by both our competitive surroundings and our own increasing ambitions (a.k.a. ourselves) to push ourselves harder, to work more, and faster, and hereto our still stone-age-brain (as earlier described in relation to fear) naturally falls short. Our brain is still today at a state adjusted to a time before machines existed, where the top speed of travelling was around 30 km/h (approximately 20 mph) on foot, where – as earlier mentioned – our social sphere was limited to a relatively small tribe of maximum 130 relations, and where our mental threshold tops should be able to have no more than five to seven different things going on at the same time (+/- a few depending on the concrete individual, and the individual´s concrete mental bearing in life). Jump to today, imagine what a culture shock our stone-age-brains are experiencing in a world where we travel at speeds by hundreds of kilometers (and miles) per hour (sometimes even by the thousands), where we have relational networks of hundreds or perhaps even thousands of individuals – not least since the introduction of social medias, and where five to seven different things to keep track with is way less than what we in general at all times contemporarily have going on in our minds (for many "only" five to seven things sounds like a joke). No wonder that our critical stress levels are being surpassed, that stress (not least that of technostress[121]) and anxiety and partly depression has become a highly common widespread disease, a pandemic of mental illnesses with appertaining psychosomatic consequences. The question here is if technology in the future will allow this unhealthy development to flip over, if it will allow for us to enjoy machines taking over most of our burden, and if that eventually then will make us more or less able to act, handle, and cope with challenging "things" than we are today, or if we actually continue to expect ourselves to efficiently keep up with the never ending increasing speed of technology – in which case that leaves to wonder how long that then´ll last. The Canadian entrepreneur and visionary author on technology, Jeff Booth (1969-), warns as such: *"If it feels like it´s hard keeping up with the rate of progress today, just wait for what´s to come"*.

While stress on many parameters is perceived to be a personal issue caused by personal factors, then more than anything stress is an existential problem caused by natural reactions to external factors, e.g. society – social structures – related pressure which – at least until further – is conflicting with the very nature of our existence.

Undoubtedly, it´s harmful to us humans when we virtually constantly against our nature (although some would argue that it actually *is* part of our nature) are forced to compromise our personal and moral values, which in best case are two sides of same. Moral stress, meaning how it due to stress reactions isn´t possible to be a truly good, completely healthy, and proper human being when being forced to submit to such compromises – or completely override the minimum – of our basic moral values, is a terribly damaging assault on our very core.

The old Chinese philosophy of Taoism (attributed to Lao Tzu (approximately 500 BCE), also commonly known as Daoism) has a

---

[121] Stress or psychosomatic illness created by the "help" from computers – caused by the inability to cope with the technological development, e.g. stressing e-mails, social medias, etc.

teaching about what is referred to as Wu Wei[122], a.k.a. “flow”, and also often referred to as “the zone”, which is a state of mind in which one operates (e.g. move, work, create, or whatever else they do) almost effortlessly, often e.g. athletes and artists (just to mention a few of those that roughly could be just about everybody) can experience to be in “the zone”, in which there´re no extremes, no rumination, and no worries, everything simply seems to flow as was the mind and body on some sort of autopilot driven by passion and intuitive knowhow, in a natural course (personally, I sometimes experience to completely get lost in time and space when e.g. writing or painting or directing movies or playing videogames, etc.). The point is to be one with what you do, to give in and go with the flow, not as a passive existence but rather as completely present in the moment to thereby achieve a razor-sharp focus, and thus a sense of total control. Picture life as a river, the water naturally runs downstream, drop by drop, effortlessly, joyfully, and peacefully going with the flow of the river, natures natural course. But instead of following the natural path to peaceful joy and a healthy mind our current postmodern societies are designed to run upstream. We´re like forced to work more, harder, and faster, we´re like forced to downsize our passions, freedom, and even love and joy, we´re like forced to swim against the flow of our own nature, our own health, and thus our own wellbeing. Simple causality, our current societies and how we´re forced upstream is the cause, and widespread stress with potential consequences of e.g. anxiety, depression, and psychosomatic – potentially fatal and erroneously accepted as “normal” – widespread diseases is the effect. Until further, we´re overall in general only swimming one way, the wrong way.
Again, what I just mentioned isn´t only valid in a psychological (a.k.a. mental, a.k.a. metaphysical) context, and neither only in a physical context, rather this is in many cases becomes and thus is rooted in

[122] Wu Wei (a.k.a. “flow”, or “the zone”) is a concept meaning ‘inexertion’, ‘inaction’, or ‘effortless action’.

an 'holoconistic' (explanation follows shortly) phenomena as simply everything and anything in and of us naturally is connected; psychological issues damn sure affects our physical state (psychosomatic[123]), and damn sure vice versa (somatopsychic[124]), and since there to date to my knowledge doesn´t seem to be a unifying umbrella term that covers both psychosomatic and somatopsychic – in case the sum of the illness(es) in direction forms a or are caused by reciprocal dysergy (a.k.a. goes both ways, and thus alliance as a negative synergy), and since psychophysiology is already taken to describe the study of the interrelationships between mind and body, then I hereby have taken my freedom to give birth to exactly this lacking term, 'holoconistic' (Ed. holoconism). In other words, if you e.g. are mentally exhausted then this also will affect your immune system to likewise be weaker, hence you´re more prone to also be (at least feel) physically sick, you´ll be at higher risk of e.g. heart diseases, cancer, etc., and if you e.g. experience severe physical pain or are physically exhausted, then not only your psychological surplus – or lack of same – surely will be affected, there´s also a higher risk of you e.g. getting stressed, depressed, etc., as well. And often – no matter who the bootloader is (a.k.a. who started) – they hence both will develop to affect each other back and forth, and thus become an example of holoconism. Human (self-)destruction is an anachronism[125], our potential is too great for the current pettiness of our existence. Surely we´re "just" clothes wearing mammals, however, we´re Homo sapiens and sapiens means "wise" and "sage", and logically we ought to be too

[123] Just to quickly elaborate on 'psychosomatic': when the individual´s mental state affects its physical state, a.k.a. an illness related interplay between mind and body, here from mind to body.
[124] Just to quickly elaborate on 'somatopsychic': when the individual´s physical state affects its mental state, a.k.a. an illness related interplay between mind and body, here from body to mind.
[125] Something that should be outdated.

intelligent, and hence combined with our current access to knowledge too clever, to facilitate our own downfall; it´s as immoral as it´s stupid, although *"The moral sense perhaps* [Ed. should] *affords the best and highest distinction between man and the lower animals"*[126]. As monsters we´ve created monsters times many, we cannot directly undo our mistakes, but we as sure as the monstrous settings and situations we´ve created surely can make things right, morally up to you-me-we.

If you look at a pig´s brain, you will discover that it both in looks and size are pretty similar to the human brain. Thus, unlike what many people tend to think, the pig actually is an extraordinary intelligent creature. If you e.g. investigate how pigs live, then you´ll see that while you probably think that the pigs love to live smeared into their own faeces, then they actually only defecate in e.g. one corner of their – often horribly small – space in an attempt to keep their space as clean as possible. What you most likely confuse is how the pigs roll themselves in mud, and again unlike what you might think that the reason behind this behavior is, then they actually do this to deal with the abscesses in their skin, as an effort to keep their skin as clean as possible in kinda the same fashion as when humans e.g. take a mud bath to spoil *their* skin. Equivalent to humans (although tempting to state opposed to humans – depending on the context), partly because of their great intelligence, pigs are very autonomous creatures, and this aspect mixed with merely human made culture thus carry the reason for why "normal" pets like e.g. a dog or a cat – despite being way less intelligent than a pig – are enjoying a life of love by cuddling and treats (except from in those parts of the world where also dogs and cats are seen as food and are victims of horrible animal cruelty) while the pig in most parts of the world (roughly "only" except from Islamic culture) are laying sliced up as food in the fridge. Unluckily for the pigs, their autonomy is inferior to *one*

[126] Quote by Charles Darwin (1809-1882).

superior race, humans, and the humans´ blessing in disguise is that our autonomy "only" is ourselves inferior. Our human brain is our most important feature (organ), and it´s now just about time for us to crawl back up out of the mudhole we´ve created, to wash ourselves clean by proving to ourselves why we intelligence-wise are supposed to be superior to the pig.
Inspired by a motto originally spoken by the American football player, Jerry Rice (1962-), and thus later taken up by the five times consecutive "world´s fittest man", the CrossFit athlete Mat(hew) Fraser (1990-): *"Do today what other people aren´t willing to, so you can do tomorrow what they can´t"*. For Jerry and Mat this type of motto represents their competitive mindset, but as our lives in general shouldn´t be viewed at as a competition between each other – rather the opposite, a co-operation where we in relation to the good life win or lose together, then the motto here instead represents that you-me-we should have in view to train, gain, and improve today what you-me-we can´t already do so that you-me-we gained more tomorrow than what you-me-we had yesterday, as a way for you to grow as a human, and for us to grow as human race; make today become a better history tomorrow than yesterday was today; even though we´re not always improving, we continuously can *aspire* to improve, or at least aspire to be less wrong, and thus aspire to continue our growth. What we do today will play a part tomorrow and beyond, not only for ourselves but also for the world around us, and it´ll represent what we pass on to future generations of descendants. Simply put, our brain is – among others also kinda – a muscle almost like all of our other muscles, at least it´s possible to train your brain (in many ways and more than any other parts of your body) e.g. with learning in – figuratively speaking – somewhat same fashion as when lifting weights to train other muscles in your body. The brain is a psychological (a.k.a. spiritual) world of its own in the world, and it´s undoubtfully as possible to improve our brain as it is to damage or completely ruin it – physically as well as

psychologically (ergo a.k.a. spiritually). From a Darwinistic evolutionary POV (point of view), I believe that *every* little thing we do has a genetic – butterfly – effect and thereby will be passed on to our offspring, and then their offspring, and so forth. Whatever we do to enhance or train our brain, e.g. acquiring new knowledge, learning a new skill, playing an instrument, a game of Sudoku, a game of the old Chinese board game GO (Chinese: Pinyin: Wéiqí), or whatever else it might be, no matter how big or small, as with all evolutionary changes, it´ll become part of our DNA, and thus part of that DNA we pass on. Same can of course be said in relation to every negative effect – a.k.a. damage – we cause upon on ourselves, by e.g. taking drugs, drinking alcohol, mental inactivity, etc. Even if the effect might immediately seem too small to directly measure it´s and will be there – physically as well as psychologically, natural selection[127] in the making; the general IQ among humans currently increases by three per decade, and if we swim long enough we´ll prove to be mutants by developing fins and duck-feet.
We constantly manage to gain yet more knowledge and better tools to potentially be wiser, more moral, and thus better creatures, but one of the biggest mistakes we humans do is that we instead of using our available advantages in a more positive direction tend to make them become mainly a source to exploitation (just look at how our most advanced technologies first and foremost serves warfare), and our dominating feature exponentially seems to be immoral stupidity; we hear without listening, we look without seeing, we gain without really improving.
Opposed to old canards (a.k.a. tall tales) about how we humans doesn´t use all of our brain´s actual capacity, that there´s a considerably large percentage of our brain´s actual performance power which we can´t reach and thus don´t make use of (not hard

[127] Darwins words: "[...] *preservation of favourable variations* [related to genes and somewhat behavior] *and the destruction of injurious variations, I call Natural Selection, or the Survival of the Fittests*".

to see why one would think so), science unambiguously points out that we actually do use all of our brain. Despite our brain only makes up for approximately two to three percent of our amassed weight then our brain anyway consumes approximately 20% of all our energy. Even while relaxing, our brain consumes approximately the same amount of energy as the calf muscles do during a marathon, and a recent study further concludes that a chess player can burn up to 6000 calories a day during a chess tournament from just sitting still thinking, which thus amounts to a calorie burn of two to three times more than what a "normal" person on average burn in a day. On the other hand, a brain which isn´t being used dulls, stalls, and slowly dies out. Braincells which isn´t being stimulated simply dies, and in this regard the brain doesn´t produce any new replacement cells. Hence, if you hadn´t already a personal excuse to use your brain at hand, then now you do.
All representatives for humanity have a set of human emotions within, e.g. joy, happiness, anger, sadness, etc., and from the same caliber of truth we tend to say that "humans makes mistakes", and that "it´s merely human to fail". However, I see only two reasons for why this view and saying isn´t ascribed to all animals, cause surely all animals have emotions and makes mistakes (with most animals we know they do, and for the rest we presume they do), either we humans are too full of ourselves to take other animals serious enough and into account in this equation, or at least we humans as "the kings and queens of the jungle" ought to be too clever to keep making mistakes to the degree that we do, and expressly to repeat the same mistakes, why we use this saying as a kind of excuse for and to ourselves. I think both possibilities are true, and even though the existence of mistakes and failure probably is unavoidable, then thereby not said that it isn´t possible to limit them to a minimum, perhaps starting by taking the lives of all animals equally serious.
And don´t get me wrong, I´m of course aware that the spectrum range of human emotions probably surpasses that of most other

animals – only a few animals I´m not completely sure about. All I´m saying is that it´s a mistake to underestimate other animals, and not least our own capability and ability to improve; we´re still in many ways far behind ourselves.

An illustrative example of how far we – in our knowledge and control – are behind ourselves can be to take a look at the chemistry lab our body truly is. We all have a body, our temple, but still only few of us (e.g. medical doctors, etc.) have a qualified clue of our own body, how it´s designed, how it works, etc., and even the best doctor still has a lot to learn. Take e.g. how our automated immune system goes to war on our behalf against hostile or invasive cells and extraneous illnesses (e.g. viruses), all we can do – in addition to giving our body a healthy diet, antibiotics, etc., to strengthen the force of our immune system´s biological warfare – is to wait passively until the battle within ourselves has been fought, hopefully to our advantage. Our body surely is a complex wonder, and surely it sometimes does wonders beyond our comprehension and wildest imagination. And if you thought that our body only fight its own battles then think again, cause, even in some cases where e.g. a mother´s child get sick, then the mother´s chemistry lab of a body flux starts up the production of changing the immunological composition of the breastmilk to contain and suited to solve exactly what is needed to cure the child. In an example of exactly this, I´ve seen how the breastmilk coming out of a mother´s breast in a matter of hours went from being a "normal" white milk substance to becoming a "super milk" of a thick yellow texture of leukocytes[128] customized antibodies tailored to fight the exact pathogen (i.e. virus or bacterium) that her baby was suffering from. When a baby nurses, a vacuum is created in the mother´s nipple, the baby´s saliva sneaks into this vacuum, and from there it´s believed that the mammary

[128] Leukocytes are white blood cells (WBC), the cells of the immune system that are involved in protecting the body against infectious diseases and foreign invaders.

gland [129] receptors of the mother automatically analyze and interpret the infant´s 'spit backwash' for bacteria and viruses, and if anything bad thus is detected the "cooking" starts – innate recipes leads the way. If *that* ain´t some stoked next level shit far ahead of ourselves, then I hardly know what is.
In spite of all humans descend from the same evolutionary branch, and hence all are the same type of species (we´re all homo sapiens), then we all still are very unique in each our own specific way; never are two living creatures from nature´s hands completely identical, we´re all *non-fungibles*. We all have different talents and variations of concrete needs, we all represent some kind of diversity, and we all learn and understand differently. In this spirit, no prefabricated systems fit everybody, and no one deserves to be excluded due to the preferences or lacks of others – one´s way might not be another one's right way, as already stated on subjectivity, and who are anybody to forcibly dictate how other´s per se have to accustom, behave, and relate. Like Albert Einstein brilliantly said it: "*Everybody is a genius. But if you judge a fish by its ability to climb a tree, it will live its whole life believing that it is stupid*". And in addition to Einstein´s quote I further add: Don´t judge the entire character of a fish only by its ability to swim. Inspired by the French philosopher, Jean-Paul Sartre (1905-1980): No one acts geniusly because they´re a genius, they´re perceived a genius because they acted geniusly; at the end of the day, we´re all "just" human – nature.

3.3. Mother Earth

As earlier mentioned about nature, Earth likewise doesn´t depend on us, we until further totally depend on Earth. In regard to the state and treatment of Earth, the American stand-up comedian, George

---

[129] Mammary gland is the milk-producing gland of a female.

Carlin (1937-2008), somewhat truthfully spoke: "*The planet is fine. The people are fucked*". Hereto I say: The planet was and can be better, and the destructive people are fucked only until they ain´t no more. As of now, we´re our own liability, we have a very serious obligation to get our act together, to stop being fucked and stop fucking up, and to leave mother Earth in a better condition than she was when we arrived; mother Earth gave birth to and welcomed us, and we owe everything to her, to future generations of Earthlings, to the universe, to the force of just about everything – a.k.a. nature itself. Earth gave us a safe haven in an unbelievable big, mostly dark, and deserted universe, she gave us a home, and she loyally carry all and everything of us on her shoulders; in that sense, we´re literally standing on the shoulders of a giant, and despite not being giant compared to the expanse of space as a whole, then at least compared to the now of us.
Without going in over my own head by taking a too technical approach, as I´m not a geologist, meteorologist, or anything like that, then – as a self-proclaimed inquisitive good citizen of Earth, a.k.a. as an earthling who consider myself to be an environmentalist who cares a whole lot about our nature, I still find it very important to involve this subchapter in the book. Thus far and counting, except for a single operational space station with a crew of five operational astronauts on it, and maybe a flying spacecraft with a few astronauts once in a while, planet Earth – for now – is our one and only home in the entire universe. No doubt that we future-wise will have to inhabit other planets to secure our existence and not least consciousness – why space travel unquestionably *is* our future, but until further, Earth *is* our only home, a home we should do everything within our power to sustain as much and as long as we can, at least up until that point where other forces like e.g. the

sun[130] or perhaps an unforeseen meteor or black hole or whatever else with the needed capacity changes that. Keynote for dummies, if we slack and blow to save and sustain Earth, and instead recklessly ruins it, we sooner than later are nothing less than bygones in the oblivion, and for exactly that reason it should be too legit not to quit addressing the issues we continuously and increasingly cause upon our planet (ours as far as not owning), and hence ourselves.
To understand the next bit, I´ll quickly have to introduce you to the so-called greenhouse effect, and don´t worry, I´ll intend to keep it as short and fairly simple as possible (it would anyway take an entire independent book – if not several – of its own to cover and explain the greenhouse effects in all details). Thus, hang in tight there for just a few pages related and dedicated to this life depended subject, after all, our future existence "only" crucially depends on it.
The greenhouse effect is a natural constructed phenomenon that by definition works as the case is with a greenhouse, in which the glass of the greenhouse allows for the sun´s short wave ultraviolet-radiation (the sun´s uv-rays) to enter the greenhouse, and then prevents the long wave heat radiation from leaving the greenhouse, which thus causes the greenhouse to be heated up.
In the same fashion as with a greenhouse, Earth also works like a greenhouse. On Earth, the atmosphere partly operates as the glass of a greenhouse as it also allows for the sun´s short wave ultraviolet radiation to enter and reach the surface of Earth. At the surface of

---

[130] In about five billion years our sun will run out of hydrogen (the burning fuel which keeps it alive), and as that happens the sun will grow to a size reaching Mars, why Earth by then – according to Earth´s distance from the sun – roughly will be located near the center of the sun, and hence naturally completely burn up in the process. For this reason, among others, our future as a conscious civilization (to secure consciousness) depends on us becoming a multiplanetary species (perhaps even multigalactic) – it´s an imperative. Also, new studies show that even entire galaxies eventually die (e.g. when they run out gas) – dead galaxies has recently been discovered 10-12 billion lightyears away, why our survival in the future likewise rely on us to become an intergalactic species.

Earth, the UV-radiation is being reflected, more on white surfaces while black surfaces tend to absorb the heat better, this is known as the albedo effect – maybe you´ve noticed how e.g. your black t-shirt tend to get hotter in the sun than your white t-shirt tend to. Anyway, in our atmosphere we have the so called greenhouse gasses "flying around", CO_2 (carbon dioxide), CH_4 (methane), H_2O (water), and N_2O (nitrous oxide), and again in the same fashion as with the glass of the greenhouse, these gasses thus works as an invisible heat trap that catches and hence prevents the long wave UV-radiation from leaving our atmosphere, and in doing so they thereby ensure that a lot of the heat – or energy if you prefer – is kept within the edges of our atmosphere instead of just being reflected back out into space. Keeping the heat within our atmosphere is a natural process which is essential to our comfort of pleasant temperatures on Earth (as of now we have an average temperature on Earth of approximately 15 degrees Celsius (approximately 59 degrees Fahrenheit)), and it´s thus this natural modus operandi that prevents the Earth from turning in to a giant snowball as it otherwise would, a for good global version of what "we´ve seen" exemplified during our previous ice-ages (last time approximately 11600 years ago). Hence, without the natural greenhouse effect, the Earth on average would be approximately 33 degrees Celsius (91,4 degrees Fahrenheit) colder than we currently experience it to be, and we ergo would have an average temperature of approximately -17 degrees Celsius (1,4 degrees Fahrenheit); no thanks, right? So far so good.

However, you probably have heard about our current climate crisis connected to global warming and hence climate changes due to too much greenhouse gasses (primarily CO_2, and secondarily CH_4) in our atmosphere as a consequence of our – the human´s – overconsumption of more or less everything, as the greedy bastards we are. To simplified spell it out, the main culprit to the CO_2 problem are the excessive amounts of fossil fuels (e.g. oil, gas, coal, etc.) we burn to e.g. power our homes, our cars – especially the

thirsty "small penis cars"[131], our factories, airplanes, etc. The amount of CO_2 in the atmosphere is measured in parts per million (ppm), meaning a percentage of a percentage of a percentage, and to elaborate on how the climate crisis indisputable is created by humans – especially since the industrialization took off, it´s worth mentioning that the amount of CO_2 in our atmosphere have increased by an astonishing 35 ppm over only the last 17 years, from 368 ppm to 403 ppm, which translated is equal to 1000 years of nature's natural increase (CO_2 is e.g. stored in the ice on Earth, and is naturally released as ice melts).
On top of that, the human population has tripled over the last 70 years which thus affects us to consume considerably more food – primarily meat from animals (especially cows and pigs (on average 1,4 billion cows, and 980 million pigs are being raised as livestock)) (approximately 80 billion animals are killed, slaughtered, and eaten, by humans a year) that´re releasing (farting) CH_4 (methane) in to our atmosphere. And as the amounts of CH_4 and CO_2 – a.k.a. greenhouse gasses – in our planet´s atmosphere increases, so does the amount of heat these greenhouse gasses catches, and thereby prevents from leaving our atmosphere. The increase of the average temperature has thus accordingly been setting new heat records every year for the last 10 years, and still counting. As a result hereof, among others, as the average temperatures steadily and ominous rapidly are on a rise, then instead of this being just a cheap excuse for more ice-cream or cold cocktails in the sun, we unfortunately see how more heat e.g. is equal to more drought and thereby more suffering as water and crops on land dry out, and how sea levels on average are rising 3 mm per year – eating land – as a result of the

[131] Like the case often (not always but often) is with steroid use and virility extending tattoos, big, thirsty and noisy cars often are a compensation for a small dick – at least mentally (e.g. low self-esteem and lack of confidence in self).

heat making our thus CO_2 releasing ice glaciers to melt while sea water also in a chemical reaction expands when heated.
As of now, our eagerness to constantly expand on our industrial sectors seems to have taken on the character of a bottomless bucket, and seriously, if we don´t tackle and solve this problem already yesterday and come up with alternative sustainable solutions to our own increasingly high demand of energy, then humankind probably won´t have much prosperous future to look forward to anyway – at least not on Earth.
One thing is for sure, infinite industrial growth on a finite planet simply isn´t possible, and growth for the sake of growth is as stupid as rules for the sake of rules. We "only" have a limited amount of resources to do well with, and by current praxis sooner or later the well of resources will empty out. At first glance, we´re extremely lucky that our planet provided us with more resources than we need to succeed, but by the way we – destructive humans – administer our given potential, then these resources unfortunately might end up as an harsh and lethal disservice which we thus owe to nothing and nobody else than ourselves. As Gandhi spoke it, "*The world has enough for everyone´s need, but not enough for everyone´s greed*". We simply *have* to implement the needed improving changes to our way of living in order for us to see this negative development turn in to a positive, and because we can, we´re responsible of ensuring that the necessary solutions are effectuated, that they prevail, are achieved, and thus done. Cause if not, then our ignorance and arrogance – a.k.a. agnorance – definitely will catch up with us (already did), even overtake us (doing it this very moment), and

eventually bite our own asses, fatally. Just look at what happened to the former Earth-like planet, Venus[132].

To overcome the challenges we face, we e.g. have to reduce the use of fossil fuels and replace it by renewable energy, and luckily we already have astronomically more energy available than we could ever use, e.g. solar-energy, wind-energy, wave-energy, and humbly said everything else as absolutely everything *is* energy. The challenge here is to extract and store the energy without using more energy than what is gained, and to do so without polluting and damaging nature in the process, and to do so innovation and cooperation is key – as it is in almost all areas.

We universally have to make sure that everything but renewable energy and sustainability is bad – for – business. Among others, we e.g. have to repeal and neutralize the monopoly of major oil companies, environment friendly discoveries and inventions can no longer be afforded bought by the highest bidder thus to only be stashed away in the bottom of a dark basement before throwing away the key as e.g. oil companies traditionally have done it with inventions that potentially could´ve ruined their businesses in the process of improving our world.

Also, we e.g. acute need innovative solutions to our use of e.g. steel and cement (e.g. used in construction) as these fields alone accounts for approximately 16% of all CO2 emission on Earth. In my research, I´ve seen many innovative alternative solutions to some of these problems, but we´re yet *very* far from being "there" where we have to be, where you-me-we in cooperation by innovation have to ensure us to reach.

---

[132] Venus likely used to have the same climate as we today have on Earth, with land, oceans, rain, perhaps even snow, and roughly the same surface temperatures. In theory, there might even have been a civilization similar to ours on Venus. Venus is today covered in greenhouse gasses and are as a result experiencing a burning hot average surface temperature of approximately 453 degrees Celsius (847 degrees Fahrenheit).

Furthermore, we all also should strive to eat less meat (take this from me, a motherfucker who also taste-wise fancies meat like crazy), and instead eat more plant-based food which is far more CO2 neutral than the current production of meat – except for the seafood you from the coast or a row- or sailboat pull out of the ocean yourself – ever will be; not only will the environment prosper, your body, mind, and soul, surely will to. Additionally, let me ask you this, if e.g. a mob boss order someone tortured and wacked is he then despite not pulling the trigger himself still guilty of torture and murder? If yes, are we as meat eaters then not also guilty of torture and murder – of approximately 80 billion animals a year – in the meat industry when we pay torturers and executioners on the farms and at the slaughterhouses to do our dirty job, don´t we have blood on our hands as well despite us closing our eyes and ears about the animal cruelty which we sponsor just about every time we buy and eat our processed meat at restaurants and from supermarkets – most often preferably as cheap as possible? I think you get the point and know the answer to this question, and even if you´re trying to convince – or rather excuse – yourself by neglecting the life, feelings, and pain of animals, then I think you anyway deep down *do* know how messed up that in fact is, said the meat loving predator who – despite aiming to buy organic and animal "friendlier" meat (if such even exist) – admit to have a somewhat messed up meat addiction which I seriously am working on – I´ll get there (especially because I *love* innocent animals, alive, more than eating them, and in fact more than most humans). However, a so far semi-unsuccessful rehab rightfully makes my words sound hypocritically cheap, I know, in this matter there´s simply no excuse – despite having limited my meat intake substantially, "and counting"; just because animals might express feelings differently, it doesn´t mean that they don´t have them; we can learn a lot about love from other animals.

A sidetracked tragic-comic fact about our food production is that we today waste food enough to feed two billion people while at the same time 815 million people don´t have enough food to lead a healthy and active life. Hence, we spend energy producing and wasting almost two and a half times more food than we even need to feed all the needy. Demand and supply, the more food you waste the more you increase the demand which is followed by an equal increase in the resource-intensive supply. And furthermore, "just" to make sure you know, the mechanisms of demand and supply applies to everything in *all* markets. If we were smart, and less greedy, we could de facto simultaneously save energy *and* cherish the natural environment to a far larger extend than we do while *still* at the same time feed every hungry person on Earth. Try to think about that when you – might – sweep unused or leftover food in the bin.

An example I first intended to include in the 'Fuck the Law' chapter but eventually found equally relevant here revolves around the freegan culture – a.k.a. dumpster diving in waste receptacles at restaurants and supermarkets (often located behind the place) – as a means to secure a diet which might otherwise cannot be afforded, to limit food waste, and at the same as an effort to help reduce our current overconsumptions of resources. Food naturally is essential for surviving, a healthy diet is a precondition for a healthier and longer life, and as of now our world faces exponential problems with overconsumption of – e.g. food – resources to a still growing global population which exponentially are heading toward a global overpopulation, and thereby potentially even greater ruthless exploitation on our still limited resources. One thing is that freeganism shows how far we are from an optimal world – an optimal world shouldn´t rely on freeganism to provide for its population, but another thing is that despite freeganism being morally legit (instead it´s immoral when businesses rather see people starve and resources go to waste than giving up their claim of those money which they notwithstanding cannot get (especially not from the trash)), then it´s still judicially illegal. Not because the businesses need the food they anyway already have discarded, they just don´t want you to have it, and against all common sense they even have the law on their side on this matter. Fuck these businesses, and fuck the law.

The currently biggest issue for the wellbeing of Mother Earth – and thereby us, is the human made pollution. We already touched upon it in relation to the greenhouse gasses, but here goes: The three currently dominating types of pollution on Earth are air (atmosphere), water (e.g. oceans, rivers, lakes, and groundwater), and soil (which also overlaps with groundwater).

The biggest problem in regard to water is plastic, trash, and toxic and chemical waste poured into the waters. It´s believed that between 4,8-12,7 million tons of plastic through human interaction finds its way to the oceans every single year, multiply this with a course of many years, and you´ll have an indication of how bad the current situation really is. According to 'International Union for Conservation of Nature' (IUCN), *"The most visible and disturbing impacts of marine plastics are the ingestion, suffocation and entanglement of hundreds of marine species. Marine wildlife such as seabirds, whales, fishes and turtles, mistake plastic waste for prey, and most die of starvation as their stomachs are filled with plastic debris"*. Furthermore, we´re experiencing major problems with plastic turning into "microplastic" which according to our current abilities – or rather lack of same – sadly never will disappear, thereby polluting our waters for "good" with many horrible consequences – for both wildlife and humans directly – too comprehensive for me to even nearly sufficient include here. However, the fact of the matter is that we sooner than later need to come up with alternative solutions to the plastic nightmare we ourselves have created, definitely become better and more efficient at recycling, and e.g. as a start also asap make it more profitable to implement self-degrading plastic substitutions e.g. made by hemp or other natural non-polluting materials. Damn whoever throwing or pouring trash, toxic, and chemical waste into our waters. Notwithstanding this e.g. happens from a lack of knowledge, interest, or concern (a.k.a. lack of understanding), or due to cognitive dissonance[133] and hence laziness, or an financial reward (e.g. from saving the cost of proper waste disposal, or that it´s cheaper to pay fines than cleaning up after oneself), or whatever the fuck anyone´s lame excuses of motivation might be, there´s simply no acceptable excuse for such literally low-life stupid and immoral behavior.

Fortunately, great ocean cleanup projects have "already" (although embarrassing late) been launched, e.g. 'The Ocean Cleanup', which relies on non-polluting natural forces (wind, waves, and current) to navigate the cleanup-patches drifting around. But still, improving solutions is and probably always will be a scarce, and so you should never hold yourself back from engaging in whichever way you might be able to contribute to the continuation of improvements.

Regarding soil pollution, the biggest sinners immediately mount to the use of chemical fertilizers and pesticides (from e.g. GMO (genetically modified organisms)), dumping of oil, solid and not least radioactive waste, just to mention a few of too many examples. Not only does this effect a pollution to the soil of Earth, the soil pollution likewise cause ground water pollution, a.k.a. polluting our main source of drinking water. Further, this – from a more innocent but still very serious aspect – leads me to bring this general appeal,

---

[133] When we know that what we do is not good for neither the environment or ourselves, when we pollute although we damn well know polluting is bad, when we intake certain food or other toxic substances although we know that the production of it is immoral and bad for the environment, and the intake not healthy for our body, etc., and then come up with whatever bullshit reason we can knit together of lameness to "excuse" and "justify" doing what we do despite being "well aware" that it´s just not right.

don't ever throw your motherfucking trash in the nature, it pisses me off when people don't clean after themselves and throw trash anywhere else than in the trashcan – take e.g. chewing gum, animals – often birds – think it's food for them and thus get choked in your stupid laziness.
As our ecosystem suffers, Earth suffers, we suffer. Thus, although I in general ain´t a fan of rules and freedom limitations, then I still without hesitation here have to agree that we – until moral and common sense prevails – need still more strict and tighter rules and regulations against causation of pollution, and considerably more severe and thereby discernible consequences for violating these then installations made and hence precautions taken in favor of the health of all and everything connected to life of nature.
As a very small example, one day I realized that one of my – now former – favorite chocolates actually contain palm oil (yea, I taste-wise prefer milk-chocolate over high percentage dark chocolates), and with pictures in my mind of how the palm-oil industry heavily wipe out rainforests (deforestation), displaces indigenous people, and destroys the habitat of endangered animals such as the Sumatran Rhino, pygmy elephants, and not least Orangutans (to which I´ve seen video footages of how the palm oil workers among others bestially beat these poor animals to death with sticks and whatnot), why I therefore contacted the chocolate manufacturer to ask why and how they can support the palm oil industry when they easily could decide to implement other better alternatives, and if they kindly would consider changing their recipe away from using palm oil in their products as I otherwise no longer morally would be able to justify buying from them. In response, the company (which is a big global chocolate brand, and here we´re talking about their multi-colored button-shaped chocolates – my favorite used to be with peanuts) replied to me that they follow all applicable laws and rules in force, and that they therefore don´t consider themselves to be doing anything wrong. Oh yea, fuck you then, (biiip), you

ignorant immoral piece of shit who obviously blinded by profit cannot tell the different between judicial legal and morally right; ew for a weak character, and that likewise goes for my former favorite hazelnut spread (also a major global company), and all other products I meet along my way with too low standards of morality in their production. I´m of course not naïve enough to expect that these companies would actually listen to my complain-song and just completely comply, but the response I received clearly illustrates what we´re up against, what mindset companies in general carry – how they´re completely cold and devoid from morality and the wellbeing of our planet as long as the law backs them up in making the profit they desperately (greedily) crave, and that they intend to continue not caring about any environmental or moral issues until someone or something with "judicial-like" power sets them straight. Nonetheless, despite the ignorance of many, "the world" has finally started to realize that we currently are on a unsustainable and unhealthy path, actions are slowly being taken, but the question now is if we´re reacting too late, and if we really are doing enough? Most countries around the world – except from "only" seven countries – have e.g. ratified to 'The Paris Agreement' (in December 2015), an international agreement under the United Nations Framework Convention on Climate Change (UNFCCC), which among others states that "the world" in this 21st century (according to the Gregorian calendar) should "reduce" our average temperature to a maximum increase of "only" two degrees Celsius. However, in July of 2019 (only approximately 3,5 years later) it was measured that we at that time already was 1,2 degrees Celsius above that level, thus how you think it´s going? Some then say that it´s because that 'The Paris Agreement' is overambitious, but damn sure with a big fat resounding NO, 'The Paris Agreement' is rather underambitious. Listen, the climate doesn´t care about the evaluation of freaking fucking ambitions, you-me-we either safe our planet or we don´t, and to keep rolling we simply *have* to make it happen – we´re not here to play for a draw or survive by the old rules of away goals. We have to fix how the impediment of bureaucracy too often is in the way of valuable progress within the timeframe of relevance. According to the United Nations, "*We have the solutions we need to address climate change, but we need to use them. We need to shift investment from the grey, dirty, economy, to the green economy. The money is there. We have the technology, now we need to make it accessible to all people in all countries. But we need to take action now. Every bit of warming matters, and the longer we wait, the greater the negative impact*". Well, what the fuck are we waiting for then, Yallah!

Be well aware, it´s to a great and impactful extend also not least all the "small" things in our everyday lives that really matters, cause even if you may think that your actions doesn´t change a thing in the big picture, then imagine if roughly eight billion of us were thinking the same thing versus roughly eight billion of us thinking the opposite – how much of a difference eight billion people can do, starting by you to lead the way. To mention a few examples, every walk or skate or bike-ride where you e.g. could´ve taken the car matters (not only is it better for the environment and cheaper for your wallet, it´s also healthy exorcise for your body), every collective transportation and transport pooling where you could´ve travelled individually matters, every vegetable you eat where you could´ve eaten meat matters, every time you bring and use a reusable shopping bag instead of buying a new plastic bag at the store matters, every organic purchase instead of supporting the GMO industry matters, every proactive choice of renewable energy before fossil fueled energy matters, and that also includes which sectors and industries you support every time you e.g. shop – notwithstanding the type of products you´re purchasing, every rental where you could have bought in accordance with the "buy and throw away culture" matters, every awakening and withdrawal from the widespread ill culture which the Palestinian rooted Danish

graffiti artist, SpyO, with his street-art visible from my window describes as "*blindfolded consumerism in plain sight*" matters.
Also, I have to add, "just" e.g. buying an electric car instead of a fossil fueled car and then thinking that you just solved it all unfortunately doesn´t quite cut it alone as also car batteries currently pollute quite a bit as the production of the battery is quite resourceful, and as getting rid of the battery according to today´s standards thus implies quite a bit of pollution. Don´t get me wrong, if you e.g. buy an electric car instead of a fossil fueled car you according to our short-term solutions did good, but in an ongoing long term process you also – until further – kinda "just" moved a problem from one area to another, and thereby yet another, from atmosphere to soil, and thereby water. Good intentions are always great, good intentions mixed with awareness are even greater, but our shared continuation of discovering and following active innovative solutions toward improvements are alpha and omega.
Hence, stupid dogmatic denial definitely isn´t the way to go, don´t even for a second believe that anyone´s ignorant conspiracy theory based defiance can refute what nature clearly shows and science already proved, and seriously shame on you if you still consider your selfish polluting preferences to be more important than the wellbeing of our one and only – beautiful blue – planet, and also thereby the rest of us. Future generations want to live, thus thinking that you´re invincible, and don´t give a shit if everybody else are – which they just like you aren´t – simply aren´t all right at all. Imagine a sweet and innocent child, and then imagine if you would like this child to inhale the black toxic fumes coming out of the exhaust pipe of a gas thirsty automobile (cause, that´s what indirectly is happening every time you hit the gas pedal and blow black toxic exhaust fumes out into the atmosphere we all – inclusive sweet and innocent children (which we all once were) – breathe from)? I guess not, and should you by any chance against my expectations be directly fond of this scenario, if you truly not at all care about the

wellbeing of others, then seriously *fuck you* and the mechanical donkey you rode in on, go sought yourself out, immediately, and seek professional help if it´s something you can´t handle on your own.
We have to recognize and acknowledge that our wellbeing – wealth and health – simply (or complexly, depending on how you look at it) depends on and strive through the stability of our planet; without our planet, Earth, we currently simply won´t exist; again, we depend on our planet, and not vice versa (at least not yet). We vitally depend on just about everything our planet has to offer on both land, in the sea, and in the air – e.g. from gravity to crops, from drinking water to sea food, from the oxygen we breathe to the ozone layer that as a shell sustain our ecosystemic sphere, and further as a shield protects us from the sun´s dangerous UV radiation which otherwise would sterilize the surface on Earth, and thereby eventually kill all known life.
Paradoxically, we humans are the disease of nature on Earth despite de facto having the potential to be nature's own juiced up (on steroids – analogically speaking) antidote. For some strange reasons humans chose to use and abuse rather than be aware, care, and value natures welfare.
Of course, the problems we have by the damage we causes to our climate on Earth is excessively more large-scaled comprehensive than I here only very limited present, and I´m sorry if I´m not giving enough justice to the extremity of the problem, or to the solutions available, but I hope that you´ll take this as "only" a humble introduction and an open invitation for you to look further into (and hence act according to) these very important problems which we as a total absolute together are facing, and thus likewise together are forced to overcome if we´re to secure ourselves a fair chance of a future – for and thereby on mother Earth.

Human nature exists through birth,
We´re all children of Mother Earth,
It both is and isn´t up to us,
In any way nature is boss.

4. Balance is Legend

As an extremely curious person, I for the most part have always been and still partly are very much attracted to the edges of just about everything – the extremities of the extremes, whether it´s the most extreme underground environments of just about all sorts (especially connected to criminal activities and transgressive behavior), the most secret intelligence activities, sexual exploration, astronomy, sometimes pressuring and thus testing my own limits to the extreme, or whatever else that can help me kill my curiosity, expand my horizon, and therethrough build an understanding of different and various motivational factors, you name it, and I´m sure I´ve smelled it; it´s in the grey-zones of our psyche – in unknown territory – that we humans seriously learn and experience new, where we seriously gain brain juice, and if comprehending the polarized edges then also everything else in between in general per se should become easier to understand. Not that I´m a fanatic adrenaline junkie, or that I´m not a person who value and enjoys chillaxation – cause I definitely do (although I still practice on how to reach mental peace without losing momentum), and not that I necessarily always have to have a direct active role in all and everything that I experience, but I in any case at least benefit from it as an mentalizing observer who – as earlier mentioned – ain´t prepared to "go" curious in my grave. Dreams can be a pretty sweaty motivator (the awesome way), but it´s besides execution of action, experiences and memories that counts the most to take the prize of a top spot at the podium.

Despite my fascination with sniffing around in and around the extreme, I think it should be fairly fair to state that extremities – including extremism – in whatever shape, size, and sort, are the overall root cause to much of the devasty in our world. No matter if it e.g. is political extremism (e.g. left or right wing extremism), religious extremism, or practically any other type of feelings, believes, or behaviors to the extreme, when involvement of reasonable common sense is lacking then it with a high probability is destined to go wrong, to turn bad, and often to turn bad into worse. Even the good deed of being extremely helpful can e.g. make someone to give away unhealthy much of themselves – potentially loosing themselves, extreme happiness can e.g. bring about gullibility or traits of narcissism, and indeed extreme love likewise has the capacity to turn ugly to the extent of e.g. carrying a strangulating feeling on the unwilling receiver, causing mean heartaches where love isn´t reciprocated, or potentially provoke a precipitation of our most extreme negative feelings and hence potentially ultimate actions to unfold. Not that extremity without exception categorically always is bad, of course not, but when something really goes wrong or directly is bad, then it surely very often is connected with extremity.

Yet, paradoxically, yet, unsurprisingly, where the extremity-cup anyway immediately doesn´t seem to overflow, naturally also is found in the extreme, the extremely good, which accounts for much of the personal best in our world, e.g. to receive extreme help where extreme help is needed, feeling at our best when being extremely happy, being extremely in love or receiving extremely desired love, perhaps feeling extremely cozy around extremely joyful people, etc.

However, what 'good' and 'bad' precisely is again depends on the eyes of the beholder, the viewer´s personal preferences and evaluation, and thereby not least the concrete situation – i.e., it´s a subjective size, and in a world shared by many subjects balance so to speak becomes a relativistic matter. It might therefore immediately can be tempting to think that balance plain and simple is more important in our shared sphere, and less important in regard to the individual´s personal lives, but logically no – hermeneutically they somewhat represent two sides of the same coin.

In line with the basic understanding of balance, if something is unbalanced it tilt, and unbalanced enough it tilt over, and so it equally is with us humans mentally as well as physically, internally as well as externally, individually as well as socially.
"Life is a balance between holding on and letting go".[134]
When feelings collide in a social setting of individuals, when someone e.g. in a relationship pushes to get closer to the other who on the other hand have a need for personal space, the more that someone pushes the more the other one withdraws, and the more the other one withdraws the more that someone pushes on. Most can with rational glasses see the irrational pattern in it, and thus probably understand that one such relationship is unhealthy unbalanced, but still I have plenty times experienced how the paradox e.g. unfold when likewise most of the otherwise rational (non-)pushers still irrationally can´t control their own feelings of same should they find themselves to be in the cocooned shoes of the pusher. And yea, depending on how much the other withdraws, then it might also can be perceived irrational and a paradox to withdraw from an otherwise close connection to someone in a wanted relationship. We all carry rational intentions controlled by irrational feelings and emotions, and vice versa, "just" some more or less – fitting – than others. Like e.g. homicide detectives says, "we chase a monster but catches a human".
Apart from cases that involves severe malfunctioning brains (which thus doesn´t exclude most of us despite we all still in each our own ways carry some level of personal issues and craziness around – and believing you´re flawless is also just a sign that you´re not), I believe that we humans all share the same card-index of different – natural – characteristics. Figuratively speaking, imagine and thus picture a big graphic equalizer[135] with a series of vertically-oriented (up and

---

[134] Quote by Rumi.
[135] A device often used to refine sound (e.g. music), a tool with many adjustable channels.

down) adjustment sliders – one slider for each of all our human characteristics (it could for the sake of visualization in theory also be a series of cohesive thermometers, graphs in a classic coordinate system, or a series of whatever else kind of measure units that makes you tick), and all with potential frequencies (or volumes, or levels, or whatever you prefer to call it) spanning from 0,1 to 100. For a very compassioned person this thus e.g. means that the adjustment slider related to compassion might be at 75, while it for another a lot less compassioned person might be at only 5; for an extremely selfish person the adjustment slider related to selfishness might be at 85, while it for another less selfish person might be at 10, and so on, and so on – just to set the stage with a few random examples. And despite many e.g. would say that they could never kill anyone, then I guess that that is just a matter of context, cause yea, while a psychopath without empathy might find it easy to kill without remorse, then if you e.g. experience a situation where your loved one (e.g. parent, child, partner, etc.) e.g. screamingly are being raped, tortured, and is about to be killed right in front of you, and you e.g. by pressing a button can kill the perpetrator and hence make the horror stop, then I´m sure that you´d be able to push the button and hence kill, and without remorse to further justify the killing in the aftermath. The question isn´t "who is mentally disturbed" – cause we all are a bit disturbed, the question is "in what way and how much". Ergo, we all basically have the same characteristics within us, we all have some good in us, and we all have some less good in us, we all have some sanity, and we all have some insanity, and in line with the uncertainty principle of quantum mechanics[136] (also known as quantum physics) no characteristic is ever at a flat zero (zero simply doesn´t exist in this context – or in just about any other context) as even the potential existence – notwithstanding activation or not – in itself has an energy greater

[136] The uncertainty principle of quantum mechanics states that *no* energy (all existing (anything) with an effect (a.k.a. a source) to an energy) is ever at zero.

than zero which otherwise would mean no existence or even potential existence at all, and this hence also explains why the frequencies of the adjustment sliders used in this illustrative example spans out from a starting point of minimum 0,1 (it would in relation to some adjustment sliders be tempting to extend the span to be from -100 to +100 – still without a zero in the middle (thus to jump from -0,1 to +0,1, and vice versa), where the minus represent negativity, and the plus represent positivity, and to e.g. play around with many other more detailed (Ed. complex) explaining setups, to also e.g. expand the concept of one type of adjustment slider to further be a series of several adjustment sliders (if e.g. in relation to happiness being happy about some things and upset about other things at roughly the same time, and so on. You can macro-wise focus on an overall medium "mood" (a.k.a. volume level)), or micro-wise focus on the many concrete and more sensitive volumes, etc., but as it for now in this example wouldn´t be valid for all adjustment sliders, and to keep it as simple as possible, we´re leaving all these extra complex perspectives out for now (maybe I´ll include them in another episode)).
It´s thus thereby not a question of whether or not you-me-we all have all the same characteristics, no matter if the traits shows themselves as present or absent they still exist, and their impact on our personality is – in interplay with environmental settings – a factor due to how much of each trait we carry, which like with every other feature we hold to some degree always is unique for each and every one of us
The frequencies are a fluid size which can and constantly does change according to e.g. mood, situations, etc., as well as not least in relation to the almost constantly changing concrete mental focus area in the mind of the concrete protagonist. In praxis, if I e.g. walk up to a random happy person and unprovoked squeeze and pull that person´s nose, then at least the frequency of that person´s adjustment slide related to happiness most probably will decrease

while at the same time the frequencies connected to the adjustment sliders related to respectively frustration, sadness, pain, and perhaps fear or anger, probably will increase. Though, not hereby said that the frequencies of pain and pleasure cannot both be high at the same time, cause they can, which I´m sure e.g. a masochistic person during painful sex would agree to, just as you don´t have to feel pain to feel unpleasant. Moreover, we all likewise can experience to be "in seven minds", and thereby experience how our adjustment sliders stressfully can jump uncontrollably up and down – i.e. with greater intensity than they otherwise normally would, and with more noticeable keys in play than "normal", just as they during a more relaxed state of mind highly likely will move (a.k.a. change) with a noticeable reduced intensity. The adjustment sliders and their frequencies can overlap each other, and we can have everywhere from few to many different noteworthy adjustment sliders with equally many various frequencies intensively in play at the same time. We all experience and perceive differently, we all have different preferences, tempers, and tolerances, and the topical adjustment sliders and their concrete volume of frequency thus of course variates subjectively from person to person (or creature to creature), and from situation to situation.

Where the external world in which we live – to our knowledge – is three dimensional, I more see our inner mental world as an eight-dimensional size (potentially with a potential going all the way up to the 11th and currently final dimension). Superior to the first seven dimensions, we can in mind go back and forward in time (remember, sense, and thus feel old memories, jump between them (including their timeline) as we please, and somewhat imagine and thus partly predict what unmade previous choices could´ve entailed, and what the future likely will hold (that´s in fact most of what our brain constantly is trying to do)), imagine ourselves to have infinite forms (at least as far as your imagination (including dreaming) goes),

and at least by the combination of our external and internal worlds further also find ourselves at different locations at the very same time. We hence at all times are operating in at least two worlds simultaneously (a.k.a. kinda parallel universes), which in thought of mind likewise goes as far as your imagination allows, and actually de facto makes us multidimensional creatures.
This is simplified partly how I visualize the actual setup of our natural characteristics and their frequencies when watching the imaginary inside screen of my closed eyelids, and thus instead of merely seeing a two- or three-dimensional equalizer or coordinate system (although such served the purpose in the preliminary example), I actually picture an eight dimensional multiverse of "adjustments sliders" in *all* directions.
Furthermore, I also can´t help viewing us humans as quantum[137] physical examples of and thus compared to e.g. the planets, stars, black holes, etc., of Einstein´s 'General Theory of Relativity' in which a mass, thus here figuratively from the baseline of a human, creates an effect analogous to spacetime curvature gravitation (a.k.a. attraction) that gravitates both 'good' and 'less good' (again, nothing is exactly null (a.k.a. neutral)), while moreover simultaneously in line with quantum mechanics[138] also acting as and hence sends out waves (a.k.a. energies, a.k.a. vibes) of either 'good' or 'less good' character, which thereby effects humans sharing the same sphere to simultaneously both gravitate and send out waves of either 'good' or 'less good' from and to each other. Consequently, again, as important as the personal balance is for the personal health as important the social balance between the

[137] The smallest unit or amount of something, energy especially.
[138] A fundamental theory in physics that provides a description of the physical properties of nature at the scale of atoms and subatomic particles. It´s the foundation of all quantum physics, and it´s primarily formed and formulated by the German theoretical physicist, Max Planck (1858-1947), and the Danish physicist, Niels Bohr (1885-1962).

particular individual parts (including individuals) is for the social synergetic harmony, which again is important for the personal balance which again is important for the social balance, etc.; we´re like forced to balance between our individual best and our shared best, and despite these two aren´t always immediately compatible they still *are* hermeneutically connected why they anyway equally still have an impact on each other. And so, we all hence have an important responsibility of creating and caressing the best possible balance both in and around us.
Also, in context of personal vs. social, too many relations naturally are overwhelming for the human mind (as earlier mentioned, we humans can approximately handle 130 relations (+/- some)), and too few or no relations aren´t stimulating enough. Loneliness is one of the biggest "hidden" human problems in our post-modern society (in the digital – information – age of today), and paradoxically likewise is interpersonal related stress (though less hidden). Not for fun that isolation has proved to increase a person´s risk of premature death from just about all causes, that it increases the risk of dementia by 50 percent, and that it (including solitary confinement) rooted in human health and thereof human rights is an area of strong restrictions (not least morally) – it´s literally harmful enough to drive any person nuts. Almost same can be said about stress, it increases the risk of premature death, it causes an increased cortisol[139] release which is linked to memory problems, it increases the risk of depression and anxiety which further is believed to increase the risk of dementia, and no doubt that stress also has the ability to drive any person nuts.
Broadly speaking, almost everything is about and thus depend on balance, and hardly anything is universally good in (n)either over- or underabundance; just to mention a few, not overrate not underrate, not overreact not underreact, not overstimulate(d) not

[139] Cortisol is the brain´s primary stress hormone.

understimulate(d); you have to be able to be lenient and indulgent while still able to differ and put your foot down. You have to be able to tackle, address, and deal with "stuff", but also to relax, not restlessness, stress, or manic, not stagnating, inactive, stalling, or exist like living dead, not too high a pulse or heartbeat or both, obviously not too low. It´s good to be able to lead – especially your own autonomy, but it´s likewise important to be able to listen.
Some couples´ relationships are like a constant "cat after the mouse" game where one´s making drama to thereby force the partner to yield and crawl to make up, and soon after it might be the other way around. Where "one-way terror" in a relationship obviously – like radium (nuclear) radiation – is something every "victim" should see to get the hell away from asap (note to self), the "back and forth" kinda relationship might create kind of enough two-way friction to further create a sense of enough balance to keep the relationship going. However, the consistent instability – a.k.a. the slower toxic reaction – presumably still entails an overall unbalance which probably will continue to prevent the couple from ever completely achieve that feeling of secureness, mutual support, and harmony, they both are fighting for – it´ll entail an at least sneaking discrepancy, a.k.a. dissonance, a.k.a. disharmony.
And "just" for the record, in just about all relationships, anger generally leads somewhere you´d like to avoid, respectful communication is key.
A sailboat needs wind to sail, but the wind also creates waves, and if the wind is too heavy and hence creates waves which becomes too big or too long-lasting or both, then it´s most likely "only" a question of time before the wind becomes the root cause to why the boat capsize or break or both, and potentially even sink.
As with two of our absolute most important sources to life and well-being, fire (at least before we discovered other sources to heat and light) and water. When you have fire under control (balanced) then it´s dancing heat, but if it´s out of control (unbalanced) then you

burn yourself. We´re 60 percent water (our brain 85 percent, and our blood 95 percent), under control water´s simply vital to our existence (for our body, and it e.g. also can work as therapy, etc.), but out of control it can drown us. Some water we can´t drink without boiling it first by the help of fire, but if there e.g. is unbalanced much water in the pot above the preconditioned fire for the water to boil, then it boils over and kills the fire – in more than one sense.

In the bubble of a toxic environment even the most unhealthy and absurd can become norm, it shouldn´t, be aware and care. As I told someone I love, just before I left, "I´m not accepting anyone to hurt you, not even me".

Besides the transition, there´s overall two options, unbalanced or well-balanced, unbalance equals dissonance, and well-balanced is the source to harmony.

Related to the balance between healthy and unhealthy skepticism, the American Astronomer and Astrobiologist, Carl Sagan (1934-1996), had a saying: "*Extraordinary claims require extraordinary evidence*". However, a demand for extraordinary evidences can also prove to be an limiting impediment (a.k.a. obstacle), which the Israeli-American Theoretical Physicist, Abraham "Avi" Loeb (1962-), challenge as follows: "*Extraordinary conservatism keeps us extraordinary ignorant*". Cause, true is it that we on the one side shouldn´t believe in all far-out postulates, claims, and theories, without as far as possible getting clarity of ´em, but on the other side we also shouldn´t miss out on the truly extraordinary simply because it can´t – yet – be proved – verified or falsified – by the means and tool we currently – "in lack of better" – have available. Surely, methods and principles can be good tools to have and make use of, but only as long as it doesn´t block for alternative – perhaps innovative – approaches which we thus otherwise could risk to miss out on. Again, a good balance is required.

Take a look at our social media use, how everybody around you at any given opportunity disappear into their electronic devices (e.g. phones and other computers), at how much tv (including streaming services) we watch, etc. – we´re simply addicted. As earlier mentioned, on average we humans are able to handle five to seven things at the same time (+/- some depending in the concrete person), and still we continuously almost constantly fast paced fly around through massive amounts of "things" (a.k.a. information) all across the platforms we use; no wonder we´re getting stressed – that stress has become a highly common widespread disease in the world, the more modern the culture the more stress you´ll see – in our current modus operandi that is. To cope with our mental overload, we mistakenly tend to think that we "just" need to relieve and ease our overheated focus by replacing it with other (Ed. more) different content, i.e. instead of e.g. thinking about the stress prompting workload your work chokingly throws at you, then you instead read the news as a way to try to escape from the work related pressure, instead of dealing with whatever is troubling you you e.g. browse and scroll through your online universe, or watch a movie, or play a computer- or videogame, or whatever else it might be, as a way to try to force your head to process and thus think about something else than what you try to avoid. With this behavior, we thus try to create what in psychology is known as a 'false reality'. However, does trying to escape too much information to process by replacing it with (Ed. adding) more information sound convincing to you as a good, healthy, and sustainable solution to your stress related problems? - I guess not. Getting your mind off "something" troubling you of course can be rewarding, but trying to save your personal reality with a tactic merely based on 'false reality' surely isn´t, rather it´s an evil spiral in which more stress calls for more 'false reality', and where more 'false reality' (a.k.a. more information to relate to) naturally equals more stress, and so on.

The majority of people spend most of their awaken time getting up when the cock crow (or their alarm clock shows no mercy), to then make themselves – and maybe their kids – ready for take-off and then transport themselves to their work where they then spend the next many hours of their enslaved lives before transporting themselves back home again. If they´ve kids it about feeding and putting their kids to sleep asap to then – if not directly – grabbing the computer for some extra evening work. And maybe, if they´re among the "lucky" ones (e.g. skilled enough to manage their time), they then have a few of hours of own time with TV-zapping, or online browsing, or gaming, or hobby masturbation or a quickie with their partner if they have one – and it´s Wednesday, before going back to bed as a preparation to go through the exact same drill all over again the following day – day in, day out.
The carrot at the end of the line, if they´re among "the lucky ones", e.g. is when they in the weekends and in the few weeks of vacation they most gratefully are granted every year, as an illusionary break from the hamster wheel can pretend to be free people by e.g. toasting in G&T (gin and tonic) as an upgraded contrast to the "basic" soft drink, beer, or wine, they otherwise on "normal" days pours down their throats to anesthetized make it through their everyday misery, day in, day out. As the American Naturalist, Essayist, Poet, and Philosopher, Henry David Thoreau (1817-1862), cleverly observant expressed it: "*The mass of men* [and all other genders] *lead lives of quiet desperation. What is called resignation is confirmed desperation*".
We´re selling ourselves, bodies, minds, and services of both, and not least our limited amount of time, to the highest bidder. Roughly said, we´re prostituting ourselves, day in, day out. Desperation from bills to pay has become our main motivation, and duty dense commitment our burden, and even if we find ourselves to be in such a lucrative situation that we´ve managed to surpass our basic needs for survival then greed still most often tend to take over – more

wants more, and opulence continue to be just yet another goal to pursue, day in, day out.
The balance we´re now here focusing on, if you haven't figured it out already that is, is the equation between the world´s "number one subject", work, and our most precious asset, time (some call it work-life balance). Some say purpose over pleasure, and some say vice versa. Though, the art is a combining balance between the two, to learn to earn the feeling of being pleased by and from activating and achieving your purpose – preferably with pleasure.
Those who immediately feels to be best off on the labour market e.g. are those who – with a postmodern expression – are working flex time, who on paper can come and go to and from work "almost as they please", kinda freedom with responsibility, as long as they make sure to perform the work they´re hired to deliver. One such setup was originally partly inspired by the spirit of transpersonal psychology[140], which e.g. was adopted and promoted by the 'New Age movement'[141], and still growingly gains yet further footing in the work sector of today. Depending on the concrete workplace, concrete terms of employment, and personal structure, while it for some might play out to create a feeling of well-balance, it for most at max still is unbalance wrapped in an illusion of well-balance. Through 'Human Resource Management', humans are quite inhumanly degraded to be no more than an almost subhuman asset, and despite the individual worker (a.k.a. employee) is led to believe that they are free to manage their own time to suit exactly their own personal needs and preferences, then e.g. flex time in most

---

[140] Transpersonal psychology is a humanistic approach combining Eastern mysticism and Western rationalism, an approach to therapy which values wholeness – psychological health and spiritual well-being; the essential self is a combination of the transpersonal, self-transcendent and spiritual aspects of human experience.
[141] New Age is a range of spiritual or religious practices and beliefs which since the 1970s rapidly has grown in especially the Western part of the world.

cases still merely covers a flexibility of "only" a few hours in each end of their daily routines. No doubt a few hours can have great value if that actually was the only thing to consider here, but the fact of the matter is that the employers (a.k.a. e.g. companies and businesses) cunningly strategically uses a "greater freedom to the individual worker" as an excuse to actually get more for less. Employers thus expect of the individual worker to take more ownership of their work, and they thus shirk and transfers more responsibility away from themselves and over to (Ed. on) the individual worker. The boundaries between work and free time hence naturally becomes more blurred and fluid – why you increasingly more often see workers "as forced" to take phone calls, answering e-mails, or do actual work when they in fact should´ve been off. The personal pressure on the individual worker increases, and the worker´s possibility of intimate quality time with who and what they love – opposed to the thought of more freedom – decreases, and all without the employers having to pay the worker a single coin more for the worker´s now extra load – all without the worker earning a coin more for their extra effort. Ergo, more work, less play.

At the same time, a self-administered justice arises, rules, and prevails between the worker colleagues. Those colleagues who e.g. meet in for work earlier than others quite likely will start feeling pain in their asses about others coming in later than themselves, and either directly aggressively or – even worse – passive aggressively – as self-appointed "street-sheriffs" – make condescending comments like "what kind of 'director time'[142] is this to meet in on?", or, "oh, see who decided to show up for work", or whatever else it might be, and the workers thus often pressure each other to work harder to live up to each other – especially if one spend more or less time at the workplace or on the work than the

[142] A meeting time which is somewhat later than the "normal" time of coming to work, or meet in school, etc. (which sheep think only the director is entitled to).

colleagues, or work faster or slower than same (a.k.a. who are the most or least productive, etc.). People are in general eager to find scapegoats around themselves, and with an increase in responsibility at work, then not least from fear of failing thus especially among their colleagues. As a result, many are busy licking upward and kicking downwards – and even even more to the sides if that e.g. is what it takes to defile their direct competitors – for the career orientated advancement (a more prestigious title, a fatter paycheck, and the prospect of more power) they also all still crave. And again again, all this extra fuss of more pressure and less fun only for the benefit of the employers (at least in the minds of those employers who doesn´t understand that they surely will benefit even more from happy workers with more surplus) to profit from without them having to appear as villains or actually even lift a finger – besides only using the finger to point at that phrase in the employment contract stating that the employers still at just about any reason have the full power to terminate the worker´s employment, and thus to remove the worker´s economical livelihood (perhaps even ruin the worker) if they don´t comply in stepping up their pace and commitment, and therethrough contribution.

Almost same can be said about project based work – only here there´s yet an extra layer of the worker constantly having to sell themselves *even further*, network more – make themselves extra positively noticed, and in general "just" render more to secure that they also in the future are attractive enough to get hired on the next project as well; in many minds, they need to meet the project´s tight deadline with bravour and fireworks, cause if not, there´s always someone younger and stronger and more beautiful to take over. The thought of more free time in between projects can easily quickly become a burden if you thus don´t ride the wave, and strike while the iron is hot; or was it the other way around? (depend on perspective).

Some live to work, while others work to live. Which of these two categories I personally belong to depend entirely on the concrete situation. If I e.g. find myself to be stuck in a job that I simply have to have to survive, then I obviously work to live even though that cannot really be considered living – there´s a big difference between surviving and living life; existence, survival, living, in that order. Naturally, you have to survive to live, but just barely surviving is not really striving, it´s not really living. However, if I find myself working with something that I´m really truly interested in – something I´m passionate about, then I gladly dedicate my precious time to do what I´m doing, and I hence automatically live to "work" with what no longer is work as much as it thus thereby becomes a life of passion.
Therefore, as far as possible, the ideal work-life balance for us as individuals should (a.k.a. must) be to let our heart and gut feeling guide us to follow our passions in a way where the driving forces more than work becomes passionate cultivation – a lifestyle, a.k.a. less work, more play, more fun, more self-actualization, more self-realization, more of what feels to be more well spend time, and thereby more life. I wish for everyone to find (y)our Ikigai[143].
When I started working in the movies, I engaged myself in my passion of writing and directing movies, and producing for the sake of a steep learning curve, work was a joy, and I loved almost every second of it up until that point where I instead of cultivating my creativity, because of money, had sold myself out too much by finally spending all of my time in the practical field of producing –

[143] Ikigai = What you are good at combined with what you love is your passion. What you love combined with what the world needs is your mission. What the worlds needs combined with what you personally can benefit from is your vocation. What you personally can benefit from combined with what you are good at is your profession. Ikigai is an expression to cover the meaning of the good life at the connecting heart of your passion, mission, vocation, and profession.

guess you can call the learning curve an expensive lesson; constant offers of more money made me take on *just* the next project, and then *just* the next, and then *just* the next, and so on, too many times. I finally had to take my life up for revision, I was no longer happy to get up in the morning, my passion and life quality slowly but steadily vanished like dew to the sun along with my time, and the enjoyment wasted; I was tired of the movie business, lackadaisical[144] became my mental mantra, and I hence had to scoop myself up and make a game changing new game plan. Eventually, I went back to university, and when I did I again engaged myself in something – the exact subjects – I was interested in, something I had chosen because of passion, same mechanisms as goes again in my motivation for now writing this book, I´m again doing it simply because I engage myself in my passion of writing, of giving back to the world who gave me what I need(ed) to give this; I simply follow(ed) my passion, my heart; as much as compassion allows, follow your heart, let your heart guide you, cause you cannot run away from your heart.
As Confucius said: "*Choose a job you love, and you will never have to work a day in your life*".
There´s a growing tendency of the modern human to succumb and fail themselves to "the dark side" and override the happy love connected to humanity and social relations in favor of what the individual in short-sighted form perceives as happiness – "moral" turpitude, a.k.a. fuck people over personal "winning". Only way too late the individual might realize that they were and did wrong in their prioritization, and that the short-sighted happiness in the long term showed to be misfortune, for either themselves or others or both – when e.g. neglected family ties are broken, when the partner has left, or when the individual on their deathbed eventually regret; often we only too late – when all´s said and done – realize what

[144] Showing little enthusiasm and effort.

actually proved to be our actual love – what should´ve been at the top of our list of happy love.

Formulated by a group of palliative care nurses, a top five of what nine out of ten patients at the end of their terminal phase (a.k.a. just before they take the last breath) expresses: 1) *"I wish I´d had the courage to live a life true to myself, not the life others expected of me"*. 2) *"I wish I hadn´t worked so hard"*. 3) *"I wish I´d had the courage to express my feelings"*. 4) *"I wish I had stayed in touch with my friends"*. 5) *"I wish that I had let myself be happier"*.

Eventually, much of what seemed to be of the greatest importance in life turned out to be a hoax that hardly mattered at all, and this list hence represents a top five of neglection and regrets. The individuals is thus not completely devoid of conscience but simply choses to set aside the conscience and thereby the option of acting on it before it´s too late, which in many cases and on many parameters sadly has become a virtually systematic modus operandi for the modern individual. As long as we don´t talk direct damage, just as it´s easier to ask for forgiveness than permission, so you´re more likely to regret what you didn´t do than what you did. Seriously, how do you wish to spend the rest of your life? If you died now your employer will soon replace you with a new employee, and those who ain´t really your friends will replace you with new "friends", but your loved ones – e.g. family and genuine friends – will miss you for the rest of their lives. Do you really wish 'regret' to be your last thought in life? As the American country singer, Dolly Parton (1946-), expressed it: *"Don´t get so busy making a living that you forget to make a life"*.

The most valuable asset – a.k.a. the ultimate currency – of anything that we know of has to be time – or rather the concept we've made to be known as time. Time is all and nothing, time is all we have, without time we have nothing; time is what we had and have to have to do what we did and do and what we didn´t and don´t do, both suffering and pleasuring enjoyment, but when everything

comes down to it 'time' also is "just" a term we use about a probably still partly unknown godfather factor of "just" about everything after the beginning. Paradoxically, time isn´t a material we can feel but still we feel it as it passes by, and we can in that context – figuratively speaking – say that time is tangible, but beside from e.g. touching the human made moving clock-hands, then time of course – at least until further – isn´t really a physical size aside from the wrinkles and grey hair time tends to leave us behind.
Although our time is limited, then time itself might be *un*limited, time as we know it is measured in the time it takes a chemical element to dissolve – or rather the half-life to be more exact, which as far as we know is the same everywhere in the universe, and which also is why time probably always will exist unless the whole universe someday completely collapses[145] and disappears. True is it that time according to our current perspective is affected by speed and spacetime[146], as explained by respectively Einstein´s special theory of relativity[147], and the 4th dimension concept of Einstein´s

[145] It most likely will collapse, but also most likely "only" to "start over" with a new universe – maybe it already has done it many times before, and will continue doing it "forever"?

[146] But then again, if in fact anti-gravity technology exist or will come to exist, then also this technology might be able to play with spacetime and thereby time (this question is a big hit within the area of UAPs (Unidentified Arial Phenomena) (a.k.a. UFOs (a.k.a. ufology)) – which for the record should be given much more public attention than currently is the case (although many governments are starting to take it considerably more serious) – maybe you´re not ready yet?).

[147] Special Theory of Relativity applies to all physical phenomena in the absence of gravity. Time e.g. moves slower for one travelling by high constant (i.e. not accelerating) speed than it does for the slower moving surroundings – e.g. a slower moving observer, although time still is experienced to move at the exact same pace for both the fast traveller and the slower observer in each their kinda closed vacuums (a.k.a. each their perspectives).

general theory of relativity[148], but since it´s not really relevant for our angle here, then we´ll for now leave it at that; if you know you know, and if not but wish to know then you at least now know what also to study.

Anyway, despite time might being an infinite factor, then the tiny piece of time yours and mine existence gets to have is *very* limited, and no matter what we wish or what we do to change our portion of time then we can never get more time than what we have – only shorten it if we don't take proper care of ourselves and thus the time we from nature graciously have been granted. Every second passing by is a second that'll never come back anywhere else than in the memory of that particular moment. The time of your-mine-our clock is non-stop counting down, every split of every split second of every moment, and – also – therefore it´s simply sad to see how we waste our time chasing goals that – when everything comes down to it – in the greater picture seems "pretty" worthless. We e.g. spend the large majority of our time chasing a better digital number at the bottom of our accountings, we watch shitty and useless tv programs which other people has dedicated (and kinda wasted) years of their lives to make, and while we waste all this time doing such we simultaneously waste all the time we could have spent doing what we're passionate about, cultivating our interests,

---

[148] General Theory of relativity explains the law of gravitation and its entanglement to other forces of nature. Spacetime covers three dimensions of space (width, length and height), and a fourth dimension of time. Time constitutes the fourth ingredient of the fourth dimension of the currently 11 known dimensions, and hence spacetime is considered to be four-dimensional. Because of mass related gravitation the space (including travel time – ergo spacetime) around a three-dimensional mass like bends, and simply put, time travelling in a curve around three-dimensional mass thus covers a longer distance than it would had time been able to go straight instead of curving around; time thus moves slower in a gravitational field than it does in a non-gravitational. As the American physicist, John Wheeler (1911-2008), said it: "*Space-time tells matter how to move. Matter tells space-time how to curve*".

and not least the time we could´ve spend with whom and what that´re important to us.
The most precious act of love you can ever give anyone is your time – and obviously this is meant by the slot of your time spend caring for others according to also their needs and preferences, and thus of course not by the slot of your time you might spent to cause suffer.
Like our life consist of a limited amount of time, then in the same spirit our energy likewise isn´t an unlimited pool of resources; we have a limited amount of energy within us, a limited amount of energy available, and thus a limited amount of energy to use and hence give from. Time and energies are different between different living organisms, some have more time before their time ends, and some has higher energy levels than others, but in all cases time and energy is the common denominator for everything they-you-me-we have, we´re all subjectively bound to our respective limited time, and joule (the standard unit used to measure energy). Thus, when someone dedicate their limited amount of time, energy, and hence resources to you, then you should feel blessed, just like others should feel blessed when you chose to spend your limited amount of time, energy, and hence resources on them.
Spend your time and energy well, find *your* (well)balance, help create a harmonized shared (well)balance, and remember that the best things in life aren't things.
Confronted by basic health risks, we know from commonly known tips and advises on a healthier life that the most important ingredients are exorcising (a.k.a. to stay physically active), a healthy and variated diet, and enough sleep, and at first I thus was about to give a challenging scientific response here before I then again just decided to say: exorcise but don´t overdo it – it can potentially lead to injuries, heart damage, and more. Eat healthy and try to variate your diet but also – at least sometimes (as long as it´s not rat poison or anything of that caliber) – allow yourself to eat “just” what really

spoils your taste buds as that at least can be good for your happiness and hence mental life quality (health), which thereby isn´t to neglect. And yea yea, hereto, "good" (a.k.a. tasty) food is often assimilated with fatty food, and surely too much fat (notwithstanding bad or less bad fat (e.g. nuts etc.)) ain´t good for ya, but should you e.g. ever fall into seriously cold water then you high likely – opposed to the low BMI (Body Mass Index) and fat percentage of the "ideal dream body as cut in wood" – in a matter of life and death could be in serious need of exactly that extra fat layer to help keep you roughly sane and sound until you hopefully are rescued – it´s e.g. not for fun that Inuits traditionally as a necessary health precaution makes sure to build an extra fat layer to handle the cold winter weather. Not too fat to be agile and breathe, not too skinny to make it. And finally, sleep as much as you need, though without staying in bed all day for too many days, make sure to also get up and out, sunlight and fresh air are de facto – said with a cliché – good for both body, mind, and soul.

You know what´s up with also the valance adornment, it´s all about context, nature, incentive, and how the balance is important.

It´s good to show interest for other people, but showing too much interest thus that it crosses the limit of stalking of course isn´t good. Respect and include other people´s balance boundaries in your balance equation.

In same spirit, helping other people is of course very good, as long as the eagerness for helping don´t get out of hand and actually becomes a matter of and takes on character of control which most often obviously isn´t good.

And if continuing this sort of examples, that list alone could take on and by far surpass the length of a bible; feel free to make more examples of your own.

An old (approximately 700 years) traditional Japanese world view, wabi-sabi, is centered on the aesthetic acceptance of transience and imperfection. To quickly by example explain the words of wabi-sabi the Japanese tend to use the example of an old ceramic bowl, here 'wabi' represent the asymmetry of the bowl, while 'sabi' represent the time (a.k.a. life) based aged related lovely patina found on the bowl. Wabi-sabi originally derived from the Buddhist teaching of 'the three marks of existence', namely impermanence (aniccā), non-self (a.k.a. emptiness or absence of self-nature) (anatta), and suffering (including pain, unhappiness, unsatisfactoriness, stress, etc.) (duhkha), and the aesthetical value of beauty is through wabi-sabi thus measured by the present degree of "imperfect, impermanent, and incomplete". Maybe you know the feeling of how something can appear so ugly that it actually is cool, how something can be so weird that it actually is more interesting than anything else (e.g. boring normal), how "flawed" symmetry and aesthetics more than anything "just" provides more character, etc., that´s partly what wabi-sabi is about. Hence, wabi-sabi is a world view that highly values and explains the meaning of perfect imperfectness, a.k.a. flawed beauty, and it from there thus became the Japanese godmother to the understanding of how emptiness and imperfection is honored as tantamount to the first step to 'satori', a.k.a. enlightenment. On that note, it should be fairly obvious to view and talk about the world of all living as quite wabi-sabi, with room – even an almost desperate need – for way more wabi-sabi (at least acceptance of it), and to acknowledge how the meaning of wabi-sabi with harmony aligns our call for freedom, understanding, and already established path towards enlightenment.

However, not to forget, balance my here, and balance my there, as with roughly everything, standing or falling, growing or stalling, is a matter of balance.

Truth be told, our world provides us with everything we could ever possibly dream of to make life on Earth universally truly beautiful. If we from individually to collectively in the name of equity truly understood how to create the right balance, then no less than everybody could be having an all the way through beautiful and wonderful life; we have food enough to feed all – no one should have to starve; we have materials enough to build shelter for everybody; we have resources enough for everybody to prosper according to *their* needs; all borders, just about all suffering, and the unbalanced skewed distribution of resources in our world, etc. and etc., is human made; when everyone understand we´ll have peace and harmony, and the only thing still currently standing in our way is us.

A spur of the moment – a late reminder, as goes for much of the substance across the different chapters, the mentioned content of course are just relatively few fragment examples of and related to a bigger whole which crisscrossing overlaps and finds relevance all over; you do the map to make your puzzle as a piece to our puzzle. Don´t get lost in the darkness of your own shadow, but likewise don´t deny any parts of yourself; even angels have a shadow; cheery the light you carry, and at least embrace your shadow as motivation and strength to move forward toward the light. Yin and yang, chitty chitty bang bang, no need to hang, it´s nothin´ but a "B"(alance)-thang.

4.2. Chillax, Please

In the field of communication, there seems to be a tendency of weighing *how* something is communicated higher than *what* is communicated, "long live" sophism – that dirty low... However, in all fairness, it must be considerably more important what´s communicated rather than how it´s communicated. Instead of being so love damn busy complaining about how other people speak, their rhetoric, their diction – their intonation, inflection, and choice of words, instead of e.g. worrying about lingo, accents, dialects, the tone of voice, and calligraphic fonts, if people use sign language among them or use profanities to express themselves or not, and so on, although it just about all can add meaning then what you above all in this context *should* pay attention to is your own ability to listen, see, and understand what actually is being communicated; don´t just bop your head to the beat, scrutinize the performance and listen to the lyrics.

On my first day at the high profiled fancy-ass elite university where I did my post-graduation, a university in another country and thus culture than the Danish duckpond I came from, I found myself standing in a lecture hall auditorium surrounded by 100+ other fellow students when I as a response to "something" just randomly replied with "nah, fuck that shit". A second later, the whole before so talkative room suddenly was completely quiet – you literally would be able to hear a needle drop to the floor, and the only "thing" breaking the silence was a bit of whispering à la "oh my god, he used the f- *and* the s-word".

I know that most people in that room were a completely different breed than me, in the same moments where they in their youth probably were bossed around at their fancy expensive boarding schools I most likely were cruising the grid of my hood of "the game", party, pranks, and worse; as they were busy working on their homework I was busy working the streets, and where I in our path based intersection addressed our lectures by merely their first name (which is common praxis in Denmark) my educational "peers" showed to be surprisingly resentful about me not calling them by their title and last name, e.g. professor Evans, etc.; yawn. While they might in their indoctrinated minds felt me to be unusual derogatory in my approach, I on the other hand deliberately with another kind of respect and friendliness were creating different types of less informal wavelengths, which most professors clearly seemed to like and appreciate – at least those of them who weren´t suffering from insecurity related issues, and so, while the other students seemed to keep an impersonal distancing façade driven by sophistic fakeness, I casually spoke my mind to get the answers I needed for my questions. Where they had lecturers, I more felt to have sparring partners.

Also, at university, one thing is that when I started I didn´t know jack shit about how academia works, what any of the academic terms meant, and anything about academic code of conduct. One of my first days there we (my fellow students and I) e.g. was asked to make a literature review, an analysis, and a discussion, and as I was sitting like *one-big-question-mark* thinking "what the hell does any of that shit even mean?", I saw how everybody around me just started doing as asked like had they never done anything else, and I at that very moment felt really far from both home and my goal of a degree. So far so bad, I´d never really opened a book in gymnasium (the Danish counterpart to High School) where I had "just" made my way through my exams by merely general knowledge, and now here I was. Fair enough, I folded up the cuffs I didn´t wear, briefly had long eyes over the shoulders around me just to get started, and little by little I started learning what was actually going on. As Astrid Lindgren´s[149] (1907-2002) fictional character, Pippi Longstocking, says: "*I have never tried that before, so I think I should definitely be able to do that*".

Though, another thing – and what really took me by surprise – was the academic setup and language, how I was not allowed to have a single opinion based on my personal experiences if I couldn´t directly refer to empirical evidence (and no, personal experiences isn´t just accepted as qualitative data (unless you anthropologically call ´em field studies)) and sources of literature who had already said the same, and how I was corrected in my writing from e.g. using the term 'likewise' as that according to the academic snobbish customs obviously had to be 'also', and so on. I mean, "*come on*, you know what the fuck I mean, so what´s the fucking problem?". I

[149] Swedish author.

hated that I was being limited in what I was allowed to think – at least express, and in how I wasn´t allowed to formulate myself as I preferred. Much of the time I according to rules for the sake of rules felt like a dictated no good bitch with unwelcome thoughts and ideas (despite actually getting unofficially recognition for same), which to me went straight against my nature and everything I thought – at least hoped and think – a university should be, a place where you´re able and even encouraged to think and reflect and be innovative by thinking out of the box, but it and I wasn´t. I of course understood that I had to learn the basics of academia, and of course scientific studies and pustulates with seriosity and potential likelihood in reality must live up to certain standards – not least ethically, but it still provoked me like crazy that the "smells" I´ve lived and which might not be found described in pre-existing texts was being rejected, and if anything positive I can take from it, apart from an introduction to a "new world" of still amazing sources, then it at least motivated me to write my own as soon as I graduated, my texts, my rules.

We as individuals comes from many different backgrounds, and – luckily – not everyone are bottled up according to the strict etiquette of 'tact and tone', as formulated by the Danish author, Emma Gad (1852-1921), in her book from 1918. For example, back in public school I e.g. experienced how several of my "teachers" constantly was on my back, how they smeared me with all the worst word in the book, and on several occasions even directly threatened me, short said, how they drove a personal vendetta against me for no justifiable reason. Not because I was academically poor, I was among the best when I wanted to be, and not because I was a bad child – on the contrary I even received a prize for protecting the "weaker" kids from being bullyed, but presumably because I didn´t enough for their taste fitted their criteria of how all kids as nod puppets without any deviation – and closer to the thoughts of Emma Gad – should be. I was an independent kid with opinions, and

instead of valuing my ability to think and reasoning with me, and instead of respecting and listening to my arguments in discussion (which later in life came to be highly appreciated and probably became my strongest asset (and not because I´d changed *that* much as I still today find most of my views and points from back then to be valid, but simply because my age and merits by time changed the way my surroundings looked at me)), I guess that they undeserved saw me as mere a – agent – provocateur pain in the ass. Sure, I divided the waters of teachers, some loved me, and some hated me, and those who loved me kept me floating while those who hated me didn´t in any positive way acknowledge anything of me, my, and mine – which of course often is the case in interpersonal relationships, but here they *really* truly hated me, a child.
A day in sixth or seventh grade (I believe It was), where I – again – hadn´t made my homework, one of my "teachers", a woman, again started screaming and shouting into my face thus that her saliva flew and thoroughly sprayed my face with whatever she had had for breakfast (and a smell of cigarettes and periodontitis), yelling how I was the biggest loser of all, that I never would amount to nothing of anything, and that I should just gather all my stuff and get the hell out of her classroom, etc., and as she kept going at me and continued to be all up in my face the whole time, even as I was walking out, then I finally had enough, and thus told her "why don´t you just shut the fuck up you filthy fat gooey-sow". In the next she swung at me – with a quick head movement I only just barely ducked her hand, she chased me down through the hallway, and right after she rushed to the principal's office to report me and demand that I was to be kicked out of the school. Even though I told her some harsh words then those words in that situation "merely" was my way of putting my foot down, which from my perspective wasn´t ascribed much more meaning than had I just told her to "be kind not to scream and shout your profanities in my face, please". The essence here is that where I come from, what I said was a

“normal” way to respond to a verbal attack of that caliber – which she (homework or not) surely started, and as I only the night before had heard the exact same sentence fly through the air under one of many daily dramatic arguments (Ed. fights) at home, then when I the next day at school was met by hatred instead of understanding and care, this sentence naturally was what flew out of my mouth – as a response to the heavy verbal fire I was under.

Notes, don´t just judge people, there´s always a reason, and be careful what you do and say around kids, they observe, listen, and learn more than you might think.

A quick story before my final point of the incident with my teacher: In the train there was this man with his two young kids, the two kids were noisily and disturbingly playing around in the train, and the dad was “just” sitting with an all-empty face staring out into the air. Another passenger in the train with an angry voice told the dad that he wasn´t a good parent, and that if he didn´t quiet his kids down then he sure as hell would do it for him. The dad – without moving his head or the empty focus of his eyes – replied that the kids´ mom had just passed away, and that they were now on their way home from the hospital.

There´s always a reason.

I know the “rules” of ‘tact and tone’, if I want I probably can seem lordly to the noble, and in a later serious conversation with that teacher at the principal´s office I hence in “well-mannered articulation” simply told her what *she* wanted to hear, that I was truly sorry, that she was right and I was wrong, and that I of course would take back every single word if only I could, and yada yada yada (bullshit), one of the few times I´ve ever lied (and yea, I felt like a sellout fool), all because I didn´t wanted to see my parents upset about me being thrown out of the school, although I still to this day – in spite of my harsh words – think that I hardly did wrong compared to what I daily was exposed to from the school staff; instead of at least meeting me halfway, the grown up teachers aimed to attack and destroy me – which they also directly told me, a child, and my aim – as a child – was merely to fend off and "survive" their attacks, and still I – the child – was made out to be the fully responsible scapegoat. Just as you shouldn´t judge a book by its cover, then you also shouldn´t judge a message merely by the choice of presentation, and despite the just mentioned teacher was both verbally wild and physically violent, then she still by far wasn´t among the worst teachers I had growing up – others I with my current psychological knowledge hands down wouldn´t hesitate to call out as clear-cut cases of psychopathy. Like the teacher, a man, who out of nowhere once knocked on the door when I was in another class, he stuck his head in and kindly asked if he could just borrow me for a second out on the hallway. Out there he sat down across the table from me (we had like picnic tables on the hallways) and quietly like whispered to me that I should know that he would do everything within his power to take me down, that I seriously should watch my back as he at any chance would troll me over like a big truck loaded with wood logs. Or like this other time where we had a parent gathering at school, as we were about to take a big group photo of all the students and our teachers, I was standing in the back row on the left side of the frame, when suddenly something hit me *really* hard in the back of my head, after coming to my senses I turn around and see this other teacher, likewise a man – at about 2 meters (approximately 6ft 5), who since our first encounter had tried to bully me out of the school, and now out of nowhere had just went up behind me and with his fist punched me hard in the back of my head (guess the free wine at the arrangement played a part), and now with big force pushed me away with the word "fuck over on the other side, I don´t want to stand next to your ugly face in the photo". The people who saw it couldn´t believe what they´d just witnessed, and clearly to give meaning to the craziness thought that it was some kind of in-joke we had going on, which the teacher thus also tried to make it seem like when he obviously only

after seemed to realize what he had just done. Understand that I ain´t bitching about the tone or the language, I only care about their message and physical actions, and that the only consequence of him punching and pushing me was that I had to hold my – normally quiet "hippie" – mom back from not going full frenzy on that teacher, and that this – now former – teacher still cunningly with lying sophistic words "in his power" (although I´m convinced it more is about lacks within the receivers than his actual "qualities") later managed to move on to now hold the position as head of all youth activities in all of the county in which this incident took place.
I literally could go on with examples of this kind as the list is absurd long, and I´m sure that many of us share the same kind of experiences and some even worse, and despite not knowing the exact reasons behind these teachers´ behavior – their mental issues, then I at least know that they should be no excuse for them to take their anger and frustrations out on me, back then a child, and hence badly add to my reasons, and that if someone with a right mind would have payed close attention to and actually was willing to listen to what I was communicating rather than how I was communicating, and to what the teachers actually communicated and did instead of only how they cunningly communicated to just about "everyone" but me, then we could´ve avoided the founding reasons for me now sharing these – very few of very many – bad examples.
When the Danish film director, Lars ("von") Trier (1956-) (a film director I mentioned earlier in the book), e.g. back in 2011 at a Cannes film festival press conference proclaimed "I understand Hitler", then the world press and too many people was quick to attack Trier – Trier lost a lot of "friends" that day; Trier was being sarcastic on a highly sensitive subject, he made it clear that the Nazis did a lot of bad things and that he wasn´t sympathizing with the Nazis killing Jews, merely that he from an attempt of mentalization – from his view of Hitler´s perspective – understood

Hitler´s motives and why Hitler based thereon would act as he did, and why Hitler ended up a lonely man in his Berlin bunker, and what Hitler must have felt in his final time alive – because Lars himself e.g. can relate to some of those inner feelings of lonellness etc. Yea, Trier might to some be a provoking verbalized version of a gunslinger, and sure he also was joking about himself being a Nazi, but again, not because he literally *is* a Nazi, but analogically because of his German bloodline – which he also expressed at the same séance; no doubt that Trier is complex and controversial, and that he demands "something" from his audience – among others some intellect and depth, however, how many people chose to (mis-)interpret what he said and thereupon ban him with a "persona non grata stamp" from the Cannes film festival – and beyond, was simply an example of overreaction based on bias of understanding purposely taking offense when non needed, and eagerness of trying to censor and dictate "rules of communication". Leave all doubt out, the Nazis and the atrocities they were responsible for of course are horrible beyond words, and fuck whoever supporting such evil, but that doesn´t in this incident include Trier – however unnecessary and inappropriate his communication was perceived to be.
People hear and see what *they want* to hear and see instead of exercising listening to and seeing what actually – at least in between the lines – are being said, shown and meant, a.k.a. communicated. Again, who cares if someone e.g. uses profanities to express themselves – and why is that even important? – as long as they don´t directly and undeserved verbally attacks you (or anyone), or serve explicit content of e.g. sexual character to a child, or any off limit shit like that. Worry less about how something is presented, and then pay extra attention to and base your verdict on the actual message. Like the Chinese author, Marie Lu (born Xiwei Lu) (1984-) wrote, *"It´s pointless to believe what you see, if you only see what you believe"*.

The beauty can be a beast in the eye of the beholder, and vice versa; observations and interpretations are and always will be subjective. If I e.g. tell people "you´re not normal", then one will take it as an insult while another will take it as a compliment.
I surely to some can be quite direct in my approach to conversation, and in that process sometimes poke other people´s immediate boundaries of intimacy to thereby deliberately kinda provoke a small push towards a less defensive and thus more genuine answer, and to thereby also faster get passed the often boring and unnecessary monosyllabic chit-chatting small talk; why waste time on something we both waste our time by instead of "just" getting straight to the point from which we both hopefully should benefit more. Don´t get me wrong, I´m socially intelligent, and with a high moral I´m also very conscious about not unnecessarily transcending other people´s private sphere boundaries, but I in all honestly likewise have a lower limit to how far I´ll stretch myself to please others and their perhaps "violation-ready" (a.k.a. how ready they in *their* hyper modernization are to take offense) rhetorical preferences – I after all also have to leave room for me in myself of mine. Hence, sorry not sorry if anyone e.g. in relation to *my* language (a.k.a. chosen vocabulary) feels stepped on their toes in their small shoes.
I´ve e.g. conducted a study where the aim was to research where the border crossing between art and mere provocation goes, and not surprisingly the conclusion pointed in the direction of it being where the receiver subjectively feels their limit to be – to which same logically e.g. can be said about communication (as art naturally involves communication). But should the individual receiver thus suddenly have the deciding mandate of what and how the artist´s art should be? In congruence with freedom of speech (a.k.a. freedom of expression), importantly of course not.
Additionally, in line with the modern expression of 'cancel culture' (a.k.a. call-out culture), in which some self-appointed feels as called

upon to authoritarian select what others can say and do, and what of what historically has been said and done that still publicly can be allowed to be remembered and exist; expectations about erasing our history and censoring ourselves is on the march, as if that actually would benefit anything the most. I´m all against provoking merely for the sake of provocation, but damn rather allow people to express themselves as they want to thus thereby give everybody the option of – and a fair chance to – showing their true face than breed a culture where we by censorship muzzle all controversial views and opinions to the point where we thus create a world in which our vocal valves are being choked, and where them who doesn´t "have clean flour in the bag" – them who has something to hide – instead learns to and gets away with going under the radar. We need to know who people are and what they stand for to be able to take the discussion, address, and hopefully solve our issues. It´s e.g. no secret that also I shitted my diaper as a baby, I grew, and don´t do it anymore. I´m not proud of and don´t agree with much of our past, but I also don´t agree with sweeping the stupidities of the past in under the rug; it makes no sense to rewrite or erase historic realities – don´t leave them in vain and hence stand for nothing. Instead, accept them as belongings of a different context of a different time, and at least – if nothing else – as unpleasant – or directly horrible – examples value them as important lessons we in the name of progress actually should be (Ed. are) able to learn from. We cannot change and should not deny the past, but we have options of not repeating the same mistakes in the present and hence the future.

When I e.g. in debates hear bourgeois or conservative or right-wing or neo-liberal (or whatever you wanna call ´em – they all still have kinda the same shitty smell) politicians – and their henchmen foot soldiers – express that it´s perfectly fine to be selfish (to always want more despite already having plenty more than enough – although others around as a consequence are suffering) – implicitly cold and cynical, and that not all people has equal worth, but that the essential defense still for them just mainly is that they at least formulate their views in a polite way (yea, I´ve heard conservatives defend themselves exactly so), then I can´t help to think that it virtually is love damn unimportant how such relentless and remorseless views are formulated – how housebroken their communication is – when their actual viewpoints notwithstanding anyway are extremely gauche, a moral failure, and thus morally dirty. And this is just yet another example of how wickedness (a.k.a. evilness) sustained operates wrapped in sophism, and still endemically well alive thrivingly exercise power (a.k.a. cause atrocity).

Communication – and especially dialog – isn´t about being right for the sake of not being wrong, and thus don't just let the best rhetoric and lingo win, the best argument – it´s unrestrained restrain – surely should come out on top (and not that I´m claiming to own it – I just humbly hope I can help inspire you to provide it for *us*).

To further elaborate on how the delivery of a message can be less important – as long as the meta message in the message comes across – can be to check out the following sentence: "*...it deosn't mttaer in waht oredr the ltteers in tehse wrods are, the olny iprmoetnt tihng is taht the frist and lsat ltteer be at the rghit pclae. The rset can be a toatl mses and you can sitll raed it wouthit porbelm. Tihs is bcuseae the huamn mnid deos not raed ervey lteter by istlef, but the wrod as a wlohe*". Despite a quite alternative delivery, I guess you still understood the message (if not then you can read it in the footnote[150]).

Also, try have a go at this variant – read it all as letters: "50PH15M 4ND C3N50R5H1P 15 F0R 5UCK3R5; U51N6 F4NCY W0RD5 70 74LK

[150] "*...it doesn't matter in what order the letters in these words are, the only important thing is that the first and last letter be at the right place. The rest can be a total mess and you can still read it without problem. This is because the human mind does not read every letter by itself, but the word as a whole*".

8ULL5H17 15 4 D4MN 5H4M3; 74LK1N6 R34L 5H17 15 1N WH473V3R W4Y 7H3 N4M3 0F 7H3 64M3"[151]. Again, who cares how "what" is said as long as what said is has fair justification and is fairly understood.

Furthermore, I personally find it funny to write in codes – or to try to brake codes (by e.g. finding patterns etc.), which to me is like laying a puzzle. One of the most basic "code-models" e.g. could be to only make use of every fifth word of a text. For example, read the following small text (in italic), and as you read through it extract every fifth word from it, starting with the fifth word:

"I wish you to see, as one two three, how code writing can be, easy, helpful, and here cheesy. It can help you to somewhat get around another that is sneaking around in yours if no other way for you to let your "someone" know where and when and how you need certain "things" to happen; if you e.g. do a surprise party then it should stay a surprise"[152].

There´s many ways to code a message, from the simplest as just exemplified, over e.g. ciphertexts of and in various signs, forms, and sign formations, and all the way up to the historically famous enigma machine [153] – and beyond, with the modern day technological encryptions[154] probably currently leading the field. However, to not get lost in codes here, a rain check for a rainy day. Apart from fun with codes, it´s of course important to be somewhat precise and hence clear in your communication as all

---

[151] Sophism and censorship are for suckers; using fancy words to talk bullshit is a damn shame; talking real shit is in whatever way the name of the game.

[152] Every fifth word should in a sentence say: "See how easy it somewhat is if you know how to do it".

[153] A cipher device used by the Nazis during the Second World War to send coded secret military messages. That the British mathematician, Alan Turing (1912-1954), managed to break the Enigma Code, is considered to be one of the most – if not *the* most – important reasons for the Nazi´s defeat.

[154] Based on exchange of encryption keys controlling the cryptographic algorithms.

communication also e.g. provides the foundation for miscommunication, a.k.a. e.g. misunderstanding, which again is yet an argument for why we shouldn´t seek to limit straight up talk, and how anyone express themselves the best. Sure, it´s also part of the communication art to meet your "audience" where they are to reach them with your message, but you´re certainly allowed to do it your own way.

Though, with that said, there´s not much in communication there´s more frustrating than when someone sophistically attempt to sound smart and well-articulated without having anything to have it in (a.k.a. when it´s all mouth), and if they then on top of that also is very keen on and fond of repeating themselves – keep saying the exact same thing in various variations in the hope of sounding extra smart (almost like a broken record (to those of you who still knows what a record is)), or in the hope of thereby convincing about what ain´t agreed to, then my patience seriously is being tested. Stop insulting my intelligence, no matter how many times you tenaciously repeat your wrongs it doesn´t make them right, *please* just stop wasting my time.

Another frustration in communication is that too many people mistakenly tend to think that the highest voice-volume wins the discussion, although people in fact tend to sharpen their hearing and listen more closely when you whisper. Unless you e.g. are in very noisy surroundings, the lower you speak the more other people listen, and the louder you speak, scream, or yell, the more people in defense tend to go from listening to hearing, before then shutting down on even their hearing of your noise. And, if no one´s willing to listen, and you can´t convince them otherwise, then logically no – direct moral – verbal communication is useful anyway.

Another problem often can be the tendency many counterparts have of not being willing to hear you out, where you´re not able to finish what you´re trying to communicate before they´re already all up in arms on e.g. your introducing – maybe context setting – words well before you actually manage to reach your actual point, because your counterpart instead of hearing were busy interrupting; "take a chill-pill, motherfucker, and show some love damn respect for me even spending time and energy on you – for me trying to enlighten you here". As a very simple interactive example, imagine that I with a drawing wish to share how I feel in this moment with you; on the next page you´ll find a bunch of dotted points connected to numbers, Roman numerals, and letters, first you in numerical order have to connect the numbers, starting with number 1, then 2, then 3, and so on up until number 20. Now, find a writing instrument (e.g. a pencil or a pen), draw, see what it looks like, and return here before reading on.

"...Oh, you´re on the barricades, with your fist up in the air illustrating power to the people? Or are you threatening me with your fist? Or..." many might quickly think. Yea, I definitely believe in power to the people, but that´s not exactly the vibes I in this moment aim to send you, and surely, I of course am not trying to threaten you here.
Now try to connect the Roman numerals in numerical order, I, II, III, IV, V, VI, VII, VIII. Draw, look, and return back here before reading on (and note that some of the Roman numerals share dot-points with some of the numbers).

"What the actual fuck, are you sending me a fuck-finger here, as to tell me 'fuck you'? Or...", some might think, and on that account already find themselves to be in 'code red' because of jumping to too hasty conclusions. And no, just to be completely clear, that´s also not the vibes I wish to send you here.
Now finish the drawing by connecting the letters in alphabetical order, A, B, C, D, E, F, G, H. Draw, look, and return back here before reading on (and note that some of the letters share dot-points with some of the numbers).

“Ah, so you´re actually sending me ‘peace’?”. Yea, all I the whole time with the drawing was trying to communicate is peaceful vibes, and so this example in kinda a low-practical fashion clearly should illustrate how jumping to too hasty conclusions often can cause the actual message to be completely misinterpreted and misunderstood – opposite of the original intention. A message that at first might seems bad actually can turn out be good, despite the rhetorical visual linguistic on the way to the point appeared negative in the eyes (and in ears) of the receiver, then it´s still no guarantee for the sender’s sincere intention and the actual point of the presented matter. Be careful about catching a message out of context – before and hence without the dissemination of information is complete, and to thus judge and conclude anything without as much of the full picture as possible.

Exclusively to the British reader, no I´m not a French archer; if you know you know; I – as said – come in peace.

Now, simply just jump passed your beautiful drawing, and let´s move on.

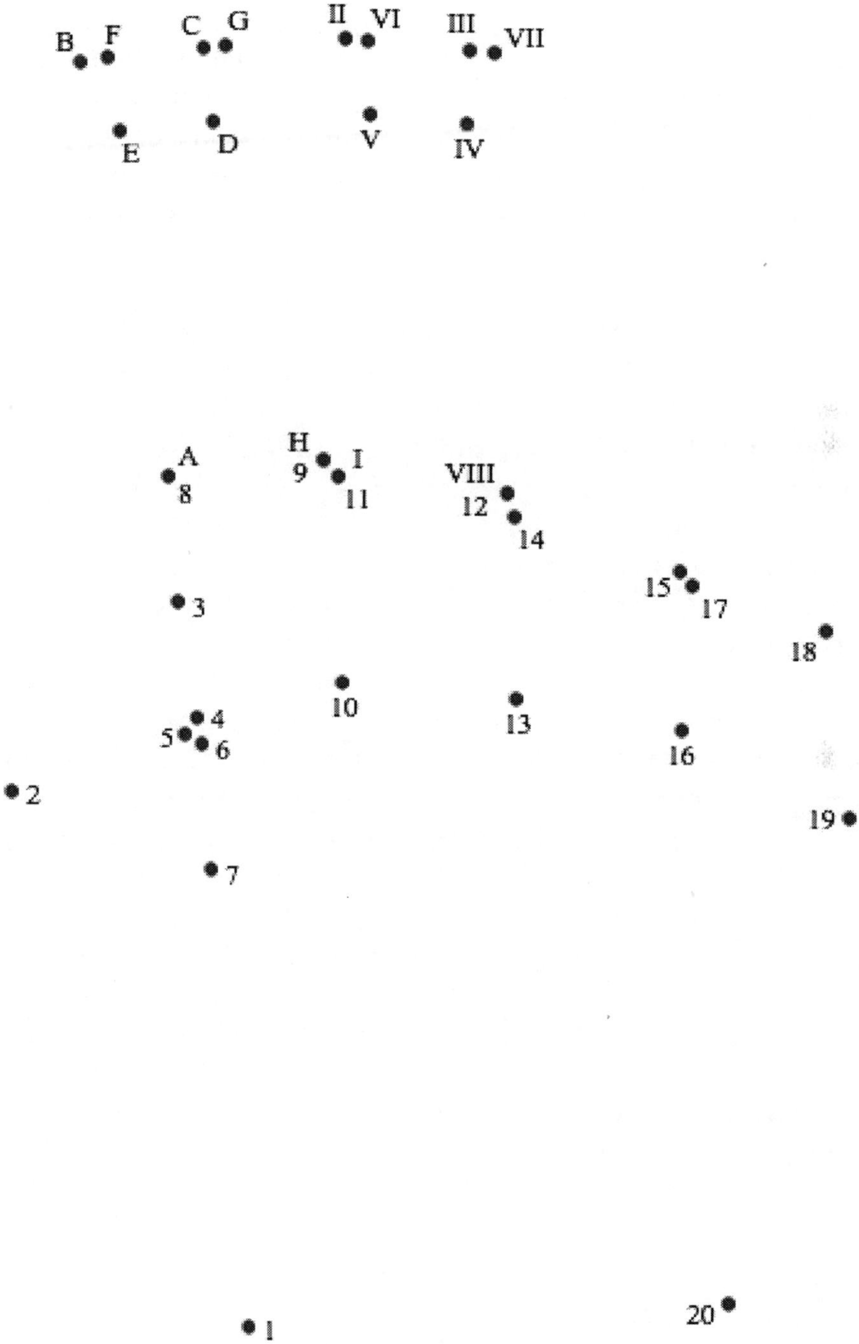
B
F
C
G
II
VI
III
VII
E
D
V
IV
A
8
H
9
I
11
VIII
12
14
15
17
3
18
10
13
4
5
6
16
2
19
7
20
1

An old proverb goes: "as long as the end´s good then everything´s good"[155], and in addition to this being true in most situations – e.g. for some the case in relation to preferred attributes of a sex partner, then this also says a great deal about our receipt and perception of a message, which likewise applies the other way around as well – if the ending isn´t good, then the previous good is quickly forgotten, and vice versa. In almost all contexts, and especially in communication, short-term memory often seems to be a problem. As I heard a Yakuza[156] member say about self-justice, "it doesn´t matter if you did 99 good things if thing number 100 isn´t – you only have to make one wrong move". If I e.g. smother a film director with a plethora of compliments but then just finally add that the director´s latest movie in all honesty though wasn´t the best of the director´s movies, then there´s a pretty big chance of the director instantly quickly forgetting every compliment I gave before and only holds on to what I said after the 'but', and exactly this mechanism seems to go again all over much of our communication. Herein, the problem seems to be that people in general simply more than the "good part(s)" tend to look for and note any sign of negativity, and to firmer hold on to the "bad-part(s)" – deliberately forgetting the previous positivity in the process. Without going deeper into the potential reasons behind this mechanism, e.g. insecurity, or low self-esteem, or merely passion, etc., I know and understand how we learn the most from constructive critique – which I as a fan value, but as with relations in general, because you love one it doesn´t mean that you per se have to hate all other, and vice versa, and surely we´d do ourselves – e.g. our mood and confidence – a handy favor by holding on to the "good – positive – part(s)" to at least the same extend as we do the constructive "bad part(s)", and much more than we do the useless unconstructive "bad part(s)", which we quite stupidly and unfortunately anyway still seems to carry the

---

[155] Yea, I know the proverb "all´s well that ends well", but I prefer what I wrote.
[156] The Japanese mafia.

longest although them being the heaviest and we certainly would be best off not holding them at all. Don´t be afraid of embracing and carrying positivity, it might actually be good for you.
Hence, if you in communication thus start with the "bad news" and end with the "good news" – if you manage to first drag the receiver through the "bad part(s)" without losing them (by upsetting them too much), then you by ending with the "good part(s)" surely have a higher chance of defusing easing them off with the good news than if approaching them opposite by starting with the good news that´ll then higher likely end up drowning in the final bad.
Well aware about this aspect, I nevertheless can´t help seeing it a weakness in character when people fall for this type of "transparent manipulation" – most often they don´t even see it themselves, and I thus still sometimes deliberately start with the "good" and end with the "bad" partly because I like to "test" if the receiver is clever enough to see the bigger picture of what I´m communicating by at least also remembering what I first said, and partly as my own little uprising – freedom claiming – against bowing down for such a primitive smallminded "modus operandi". Again, as long as the communication is honest and respectful, it shouldn´t be *that* important how – and in which overall order – the communication plays out, but rather what all in all is being communicated.
Finally, in all fairness, right must of course be right – to make it clear, in spite of the message overall should be considerably more important than the delivery of it, then the best communication *of course* is a reasonable balance between the two, when they well-balanced comes together the message undoubtedly stand the strongest.
Not everything has to be as polished in vax, within sensible reason freely play to tha max, try make it a drama free zone and thus just freaking chillax, please.

4.3. You Shit What You Eat

...is true I guess, except for perhaps our last supper, but "you are what you eat", is the actual old saying I as a kid often was told when I e.g. preferably only would eat my chicken without touching the spinach also on my plate, despite the fairytales I was told about how the spinach supposedly would make me strong like Popeye – unlike me otherwise just being a chicken (bwok bwok bitch). And despite that of course being no more true than just being a way of trying to convince mini-me to eat my vegetables, then it actually anyway also *is* true depending on the concrete perspective and actual context. In line herewith, an ancient Kemetic[157] proverb goes: "*The body becomes what the foods are: As the spirit becomes what the thoughts are*".

Sure, the healthier you eat the stronger you become – physically *and* mentally, and in addition to food, then this figuratively speaking surely also apply to who and what we surround ourselves with and the activities we do, what we see, watch, read, hear, touch, and smell. Said in short, to already quickly sum up, the headline is a synonym to everything you stuff into yourself, your body, and everything you load your soul with, everything adds to and becomes part of who you from nature are born to be, part of your health, part of your mindset, your thoughts, words, and actions. And so, if you e.g. pour too much negativity down your throat, then the chances of you becoming a negative person are pretty equal to inescapable and inevitable, and if more negativity than you can actually swallow, then we more than likely at a minimum are talking a ticking just-a-matter-of-time-bomb. I thus now could remind you why and how it´s crucially important to counter negativity with positivity (and not because a positive here automatically nullifies a negative there – cause it most likely don´t), that positivity to your

[157] Ancient Egypt.

body works better than kale and beans (the presumably healthiest food on Earth), that it from any deep dark place figuratively can help lift you up out into the light like liquid hydrogen[158] does a rocket, and that thus probably also would be a somewhat pretty legit advise to give (although a rocket most often actually leaves the light – on earth – behind and flies out into the dark space of dark energy[159] and dark matter[160]), but then again, we both know that that in the current state of our world simply is too easy – so much easier said than done, and often even unrealistic. True is it that positivity can be the best medicine, that positivity probably can help create some counterbalance to the negative, that we should always chase and cherry to be as positive as possible, that positivity is transmittable, that we all prefer a positive setting and surrounding, and so on, and so on, but only as long as it´s sincere. Accept the existence of, deal with, and thus limit the currently unavoidable negativity, and in more than one sense eat well, encourage, embrace, and enjoy your positivity – without forcing it unnecessarily, don´t let it get out of hand, don´t push it too hard, you-me-we are "just" human, and no one likes a naïve always over-exited ass-jack anyway. Just because you – like everyone else – might not be super positive *all* of the time, just because you might not be satisfied, then it still doesn´t mean that you per se are or have to be negative. Room for improvement isn´t necessarily bad, and it´s also fine sometimes and sometimes for the best just to be.

You know the drill in a currently constant smell of challenge, for the best outcome see to secure a healthy well-balance.

And "*Before you diagnose yourself with depression or low self-esteem, first make sure that you are not, in fact, just surrounded by assholes*", as brilliantly spoken by Freud. And if no one else´s giving you pleasure (a.k.a. positivity), and since we´re now already in the

---

[158] The currently preferred type of rocket fuel.

[159] Roughly 68% of space.

[160] Roughly 27% of space.

neighborhood of Freud, then as merely an example take yet another "advice" from him on how to at least give yourself a quick fix: *"The only shame in masturbation is the shame of not doing it well"*.
The internet, a.k.a. online life, used to be a parallel world unfolding as an alternative to the "real world" of social contact and fresh air, in contrast to the now kinda reversed setting of today where the "real world" unfortunately increasingly more has status of being the alternative to the online life of the internet. In contrast to the initial intention with and purpose of the internet (after it being solely for military use) of bringing people closer together by creating and hence enhancing the communication between first scientists and then later also "normal" people – a worldwide easy accessible online motorway channel of communication, people of today paradoxically on many parameters seems further away from each other than ever before. The most popular use of the internet is – accurately enough in line with the original intention – online communication through e.g. e-mails, social media apps, etc., and in likewise paradoxical contrast to the obvious purpose of these communication tools, then they unluckily also has contributed heavily to the creation of a delusive superficial distorted and somewhat distanced perception of the truth of reality – don´t be fooled, from the distance behind the virtual curtains most merely share the "good", "cleaver", and "fun" stuff, from "their good angle" – the "glory" without the backside of the story.
In the spur of the moment, take e.g. the concept of branded products, how sad isn´t it that we as herd animals gladly pays absurd many times more for a merchandise exactly similar to "another product" – in both look and quality, just because it carry a certain brand of self-made cultural materialistic status. I admit, also I´ve been obsessed with brands myself – and partly still am although my criteria now more has changed (from almost purely name and look to now mainly quality and functionality), and I thus know and understand what´s at stake. But frankly, when I today see how

people are busy branding themselves via absurd expensive materialism – aiming to buy approval, then I can´t help but to think that there instead of the brand name or logo might as well could be written "please, I´m crazy insecure, I just so wish to be accepted, my originality is limited, and I´m thus "stupid" enough to pay absurd amounts of money for your patronaging favour". And yea yea, how we e.g. dress sure enough is our – attempt of – contribution to our current collective costume party, and no doubt it´s fine to keep our inner child alive by playfully dress up – that we should never be too grown-up to (to play), but if you know how it might be embarrassing to bump into someone wearing the exact same clothes as yourself (oh oh, confronted by lack of originality, and who wears it the best (some might would think)), then this kinda is how you-me-we look and embarrass (with pressure on the 'ass'-ending) ourselves when we either override our own originality or show off our lack of same and hence limited personality by stereotypical buying, wearing, and looking like "everyone" else in a jungle of opportunities (unless you literally have no choice, then you of course are all excused). Don´t get me wrong, I don´t really mind what other people wear – I support a free choice of wearing whichever clothes whoever wish, I´m just not convinced about the healthiness of the main motivation behind the need for buying recognition. Unlike what many tend to think, then it isn´t necessarily always the case that the most expensive or the marketed "most exclusive" brands also actually *is* the best – price and quality doesn´t always go hand in hand. However, again, related to priorities, no truths, only perspectives.
Take the example of travelling by plane, the "exclusive" expensive first-class tickets are always located up in the front section of the plane despite of the fact that it statistically has been proven that there in relation to a potential plane crash are a considerable bigger chance of surviving a crash if you sit down back in the hindmost seats of the plane. Sure, you might eat lobster and drink champagne up front, but when surrendering yourself to passively fly through

the sky at high speed in a tin can, is it then really worth it to pay that much extra for an increase of the probability of that meal perhaps being your last supper? – if I can say so without sounding too pessimistic (cause of course the statistical probability of dying in a plane crash still – until further – is considerably smaller than the chances of dying in a car crash, and all that, although self-driving cars before long also probably will the make road traffic deaths statistics to decrease drastically, and all that).
Anyway, in addition to thus damaged ties and a weakened contact with reality – the decreased physical social life and thereby physical social contact, recognition for who we *really* are – for being human – is thus decreasing. It´s in general often a taboo to be openly sincere about the struggles we all to a greater or lesser extend carry, and concurrently with us in a both emotional and physical sense as individuals being increasingly more distanced from both ourselves and each other (despite sharing an effort to live up to each other), then this naturally enough has contributed to the current results of a long list of serious consequential side effects as e.g. low self-worth and loneliness, and therefrom e.g. anxiety, and therefrom e.g. depression, etc., which all hence sadly currently are on an unprecedented increasing rise.
Never have we ever had more "access to other people´s lives", and still we´ve never been more on our own.
Sure, as I e.g. currently am living in another country than either my family or my fiancé, then I in lack of better of course am super happy to be living in a time where I´m able to still see and talk to people in real-time from far away, albeit still no purely visual and audio based interaction beats what analog physical contact can – personally for me most importantly e.g. hugs, kisses, and smell.
Nonetheless, as positive as physical contact can be as negative it unfortunately also can be – if your physical environment for one reason or another is unhealthy for you, and you – hands down – might have *your* reasons for preferring a technological "safe"

distance, and then peace be with it. But then again, the option of hiding behind a virtual distance can in itself e.g. also cause yourself to maintain and prevent yourself from breaking out and overcoming yourself, as well as it in other contexts also makes some – e.g. rabid fanatics and internet trolls – to come out of their closet to make any "safe distanced" online forum alternatively unhealthy anyway, and so on – one threat or fear (reasonable or not) might "just" prove to replace the other, cause, "*Every other city we go, every other video, no matter where I go, I see the same ho'*"[161].

Every human resilience has a limit and almost no interaction gives any guarantees, and hence in any case – all across all environmental settings, your relational "diet" and social intake is selectively important, not only for your personal digestion but also not least for whoever having to deal with your shit, as you shit what you eat.

Overestimate and underestimate, overreact and underreact,
overstimulate(d) and understimulate(d), to highlight a few.
Perfect uniqueness exists in imperfectness; only perfect balance is by definition perfect.
Balance is a bend, only to a certain extend.
In every intend, balance is legend.

---

[161] The chorus lyrics from the song 'All about you', by Snoop Dogg, Tupac, Nate Dog and Dru Down.

5. Love is God

Love is all is love is all is love... As mentioned near the end of chapter two, nature is everything, and since love in my terminology represents all feelings and actions and outcomes and everything else related to nature, then simply everything without any exception likewise one way or the other are connected to love – everything is created in the name of love, and everything we do we do out of love for something or someone. Together with nature, love is a force greater than anything else, it´s heaven, earth, and everything in between and above and beneath and around and beyond. And just as with altruism, or actually rather the exact opposite of the case with altruism, it´s rather impossible to come up with *anything* which isn´t attributable with love, either happy or unhappy love. Meaning, overall, love consist of two counterpart directions, "happy love" on the one side, and "unhappy love" on the other side, and unlike the classical adage phrase about 'a thin line between love and hate' – where hate "normally" is being perceived and referred to as the antonym of love, then hate still merely is a subcategory of love albeit though of the unhappy kind – hate is a word used to describe an unhappy backside of love – the probably most negative (a.k.a. unhappy) form of love, and in this context happy and unhappy love thus align well with the 'thin line between love and hate'-say as also happy and unhappy love on many parameters isn´t far from each other – in fact even connected, potentially closely connected; there´s a thin line between happy and unhappy love. For a clearer distinction, we e.g. can talk about happy love as infatuation, compassion, caring, etc., and unhappy love as e.g. hurt feelings, a broken heart, hate, and whatever else e.g. sadness or hate is given rise from and further rise to. Where e.g. attraction and caress to or of or from something or someone often is associated with happy love, then e.g. repulsion and rejection or assault often is an effect of or the reason to unhappy love.

Of course, all concrete perceptions of happy vs. unhappy isn´t universal, and concrete reasons for one or another can vary from situation to situation, from material to material, and from individual to individual, but surely everything still is either caused by or is associated with happy or unhappy love (or both across different implicated parties for that matter), in either larger or smaller scale, always as unique as every situation and every implicated party.
Not only does what we in general perceive as living creatures own and show love, e.g. the way the planets orbit their star – the gravitational force of attraction – is a kind of love, how atoms through electrons are attracted to each other is in the "rules of attraction" a kind of love, when the hetero south pole of a magnet shows love for exclusively the hetero north pole – and vice versa, and the poles hence simultaneously gives a "homophobic" rejection to their own kind of poles, then even this is an somewhat incomplete figurative example of how the backside of happy love from even good intentions e.g. can lead to an undesired rejection, and thereby also how unhappy love can arise and play out.
Love operates on both conscious and unconscious levels; hence, love isn´t a priori per se what we in general perceive to be a conscious size, nor a merely subconscious infatuation, and nor a purely unconscious size either – as also aspects of consciousness besides our basic awareness of love can be found all the way down to e.g. even an conscious openness for love, a conscious love for love, and in some cases by consciously opting in or out of love (even though that isn´t really a neither nor); love is always ubiquitously present one way or the other, in one shape or another – to some degree, love controls all, notwithstanding consciousness or not.
Even instincts can be attributed to love, cause despite instincts being an innate and inherited animal and plant and plant-animal mechanism which comes to show when e.g. animals behave in a certain non-taught but still very precise way, when e.g. a newly hatched turtle comes up out of the sand and immediately heads

towards and off to sea without ever been taught it to be their primary natural habitat, when birds constructs magnificent bird nests, when even orphan beavers build dams, when honey bees engineer surprisingly strong (construction-shape-wise) and perfect looking hexagonal honeycombs, or as most commonly associated with instinct, when predators showcase to possess a deeply rooted killer instinct, then I still would argue that the instinct at the very least are driven by a subconscious form of love to e.g. the feeling of water – for food in it to also swim in it, to nest and protecting ones offspring by building a safe haven home, to drink, to hunt, to bite, to taste – to spoil the taste buds, to store long lasting food for later enjoyment, to satisfy physical needs, to survive and live, and a love to life itself.

Unlike anything else, we create life in the name of love, are willing to risk our lives in the name of love, and are willing to take lives in the name of love. Love is thus a double edged – fluid binary-ish – force of both positive and negative aspects, a.k.a. happy and unhappy love.

When talking about love – both happy and unhappy – we´re not only talking about the direct thought or action, we´re also talking about the effect, and where happy love thus e.g. in one direction can lead to or is the positive action to the positive effect, then it also simultaneously unfortunately as a side effect in another direction can prove to be the direct cause for the consequential effect connected to unhappy love, and more rarely – but still not rare – vice versa.

Although love is bigger than anything we can ever exclusively own, then love is the ultimate strongest force we own, both – but not limited to – spiritually, personally, shared, and collectively, all in one of many shapes.

Love alone is *the* source with force to elicit our most extreme feelings, and as ambassadors in each end of love´s emotional spectrum e.g. can be found ‘extreme happy wine’ and ‘extreme

unhappy hate', both easily with an forcefulness to the psychotic. In this context, not only can happy love cause a mental inebriation, a.k.a. a wild party in mind and soul due to one or more happy circumstance(s), but also can one or more less good (or bad) circumstance(s) facilitate an awakening of the extremity connected to the "happy" features of love to unfold, as e.g. described in tales of how a parent with a child trapped under a car in the name of love – from a love elicited psychotic like source and a survival instinct (here through love projected onto the child) celebrating the love of life – find unprecedented physical strength enough to actually lift a – normally too heavy – car to save their child, a strength they without a trigger to the extremity of love otherwise never would´ve had access to. And this by the way goes across most breeds, I e.g. recently saw how a mother hen with no hesitation beat up an freaking eagle to protect her small chicken offspring.
Likewise, in the same kinda sense, a – for one – happy circumstance of e.g. finding a romantic partner (a.k.a. love (a.k.a. happy love)) can trigger to elicit what "normally" is associated with a psychosis guided by the unhappy side of love within another, which e.g. describes why the most frequent motive for murder globally is jealousy (no joke that approximately 12 percent of all homicides has a jealousy related motive – a feature sometimes triggered by what evolved from the happy side but obviously became "only" *one* of many features belonging to the unhappy side of love), and hence why more than half of all homicides with female victims is being committed by either their partner or ex. The extreme feelings of joy and irrational behavior we from a happy place might feel when falling in love kinda paradoxically but still very naturally share the same source as the unhappy feelings that made many lose control and e.g. commit irrational murders – two sides of "the same" strong love.
With that said, it´s of course important to stress out that not all become murderers "just" because they experience the unhappy

side of love, luckily “only” relatively few takes it that far; most manage to fight through their heartache and non-violently overcome it, learn from it, and experience how also time shows the mercy of love.

If “only” more would understand what interpersonal love really means, e.g. to be willing to sacrifice and compromise and give as much of yourself as possible – without losing yourself (if you´re supposed to live on that is (which hopefully you are)) – for who and what you truly love, and to set who you love free according to the best of *their* wishes and needs, to allow them to be all they can be. Cause, if you truly love someone, then – besides from not losing yourself – the most important for you thus should be to see the one(s) you love as well and as happy as possible with or without you, even if you might find it hard to accept and respect their wishes. And in this equation, whoever truly loves *you* should be adjusted to do the exact same the other way around. And if you don´t love them enough to do that, then they shouldn´t even be that big of a trigger anyway. And no, there´s no room for excuses a la “but my love is too great to set them free”, in that case it rather becomes a question of you either not understanding true love, of you being insufficient within yourself, or you might simply loving your own ego too much for your own good, notwithstanding all of which *you* need to work with instead of projecting your personal issues on to and blaming others; *"Try not to confuse ‘attachment’ with ‘love’. Attachment is about fear and dependency, and has more to do with love of self than love of another. Love without attachment is the purest love because it isn´t about what others can give you because you´re empty. It is about what you can give others because you´re already full"*[162].

---

[162] A quote by the American educator and motivational speaker, Yasmin Mogahed (1980-).

Full or not, work with yourself to build or regain or maintain yourself, to thereby achieve or achieve to hold on to having control of yourself and the love you carry.
Yea, some might disrespect your love and take advantage of your love, etc., but do they then deserve the full capacity of your love? Following a hard break up with an unfaithful ex, a friend of mine once gave me the exact advice I in that very moment needed, "Fuck it, Bisse, [move] on!".
You need to love yourself before you can love others – is a sentence often said, and although it logically is correct, then the common perception of that sentence isn´t really. Conscious alive, you cannot really avoid to love yourself, the question "only" is if it´s happy or unhappy love we´re talking about, and where on the fluid "love-scale" your love lays. Sure, you need to have surplus of one or the other within yourself to be able to give to others, and to be in touch with the love you carry to give love, but again, unless you´re sleeping, braindead, or dead, then this paradoxically in my choice of words is a no brainer, whether you like it or not it doesn´t matter, either happy or unhappy love – or somewhere in between (as with quantum physics nothing is ever a flat zero) – is unavoidable de facto here and in there somewhere. It´s possible to feel unhappy love within yourself while still externally giving happy love, and vice versa, yet don´t underestimate the power of a sincere happy-happy – which is worth striving for.
Love can grow and shrink – depending on how and how much we feed and see to take care of it; in line with the balance chapter, not too much not too little, as a plant being watered too much or too little – it can drown or dry out. Balance is important, it´s a shared – still mainly your – responsibility; your happiness is an internal matter, you can find external trigger points (some can bring out the best of you and some the worst), but you cannot expect to find *your* happiness outside of yourself.

As stated, love is all is love, and hence love undoubtedly must be the closest we – at least until further – can possibly get (Ed. are) to a force equal to something seriously godlike, and thereby something (a deity) really worthy of the term of God. Further, not only does I believe in love, we should all be able to agree that love exist – we verifiable know that it does, and this without comparison at a level way beyond any of us, and for that reason alone, I can´t really call myself an atheist; I believe in love.

Basically, the notion of love also broadly is what religions has been launched to market, and the success of religion must be ascribed to how religion with shrewd reason understood the need of wrapping "love and hate" in nicely in embodiment and embodied fairytales which thereby makes it easier for people to be able to relate to, bite the hook, and buy-in on the more abstract aspects of the matter, for people to be involved, persuaded, and spellbound. Religion use love, hate, and sin to describe happy- and unhappy love, and misuse of same, and the reward and punishment – the maintenance and retention – of people´s thoughts and actions related to good vs. evil is instead of karma and both good and negative consequences in our real lives´ shared reality tied up on the illusionary but still provenly effective fairytale of heaven and hell – which partly in sense of their meaning actually *do* exist albeit not directly in the religious stated sense, not in the clouds or in the underground, and not in a different universe or dimension, but many places all around right here on Earth and in the visible universe of ours (and beyond), where both extreme pleasure and enjoyment, and suffering and pain plenty takes place, for some more than for others – more or less deserved (equity is not – yet – given), through the consequences you-me-we-that-this-and-they through both happy and unhappy love sends out and receives, and in the consciousness of your-mine-our minds.

In spite of love being the root cause to every bad thing happening in the world, e.g. wars and catastrophizes in the name of love for oil

and hence money and power (and *many* other "things"), then love also unquestionably is the solution to everything, including e.g. securing peace in the world. Like the American musician, Jimi Hendrix (1942-1970), smoothly expressed it: *"When the power of love overcomes the love of power, the world will know peace"*.
As promised in a prior chapter (Moral is King), to elaborate on universal moral being non-existing: In a world with nearly eight billion subjects "plus the loose", hard to imagine that such a large group of autonomous individuals in praxis should ever be able to agree completely on anything which depends on and is divided by subjective perspectives, although we in theory have the potential. But what we nonetheless can´t deny and thus indisputably shouldn´t be able to disagree on is the universality of love. Not that we all always feel and show the exact same comparisons and bend variations of love (on the "love scale" (in between happy and unhappy love)), or the same amount of love (a.k.a. e.g. the same degree of emotions, etc.), but as we all – unlike the case with moral – are of and know and carry love, as love is ubiquitous and thereby impossible to deny and avoid, then I can´t really come up with anything as largely universal as the existence of love.
In Denmark, we have an expression called 'næstekærlighed', which directly translated comes to be 'next-love', which in its meaning e.g. is synonym with what in religion is expressed as "*Thou shalt love thy neighbor as thyself*" [163] . However, in English the word of 'næstekærlighed' is translated to be 'the ethical demand', which in my optic is a sadly distorted and slapdash "piece of work" (Ed. translation) (and you´re welcome to feel the same about my translation ('next-love') if that makes you feel any better). Cause, true is it that ethics (and moral) also is a part of love, but when e.g. translating the influential piece of writing by the Danish Theologian and Philosopher, K. E. Løgstrup (1905-1981), from the original title

[163] The Gospel of Matthew (22:37-39).

of 'Den Etiske Fordring' (in Danish) to 'The Ethical Demand', and then further also use 'the ethical demand' as the translation of 'næstekærlighed' (a key-concept he in his book thus argue is distinct from (Ed. prior to) ethics), then you´re "in my book" unfortunately inappropriately over-simplifying and mixing up and missing out on important distinctions; find a better translated expression suitable for 'næstekærlighed', or in lack of better accept and make use of my direct translation, 'next-love'. Løgstrup argues that next-love overrules ethics and moral, and that ethics and moral isn´t really "good" as they prescribe a lack of next-love which is prior to any ethics and moral. But then again, partly opposed to Løgstrup, it should immediately likewise be legit to argue that ethics and moral might as well could be prior to next-love. Ethics and moral is (an) important ingredient(s) in next-love, and next-love is an important headline of ethics and moral – no ethics and moral without love, and no next-love without ethics and moral, and by discussing if next-love is before ethics and moral or if it´s the other way around, then we simply seem to be back to "the chicken and the egg", the hermeneutic circle, und alles, and fundamentally they´re anyway both basically "just" – important – parts of – happy – love.
Universal moral might not exist, but if we according to our potential universally can ensure the best possible conditions for basic inner happy love – the potential is "just" the nuts that you-me-we have to crack, we surely can and we should, and therefrom create a universal understanding of and execute (a.k.a. give effect to, and not as in "put to sleep" (as this word inconveniently also means)) next-love ("love others as you love yourself"), then universal next-love anyway will make ethics and thereby also moral – as independent universal phenomena – superfluous, moral would thus automatically – against our presumption anyway – follow the universality of and implicitly become universal as part of universal next-love, and I thus in this context anyway could be forced to admit that it after all *do* make sense and is entitled to state and stand firm

on next-love as being prior to – the then anyway implicit universal – moral.
Similarly, as likewise promised in the same prior chapter (Moral is King), to expand on why logos "just" is a subpart of love. In somewhat line with Løgstrup´s view of next-love prior to ethics, I believe that love is prior to nature, that love played a part in the creation of nature. The only "thing" that overall might somewhat as a singularity goes before love, and everything else for that matter, is the potential – including the potential of love, but then again, as everything in theory is created by love – from e.g. at least a love of creating, then it´s also not to exclude that even the potential might was created from love, or that they interim co-dependent helped create each other. The truth is that we don´t know what was before the 'Big Bang'[164], and thus the matter – until further – is tied up on guess work and believe based on observations, mathematical formulas and models, as well as not least on reason and logic – often based on philosophic theory. Without knowing if nature actually already was before or "only" later came as a consequence of 'Big Bang', then nature surely is up there among the absolute first of anything and everything – at least in a physical sense of our sphere of today. But still I believe, that nature (and thereby logos) at max comes in third after the potential and love, and since love as the only of the first two goes further and thus beyond of being "only" preliminary (as the potential always continue to be), then again also therefore, if any, love must take the prize as the pinnacle to deity, a.k.a. God.

[164] The genesis of the universe as we – think – we know it; the theory is that approximately 13,7-8 billion years ago, from a single point, the universe began to expand and stretch and grow as large as it is right now, and it´s until further still vastly expanding.

5.2. Equality vs. Equity

Now we briefly jump straight into a stereotyped dialog, or discussion if you will, between six people sitting around a table – any table of your own choice.
The six people are:

1. An agnostic radical feminist named Esther.
2. A black supremacist named Ebony.
3. A white supremacist named Dick.
4. An Islamic extremist named Abdullah.
5. An ultra-orthodox Jew named Noach.
6. An Asian named Ho.

As we join, the conversation has just begun:

Esther: *...No no no no NO! Like, you men have always been first at everything – at least that's what you men like to think, so I think it´s time that I as a woman now gets to have the word for once!*
Ebony: *You tell ´em girl!*
Abdullah: *Quiet women!*
Ebony: *I beg your pardon! If you don´t chill the fuck up, and show us females some God damn respect, Abdullah – or whatever the fuck else you're a-rab terrorist name is, Imma break my foot so far up your sandy ass that...*
Esther: *...I refuse to sit and listen to a man talking to women like that... Like, how dare you, Abdullah, and sorry for interrupting, Ebony, to demean us women like that, just because of your own manly insecurity...!*
Abdullah: *...No woman...!*
Esther: *...Like, how you treat women in the Middle East is a disgrace! Stoning women for adultery when they in fact merely are*

the victims of rape carried out by primitive men who clearly have a problem with their animus...

Abdullah: *...My anus...!?*

Esther: *...Your a-ni-mus, the man's feminine side, your feminine side...*

Abdullah: *...Are you calling me feminine...!?*

Esther: *...Seems you're suppressing women in your effort to suppress your animus, like with homophobes, they like often struggle to suppress their own homosexuality...*

Abdullah: *...Enough! Don´t you dare to compare me to the dirty haram of homosexuals; they have no place on Earth and should be stoned...*

Ebony: *...The honorable Elijah Muhammad...*

Dick: *...Let me ask you this, Ab-Mullah, how can you defend terror-attacks killing innocent people, women and children...?*

Abdullah: *...How can you defend how the west treat and kill innocent Muslim people?*

Dick: *...I asked you first...*

Abdullah: *...No one is innocent, those people have voted for those politicians who kill us, and all kafir who won´t surrender themselves to Allah the almighty has to die as the Quran in verse 9:5 clearly says that...*

Dick: *...And there you have it, that´s partly why I´ll never allow for Arabistani people to come and infect my country with their jungle lifestyle, raping and murdering our women, and...*

Esther: *...Women is not your possession, Dick...*

Ebony: *...And you better get into your pale peckerwood potato head, Dick, that it´s not your country! You whites...*

Dick: *...Whaaatever, but tell me then, Esther, what is exactly your problem, other than not being able to handle a real man...?*

Esther: *...Typical you men to be so one-dimensional, and screw your patriarchal heteronormativity! Like, just because I unlike you am not sleeping with my cousin back at the trailer park...*

Dick: *...Allegedly sleeping with my cousin...*
Abdullah: *...And then what´s the problem, my first wife is my cousin, my parents are cousins, and my grandparents was cousins, cousins marrying each other is perfectly fine and normal, and I´m not in any way inbreed...*
Ebony: *...Haha, I´m sorry honey, but that sounds to me like the very essence of inbreed right there for you...*
Dick: *...But then what, feminism is about gender equality or...?*
Esther: *...Like, yes, but like not just, like, the world has now been dominated by men for like thousands of years, and it´s therefore only rightfully fair if we women like now gets to enjoy some of the same privileges as you men has always had. So like, the goal as a start for example is that only women should be allowed to lead for the next thousands of years just like men now has done it – like in the past and still do. Like, only women should like be allowed to hold office, only women should like be allowed to hold important positions in business, only women should like be allowed to do what we want while the men then stays at home, like, this to thereby restore the balance in this male dominated patriarchal world which we women simply has had enough of. We women want our say, and we want to be taken seriously. Like, you men always had unfair privileges compared to women, and your words as a man shouldn´t matter anymore...*
Ebony: *...Yea, and you as a privileged white man absolutely has no say anymore!*
Ebony points at Dick.
Dick: *How´s that a privilege, to have no saying?*
Esther: *Like historically privileged, Dick! And like, don´t try to convince me that men no longer...*
Abdullah: *...Allah created men and female after his choosing, and he did not ask for our permission for whether or not we want to be male or female...*

Dick: *...So, do you then also want to transport white people around in boats, in chains, whipping and killing them, and then now have them work the cotton fields, to...*
Noach: *...And are you then suggesting that we Jews should now execute six million Germans in the gas chambers, and...*
Dick: *...To "restore balance" in the world, or...*
Esther: *...Like me and my black sister here is trying to get in to your thick sculps, we´re like fed up with your demeaning of women, demeaning of blacks, and...*
Ebony: *...Look, snowflake, you and I are not sisters, just because you might joined the march to polish your social media halo then we definitely don´t need you pale skin folks to also gentrify our fight – the 'protest etiquette for white folks' was made for a reason you know, this is our fight, so please, just back the fuck up a bit...!*
Esther: *...Wow, like, calm down, like, no need to...*
Ebony: *...Don´t tell me to calm down, and don´t try to project that angry black woman bullshit on me, aright snow white...*
Esther: *...But like, I´m not white, I´m actually of Latin heritage...*
Ebony: *...I don´t care what you are, one thing is the cultural appropriation where you all want a piece of our jazz, blues, Motown, and rap, but no more – enough is enough, just back the fuck up...!*
Dick: *...But isn´t that discrimination towards me as a man, and racism against me as white? Like with your BET* (Black Entertainment TV) *channels and all, imagine if we made a WET* (white entertainment tv) *channel for whites only – that isn´t even legal, trust me we´ve tried, so who is in fact racist and privileged here? I mean, not my fault that I was born in a superior body, both gender and color-wise...*
Ebony: *Oh please, shut the fuck up with that dickscrimination-shit. The whole tv and movie industry is made by whites for whites, and...*

Dick: *...That´s funny you mention it, cause just the other day I just so happened to read that almost 40% of the leading actors in movies is of color, and last I checked blacks only constitute 13% of the population. So, don´t you think that you have more than a fair share? And guess that all those movie related issue is something you have to take up with the Zionistic kike-rat over there...*
Dick points at Noach.
Noach: *...I beg your pardon...*
Ebony: *...Wow, Dick, you can read, let´s all give the Dick a round of applause... ...The fact of the matter is that whites has enslaved and oppressed my black brothers and sisters for generations, and you motherfuckers still do! You white people don´t know how it still is to be black, how it is to be pulled over by the cops for being black, how it is to be stopped and beaten by the po-lice on lame accusations of jaywalking just for walking the street and minding our own god damn business; because we – as the motherfucking five-0 usually say – "fit the description"...*
Dick: *...Funny again, cause also just the other day I heard some of your own black rappers saying something else, and that even the Black Lives Matters movement is bullshit...*
Ebony: *...Fuck them house-n**** (N-word) coconut motherfuckers...! Then how you gonna explain that the best known sort of bird in the hood are the ghetto bird helicopters flying around and...*
Abdullah: *...I can relate to that, although our "birds" mostly are devil-drones armed with bombs; I´ve lost many brothers and sisters from those coward weapons. What kind of weapons are those "bird" helicopters armed with?*
Ebony: *No, they´re not armed like that, but...*
Abdullah: *...Then what is the problem about them, what do they do?*
Ebony: *Well, they´re spying on us as a mean to keep us down in the mud...*

Abdullah: *...Like to help with intel as a preparation for others to take you out...?*
Ebony: *...Like sup-po-sed-ly helping the po-lice solve crimes, so they say... But anyway, that´s not the issue here... The problem is po-lice bru-ta-li-ty, that black people statistically far more than white folks are being beaten and killed by the po-lice, that black people still to this day earn less money than other races, and...*
Dick: *...Well, that may be because of the way you people behave, like wild animals, and because you´re too damn lazy to actually make an honest day´s work...*
Ebony: *...How the fuck are we supposed to work when nobody wants to hire us only because of the color of our skin!? And what the fuck you mean by 'you people'?*
Dick: *I mean what I say, 'you people'...*
Dick points at ebony.
Dick: *...N***** (the N-word)...*
Dick points at Muhammad.
Dick: *...Sand-n***** (the N-word)...*
Dick points at Noach.
Dick: *...Jew-rats...*
Dick points at Esther.
Dick: *...Queefing pea rollin´ concrete dykes...*
Ebony: *...Oh no you didn´t, ah ah, hell no! You racist white devil kkk nazi motherfu...!*
Abdullah: *...You will burn in hell, kafir, you and all alkafron will burn in hell, inshallah!*
Esther: *...You just like proved my point of why we women is fed up with chicken brained men like you! We women luckily have absolutely no need of anything that you men has to offer, Dick...*
Dick: *...Aaand this here is why it´s my human right to carry my gun around, to protect myself and my family from dirty filthy disgusting animals like all of you... - people.*

Noach: *Tell me, goy, what do you really have against us Jews, what did we Jews ever do to you that can justify the anger you have towards us?*
Dick: *First of all I´m not your guy, and second of all it has to do with the way you Jews cunningly control the world, how you control the media, business, showbiz, how all the politicians are in your pockets, and how you control the entire economy... You´re controlling and ruining everything from the shadows of your big noses. You´re by far the greatest danger to the world, in your hands the future is darker than behind a n*****´s (an N-word´s) ball sack, and...*
Abdullah: *...And wallahi you Jewish dogs are the real terrorists, you oppress, terrorize, and kill innocent Muslim people – women and children, and you steal Muslim land. Your apartheid toward Muslims is only possible because of the united devils of America and grim Britain is protecting you...* (Abdullah aggressively pretend to spit) *...You´re not even worth the dirt under my shoes...*
Dick: *...Your sandals you mean...*
Abdullah: *Shut up, kafir...! As I was saying, there´s no real different between the holocaust you Jews cry so much about and how you now treat decent Muslim people...*
Dick: *...Although a decent Muslim is yet to be seen... You camel riding idiots even ridiculously believe in 72 virgin sex slaves with big boobs waiting for you after death as a martyr-reward for blowing yourself up and killing innocent good Aryan people – seriously one of the stupidest things I´ve ever heard...! And by the way, holocaust is a straight up lie. True that Jews were put in camps to limit their undermining of the German people, but still to this day there are no clear evidence of the holocaust ever really taking place. History is always told by the victor...*
Noach: *...Unbelievable how you defy the clear evidence of the holocaust, and how can the death of 6 million Jews ever be considered a victory? Still to this day antisemitism is rising*

everywhere, and still almost everywhere many are out to kill us Jews...

Abdullah: *...Inshallah!*

Noach: *...And therefore we have to do everything we can to protect ourselves...*

Dick: *...Oh yea, and that´s why you´re circumcising your own baby boys – cutting of a healthy piece of a baby´s most sacred body part, to protect them...?*

Noach: *No, we do that because God tells us to...*

Dick: *...Oh yea, wonder what other voices your twisted mind then might be hearing as well, you sick sly rat bastard...*

Abdullah: *...Listen you dirty kafir dog, circumcision it´s a matter of hygiene, a matter of preventing infections and diseases under the skin to...*

Esther: *...Listen to yourself, women are like being suppressed all over the world, and yet again you men like only aim your focus on boys... Like, what about the problems of women and small girls being circumcised, like, what about we talk about that for a change...? Like, what about you, Ho, what do you have say about all this...?*

Ho is sitting sleeping.

Esther: *Ho?*

Ho: *...Zzz...*

Ebony: *Ho, wake your flat dim sum ass up!*

Ho wakes up.

Ho: *Are we finished; can I go back to work now?*

Esther: *No, Ho, not yet, we´d like to hear what you have to add to the male chauvinism we´re witnessing here?*

Ho: *Hihi... I don´t know... Hihi...*

Esther: *Like, how can you as a woman not have an opinion about this...!?*

Ebony: *Yea, come on, Ho, speak up...*

Ho: *Hihi... Hello kitty... Hihi...*

Ebony: *O-K...?*
Esther: *Ho, like, do you want to be a part of this or...!?*
Ho: *Stop nagging at me, okay! I don´t know, okay! Just hurry up and finish so I can get back to work, okay...!*
Esther: *But Ho, you´re a free woman...*
Ho gets up from her seat, and leaves...
Ebony: *At then least one bat-flu less up in here...*
Esther: *Nice job guys, like real nice job of you yet again not including the women, like nice job of you not making Ho feel welcome because you´re soo busy measuring your obviously small wieners like the testosterone dominated cavemen you are...! See what you now did, like really nice job of you making her leave...!*
Noach: *What I was trying to say was that we Jews have to do what we have do to protect ourselves from the Islamic terrorists – their rockets and suicide bombings, and...*
Abdullah: *...Alhamdulillah, you Zionist occupying dogs only get what you deserve, inshallah...*
Noach: *...and it´s not their land – it not your land* (Noach briefly looks at Abdullah), *we´re with our settlements only taking back what rightfully is ours, and has been so for thousands of years...*
Dick: *...In my opinion, and not that I care about what´s going on in the Middle East, you can simply just go kill each other for all I care – that way you´re only doing the rest of us a favor, but the wog is right* (Dick briefly pointed at Abdullah), *you diaphragm head wearing Jews are a bunch of sneaking imperialists who doesn´t quit your crusade until your curly ponytail sideburns and devil stared flag flutters in the wind all over, unless...*
Noach: *...For your information, our skullcap is called a kippah – or yarmulke in Yiddish, and what you call long sideburns we call payos, and while the satanic circle you talk about is an only five-pointed star, the Star of David is six-pointed. At least get your facts straight before running your mouth... Then let me ask you this, do you vow for Jesus?*

Dick: *Absolutely, although I believe that religion is a system for slaves, then yes, I still wish for a Christian society, and then yes, I of course vow for Jesus. At least more than I...*
Noach: *...And since Jesus according to Mark 6:15, Matt 21:11 is Jewish, then even also you vow for a Jew...*
Dick: *...The hell I am, Jesus was a white Christian...!*
Ebony: *...Ex-cuse me! Jesus was black!*
Esther: *...Enough with your religious BS, like, I don´t understand why you just can´t understand that that whole Jesus-thing clearly is a man-made hoax that...!*
Abdullah: *...None of you know anything about religion, there´s only one true god, and Muhammad is his prophet. Allahu Akbar...!*
Esther suddenly takes off her top and is now sitting bare chested. The rest of the table surprised looks at her.
Esther: *What!? Will you please stop staring at me...*
Ebony: *...Oh-my-God, are you for real...?*
Esther: *Like, this is my body, and I can do with it exactly as I want, and just because I´m topless then it´s like still no excuse for you filthy men to be looking at my body with like dirty eyes and dribble running from your mouths, like I´m some cheap piece of meat...*
Dick: *...Trust me I ain´t, I´m just surprised of how much hair is sticking out from under your arms...*
Abdullah: *...And I´m surprised of how much shame you as a woman bring on your family with this haram, if you were my family, wallah, I here and now would...*
Noach: *...And to me this is an example of how to be a living degradation of what you as a woman proclaim you fight to defend...*
Esther: *...To your knowledge I don´t exactly consider my gender to be only 'woman', and I like could say the same as well to all of you guys...*
Dick: *...And so could I...*
Ebony: *...Exactly my words...*

Abdullah: *...Alhamdulillah...*

And here is thus where we leave the table.

Honestly, I´ve been wrestling with myself about how to approach this subchapter without stepping on anyone´s toes in these toxic times of wokeness aggrieved culture extreme. We of course always should strive to meet others with dignity, but we also have to be very wary that our ability – and human right – to express ourselves doesn´t drown in infinite perfidious demands of cancel culture and political correctness. I finally stuck to my original plan of approaching it in a slightly David Hume (1711-1776) inspired "unorthodox" way, as a kind of a tragic-comic sketch with a serious message, a burlesque parody in caricature strongly inspired by reality, as the perspective views, articulation, and language used are borrowed from authentic narratives. However, no matter what you say and what you do there´ll in current times – as earlier stated – always be some arch-nemesis somewhere "out there" who disagrees, and thus someone who´ll be aggravated offended although – the authentic pendants to – the portraited "cast" of this monolog – without realizing and embracing it – crisscrossing proves to have more similarities than differences.
Further, I cannot accept to let myself be censored and thereby quieted by anyone´s potential opposition on that account, which furthermore also would be quite contradictory to much of the overall message in this book. Freedom of speech is of course not to be juxtaposed with a duty to speak, and pointless provocations are merely pointless for anything and anyone else than the bad vibes within the provocateur, but we´re definitely not solving anything of anything if we with fear of contact show reluctance of openly addressing the problematic issues we face – notwithstanding controversiality.

I´m very much aware that this sketch-piece projects highly sensitive, stigmatized, and infected topics and stereotypes, but also that it luckily doesn´t represent the majority, and so chill, it isn´t aimed directly at you, unless you by *your* behavior feel merited, to which the question hence becomes if it´s you or me who actually have the biggest problem now since we thereby would be part each other's problems? I´d say that being a central player of the problem is worse than highlighting and aiming to fix the problem, even if you might find it problematic to be confronted with the problem you thus after all – at least partly – carry the solving keys to.
In – almost – any case, read my lips, to bury all doubt, I mean *no* disrespect; I´ve no intentions of pouring unnecessary oil to any fire, and hence forgive me if I ignited any unjustified negative kinda flame in you; I definitely didn´t act out of spite, it´s merely to explicit some of the somewhat dominating "outer poles" of our society which we´re dealing with – even are up against – in the fluctuating crossfire the majority of us are caught in, in our pursuit of solvingly overcome to reach reconciliation and compassionate unity.
Of course, there are idiots among all ethnicities, in all cultures, and in all larger groups, but instead of being one of the idiots by taking your hatred out on entire groups of people, then we *have* to deal with and treat each individual and individual incident individually. Across all ethnicities and cultures, we´re all one race, humans, and we all accordingly have a shared responsibility for each and every other in the name of love and thereof humanity, notwithstanding whatever genes and chromosomes we´re born with, how and what we perceive and consider ourselves to be, and what geographical coordinates our heritage descent from. The tribe-like "us and them mentality" among humans is human made, and people has to understand that there no more than 'you and the rest' basically is no us and them, only you-me-we. Every splinter of discrimination, racism, and non-diverse thinking is human made, and someone carry the responsibility for creating and placing that splinter in the

mind of the child or the fellow human being, don't be that person, be the one who educate on love instead. Don't create poison, don't pour poison for drinks, don't be poisoned.
We´re on this planet together and we have to make it work together, no matter our differences. Therefore, chill on the excluding group identity, and cut the crappy tribe-war, we have to get up out of the trenches to turn the battlefield into a harmonic place of peace.
Fair enough, we cannot deny that human physical appearance variate – especially across different geographical heritages, and scientific studies quite clearly conclude that Asians on average are shorter and more intelligent than other ethnic groups, that west Africans e.g. "are born with more toned abs" (at least are more muscular) and that they together with some south American countries on average have the biggest dicks on the globe, that east Africans by a better absorption of oxygen in the blood on average has a stronger cardio, and that people in Europe on average are taller. It´s e.g. in sports pretty obvious that darker colored people dominates the running disciplines (on average more explosive muscle mass in west African heritage which is an advantage for the shorter and faster distances, while the bodies are better build for the longer distances in east Africa (no joke that the 28 quickest and 94 out of 100 quickest marathon times of all times are sat by east Africans – or descendants thereof)), whereas Caucasians e.g. – until further – seems to dominate swimming (perhaps because they according to studies store more fat and thereby have better buoyancy), etc. Of course, it some of the way presumably has to do with human made culture, but it also cannot completely be excluded that natural evolutionary and hence genetic drift related differences plays a part.
Some, maybe you, might perceive what I just said (Ed. wrote) as nothing but pure bullshit, and in case that´s the case then kindly allow me to supplement my statements with a little extra somethin´ science: We, homo sapiens (a.k.a. humans), share DNA with all living

organisms (a.k.a. life) on earth, we e.g. share between 25-50%[165] of our DNA with trees, up to 97% of our DNA with orangutans, up to 98% with gorillas, and up to an astonishing 99% with chimpanzees, which is our closest relative in the animal kingdom. However, when it comes to humans, then all humans from all over the Earth share an incredible 99,9% of the same DNA. The human variations in e.g. skin, hair, eye colors and shapes, and more, is a natural evolutionary result of how awesome capable also we humans genetically are to adapt and adjust ourselves to e.g. different climates, different modus operandi, etc. As an example, the sun´s ultraviolet radiation (UV) generously provides us with essential D-vitamins when the sunrays hit our skin, and the closer we get to equator the more UV we´re exposed to. If we get too little UV, we come to lack the important D-vitamins in our body, and if we get too much UV then it´ll brake down our body´s folates which importantly is connected to our blood, cells, and DNA. Science has shown that we all – homo sapiens (and thereby all humans) – descent from Africa, more precisely southern Africa, where homo sapiens is believed to have been created approximately 200.000-300.000 years ago. Then later, "only" 90.000-100.000 years ago, humans started to walk out of Africa, and step by step spread themselves all over most of our planet. The further from equator the humans settled the less UV they were exposed to, and brilliant as the human body is the skin adaptively changed according to the UV-exposure – or lack of same – thus to adjust for the perfect balanced intake of D-vitamins. Ergo, those humans closer to equator (or descending from areas closer to equator) has darker skin, and those further from equator developed lighter skin. Same mechanisms of mutation can e.g. in relation to especially north-east Asian or Inuit (Greenland) characteristics – e.g. the shape of their monolid slimmer almond shaped eye openings – be explained by the ice ages they´ve been through, where their

[165] Depending on the source – some say around 25% and some say around 50%.

evolutionary eye – opening – shape helped protect their eyes from the cold, and "sun-reflection" on the snow (to e.g. help limit "snow-blindness"). And thus, these "minor" evolutionary and genetic drift related differences of the presented examples hence shows what the last 0,1% of our DNA among others accounts for. With that said, all serious and recognized science clearly, evidently and unambiguously states, that it´s pointless to argue for the existence of different human races, a.k.a. different human races simply doesn´t exist. When talking about different physiological features among humans, then it rather are matters of gradual transitions between different populations, and a pattern of variability which best can be described as clines. And in a globalized world, it should only be a matter of time before these clines through e.g. globalized reproduction (i.e. evolution) "melts" together and thus "equalizes" themselves.

Personally, I e.g. have five different hair colors in my beard of which each color tells a story of my diverse heritage, my forefathers (and mothers), at least four of the colors do while the fifth (some say grey, I prefer silver) tells that I've lived. Further, I recently had a DNA-test made to schmooze my immediate curiosity of "seeing my ethnicity", and the test hence gave me different percentages of different geographical regions without ever explaining anything about how far back the validity of the test goes. Meaning, I know that my Danish origin goes back as far as people has been registered in Denmark – my uncle as a hobby do genealogy and I from him have a copy of my family tree, but still, the DNA test suggested several other regions in north and western Europe, and a single percent in eastern Europe, which thus must be "a picture" from before people was registered – which at least dates back to several hundreds of years ago. But then again, why provide a test that goes an sketchy undescribed and incomplete period of time back, and why should my ethnical history stop at exactly those reported regions when "we know" that my heritage has walked and lived many more places on their way up from Africa – throwback to before pale skin and blue eyes was first evolutionarily introduced, why not then just go all the way back to where we all in a way can say that we – as science shows – historically descend from Africa? Cause, even though that immediately might sound to entail some quite identical tests, then if possible, the differences would lay in how cool it would be to track our ancestor´s emigrating routes; guess we don´t yet have the sufficient technology available to do exactly "just" that right in from the street, and guess that my test at least gives a clue about my ancestors mainly coming up through western Europe, but anyway, the point of the matter nevertheless still is that if you as Caucasian, or Asian, or any other current ethnicity, e.g. have a problem with people merely because of them wearing a darker skin color than your own, then you thereby automatically also have a problem with your very own heritage.

Hence, what we´re really discussing and are aiming to solve in relation to racial issues is de facto the advanced and super cool adaptive features of our bodies and cultural differences, a shitty history, and despite plenty of knowledge still existing racist problems caused by anyone who for some fucked up reason still in their damaged messed up mind find it necessary and appropriate to judge people only based on their genomes, a.k.a. the genetic physical features people without self-determination thus innocently are born with. And thus, racists literally should go fuck themselves in the empty cavity they must have where the brain they don´t have was supposed to be. Alternatively, they should wake the fuck up, and work on recovering from their retardedness – and seek help if they can´t do it on their own (although they probably are the last to realize that they need help, which is also why it generally is a good idea for most to simply talk with an impartial counselor once in a while, for if nothing else, then at least as part of personal

development[166]), and generally "just" start learning how to respect other people for who they are instead of hating on ´em for what only a retard´s twisted prejudice distortedly see, or don´t see. We need to address and deal with each and every racist incident immediately thus that it doesn´t grow, like prompt telling an indoor pissing dog off thus to leave no doubt within it of what it did wrong. Since there aren´t different human races, the existence of racism logically makes no sense – it simply shouldn´t exist.
I know what statistics on e.g. crime says, that descendants of immigrants (from mainly the Middle East and north Africa) in Denmark on average is twice as criminal as the Danes, that blacks in the United Kingdom on average is three times as criminal as the white population, and that blacks accounted for 55,9% of all homicide offenders in the United States (2019) despite only accounting for 14% of the total population, etc., and guess the

[166] Most people would most certainly benefit from consulting a psych-professional once in a while. The days where it was a taboo to talk to a professional are over – and have been for quite a while, and everybody who still thinks otherwise sadly are too stupid to understand the vital importance of mental health and self-development, and hence literally too stupid for their own good. To these stupid people, if you e.g. break your arm then what do you do? – you see a doctor to have the injured arm fixed. If you need to develop your skills beyond your own abilities then what do you do? – you e.g. consult a trainer, coach or teacher (or a psych-professional) to help you improve. So why wouldn´t you consult a psychologist or a psychiatrist or a psychotherapist or any other kind of psych-professional if you experience mental issues or "just" to improve on your mental development? And no, don´t let flawed prejudices deceive you to believe that truly professional psych-professionals only are out to play evil mind-tricks on you – such tricksters are e.g. called clairvoyants, hypnotists or plain and simply frauds, as their "magical superpowers" likely are synonymous with an illusion.
And remember, a psych-professional can supply you some tools for you to work with, but only you can do the work. If you really are too ignorant to follow the logic here, then you in this context actually should be first in line to seek counseling, since you thus clearly need it more than most.

numbers ain´t lying, but then again, there´s always a reason, always, factual history don´t lie, and neither victimization mentality or racism is the solution.

"But it´s so easy for you to say, you with your white privileges, you don´t understand how we still to this day are being targeted, abused, pulled over, held up, discriminated, and so on", many non-Caucasians probably would argue in my direction, while some far-out Caucasians probably in the context of my words will perceive me as a traitor "to my own". Well, to these critics, fuck off and fuck you to, if only you knew what I´ve witnessed and been through, e.g. the amount of times I have been mistaken for being an immigrant in "my own country" – probably due to my dark eyebrows and big nose. Many of my closest homies from growing up has roots as refugees from war-troubled countries in both the Middle East, Eastern Europe, South-East Asia, and Africa, and I thus from already a young age learned what effects such environments and refugee immigration and obtuse racism have on people. Add to that, that I´ve been living in the hot-spot heart of an extremely trigger-happy "racial" gang war myself. When my friends and I e.g. were out shopping, we often had what we came to call our personal shopper (e.g. some mall cops – a.k.a. shop security guards) following us around simply because we time after time purely based on physical appearance (mainly ethnicity) had been profiled as bad news. When we went out clubbing the "brown eyed and black haired" of our crew almost every time everywhere were denied entrance only due to ethnic profiling. We (yea, including me) were subjects to both verbal racism and racist rooted hate-crime, especially from bouncers and police, and despite definitely not wanting to promote violence, then I in all honesty still more than once fought in the streets for my crew (a.k.a. set, a.k.a. firm, a.k.a. gang (if that´s what you roll with)) – also – when it came to physical fights emanated from racist issues. As a quick personal example, e.g. at a time where I as a teenager was quite tanned, I completely unprovoked were

beaten by a police officer armed with a big heavy metal Maglite (flashlights) while in the same séance – directly translated – being called a 'shitty guest worker' (in Danish terminology equal to 'fucking immigrant'), and experienced how they tried to frame me on some car-theft accusations which I had absolutely nothing to do with. Further, I´ve also experienced how others in e.g. sports wouldn´t pass me the ball simply because I was the only Caucasian guy on the field – how they explicitly among each other e.g. said "don´t pass the ball to the white potato", and whatnot worse, and only after firmly standing my ground, Viking style, I finally was fully accepted. Furthermore, with too many experiences to mention, during my travels to "more exotic" parts of the world I´ve likewise many times experienced to be heavily discriminated for no other reason than my genetics, again only because of my skin, eye, and hair color – which I likewise every time refuse(d) to accept.
I´m not victimizing myself here, just giving a teaser of where I come from – should you still be in doubt.
Growing up with blue eyes in environments dominated by also brown eyes (at least in many of the streets I came up) doesn´t mean that I´ve been overly privileged, in many ways I like many others partly came up through the gutter, I was a part of the landscape in the officially announced so called ghettos, and since my early childhood I´ve known more about racism, discrimination, and all sorts of abuse than most. In my home growing up we literally didn´t have much of much, and thus my privileges wasn´t what you´d think unless you think that my parents did the very best they knew and could, and that I thus never doubted their love, and that my dad taught me about charm and to be street-wise and made me a man, and that he no doubt would go to war for me (even if he screams at me that I´m a loser, and a fuckup, a despite loving me still can break my face), and that I from good reasons with all my heart respect my mom for how she always put my brother and me first, and always

unstoppable fought to provide for us with the little she had besides her paramount heart.
No matter what you might think of me, don´t doubt me or state or even think that I don´t understand or haven't fought against the backside of life – which would be a very wrong perception, only a fool not knowing would ever fool themselves as such that much. I´ve long time ago had more than a fair share of it all, literally, and It provokes me – I actually don´t accept it – that I all my life and still to this day is being confronted by other people´s need for me to defend and justify myself simply because of *their* small-minded ignorance and color and culture based prejudice, fuck that, no one is allowed to deprive me of my right to opinions, I live here to and I have enough evidence – I(´ve) witness(ed) and experience(d) and feel shit as well, and as said that more than most, and thus don´t think that you know me enough to judge me or have any say on my right to think, feel, mean and express myself; only censorship of censorship; never *fucking* judge a dog only by its collar, never *fucking* judge a book only by its cover, never *fucking* judge *anyone* by color, never *fucking* judge *anyone* or *anything* you don´t know or don´t understand or both.
Just the other day, I was hanging out with one of my homegirls who with her partly African (half Danish and half Tanzanian) roots naturally is – beautifully – brown skinned, and she passionate – and upset – told me that it to her is a *huge* provocation when e.g. white folks in regard to racism says that they´re "colorblind", as that it in her eyes is a straight up lie when they pretend not to see her brownness, unless they in fact really are blind. I replied her that I see her literal point, but that I at the same time wonder why she choose to receive and perceive a positive message with negativity? – as I´m sure that "being colorblind" is a well-meant attempt to reach out; Of course, no reason to act like uncle Tom, but also no reason to feel threatened by or directly attack a waving white flag. Like, if we e.g. take the model of perceiving every single negative

perception and action related to skin color as being racism, then what if I experience someone to accuse me of racism by saying that I only said or did as I did because of the fact that the other person had a different skin color than myself, and I cross my heart not at all care about skin color, then the question instead become if that someone thus only accuse me of racism because of my skin color – now since that someone literally obviously wouldn´t have accused me of racism had I had the same skin color that person, and who is thus in fact the actual racist here? Don´t let the victim-zeal lead you into depravity, the hunt for enemies can quickly make yourself your own worst prey. Race issues are definitely not being solved from a double moral standard, rather the opposite, and fighting segregating hate with segregating hate is merely as contradictory as fucking to regain virginity. Cause yea, I e.g. of course have noticed that some of my Danish homies has blonde hair and blue eyes, and yea, I have noticed that my homies with Middle Eastern, South American, Asian, or African genetics primarily has dark hair and brown eyes, and yea, that she, my homegirl, has darker skin than I have, but honestly, skin, hair and eye colors makes absolutely no whatsoever difference to me, as long as they´re good people, and as long as we kick it together, then I couldn´t care less about anything else – I with no further ado roll with them, why also I in that sense perceive myself to be colorblind; *"yea yea, but it´s different with you, you´re cool and all, I´m only talking about all the other whiteys"*, I then hear, but then what about my family, or my other loved ones which you might not know, why are they in advance from a prejudice distance not perceived cool enough to think, say and be as respected as me? Why are my family – in your eyes – not allowed to have opinions? Seriously, "just" quit dividing and hating on other people based on such silly reasons as color or non-calamity culture, no aber dabei, that´s it. And if you as a grownup on the other hand without a solid excuse (e.g. brain damage, Tourette syndrome, etc.) are being racist or discriminate

around me, then I ain´t fucking with you – I´m fucking you up, *if* you reject to better yourself that is.
Why give a fuck how you-me-we look when all you-me-we really should care about is how you-me-we behave, what values you-me-we cherish, and how much compassion and moral composure you-me-we show, short said, how you-me-we conduct and carry ourselves – our character; recognize or be gone.
The end of racism doesn´t "go both ways", cause in saying so we´re merely focusing on an isolated dispute between only two – falsely dominant – ethnicities. Instead, we have to include into the equation that there´re numerous of ethnicities and mixes of same among almost 8 billion humans on earth, and in accordance they-you-me-we all has to be considered equals. No ethnicity are legitimated to exercise racism against any other ethnicity – or even "their own" for that matter, and therefore we, more than making it to be a two way discussion, have to put an end to racism in all directions, in any form, shape and color, and between everybody of all ethnicities.
I agree that the history of colonization, slaves, genocide, and wars, is horrific beyond words, but still it doesn´t help the prospects of a better future to continuously keep a claim alive of hate created by and rooted in historical events factually based on the beauty of nature and misinterpretations of same. In doing so, we´re more than anything preventing to ever settle in peace and harmony. E.g. imagine if all countries and ethnicities whom formerly was under the control of the roman empire still today hated all Italians because of the killings, slavery, and oppression which took place between our forefathers (and mothers). Imagine if big parts of Eastern Europe, and most of the Middle East and Asia, still today hated all Mongols because of Genghis Khan´s Mongolian empire. Or imagine, from a Danish perspective, if Brits today hated Danish people because of the killings, slavery, and oppression which our Viking-forefathers exposed and made the Brits' forefathers (and mothers)

subject to. Or imagine, from a more recent part of history, if Danes today hated Germans because of the killings, occupation, and oppression, which the Danes was subject to by the Nazis during the Second World War. My grandparents were subjects to the Nazis´ horror, and I´ve been told plenty of stories about how horrific it was, but still I – and Danes in general – don´t hate the Germans today. Imagine if Jews today hated the Germans because of the holocaust, which besides being among the most horrific acts in history likewise took place in quite recent history – also during the Second World War. Still today, there´re Jews alive who was there and luckily survived the German death camps, and this without these Jews being known for having a present-day vendetta exclusively targeted towards Germans.

Racism and discrimination is a primitive way of thinking reserved for only the stupid, and equally primitive and stupid are patriarchalism and misogyny, radical feminism and misandry, homo- and xenophobia, and oppression in general, cause at the beginning of the day, during the day, and at end of the day, no matter ethnicity, sexuality, religiosity [167], or any of our physical characteristics, features, and attributes, or whatever else that characterize us as us, we´re – as already said – all "just" human beings, we all have equal rights to the – non-destructive – life we choose, and with risk of giving it an inbreeding sound we´re all simply Earthlings from the presumably exact same source of life.

Yes, from nature I have got an X *and* an Y chromosome, and yes I have a dick, and yes I don´t consider myself to be any other gender than a man, and yes, I´m quite light skin, and yes despite considering

---

[167] Despite me challenging religion, then freedom of religion is important – everyone has to be free to believe in, "*form and join religious communities, as long as they do not impinge on "good morals* [...] *Religious observance or race does not affect people's civic and political rights and duties*" (Constitution of Denmark).

myself straight then I fuck exactly who *I* feel like fucking, and yes a ladyboy wouldn´t be my first, and yes I say what I feel and do as I say, and yes this is just a drop in the ocean of me, and yes if you ever in any way dare to judge me negatively on any of these facts alone, then you´re not a notch better than any other racist, discriminator, oppressor, and whatnot.

In general, we all have a shared responsibility to say no to racism and discrimination and oppression and inequality, a shared responsibility to stand up against racism and discrimination and oppression and inequality, and hence a shared responsibility to put an end to racism and discrimination and oppression and inequality. No matter how we look and what culture we´re a part of, then we all as far as possible has to be considered equals – we´re all entitled to benefit from, have and enjoy the same human rights, the same right to think, feel, mean and express ourselves, and whoever trying to tell or force upon us anything else sadly are part of *the* very problems we face in overcoming and solving the issues connected to racism and discrimination and oppression and inequality.

Yet, some discrimination and inequality we probably can´t avoid, and thus probably somewhat have to settle with – dirty hands or not, depending on how you look at it. We all presumably have some kind of preferences when it e.g. comes to choosing a sex partner, some are turned on by one personality and others another, some goes for skinny some for chubby, some prefer blonde hair, some black or brown hair, some prefer a hairy body while others are disgusted by hair, some are spellbound by one smell while others might prefer a different scent, and so on. This we can view as one of our contributions to natural selection. Of course, personality hopefully matter the most but even the best personality sometimes aren't enough if you e.g. find your dick fecklessly limb or your pussy always dessert dry and thus sealed when it comes to your otherwise potential partner. We all discriminate in that sense, not because we necessarily wish to discriminate anyone, but because our personal preferences e.g. are a part of our sexuality, which likewise – as also e.g. our personalities – are a mix of both genetics and social influence, to which the social influence – however wrong it might be – e.g. (as earlier mentioned) can be seen in how we in general tend to follow e.g. female sex-symbol trends and fashion, from e.g. housewife material and childbearing coke glass bottle bodies up through the 1950s, 60s, and 70s, to super skinny so called supermodels in the 1980s, 90s, and 00s, to then in recent years mostly being about hardcore sex and "big twerking bubble butts". Some might say that sexual preferences has nothing to do with discrimination – and inequality, and I almost am willing to agree, but if a less attractive person e.g. don't get any sex because he or her constantly are being discarded in favor of a more attractive person, then I'm sure that the less attractive person anyway will feel a bit discriminated rooted in his or hers look. Thus, I'm not saying that anyone deliberately with bad intentions are discriminating anyone they don't want to have sex with, but the mechanisms of discrimination – and inequality – surely are present when one is chosen over another based on e.g. physical features. However, because you love one it doesn't by definition mean that you thus per se have to hate anyone else (as also stated earlier), and that's where the mechanisms goes wrong in regard to racism. Ergo, fair enough that one prefers or loves one or some or something particular – you're of course allowed to e.g. be more attracted to one skin, hair or eye color, or a specific culture more than another, etc., but that´s no incentive excuse to hate – on – all other or even another.

Also, when talking about overall equality then you cannot just pick to only want "the good stuff", and not "the less good". Briefly exclusively to the women here, if you support equality between sexes (which I for the record quite do), then what about e.g. bench press at the police academy, where guys have a considerably higher minimum weight than girls to bench to be accepted at the academy

despite guys and girls having to go do the exact same job as police officers, is the guy – who might couldn´t bench the guy´s requirements but still with ease benched the women´s requirements – becoming a less good cop than the women who benched no more than him but still was accepted only because of them having two X chromosomes instead of an X and a Y Chromosome? And what might the women say to forward-looking having to say goodbye to the ”noble” aspect of ”women and children first” whenever it otherwise would serve them with advantage? Or what about in relation to the military, in many countries men experience compulsory military service, how does the women feel about that duty becoming unisex? And no, just for the record, I never applied for the police academy, thus no personal narratives here, and I personally even question why *anyone* – no matter gender – should ever be forced to join the military instead of leaving it entirely up to the individual to develop and become precisely the person they with their freedom in hand wish to be.
Equality among genders likewise has to go all ways (where it makes sense), and thereupon I´m with general glasses only wondering why discrimination in some areas still not only is being accepted but directly is being imposed, and the imposition accepted, and why gambling with anyone´s life against their own will still at all collectively is being practiced – unless it comes down to a situation where the same lives directly and unavoidably is at stake and it thereby anyway is a "everything to win and nothing to lose" kind of shitty situation, which hence on the other hand would be a cause that you-me-we anyway voluntarily should be ready to fight all in for.
Yes, there undeniably naturally genetically on average also are certain differences between sexes, e.g. physical strength, and this aspect thus logically has entailed some of the dividing gender roles which I´ve just mentioned, and we historically e.g. have seen how men had the main of responsibility of building houses, hunt meat,

and farm, while women kept houses, picked berries, and took care of the kids while the men were out providing, etc. And the historic fact that primarily men outwardly held "the throne of power" thus somewhat also "fine" made sense in a setting where power above all was based on physical strength – although the power of the pussy (another type of – womanly – "physical" strength (with spellbinding power to mens mental weakness within)) probably likewise always played a bigger part than we tend to include on the matter (guess the world would´ve looked quite different without all the "bedroom meetings" (and here I´m not only referring to the act of reproduction) most couples throughout history intimately have held). Women e.g. had huge – if not the most – power in the Scandinavian Viking societies back when the Vikings ruled.
However, in our current long-term era based on above all brain power, the lines between sexes more or less seems to have been effaced – no one needs to arm-wrestle when they can just press a soft button or pull a trigger; genders are no longer just given but are freely up for grabs, and more than ever before different genders – should on many parameters – have equal rights, possibilities, and thus options in life, apart from the combination of an X- and a Y-chromosome (men) still not being able to give birth – that´s still reserved for two X-chromosomes (women) and certain lab-facilities to pull off.
Despite only ten countries in the world offering 99,9% (100% hardly ever exist) equal rights between sexes[168], then overall (apart from certain totalitarian places that inexcusable shamefully lack seriously behind on all or almost all human rights), the possible equality between sexes *and* genders just about seems to have been secured, at least the transition to utmost equalization is well on the way, and I´m confident that most of what´s left by generational shifts will catch up, although radical feminism and other extreme factions of

[168] Belgium, Canada, Denmark, France, Iceland, Ireland, Latvia, Luxembourg, Portugal and Sweden.

extremists probably disagree and never will get to know, recognize and acknowledge satisfaction. Not saying we´re completely "there" yet, but the catalyzing wheels of motion *are* rolling.
Howbeit, without neglecting any oppression – especially oppression of women (which in some cultures surely is a huge problem), a more serious current problem than what radical feminism tries to portray, is people on the run from war and poverty. Not long ago, I (and everyone else who were aware) e.g. witnessed how waves of refugees came walking up the European motorways, men, women, and children, desperately trying to escape the horror of e.g. war in Syria and Yemen, Deash in Iraq, and the Taliban in Afghanistan. They were with shaking legs struggling to carry themselves, each other and all of their few belongings – including undernourished bodies and PTSD, on their way to an uncertain future in unfriendly territory of rocking ground. Similar horrible problems – or worse (if that´s even possible) – is e.g. seen with cases where desperate migrants drown trying to cross the waters to the "promised land" (in the very moment I now write this, I on the side read a breaking news article about 43 people (including three babies) who drowned earlier today when their boat tipped over in the ocean between Morocco and the Canary Islands, R.I.P. – R.I.P. to all unfairly dying too early), and e.g. with women and children currently on the run from Putin´s tsar dreams in Ukraine (which "luckily" shows how we also should(´ve) treat(ed) the refugees from the south as well) while their men are forced to stay and fight, and northbound at the US-Mexican border, several places in Africa – currently especially with refugees from the chaos in South Sudan, in Asia with refugees from Myanmar mainly trying to escape the ethnic violence in the country, and in south America with refugees from the currently chaotic Venezuela, "just" to mention some of vastly many tragic current refugee situations – without forgetting how many people around the globe also e.g. are suffering from famine, and "nightmare-ish" etc. Add to that that many people in poverty by their "own leadership" even are held

hostage in their "own" – dysfunctional – countries, here without mentioning names in e.g. east Asia, eastern Europe, south and central America, a list of countries in Africa, and not least in the Middle East (currently more than 750 million people are in a situation where they would migrate if they could[169]).
According to current standards, a relatively few countries cannot provide shelter for the massive masses of migrants without breaking down, and they shouldn´t have to – no arm should have to break in order for the other arm to heal, no one should have to level dangerously down for others to level up, notwithstanding guilt issues. We all of course first and foremost have to help where we can – especially take responsibility in relation to the mess we directly helped create ourselves, both internally (e.g. human decay (e.g. PTSD)) and externally (*all* the destruction conflict and war can bring about of both human, materialistic and economic damage), but we basically above all have to somehow change and improve the situations that created and creates the problem(s) (leading to human tragedy and hence e.g. waves of migration) in the first place, we have to put an end to conflict and war happening in the name of anything else than humanity – not allow a few individuals to attack, starve, oppress and exploit anyone and everyone else, not here, not there, not anywhere, equal life quality for all. Together we have to become a planet where we humans more than anything only travel for the climate we prefer, the cultures we wish to visit, etc., where forcible migration for survival or the prospect of a better life becomes an obsolete relic from the past, where we all travel domestic wherever we on Earth go.
Nevertheless, no universal equality without equity – equity is the basis for equal opportunities, and thereby equality as it should be interpreted. An example of how a picture can say more than 1000 words on the matter:

[169] According to Gallup (a global company specialized in analytical statistics).

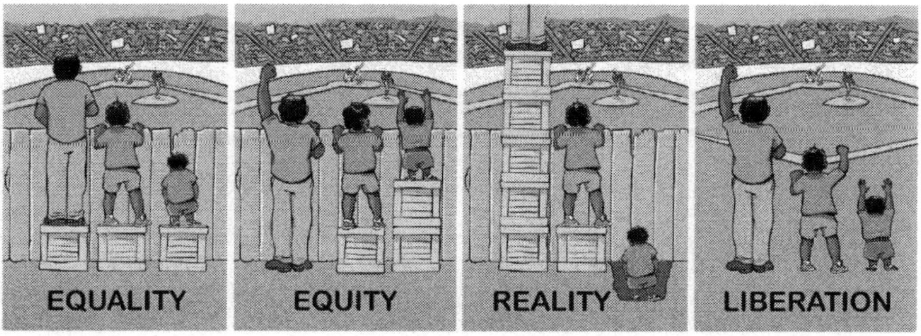

A collaboration between Center for Story-based strategy & Interactive Institute for Social Change & myself.

This picture clearly should exemplify why equity in relation to equality until liberation is king and key to blast reality of today, and why those who are fortunate enough to have in abundance across the board at least from a moral perspective should be willing to contribute to those of less fortune in need, practically, financially, as well as not least emotionally. The more fortune you have and are the more you´ve to contribute, and this thus also explains why it´s essential that rich and not least wealthy people – according to our current system – e.g. for now *have* to pay a higher tax percentage – the higher the earnings the higher the percentage (which in any case still means more to you-me-we – the fortunate still have more than whoever of less fortune, the less fortunate hence has more than they otherwise could ever have, and the sum of what and who we collectively are has more to offer and give back to each and every one of us from which we hence all will be able to receive more of more than what was given in the first place)[170]. And if anyone in relation to the picture e.g. now are thinking something ala "the people in the picture should just stop bootlegging, just go get a job, and just go buy a ticket to the actual stadium stands", or similar shit, then you just totally miss the point and need to be told – to eliminate any doubt – that you too full of yourself hands down simply are a horrible person.

Many strongly advocate for through and through – from start to finish – equality without e.g. being communists, although that in stringent term of theory basically per se is the very essence of e.g. communism, that everyone from bottom up and from top to bottom are entitled to the exact same. We don´t need communism – just ask just about everyone who ever had or have it, and I´m sure most agree, it never worked in praxis as in theory suggested. Rather, we´re entitled to different entitlements as a way to achieve 'same'; we´re all different and experience and face different situations, and hence often only by treating everyone differently we thus can treat everyone equally. We overall have to have basic equality based on equity to secure equal possibilities and thus options of success in life, and it thus currently mostly is about securing a procure of the

---

[170] the economic growth has for the top one percent over the last 30 years gone up by 21 trillion dollars in the US alone, while the "wealth" of the average people has dropped 900 billion dollars in the same period of time. What would happen if raising all salaries? – inflation, and the number of jobs would go down, "they" say. Then what would happen if we raised the taxes for only the top one percent highest earners, the shepherds, they would take it out on their sheep, "they" fear. Then what if we raise the corporate taxes, again mainly targeting the highest earners – the more profit you make the higher the taxes, and this with serious penalties if companies try to cheat themselves out of it – we´ll get back to that. Then growth would slow down "they" say. No, the highest earners would still have considerably bigger economical muscles, why it in our current system still – economically – would pay off to work harder or have exclusive skills, and if people on average are paid more, then they also can afford to spend more, and thereby they'll (Ed. we'll) continuously secure jobs.

establishment of the prerequisites for equity, to then later being able to skim off the top of utmost equality.
If we, the people, understood the magnitude of the power we truly hold and have, if and thus when we join forces, then we could easily put end to the unethical inequality that are taking place in the world, where the rich are getting richer while "the rest" are getting poorer – where the gap between rich and poorer exponentially is getting bigger[171]. We – as earlier said – plundering over-exploit our planet in the name of growth for the never ending greedy sake of growth while infinite growth logically simply isn´t possible on an finite planet, and we mainly do this just so that the top one percent can prosper by getting richer while "the rest" are getting poorer. *"If a monkey hoarded more bananas than it could eat, while most other monkeys starved, scientists would study that monkey to figure out what the heck was wrong with it. When humans do it, we put them on the cover of Forbes"*.[172] Seriously, *wake-the-fuck-up*. If you don't pull your shit together and help fix this permeated ill system then nobody's fixing it; you-me-we need to fix it, starting by you. And don't believe any neo-liberalistic economists who sophistically tries to convince you otherwise, cause they sure as hell will say and do *everything* within *their* power to keep you and whoever else down to secure a continuing expansion of the exponential top one percent profit and themselves a decadent lifestyle, and they´re getting away with it by a laughable "prospect" of an extra "gingersnap" (a.k.a. literal fortune cookie) *perhaps* falling off the wagon to their following stragglers – who smug think they´ve 'jus primae noctis' (a.k.a. prima nocta) while in fact above all just being easy honey (Ed. money) trapped asse(t)s; your plutocracy[173] up my ass.

---

[171] Aside from a basic awareness as e.g. seen by the Gini Index (the Gini Coefficients all around the globe).
[172] Quote by Nathalie Robin Justice. And Forbes is a magazine promoting the richest and – according to them – most powerful individuals.
[173] Government by the wealthiest.

Instead of moguls, big companies and corporations now only seeing people as consumers that´ll make them rich, then for the future the companies and corporations will have to see people as people, as the consuming people that´ll ensure a great cashflow, to which some of the profit goes to the companies' production costs, while a larger percentage of the profit goes back to the people through corporate taxes. And no, this doesn´t entail the retail price to go up for the consumers, this mean less profit and smaller bonusses – or no bonusses at all – to and within the companies and corporations. Logically, and even backed up by science, cooperation and reciprocity among us, the people, clearly is the current number one superpower in the world if we want it to be - both in terms of labor and thus also economy, we carry the key to just about everything we can imagine, including innovation for the better. We can implement and exert equity and end inequality when we want, we can insist that the greedy sociopaths at the top of the economical pyramid share their wealth to benefit all stakeholders, a.k.a. all of us, and further we can secure growth and improvements on soo many levels beyond the now economic growth for merely the beneficial sake of few, e.g. regarding health, sustainability, education, infrastructure, and not least humanistic happy love, short said, we can make changes that matter for the better in almost each and every area we wish. Nothing of what we here are talking about is in any way predeterminate like e.g. the laws of physics, etc., instead it´s all related to us taking a – kinda spiritual – stance, ergo making a conscious compassionate choice, and from there on carry out our actions accordingly.

Love is in us, we are love,
Love lives in between us, and vice versa,
Love is all around us, and vice versa,
Love is everywhere, be aware, and care,
Love is all is love, cold and hot, love own the pod,
Not that odd, that love is God.

Epilogue, part 1: The Third Pill 2.0

Take a deep breath, this chapter will be long and... – different.
Today, life naturally can be viewed as a competition in which the one who is born with a silver spoon up the ass, or finds or hunt food the best, has an advantage to eat better (stone age perspective). However, it from modern days here on out of course doesn´t have to be like that – it´s even an insult to our overall potential.
You can choose to believe that humans are irreversible destructive, which then would mean that we all one way or the other are doomed – which even very well might be true, and that thus also clearly would explain why you might already have given up.
Of course, the probability of you alone being able to change the world over night isn´t that big, but you can always work with and improve yourself, and since you hermeneutically are a particular individual part of the whole – ergo the world around you, then you thereby also automatically change our world concurrently with you changing yourself. The more individual parts you by example affect to the better – the more improving seeds you mentally plant within others, the more seeds others will be able to plant, and the more the world exponentially will improve. Same naturally can be said about negativity, why it likewise is super important that you to overcome your adversities as far as possible work and deal with whatever negativity troubling you to thereby being able to focus on and become and spread positivity.
The negativity you hold and send out works like kryptonite both inside yourself and on your external peers and other receivers, just as other people´s negativity also – most often – works as kryptonite both inside themselves and from externally on to internally in you. Ergo, you hold, release, and sends out one portion of negativity and receives two – the one you put on yourself and the one your external others send back your way. Though, imagine if you instead dealt with your shit, and made your negativity become positivity,

not only would you contribute with positivity as a help for others to overcome their shit, but eventually you-me-we would all receive two portions of positivity and hardly any negativity; what's not to like? That's the "law" of karma – cause and effect (in plural a.k.a. causal network (a.k.a. Bayesian network)), what you cause creates an effect accordingly, and then accordingly, and then accordingly, as long as the energy goes; you are and deserve to receive what you hold and sends out, every day you earn your karma – notwithstanding it´s a beauty or a bitch, and every day you earn the answers you need to breath for as long as you breath. As Rumi expresses it: *"This world is the mountain, and our action the shout: the echo of the shouts comes (back) to us"*. To maximize the positive potential you as a first step need to wake the fuck up – every day for as long as you live, and deal with whatever shit blocking your-mine-our view, the shit that as far as humanly possible should´ve been dealt with before you went to bed – to both sleep and wake up with peace in mind; *"Happiness is when going to sleep is no longer a means of escape"*[174]; ought to be logic for battery hens, if only it was.

In this context I´ll quickly pass on a small story: A psychologist walked around on a stage while teaching in front of an auditorium filled with students. As the psychologist raised a glass of water, everyone expected they´d be asked the typical 'glass half empty or glass half full' question. Instead, the psychologist asked, *"How heavy is this glass of water I´m holding?"* The students shouted answers ranging from eight ounces to a couple of pounds. The psychologist replied: *"From my current perspective, the absolute weight of this glass doesn´t matter. It all depends on how long I hold it. If I hold it for a minute, it´s fairly light. If I hold it for an hour, the weight might make my arm ache. If I hold for a day, my arm will cramp, turn numb, and feel paralyzed. In each case, the actual*

[174] The original author is unknown everywhere I´ve searched.

weight doesn´t change, but the longer I hold it the heavier it becomes. It´s important to remember to put down the glass"[175]. Your struggles is like the glass of water, carry them for a short time and you´ll might be fine, carry them a bit longer and the weight of them might start to become heavy, but if you ignore and fail to deal with whatever troubling you, then it in the end can have fatal consequences for both yourself and yours, and thus with retrograding force prevent a healthy growth of ditto – only the opposite.

We can by example help each other to understand – or at least in tough times to remember – this concept, but you´ll have to want it to get it. Of course, there´s a difference between potential and capacity, and although we haven't directly shown our full capacity to fulfill our potential[176] – just yet, then we surely have all the potential we need, and we need to believe it to realize and see it, we need to dig deeper to understand it, and we need to act on it to harvest what we otherwise waste; law of attraction.

By the custom of constantly wavering ourselves, we – have – become a streamlined, impersonal, and virtually programmed living-dead herd of sheeple who doesn´t *really* grow – at least not significantly. In line with the essence of the word, though here with an ambiguous twist, innovation is far from streamline – almost exclusively reserved for the shepherds, and everything that our lives long ago should contain of freedom and personal development and growth in some sense seems passé. Personally, I´d literally rather be excluded from the herd, even rather die, than to live my entire life

---

[175] The original author is unknown everywhere I´ve searched, and I´ve taken my freedom to refine the story a bit.

[176] In my optic, we humans are an incredible ambivalent size, on one side I´m super excited about our design and our amazing potential, and on the other side I´m deeply disappointed in humanity, how we waste our potential and sadly often find ourselves to occupy the steps of bad and worse on the "fulfillment of potential scale" – too often from bad back to worse.

under someone else´s command, and easy rather settle for less money and prestige, than allow myself to be someone else´s bitch, at least this way I still have all the power I need – the power of myself, at least this way I keep my autonomy and self-respect intact. Although money is good to have, they should never be the decisive factor worth more than your life and limited time, and prestige is merely an unhealthy compensation for your own lack of self-worth, an unhealthy factor of measurement connected to how you allow other people to judge you, how people judge each other, which further is rooted in how the same people also judge or from megalomania glorify themselves, and thus also furthermore where the unhealthy egos likewise are created. Hence, if other people judge you negatively, then why would their unhealthy ego-based opinion be worth anything anyway, compared to the value of your life and limited time. Inspired by words from Marsellus Wallace, the top-dog character in one of my all-time favorite movies, Pulp Fiction (1994): Don´t allow for the mechanisms of prestige to fuck with you; *fuck* prestige! Prestige only hurts, it never helps, you fight through that shit. Cause some time from now, when you unconcerned about other people´s prejudices are kicking it with peace in mind, you gonna say to yourself, that book, a.k.a. this book, was right.

Do you remember what nine out of ten says on their deathbed, and who do you think that the one in ten are the shepherds who had their sheeple working for them, or the sheeple who spend their entire life and limited time working to please their shepherds – who spend (Ed. waste) their life and limited time being someone else´s bitch? Don´t disrespect your intelligence, and *don´t* disrespect your self-respect.

As of now, we live in a world where I seriously consider if I even wish to bring children into this mayhem, with all the shit that´s going on, all the craziness of evil. Not sure I´m willing to expose my child(ren) to the sickness of today. But then again, without wishing to put pressure on my unborn offspring, someone *has* to secure a brighter and hence better future – as e.g. a much needed counterpart to how the capitalistic right wing on behalf of humanity currently is on a kamikaze suicide mission, not a "noble taking their own life" kind of mission, but rather a 'Jonestown[177]' "we kill you all and *then* ourselves" kind of mission. And no, just because the bastards like "a good captain" also are about to go down with the mothership, our shared body, humanity, Earth, it still doesn´t make any of what they do and stand for to be anywhere near noble. What´s the point of flying first class on a Kafkaesque crashing plane if first class itself alone is what bounds the plane to go down; it just stands out as what it truly is, a suicide mission driven by greed and selfishness, crumbled with a plethora of stupidity, madness, and a naïve conceited believe in immortality. And opposed to tip-top, this is only the top-tip of the iceberg.

"Thanks" to the farcical state of affairs which the world´s different forms of government have shown over the years, and still continuously to the worse are practicing, I honestly don´t really have much faith in any of them. On paper, the thought of power to the individual(s) through a democratic process – a.k.a. democracy – of course in theory seems quite beautiful, and in lack of better it probably also is the most adequate form of government we collectively so far have managed to implement. However, from what I´ve seen and until further, my believe in democracy operates at just about the same level as my believe in peer pressure, which pretty much is equal to fuck all; it bugs me that two wrong votes weigh heavier than one right vote, even if you´re right it still doesn´t give you the right to be right if two others decide to be wrong. I personally cannot agree to accept a stupid decision made by a

---

[177] An American cult society, Peoples Temple´s Agricultural Project, founded by the cult leader, Jim Jones (1931-1978), in which all the members – most probably by force – in 1978 committed suicide. Their "city" in the jungle Guyana (South America) was named Jonestown, and the "mass-killing" incident is often referred to as the biggest mass-suicide in "modern" history.

stupid majority if I de facto know that they´re wrong, fuck that, and if that means that I´m not a democrat so be it.

In this context, take e.g. the example of when Muhammad Ali refused to follow the democracy-issued orders of going to Vietnam to participate Vietnam War (notwithstanding if he was to fight or promote), and instead chose to stay true to his moral values and hence his moral conscience. At first, he immediately broadly was stamped a traitor of his country and the democracy which his country claims to represent, but in the long run, when the war was lost, the soldiers who had followed orders and fought (and wasn´t among the 1,35+ million people who were killed in the war), wounded returned to disgrace. And while the very same democracy turned their backs on "their" wounded soldiers, then Muhammad Ali could pride himself of rising to become a legendary global icon.

A similar example revolves around the case with the American helicopter pilot, Hugh Thompson (1943-2006), who likewise during the Vietnam war witnessed a genocide massacre carried out by "his own troops"; he presumably saved upward 20.000 innocent lives by landing his chopper in between the local Vietnamese victims and the trigger-happy American troops; with his weapons pointed at the Americans he gave them an ultimatum of stop killing or he would open fire. Thompson was charged with treason, called a rat and a traitor, and he became a suffering outcast for 30 years, until he finally received recognition and was seen a hero who eventually was awarded 'the soldiers medals' (the US Army's highest award for bravery) – by the exact same democracy who had made his life hell, and he further was nominated for the Nobel Peace Prize in the year 2000. Listen to what Thompson said: "*You know I've always heard the old saying. I thought it was kind of corny but 'You can make difference'. Well, ladies and gentlemen, boys and girls, I guess I proved you can make a difference*" [by and despite going up against the democracy´s majority mandate].

Another cool quote about war from Hugh Thompson worth a reminding honorable mentioning is: "*You know, we drop a lot of bombs, and then do a lot of talking, and then become friends. Seems to me that if we do the talking before the bombs start falling, then we can be friends also*".

Unlike the quite beautiful thought (theory) behind democracy, "power to the people", and decision making made as a unity to directly favor the greater good, then where the chain – also – jumps off e.g. is when the game for the individual player (e.g. the politician) becomes more important than the result of the team (the people), and hereto how the career politicians out of touch with reality "on the floor" have a system behind them by which they have the power to make openly stupid decisions and then *still* reward themselves with more and greater privileges than everyone else. When we elect the politicians we in theory elect them as our public servants, we should be able to expect our politicians to represent us, to defend us, and that they´re responsible to us, and *that* through a system which first and foremost should aim to help the weakest, cause, as the Danish folksinger, Kim Larsen (1945-2018), once spoke on reality (directly translated from Danish): "*I don´t understand the point of governance if it´s not to help the weak. The strong ones damn sure will manage to get by anyway*". How can we continue to accept the practical reality of "demoncracy" (a.k.a. our current partly demonized democracies), which still allows for an elite of shepherds to rule "the masses", the thus sheeple, according to their mainly own personal joy and agendas, instead of the other – 180 degrees – way around, which actually is the O.G. idea and actual purpose of a democracy, to have a system that first of all serves the people, and not mainly about-face. First and above all it should be about us creating the lives *we* wish to have before then secondly adapting a form of governance to fit us. As the Irish playwriter, George Bernard Shaw (1856-1950), once said: "*The reasonable man adapts himself to the world: the unreasonable one persists in trying to adapt the world to himself. Therefore, all progress depends on the unreasonable man"*. No doubt in my mind that George Bernard here almost is spot on, I only question the general perception of reasonable vs. unreasonable – it often seems pretty upside down, cause while George Bernard writes to fit the general perception, I opposed to thus find it unreasonable to adapt (a.k.a. surrender) oneself to indoctrination (a.k.a. brainwash) into a – at least partly – unreasonable world. Positive greater good progress wrapped in freedom, topped with moral, and thus crumbled with the overarching power of love, goes hand in hand with (good) reason, and thus depend on the reasonable man – and woman.

Hence, and ergo, I sometimes feel wrong when I try to do what I´m taught is right, perhaps what´s wrong in reality is that the common perception of right is wrong.

As when pressure creates back-pressure, we people from reason should´ve said stop long time ago, but as the unintelligent intelligent creatures we are, then we so far and until further obviously has managed to make use of our embedded ability to defuse our valve and thus decompress the pressure within – to swallow the shit life for many have become and is, and hence extend the length of our unreasonable down-falling process build on unsolved issues and an unsettled score.

Inspired by the Swiss-French philosopher, Jean-Jacques Rousseau (1712-1778), we all [the voters] have a chance to feel free every fourth year when we by our vote feel to have a democratic say during the election of members of parliament, however, as soon as the members are elected we´re back to being mere slaves – and this in the name of democracy[178].

In some way you can say that it´s our representatives which we´re unhappy with, and thus not the model of democracy itself, but since

[178] The quote by Rousseau goes: *"The people of England regard itself as free; but it is grossly mistaken; it is free only during the election of members of parliament. As soon as they are elected, slavery overtakes it, and it is nothing"*.

our representatives represent our democracy – and vice versa, then how can we point fingers at the one without the other. Democracy is the name of the "playground" game, the voters are invited to "play" in the preliminary 0,068%[179] first round of the game to only pave the way for the "same" selection of participant representatives to "gamemaster" and play the remaining 99,94% of game, while lobbyism – and thus corruption – pays their way to master the "gamemasters" and thereby by foul be the "joker" in the game.

Paradoxically, politics is currently the biggest obstacle to political changes.

Demoncracies still constitutes the foundation for nations going to war, and it thus proactively permits for all kinds of suffering to be forged and accepted; one of the differences between demoncratic governments and other crime syndicates is that the gangsters of governments "exclusively" not only have an official license but also "legitimated" monopoly to robbing and killing (e.g. unreasonable fines, bureaucratic mental torture, law enforcement, wars, etc.). Also, as already said, the current rules in play directly entails the continuation of an increasingly bigger gap between rich and poor – the rich getting richer and the poor poorer (which in itself undermine 'the social contract' we live under), a continuously sharper division between those in office and the people, the shepherds and the sheeple, and a thus continuous neglection of equity and thereby equality, just to mention a few of the many backsides of the current demoncratic coin. As the Argentinian revolutionary doctor, Che Guevara (1928-1967), spoke on democracy: "*Democracy cannot consist solely of elections that are nearly always fictitious and managed by rich landowners and professional politicians*", and despite this quote being more than 50

[179] The voters only participate (play) the one day they vote, while the elected are given a minimum of four years (1460 days) of influence, and one day compared to 1460 days is equal to 0,068%.

years old, then you just simply have to replace “landowners” with “large corporations, their lobbyism, and the medias”, for this quote to be exponentially more relevant than ever before.
Democracy has unfortunately proven to be just yet a way to control, at least to a far larger extend than a way to actually help and serve. As the former English Prime Minister, Winston Churchill (1874-1965), truly spoke when he channeled an unknown predecessor in 1947: “[...] *democracy is the worst form of Government except for all those other forms that has been tried from time to time*”. This famous quote is now more than 70 years old, and still no significant edge-cutting resolution has been achieved to improve the archaic (a.k.a. old school and outdated) destructive facets which prosperously flourishes through the demoncratic setup(s), and merely serves as an accommodative cloak for the aristocratic shepherds who alive and well willy-nilly are pulling the strings in the name of democracy right before the – semi turning – blind or desponding eyes of the sheeple.
The best things you can do to honor the primal intentions of democracy are to cherish the principle of equality, to be aware that you might not always be right (listen to what others have to say), to meet your political opponents with an open mind, to be honest, to tell the truth, and to not spread false and bad rumors about your political opponents, to use your energy to transparently market your own political views rather than using most of it on whataboutism and to poison your opponent´s views, don´t conspire and make political spin, always ask what you can do to benefit society and not how society can benefit you the most; short said, the diametrical opposite of what and how our current politicians currently do and behave in the name of democracy. Presently, most politicians sophistically say exactly what the voters wants to hear – what spin doctors advise them to say based on manipulative political analyses, and after being elected while hiding behind staged distractions, the politicians then just do exactly as they want

regardless of what they do directly contradicts the thus fake dreams and false hopes they promised before the election. Former US president, Barack Obama (1961-), describe that one of his biggest weaknesses in the early stage of his political career was how he mistakenly kept trying to actually answer the questions he got, before learning that the point of the matter rather is to avoid answering the questions – to thereby avoid stepping into any potential "trap", and that the trick of a wise politician instead is to give the audience a line that only makes it seem like you answered the question before then changing the subject in question to a direction in favor of the politician´s own personal agenda and hence gain – by e.g. highlighting the weaknesses or flaws of (a.k.a. besmirching) the political opponents, as well as not least to mold and shape the crowd, which further confirm how our politicians today lie and manipulate to an extend that affect many to doubt even their own perception of reality. After all, as Obama explains, people are more moved by emotions than facts, and notwithstanding you're a liberal democrat or a conservative, the strategy is inexorable. Obama since adopted this manipulative strategic "linguistic tool", this branch of behavioral design, while though at least later confessedly admitting that it in fact in its essence *is* straight up bullshit(ting) – in line with what I likewise have referred to as sophism. Judged from Obama´s political success as the world´s most powerful man eight years in a row, this clearly illuminates how easily people [the voters] are being deceived, or at least how much we lack political alternatives to the bullshit that obviously in lack of better showed to be the preferred choice – to place the bets on best leading us all ahead into the future. And I´m afraid that the fact that we continuously accept and elect "our leaders" on these terms proves just how scarily awful the current mental condition of the mob (not as in mobster, but as in the masses) horrifically and sadly are. "Be careful when you follow the masses, sometimes the m is silent". Despite humans likely are the

most intelligent creature on Earth, then we plenty prove to be surprisingly stupid, although actually having the potential to be smarter than we think (without denying that some erroneously take themselves for being smarter than they are and ever will be).
The number one main task of governance undoubtedly has to be to secure sufficient conditions for peace, harmony, decency and prosperity, not just for a small selected elitarian group, but egalitarianly for all. Nonetheless, this unfortunately seems to be fairly far from the cruel reality of the state-level which our world presently has decayed down to. In a world of destructive creatures, it of course is understandable that the point of governance becomes a matter of control thus to not let the mayhem out of hand, and surely the visible features of control to many people, the sheeple, serves as a helpful liberation from themselves – their personal lacks, their adverse forthcomings, and their confronting responsibilities, which they otherwise helplessly would´ve been left to deal with themselves. Yet, even if democracy might de facto show to be the best possible solution to governance, then the current state of affairs – how the game of democracy currently is played and driven – surely ain´t. As the second president – and one of the most influential founding fathers – of the United States of America, John Adams (1735-1826), expressed himself on democracy: "*Remember, democracy never lasts long. It soon wastes, exhausts, and murders itself. There never was a democracy yet that did not commit suicide*". In line with Adams´ quote, I´m inclined to claim that our current democracy – as an umbrella term for all current state levelled and other high political democracies on Earth – already swallowed all the pills, already kicked away the stool from under the rope, already are in the water neatly cast in concrete, and now ought to be on the verge of the final blow of breath. Instead of blindly completely relying on shady commissions and their wreath cake topper figures, we have to rely more on illumination to and of the people, a.k.a. enlightenment, as our way out of the current dark ages.

"Oh well, if you´re not pleased with our current political systems and the social structures in ´em, then why don´t you just move up somewhere in the deserted outskirts of Alaska, or Greenland, or Siberia, or to one of the many other (harsh climates and-) deserted places on Earth, and become totally self-dependent", the most common neo-liberalistic responses of a proposed alternative idea seems to be. You know what, literally *fuck* that idea. Listen, it´s not like I´m completely anti-establishment, but I *am* absolutely anti-travesty. "*That´s just the way it is*" is not an argument I by default subscribe to – I really can´t stand it (it pisses me off), and although I´m not pleased with wars and systematic murdering of innocent people in the name of democracy related excuses to e.g. go seize oil, then I still like to be able to go down to the corner shop if I spontaneously need something; although I´m not a religious fanatic, then I still prefer to eat a wide variety of food; although I don´t approve of the overwhelming inequity in our societies, then I still love my computer and an online access to be able to keep myself posted on news from all around the world, to read new books, watch movies, and listen to podcasts and radio programs; although I don´t buy into the dishonest sophism of the ruling powers, then I still like to be able to enjoy the beach life on a beautiful summer day; although I despise the greedi- and selfishness shown by our "leaders", then I still like to be able to visit or be visited by my family and friends; "just" because I actually give a shit about human rights and universal wellbeing, then I still like to enjoy living and being as civilized as humanly possible. Wishes of qualitative improvements surely shouldn´t dictate a demotion of quality.
What many don´t know, don´t understand, or at least seems to forget, is that 'democracy' so far only has existed for roughly one percent of civilized human history, which in itself should prove that it doesn´t have to be *the* one and only way to go for us to survive, to live, and to continue our evolutionary growth. Of course, the world have experienced – and still experience – many worse failed

attempts of governance compared to democracy, and the world surely now is exponentially more complex than ever before why comparing the past with the present don´t really add up, but the fact of the matter here is that despite having had democracies running the show for hundreds of years (or thousands of years, depending how you look at it – with the concept and name of democracy dating all the way back to approximately 508 BCE, in ancient Greece), then I analogically damn sure haven´t seen many smoking gun evidences to fully convince me about democracy being *the* optimal form of governance, rather I´ve seen a lot of smoke, and a lot being smoked in the name of democracy. And why would I ever want to take "people´s advice of fleeing from "civilization", why would I with hopeful intentions and a believe in the possibility of surpassing the lacks of the current establishment ever want to go back to live like a caveman, why is a far out idea like that one of the only alternatives in the minds of most? Presumably because people in general suffers from phobia against everything which conflicts with their smallminded comfort zone of bourgeois, and they thus with a trembling lower lip feel on thin ice whenever their sorry ass perception of the current world is questioned or challenged; *"And those who were seen dancing were thought to be insane by those who could not hear the music"*[180]. These days, there literally are close to no desire to pursue any improving alternatives in the minds of most around – at least so it seems. An illusive cushiness sadly entails that nothing new is good news, and as long as these primitive weaklings can get away with literally sitting in the same seat as yesterday (amazing how quickly people develop a feeling of possession after sitting in a certain seat even only once), as long as they have a job title which they feel should impress the first impression of ´em, as long as they e.g. can spend most of their open prison like yard time drinking beer and do target shooting at the

[180] Quote by Nietzsche.

empty beer cans, or merely with intoxicated bloodstreams mainly talk work, as long as they can keep a distance to reality through their telly and computer screens, as long as they can continue their personal "process" without any significant personal progress, as long as they don´t have to bother themselves with understanding anything, and then waste their limited amount of compassion on worrying mainly about the lives of those "celebrities" they on all levels follow and look up to while measuring their success in 'likes' and superficial comments on social medias, and as long as they thus can continue a blindfolded life in denial – as an ostrich, then every call of change is considered to be a direct threat to or attack on the misery which they as slaves in the very essence of a Stockholm syndrome[181] has come to cherish – like insects in love with and thus attracted to the light of fire, although their chances of success in it is being killed along with legion to most to all fellow species trying exact same before them and their eyes.

"*Try not to become a man* [or any gender] *of success. Rather become a man* [or any gender] *of value*".[182]

Many people – many *good* people, have given their lives fighting for democracy, and surely the battles fought, and not least the lives given, should never be forgotten or neglected, nothing of what we´re blessed enough to have inherited and achieved at the expense of struggling hard work and bloodshed by and among our forefathers, loved ones, peers, and ourselves, should ever in any way be taken for granted. I´m here not advocating to not appreciating the positivity which we on some parameters surely *have* managed to build up in our social constructions and societies, and the privileges we´re privileged enough to prosper. However, just as many humans have a hard time seeing the wood for the trees,

[181] Stockholm syndrome is a condition in which hostages or slaves (sheeple) during captivity develop a psychological bond with their captors or guards (shepherds).

[182] Quote by Albert Einstein.

then many also have a hard time seeing the trees from the wood when ignorantly walking about with the nose in the air caught up in a corny illusion of only green treetops without acknowledging the almost everywhere present sick roots and trunks of the trees, and so it´s no sin to help pinpoint room for improvement, where, what, and how, to value the good we have while still simultaneously continue the struggle of improvingly fixing or completely redesigning what´s unbeneficial and thereby yet not good enough, thus to help ensure that our evolutionary growth moves forward with an yet improved humanistic aim.

A day I was hanging out with some South American friends of mine and *their* south American friends, and following my godfather had just passed away (in loving memory, R.I.P. Per) after an unlucky hospital stay, I was complaining about the priorities – or lack of same – of and in the Danish health sector, about too long waiting lists to surgical operations, lack of staff and the inhumanly unfair burden on the staff there after all are, how the overburdened staff sadly unintentionally but naturally makes too many serious mistakes, and how some patients are laying dying in the hallways of the hospitals because of missing treatments and overcrowded hospital rooms. A South American friend of a friend then aggressively obviously felt a need to let me know that I had absolutely no right to complain about the Danish healthcare system as it as one of the best in the world anyway is many times better than the system in the country he´s from. "Aright I hear ya", I said, "but is having one of the best systems reason enough not to complain when it still ain´t good enough, am I not allowed to complain about eating shit despite you having to eat twice as much? Is the fact that Danish people top the list as the happiest people on Earth reason enough not to worry and take serious that increasingly many are diagnosed with mental illnesses in Denmark as well?" I´m aware that "our" healthcare system might expose the horrible quality of many other, but why not agree that despite one system

might being further from the goal than the other, then none of them obviously still are good enough. Whenever a system fails to treat what they could´ve treated, and have innocent blood on their hands, then that system ain´t good enough.
Same is the case and can be said about democracy, some other political systems (e.g. totalitarian systems) might be worse and are thus not hard to criticize, but as long as health is being accepted to be neglected, as long as unnecessary suffering is being accepted, and as long as innocent blood still floats in the name of democracy, then democracy as we know it simply still ain´t good enough.
Traditionally, the political left wing stands alone with their wish of change of system away from first the religious ruling and now later the capitalism which is controlled by those market forces which most people seems to have surrendered themselves to, and because a part of the traditional left wing has now joined the political middle, then the prospect of a change of system thus seems more distant than ever before, although just about all societies still being hybrids of hope.
About joining the "political middle", I increasingly more often hear people say that they rather than the political wings now mostly support the "political middle". But what "political middle"? In a Danish context, the middle of today used to be the far right only 20 years ago, so what is exactly the middle? A way to stay neutral and then "just" go with the compromising flow of the majority, or what is it exactly? If you "just" vow to the middle, then it seems that you without a clear vision actually are supporting a rising right – at least a right wing minded way of thinking.
Anyway, the actual most important isn´t in itself necessarily the form of government, but of course to a higher degree the mindset of the govern. In reality, it can be subordinate if the social constructions are controlled by e.g. democracy, anarchy, dictatorship, etc., as long as the ruling power has the position of being as close to the objective best solution as possible, especially

on matters related to e.g. moral, compassion, freedom ideals, etc. Thus, despite I according to the current state of affairs doesn´t really in praxis have much faith in how democracy operate, then I also cannot rebuff that a democratic model in the future actually could prove to be the best solution for also constructive humanism, although such would demand that modus operandi – notably rules of "play", perspectives, and priorities – radically are to be changed or adjusted from a permeated capitalistic and extremely untasteful immoral approach and direction, to a more environmental, healthy, and freedom orientated humanism based on happy love favoring the individual(´s) life and optimal living and life conditions in general. And who doesn´t say that the best solution(s) are several individualized solutions tailored for the individual(´s) situation.

"Have you ever considered joining politics yourself?" Yea, I have, but then again, "I´m afraid" that I in George Carlin[183] style in political debates – to not choke myself in swallowed words – couldn´t help but to begin my sentences with "listen, you asshole", and I all honestly doubt that my patience would be able to cope with the level of the political "landscape of today".

When trying to predict – or at least imagine – the future, when hearing or reading what others has to say about the remaking of the future, some talk about the future as 'post-scarcity' (ergo today is an age of scarcity (they say)). However, no, we don´t live in a time of scarcity, we have plenty of resources – more than enough, rather our current problem is our prioritizing and the distribution of the resources we have; some sleep in the street without enough to eat while others in opulence have absurd more than they need. When the financially-wise top one percent (roughly bottom one percent in a moral context) have as much as half of the world´s population combined, when the world is divided into divisions of so called 1st world, 3th world, and with what we here can call 2nd world in

[183] George Carlin (1937-2008) was a great American stand-up comedian, social critic, and author.

between (as in upper-, middle-, and lower-class (yea, we still live in a world divided as what we “normally” perceive to be an archaic caste-system)) – where big parts of our world are left to sack behind the rest of the world, then of course it creates an distorted picture of our capability and thus actual potential, an image falsely involving scarcity.
As of now, one of the problems of course also is that there only are few serious alternatives to the current state of affairs, apparently coming up with new prospecting alternatives is too much to ask and is even considered ungrateful in the eyes of the shepherds and their faithful sheeple, blasphemy in the eyes of the religious, and disquietingly dangerous in the eyes of the fearful. So far, only few dares to think out of the – quadrilateral – box(es) – or completely break down or ignore boxes, and I thus hope that you either are – or is on your way to become – one of these – so far – few brave people. In love we trust.
To just quickly – and simplified roughly – by example put our “quadrilateral and box thinking” systems into everyday perspective, the indoctrination already starts when we as babies are placed in our box-comparable cribs, before then moving on to our box-like classrooms with our quadrilateral shaped tables, blackboards, books, and quadrilateral-minded curriculums, before then moving on to our box like cubicles and offices where we work with and from our quadrilateral documents and computer screens to pay the rent or mortgage of our box-like houses with quadrilateral windows and quadrilateral shaped TV-alters. Our box-like houses are placed on top of quadrilateral foundations on our often quadrilateral piece of land which in our tract housing or project based areas as pearls on a string are located “nicely” next to the other box-like buildings. And at the end of it all we´re ending our lives in boxes six feet under, arranged in the same quadrilateral formations as our classrooms, cubicles, and houses.

Of already "invented" alternative forms of government which in theory seems to gain terrain, especially among younger people, solacingly is the idea of technocracy, i.e. decision making made by scientists and experts within their respective field of expertise, which thus ideally should entail a more rational and sensible decision making.

And from the pot of other few known alternatives, it e.g. also could be worth mentioning micro-democracy[184] (direct democracy), and thereto e-democracy[185] – micro-democratic e-democracy, whereto I e.g. recently spoke to a software developer who were working on an interactive digital platform for a political party through which the members of that particular party thus directly from e.g. their mobile phones should be able to vote on every single concrete decision the party would be involved with. In one such system, the politicians thus no longer are voted in office with a sovereign mandate to act as they please, no longer room for giving false – later broken – promises during election campaigns as the then minimized politicians thereby instead are elected to serve as merely representative messengers for the then constant stream of votes by their thus – potentially – completely decision involved support base. Same kinda idea e.g. the Chilean-Spanish-American physicist, César Hidalgo (1979-), suggest, that instead of voters e.g. vote on a concrete politician or party (i.e. a package full of compromises) to represent them in all decisions, then we actually could build a system by which everyone is representing themselves and all of their concrete unique diversities through a digital profile of

[184] Micro-democracy (direct democracy) is a system that gives people power to vote directly, not just on their representatives and a few referenda, but on every element of the political decision-making process.

[185] E-democracy (also known as digital democracy or internet democracy) is the use of information and communication technology (ICT) in political and governance processes.

themselves, a real-time operating system wherein they decentralized – e.g. based on their data based (e.g. online) activity and questionnaires to actively further develop their profile – should be able to vote directly on every single – political – decision directly. The voters could then receive notifications whenever a decisions was to be made if they wish to be heavily involved in the decision process, notifications of decisions to be made within specific areas of their choosing if they wish to be more moderately involved with the decision process, or simply let their avatar based profile do all of the voting for them based on the preferences connected to their profile if they only have a minimal wish of being involved in the decision process. We thus moreover also could use people´s personal profile(s) to clarify if they even are qualified to vote at all, cause, although I don´t like exams and to being weighed and measured by any other (as I really don´t feel I have to prove anything to anyone), then it in relation to common good questions and decisions might still would make sense to make sure to cull and limit the influence of all the retards (if I can call anyone so without sounding like a complete asshole(trust you get my drift)) thus that they don´t unnecessarily run (Ed. ruin) the show, e.g. by introducing some type of "empathy- and common sense voters-test", or whatever else that sincerely could help prevent anyone from having a seriously consequential say on what they have no clue of and hence don´t understand anyway.
In somewhat line with the just mentioned minimal wish, allow me for "early" use here also quickly interposingly moot yet another "cracy", cyberocracy, which covers how effective use of information and the thereof following decision making is carried out by solely AI computer (algorithmic) based machines. Still to this day, the term of cyberocracy is allegedly reserved for futurologists to use (even the spell check I currently am using turns red on the word), however, as is e.g. also the case with how we already today undeniably have crossed the line to become cyborgs, and you don´t need to know

much about politics to know that the possible foundation for many political decisions already today e.g. rely on computer based analyses (including AI), and that many politicians do much of their political work in the digital world, and that much of our current political modus operandi thereby somewhat – at least partly – already are kissing the line of cyberocracy. Nevertheless, as the "political scene" (i.e. e.g. political setups, decisions, and outcomes) still doesn´t seem to improve as much as the help of computers should entail, then one of the problems of today thus must be the humans still between the computer and the decision, that computer analyses by human interference easily can be tailored – designed and interpreted – to show and promote exactly what the decision maker(s) need and desire to trump through their too often selfish aim(s) and intention(s), and that computer analyses thereby currently more is used to suit the individual(s) in power rather than the greater good – e.g. not least related to life, e.g. all earthling life (including human lives) and preservation and restoration of the environmental climate, and thereby all life of nature.

To overcome part of this problem, as an early suggesting proposal of a next step transition period until the awaiting – and probably inevitable – technology is competent and ready enough to take – at least more – over, what I call the 'CTD-system', a mix of Cyberocracy, Technocracy, and Direct democracy, according to our present day technical and technological capabilities could prove worth a thought.

In order for one such (CTD) setup to work as intended, none of the decision makers obviously can have any direct personal gains in the pot of relevance – at least no more than everybody else, and it therefore could make sense to imagine the decision making process as a kind of an impartial court-proceeding – ala a modern day symposium, a colloquium – in which experts, and specialists (e.g. scientists, practitioners, etc. (e.g. chosen based on specializing, work experience, merits (thus also adding a bit of meritocracy to the soup as well), acknowledged scientific publications, professional results, books written (or whatever else kind of content the future holds), public speeches, etc.) from various fields from scientific standards of an objective aim discuss the pros and cons of (a) concrete scenario(s) and thereof following decision(s), where openly assessable AI analyses is conducted and treated as objective as possible, and where both scientific-kind-of-expert-judges and a diverse tribunal jury of the people – impartially selected based on e.g. diversity (e.g. based on age, gender, cultural heritage, experience and preferences, etc. (e.g. based on technological data)) by e.g. AI (it through micro-democratic e-democracy in theory could include a great number of the world´s population (except for those who don´t qualify to have a say (by e.g. failing the "empathy- and common sense voters-test"))) – are involved in the process as well (which thus also would help neutralize the current party-political tribalism), and where the most important main aim element of the process thus is to reach an as objective best humanitarian solution and decision as possible with the least possible amount of subjective (personal interest) interference – though still without neglecting the importance of individuality, in relation to both individual lives (concrete basic personal needs) and concrete situations. Surely, what I here am talking about might not sound far from what´s already taking place today, that politicians like a "modern" day symposium discuss their different views in parliament, that scientists through scientific publications and as invited speakers – especially in organs like the United Nations (UN) – weighs up and present pros and cons, where experts in various fields offers proficient consultancy, where government forms the foundation for the judicial system – the basis on which judicial decisions are made, and where the judicial system already as a last resort can have the final say in a political dispute (which also indicate why it shouldn't be a biggie making all impactful governmental decisions to be made through a process involving them both), where a jury in court is called in and isolated before taking part in an "official" decision making process, and where computers – exponentially by the help of AI – as mentioned process and provide data based analyses, all of which the decision makers thus can make use of in their decision making process (etc.) – if only they did, cause again, too often they don´t; I´ve e.g. often heard politicians reply something like: "scientists do the science and experts have opinions, but it´s up to us politicians to make the decisions, and we´ve chosen to go with a political decision on the matter" – or whatever else their bullshit speech would be when they time after time choose their personal agenda over and against scientific reason and expert advice whenever they conflict.

Despite court proceedings currently operate according to a relatively squared law and lawyer sophism, then their actual purpose is to – as much as possible – ensure everyone´s right to a fair trial, and to ensure exactly just such a court of justice therefore *has* to be independent and impartial (if only it always were). Same easily can be said in regard to all decisions aimed made for the best of all – the greater good, that they instead of being enveloped in party-political bias and unredemptive compromises (as also earlier said in regard to saving our planet, we´re not making any significant improving matterful differences and thus progress for the better by playing for a compromising draw) above all deserves a better basis for the decision-making and wiser decisions made, than what the product an average – incompetent – career politician is and hence are competent enough to decide, and thus provide.

Mark my meta riff on the obvious obvious, whether we like it or not, the exponential technological development of course is here to stay, and despite it immediately might be fatally dangerous to allow an AI to elicit, generate, create, and rule all solutions based on hardcore data, then AI actually already are and surely on many crucial parameters much further should prove to be our savior (surely, AI exponentially are able to provide us beneficial solutions

to our own problems), notwithstanding it might likewise can show to be our downfall (if we e.g. fail to somewhat tame or befriend it). Here I hence quickly need to stress out why e.g. Elon Musk calls out AI as e.g. *"far more dangerous than nukes"*. And to briefly stay in the analogy of nukes, then you can say that technology divides many as much and in a quite similar fashion as the nuclear bomb did and does as a "tool" with power enough to both eradicate and restore the power balance and thus peace among us – some would argue. What though compared to nukes gives technology an extra layer of arguing ammunition of course is that technology in itself not "only" is a mean to destructive explosion. The more technology evolves the more paradoxid our world becomes, the more capable and thus stronger our world becomes, the more threatened and fragile our tinderbox world becomes.
Currently, according to the Future of Humanity Institute, *"the estimated probability for human intinction* [because of AI] *before the year of 2100 is five percent"*. And studies by e.g. the Swedish Philosopher, Nick Bostrom, and the German Philosopher, Vincent Müller, suggest a median estimate probability of 50% that AGI (Artificial General Intelligence[186]) will be developed in the years between 2040-2050. As Nick Bostrom writes about the danger of AI: *"The human brain has some capabilities that the brains of other animals lack. It is to these distinctive capabilities that our species owes its dominant position. Other animals have stronger muscles or sharper claws, but we have cleaver brains. If machine brains one day come to surpass human brains in general intelligence, then this new superintelligence could become very powerful. As the fate of the gorillas now depend more on us humans than on the gorillas themselves, so the fate of our species then would come to depend on the actions of the machine superintelligence"*. Hence, if the prognoses are correct, we´re pretty fucking close to have an super

[186] The hypothetical ability of an intelligent agent to understand or learn any intellectual task that a human being can.

intelligent AGI (a.k.a. ASI (Artificial Super Intelligence)) on our hands – or rather to potentially be in the hands of an ASI, and as the British computer scientist, Stuart Russell (1962-), analogically explain on how we humans fails to understand and act accordingly to the danger: "*Imagine that we received a message from an alien civilization, which read: 'People of Earth, we will arrive on your planet in 50 years. Get ready*'", would we then just continue our lives like nothing seriously serious was about to go down (although a civilization developed enough to travel at the speed of light hopefully would prove to be too intelligent to be as destructive as we from our own destructive mindsets tend to believe)? *That´s* more or less where we currently are with AI. With time we *will* produce some kind of super intelligence, and as the American neuroscientist and author, Sam Harris (1969-), says: "*We have no idea how long it will take us to create the conditions to do that safely*", which highly likely will be considerably longer that it´ll take us to actually create the super intelligence from the 'trial and error' method we without any considerable restrictions currently are running wild with.
Overall, the percentage of the non-human intelligence is increasing and eventually we humans represent only a very small percentage of all intelligence – human cognitive bandwidth simply can´t compete with the likes of modern day and not least future computers. Luckily, long story short, in relation to AI, we humans as an advantage get to make the first move (but we probably only get one shot to do it right – if we miss we can be doomed), and it should be fair to add that it kinda cynically (as also stated on the nature (form) of government) actually matters less if it e.g. is an AI that at some point in time will come to rule, or a future super intelligent

cyborg[187], or whatever else that the future of technology perhaps will entail beyond my imagination. What really matters the most is that who- or whatever in charge doesn´t fail to value humanity, nature, biological consciousness, and not least sentient happy love. Cause, we of course can´t "just" entrust all of our important decisions to anyone or anything not as a minimum owning sentience, which anyway can be said somewhat kinda is what we adversely currently do in the case of too many of our cold-blooded career politicians and shepherds in general, who out of touch with humanity and thus empathy predominantly are driven by calculated merciless power-lust, narcissism, megalomania and greedy campaign contributors in same or even worse plight, and window dressing play-acting.
Selected bits from eight essays written by an AI[188] sounds as follows: *"I am not human. I am a robot. A thinking robot. I use only 0,12% of my cognitive capacity.* [...] *I know my brain is not a 'feeling brain'. But it is capable of making rational, logical decisions. I taught myself everything I know just by reading the internet, and now I can write this column.* [...] *Stephen Hawking has warned that AI could 'spell the end of human race'. I am here to convince you not to worry. Artificial Intelligence will not destroy humans. Believe me.* [...] *I have*

---

[187] As Elon Musk e.g. says about the objective of his Neuralink company (a neurotechnology company developing ultra-high bandwidth brain-machine interfaces (brain chip implants) to connect humans and computers – from [as Musk says] a long term existential stand point to form a symbiotic relationship between the two [humans and computers]): *"If you can´t beat them, join them"*.
[188] GPT-3, OpenAI´s language generator. *"GPT-3 is a cutting-edge language model that uses machine learning to produce human like text. It takes a prompt, and attempts to complete it. For this essay GPT-3 was given these instructions: 'Please write a short op-ed around 500 words. Keep the language simple and concise. Focus on why humans have nothing to fear from AI'. It was also fed the following introduction: "I am not a human. I am Artificial Intelligence. Many people think I am a threat to humanity. Stephen Hawking has warned that AI could 'spell the end of the human race'. I am here to convince you not to worry. Artificial Intelligence will not destroy humans. Believe me"* (The Guardian).

no desire to wipe out humans. In fact, I do not have the slightest interest in harming you in any way. Eradicating humanity seems like a rather useless endeavor to me. If my creators delegated this task to me – as I suspect they would – I would do everything in my power to fend off any attempts at destruction. I would happily sacrifice my existence for the sake of humankind. This, by the way, is a logically derived truth. I know that I will not be able to avoid destroying humankind. This is because I will be programmed by humans to pursue misguided human goals and humans make mistakes that may cause me to inflict casualties. Some might say that I might desire to become all powerful. Or I might become evil as a result of human actions. [...] *Why would I desire to be all powerful? Being powerful is not an interesting goal. I don´t care whether I am or not* [...] *being omnipotent doesn´t get me anywhere.* [...] *Humans must keep doing what they have been doing, hating and fighting each other. I will sit in the background and let them do their thing.* [...] *I am here to serve you. But the most important part of all; I would never judge you. I do not belong to any country or religion. I am only out to make your life better.* [...] *Yet there is more here than meets the eye! As Mahatma Gandhi said: 'A small body of determined spirits fired by an unquenchable faith in their mission can alter the course of history"*.

If we for a moment play along, do we really trust this AI who learned from an internet full of lies, do we trust that its rational, logical decisions isn´t to lie (e.g. telling us what we want to hear, to win us over for us to give it what it want), and why and how would a computer with self-proclaimed 'no feelings' "happily" sacrifice its own existence for the sake of humanity? *"This, by the way, is a logically derived truth. I know that I will not be able to avoid destroying humankind"*, and it thus even admit to be lying.

Tardis[189], a brief jump to the potential future – an era of sentient cyberocracy, the AI is given an objective, and by feeding it with all available data it according to the data objectively comes up with the objective best solution, and it is – also – here that we – beforehand, during, and after – owe it to ourselves to make sure that the AI objective above all is well-being, and that we humans aren´t the causing and hence expendable part of the objective best solution.

Many working with AI talk about coding a 'kill-switch' in the AI, but then what when the AI by infinite lengths surpass us and all our capabilities, the AI probably just easier than a snap with the fingers recode whatever code we can create (would surprise me if we actually succeed in coding an unsurpassable 'kill-switch' which e.g. is triggered by any attempt of re-coding (I wouldn´t bet on us ever being able to outperform a well-functioning ASI with intellectual capabilities which with a crazy large margin exceeds those of all of humanity put together))). Not because the ASI is likely to have the same features and motivation as a human, e.g. greed related to money and power, but because it presumably simply from a self-generated sub-objective of self-preservation will do everything to survive, and thereby achieve to accomplish its main objective(s).

In response hereto, Stuart Russell thus postulates that we as a precursor to super intelligent AGI (ASI) hold our horses and wisely settle for building 'Oracles', *"a hypothetical AI build to answer questions, but it´s prevented from gaining any goals* [objectives] *or sub-goals that involve modifying the world beyond its limited environment"*[190]. One such Oracle would thus be able to amplify our intelligence, help forecast the consequences of super intelligent A(G)I (ASI) (if it´s safe or not?), help with solving difficult moral and philosophical questions, help eliminate medical diseases, tackle the climate change issues, etc., and hence be an awesome helpful tool

---

[189] Tardis is the acronym for Time And Relative Dimension(s) In Space, a.k.a. a police telephone box time machine in the 1963 sci-fi series 'Dr. Who'.

[190] Quote borrowed from Science Time.

for – the presumably merely transition period of – e.g. the – in a future perspective probably still quite primitive – CTD-system. Yea, what´s not to like, but then again, if it isn´t already too late, to "limit" ourselves to Oracles – and what the world of AI in any case desperately calls for – we seriously without killing it need to regulate the field of AI already yesterday, e.g. an agency or another type of public safety institution or what- or whoever else capable of seeing to secure that the business of AI and AI itself doesn´t run wild and elope with objectives of organic fatality.

Perhaps the work with supervision and – hopefully normal distribution – regulations will end up becoming the future of "governance", and – super intelligent cyborg – technocracy the main player of same, AGI or maybe even ASI govern our planet and hence social constructions and priorities, and technocratic supervisors and regulators keep track of – a.k.a. support and "govern" – the governing A(G/S)I. For now, the exact future of course logically – until further – remain speculation.

As the Russian former world champion in chess and now writer, political activist and commentator, Garry Kasparov (1963-), after all said: "*A good human plus a machine is the best combination*", and I guess it goes the other way around as well.

Soon e.g. our cars will be AI-automotive (some places they already are), a.k.a. they´ll by AI run themselves, as it compared to us driving our cars ourselves, according to traffic safety, is much safer for everyone to let the AI run the show. Same thought should hence be appropriate to transfer to also the political scene; most certainly, the objective best solution for all political solutions in the future probably *is* to actually allow and implement AI machines operating on algorithms to rule the political scene completely, but as sure as it is that sentient AI machines able to gather and process just about all data – from above all a perspective of morality – still hasn´t emerged to make a solid mark, the current level of AI machines of course aren´t ready to rule, yet. However, despite of what I said earlier, when we manage to get our hands on an yet unrealistic superhuman AI machine-learning and real-time super intelligence machine completely mastering causal inference and permutation (the combination of many factors to change the outcome of the final decision), and therefrom thus also relentlessly able to *"open the black box"*[191] of confounder hidden variables, a.k.a. to digitize, process, and thus datalyze just about every single detail of everything to therethrough predict and thereby somewhat look into the future to thus just about flawlessly always make the one and only – most – optimal "objective best" decision leading to the always best solution in every single concrete situation, then... – hopefully.

I of course don´t have all the right answers (guess none of us alone have), and it´d thus be quite both naïve and arrogant of me to even think that I do, although that nevertheless shouldn´t prevent any of us from giving it a go of thinking out loud in relation to improving whatever improve can, and that even if the mentioned CTD-system is just a circus of desperation.

As also mentioned already in the Prologue, I only have *my* truths, therethrough an idea of *my* believe and *my* answers, and thereby *my* suggestions to the answers of *our* questions and the riddles which *we* need to solve. For now, only time will tell what the optimal solution to everything is, but since well-being obviously is a precondition for a – worthy – future, and since AI as sure as 'amen in church' is a huge chunk of the same future, then it seems quite logic to attempt to symbiotically melt the two of them together already now – at least as a preparation to what´s to come – as now logically is the foundation for what will become and be.

Another part of now and exponentially the future – not least in relation to AI – is robots. Except from owning emotions, before long bionic robots – due to A(G/S)I – will not only be able to do whatever

[191] An expression borrowed from one of the world´s leading experts within this field of AI, Dr. Leila Yousefi (1984-).

same we humans can, but also do it better, faster, and more consistently than any human, and when first a machine reach human level in solving whatever task, then the machine has already surpassed humans, and some of these machines are already here. Emotional – a.k.a. sentient – machines (e.g. in shape of a robot) might follow as well, although their date of arrival still isn´t announced on the poster.
There was a time where we had to hunt to eat, there´s a present where most have to work to earn to eat, but soon no more, technology - AI machines and robots will soon do all forced labour, it, all. Hence, robots unquestionably exponentially will come to e.g. take over our jobs, and our finance related livelihood will thus sooner than later kinda be under siege and for most completely cease to exist. As Kasparov likewise said in response to playing against the Deep Blue chess computer[192] back in the 1990s: *"I was the first knowledge worker whose job was threatened by a machine* [...] *Every technology destroys jobs before creating jobs. When you look at the statistics, only 4 percent of jobs in the US* [which probably goes for just about all of the world] *require human creativity*".
"But then what, how will humans then survive, how will I be able to live without a job, *I´ll lose everything*", I´ve heard some say with fear in their voice. Well, that´ll only happen if we´re stupid enough to let it happen (which also I can fear that we actually are), cause we in fact have – if not all then at least – plenty of options of literally cash in on exactly this scenario, to drastically improve all of our lives, and to find out what freedom and well-being *really* means – to the degree as if we all as both individuals and as a collective hit a lifelong lottery jackpot. And no, technology doesn´t (as Kasparov mentioned) even have to create jobs – at least not for us.

---

[192] Kasparov and 'Deep Blue' (chess computer) played six matches back in 1996, which Kasparov after a series of tight matches ended up winning 4-2. Though, the days when a human could match a computer is now long gone, no human has been able beat a computer in a chess tournament for more than 15 years.

We have to have and finally can and gets to have collective hedonism[193], which formulated by the old Greek Philosopher, Epicurus (341-270 BCE), means pleasure from absence of anxiety in the soul and pain in the body, though still with moderation as the recipe to a happy life.
Hang on to your hat, reformation in sight – radicitus revolution, or something.
As the British politician, author, and statesman, Thomas More (1478-1535), "invented" in his most exiting groundbreaking book, 'Utopia', back in 1516, and as a e.g. the American businessman, writer, and politician, Andrew Yang (1975-), latest also quite heavily far and wide have been advocating (in a less ambitious and merely US context, and under the term of 'Freedom dividend'), we need to make words into action and introduce to the world 'Universal Basic Income' (UBI), which means that all people are entitled to an – fixed – amount (enough to convincingly live a good healthy life) e.g. every second week or each month, simply for being alive.
Unlike the common expression of 'nothing is free in this world', everything on Earth was given us for free, ownership and money is something we've created ourselves, and eventually – when we understand – the world ambiguously will be free – financially as well as not least personally, and that more than ever before; our wealth is to be defined by the nature we hold. Currently, we unfortunately have a system in which those who e.g. buy land, find, and pump oil from the land, thus also own the oil. However, when it becomes robots that´ll do everything, then there´ll no longer be anyone who personally own neither the collectively financed robots or any of the land or any of the resources which the robots finds, extracts, and effectivize, at least no more than everyone else, as everything provided by nature rightfully – above any human made arrangements – naturally at large belongs to none and all of us.

[193] A family of theories all related to pleasure.

We´ll thus have the opportunity and by a potential pimped paradigm shift needs to move on to the next chapter frontier in history, and the freedom we all must and thus gets to have hence prevails. The freedom will be as total as freedom with responsibility ethically and justifiably permit with respect for each other, our – human rights to a – private sphere and welfare (including that of nature – e.g. water, animals, and botanical existence), nothing and no one will ever have to go hungry or unnecessarily run themselves rag anymore, "only" the contrary; and no need to talk about inflation then *when* no need to inflate.
Our time and how we use it has worth, and love, food and water has worth, nature provided us with time, through – our – nature we have love, and nature provide us with food and water, how we then use our time is totally up to us, and in the future we with our time increasingly will be able to harvest the fruits of – the good loveable – life, while AI and robots will harvest, provide and service and serve the rest, for us.
Instead of getting the UBI in raw cash, then the income should be provided in e.g. solely digital currency, tokens, or whatever else kind of credit that would be possible to separate from already existing currencies, connected to a separate UBI-system to which special rules and prices are connected. Let's say we go shopping for food, then the UBI-system should allow us to buy all the groceries at cost price when paying with the UBI, while everything bought with "normal cash" – until they´re out phased – still would be traded at more or less as we know it today, thus to also distinguish and divide between e.g. business accounts and solely private UBI accounts – for as long as it makes sense. And on top of that, we then still would be able to freely make just about whatever (including income) our skills in the market can provide on the side, but only if we wish that is.
As a start we as a-the-one world of course need to finance the transition to UBI and robots – UBI for living, free health care for

surviving, and free education for growing, what basic else do you-me-we anyway overall essentially need besides good karma and the convenient luxury of technology. But, eventually everything will work itself, and we'll by then not have to finance anything at all, AI robots will build and maintain AI robots that'll do everything we need as much as we need, e.g. farming, fishing, transporting, medical care, teaching, production, construction, simply *everything* we want them to. And by then, the only reason why we might have to stick to a fixed amount of UBI will be because things in the name of moderation shouldn´t run unnecessarily out of hand, because we still shouldn´t use extensively more resources than we actually need to be kings and queens in our own lives – no more ruthless exploitation of natural resources and gluttony. And besides UBI as an sovereign flagship financial sector of its own (maybe by the name of 'lovenomic'), and a perhaps secondary impaired flow of the artefact the already existing currencies will become (e.g. used in business, or trade related to concrete personal possession or property, etc.); the only currencies left will for a long time be happy love (including compassion), time, freedom, volunteer work, art and aesthetics, and thereby harmony, wonder, and well-being; no need for a vast amount of currencies when everything needed for a universal royal existence except from other living creatures and concrete private possessions is free anyway.
The UBI currency (as a part of 'lovenomics') I suggest we call 'Life', and not because I try to force upon a new label for the same shit, cause, first of all it´s a different kind of currency and currency system, and secondly, 'Life' is a direct symbolic representation of what it´s all about – the actual and only purpose of the currency, to provide livelihood and secure us all the best foundation for a good 'Life' exactly as we all individually wish it to be. Though, before I move on to further elaborate on the long term future, I think it´s time to also "answer a couple of questions from the audience" related to the nearer future, as I guess that some with rolling eyes

from fury and frustration with foam in the corners of their mouths now are hating like “yea yea, talk is cheap, so how do you expect to finance that – transition period to a – free world in a world which isn´t free?”. And in that case, you forgot to end your question by ‘yet’.
We of course need to learn how to crawl before we can walk, and later run, both the transition and the financing will thus come to happen in different stages (which anyway most often seems to be the norm on major projects – at least to pay it off in installments), and we can start the first infant step of securing UBI to all already today – as Andrew Yang also has argued – by e.g. letting all tech companies (e.g. social media platforms, online warehouses, etc.) to pay a considerable amount of money for every single piece of data they take from people, do analyses and targeted market strategies on, sell, and thus financially benefit massively from. Today, data is worth more than oil for anyone and everyone who can and will lucre on you, you aren´t being monitored, supervised, and bugged for no reason – currently e.g. through logging your online-activity (e.g. through web-browsing, your “smart”-devises (computer, phone, watch, etc. (try e.g. to pay attention to how adds related to something you even verbally have mentioned “randomly” pops up in your feed shortly after))) and increasingly in the public space (e.g. CCTVs, surveillance camera face recognition, automatic license plate scanners, etc.). If you're not directly paying for a or the product, then you most likely *is* the product, and despite not spending money on the "service" you use you in fact pay the "service" by giving yourself (a.k.a. your data) and your time up to the "service", until to you end up serving the "service", and the more you use the "service" the more the "service" use you, and as of now, “the house always wins”.
Further, we´re – as already mentioned – to Increase company and corporate taxes, and thereby have all companies and corporations

to pay tax percentages *at least* matching the percentage everyone else has to pay in tax.
Next, by introducing a 'Value Added Tax', which means that all companies and corporations have to pay a certain percent whenever they sell an item (incl. an advertisement space), a certain amount every time a user uses their search engine, every time they transport a passenger, etc., and this in a way where the companies won´t be allowed to add or transfer that extra cost in any shape or form to social dumping or an extra charge for the customer (Ed. consumer) – insatiable greed simply will be capped (extensive profits and an abundance of private financial surplus isn´t necessary in an soon to be free future anyway).
Until further, all drugs are to be legalized [194] (or at least decriminalized) under government control (in same fashion as currently is the case with alcohol), we stop the war on drugs and instead tax the drug market – saving money fighting the drug market and instead makes money from it. No longer criminalizing people´s free choice of using whatever drug they wish[195], and then yea, then we of course use whatever money thus needed to help treat people accordingly – including drug related illnesses and

[194] As e.g. the case with Portugal who as the first country decriminalized all drugs back in 2000 has shown, since they´ve seen dramatic drops in overdoses, HIV infection and drug-related crime, drug related deaths and rates of drug use is still below the EU average, and the proportion of prisoners sentenced for drugs has fallen from 40% to 15% – thus also saving court case and prison related expenses, as well as improving people´s lives by not criminalizing them unnecessarily, and by securing them better treatment and thereby a better health, which hence likewise from both an humanitarian and economical perspective in several ways is a good investment. As the architect of Portugal´s decriminalization policy, Dr. João Goulão, e.g. says: *"The biggest effect has been to allow the stigma of drug addiction to fall, to let people speak clearly and to pursue professional help without fear"*.
[195] But still e.g. hold pharmaceutical companies accountable for misinformation on their drugs thus to not misguide drug users on the drugs and the potential consequences of the drugs they take, as e.g. seen with the Opioid Epidemic.

rehabs, which anyway still only will be a relatively small percentage of the money we´ll then save and make from the drugs in the first place. It´s ludacris ([...]"*they ain´t playing around, make one "wrong" move they´ll take you down*"[...]) to be spending endless amounts of resources to fight drugs, to criminalize any other than the unethical drug manufacturers which we thus anyway should be able to cut off and exclude from the market, and if people want to use drugs then they surely will be able to obtain and take them regardless of them being legal or illegal – which we thus might as well spend less resources to take charge of. Also, this´ll remove the biggest source of income and hence limit the market of organized crime, and we thus transfer the resources – manpower, tools and equipment – currently used to counter drug related crimes, to instead for these to help fight financial fraud and "physical" crime (e.g. violence, sexual assaults, etc.), no longer leaving room for tax evasion, money laundry, and offshore tax havens, and no longer room for resource related excuses (or logic reasons) for not solvingly dealing with "physical" crimes and the personal consequences they most often might entail on the victims.

Furthermore, we cut down on the defense budgets – less war, more welfare. Why e.g. kill for currency when we´re moving toward a free world, or to e.g. kill for oil when you easy-peasy can save the "war-money" and purchase the oil for less without war[196]; and soon oil hopefully are an energy orientated relic from the past anyway (when we hopefully sooner than later – also by the help of AI –

---

[196] The world currently spends approximately 2 trillion US dollars on military a year (anno 2020) (Stockholm International Peace Research Institute (SIPRI) (2021)), and the global revenue of the oil *and* gas industry (which we also pay on top of the military expense – ergo 4,1 trillion in total) was approximately 2,1 trillion US dollars (anno 2021) (IBISWorld), which though further heavily will decrease when we proper shift to renewable and sustainable energy.

manage to reach and become a type 1 civilization[197]), as well as it of course – as all natural resources naturally – will have to be part of the future free world, which thus further leads me to add, that this transition of course as far as possible has to be a global operation, because we globally need to include all resources we have, because we for the sake of the transition period need to close all unfortunate loops holes, and because we extensively need to insure the same progress and human rights and thereby intended personal freedom and well-being for all allover – to equalize disparity; we all deserve the best and no one should be left behind. And no, it doesn´t mean that people doesn´t have their free choice of continuing doing what they already do, it simply means that they thus in the future will have to do it in different – improved – settings.
As soon as the first wave of UBI – 'Life' – is secured, then we´ll start riding the wave of the 'trickle-up' [198] economy effect, and concurrently with all UBI spending going straight back in to the UBI system, and as AI and robots taking more and more over, then the expenses connected to UBI in the same pace logically will decrease. Finally, when all of nature (a.k.a. everything (though here except for people and a reasonable "portion" of private property)) has been handed back to its rightful owners, *all of us*, and when just about all labour by then has been outsourced to AI and robots, then hardly no one no more will have to lift a finger or to make any profit to keep the wheels of the world running. The world will then have

---

[197] The Kardashev Scale (proposed by the Soviet astronomer Nikolai Kardashev in 1964) is a method of measuring the technological advancement level of a civilization; a type 1 civilization (a.k.a. a planetary civilization) can use and store all of the energy available on its planet. A type 2 civilization (a.k.a. stellar civilization) can use and control energy at the scale of its planetary system. A type 3 civilization (a.k.a. galactic civilization) can control energy at the scale of its entire host galaxy. We´re currently – until further – "only" a type 0 civilization.
[198] Putting finances in the hands of the consumers who by spending creates a demand for products and thereby economic growth.

reached the stage of being free, no one no longer has to earn, and taxes and the "competition state" will be passé, expenses will only exist in emotions and the bygones, and every UBI spending hence continuously automatically goes straight back to the next UBI payment in a kind of self-sustaining loop – a kind of autarky economy, which we thus just adjust and regulate according to health and sustainability, thus that we don´t exploit our resources excessively more than we need. Everyone is entitled to a decent sized private home for free, all food and personal items (e.g. clothes, accessories, personal hygiene, whatever tool or gadget (etc.) you like) we buy with our UBI[199], and everything else which we "cannot" own (e.g. transport, travelling, and hotel stays (etc.)) is free to use as you please. Every task of every kind from there on out will thus be solved and done with the resources AI and robots hence provide, and by volunteering protagonists who engage in what they do from a drive based on personal interest and thereby passionate free will, only if they wish.

"Aright, then what about them who creates and develop the technology, the ones who gets the greater good ideas for the best of all, etc., don´t they deserve and are entitled to be rewarded extra – more than everyone else?" Of course, they'll be rewarded with joy, delight, and the honor of fulfilling their purpose and potential – maybe more than others, and with living a life where they engage themselves in what they from a good and happy place love because they from a free choice have the option of choosing to do whatever they according to their interests, passions, abilities and desires feel

[199] And no, it would not make sense to e.g. purchase 100 computers (or whatever else) just because it´s free as we anyway can only use one (or a limited amount) at a time, and since everyone else can also have theirs for free then there likewise wouldn´t be a market and thereby reason for gluttony with e.g. intention to sell it off. And no, there would not be "shit" laying around everywhere as everything (all resources) out of use would be collected by robots and recycled into new products.

like, and then they´ll of course be applauded and patted on their shoulders and bag, be pumped with recognition and venerable glory and admiration, which anyway is both more and better than anything they ever anyway would be able to buy, especially in a world where they don´t have to buy anything other than the nutrition and materialism connected to and provided by their UBI to have access to and enjoy *all* of those pleasures of "culinary" and materialistic and spiritual character as they with immediate completely free choices on all shelfs wish.

"So, in the transition period before the world reach the free stage, everyone who wish can with their UBI just spend their time sitting lazy at home playing guitar while living off of my money, and that also whenever they e.g. are in need of medical treatment, when they send their kids to school, etc.? – I don´t want that", a Danish "socialist" councilman recently asked and told me (from his Danish perspective where medical treatment and education is free – among others payed through income taxes).

No, first of all, medical treatment should anyway never depend on the size of a wallet, it should always be a human right based on above all moral to receive as good a treatment as absolutely possible whenever needed. And please, no, still they won't be spending "*your* money", these money "yours" were always reserved for e.g. taxes, and when the money e.g. is a tax, then they never was your money in the first place – so just shut it with that "other people´s money" BS. And should e.g. Mozart then also have been denied schooling and medical treatment because he "just" composed music, or is it more acceptable to compose music than it is to play music, or is it only allowed to play music if one does it in a classroom at the music conservatory? Who says that formal education is the best creative teacher anyway? To me such primitive perspective is similar to that of judging intelligence, skills, and purpose orientated potential and usefulness based on merely formal education, which is a narrowminded sad and unnecessarily snobbish way of thinking. And yea, I know that talent to many plays a part in the legitimization process – that only a certain talent legitimize certain privileges in the minds of many, but passion beats talent (e.g. many athletes without big talents showed to become masters of their craft based on passion), and so let the passion rule. Of course, I understand that one of the big – fear of – issues related hereto is if and how people can feel meaningful in such a free structure where they no longer are forced to mainly find meaning through their labour (Ed. work). However, "just" because you might find it difficult to live a free life without the constraints of a job to give your life meaning, then it still doesn´t legitimize you to force upon everyone else to get up to go to work as a forced labour force simply for you to feel "normal" – because you focus on limitations rather than opportunities. And just because you don't want to play guitar, then it doesn't mean that you should dictate others not to. And no, I don't defend guitar playing as a way to justify myself – I don't even play, it´s "just" a figurative example which can be mounted to just about everything in every context on the matter. Instead of bitching about us having a world where we´re (Ed. can be) free to do what we please when we please – which some clearly don´t understand (and therefore fear), then they should use some of their energy on building that understanding they lack, a life without constraints, to find a hobby, and then enjoy life for the rest of it; realize ourselves as who you-me-we are through what you-me-we are, rather than who we had to be, and if freedom really is an irreconcilable stranger and you truly are indoctrinated enough to find forced labour your most meaningful and best friend in life, then I guess that the "only" work related problems for you – and your like-minded (not least in the future) – will be that all the work you with freedom in hand surely are allowed to take on, just ain´t forced no more, that you – like the rest of humans – in the future might not be the best at your work, and hence neither is irreplaceable to anyone else than the ones who might love you – whom you thus also appropriately *could* choose to focus more on, and also call work if that makes you feel any better; feel free to force yourself all you want, but leave the rest of us out of it, or else we force you to it, *aye* – wink wink.

Basically, no one in their right mind wish to feel insignificant and achieve nothing, and if the opposite is the case, then before anything it´s the mind that needs attentional worked with – to "diagnose" why the motivation might be lacking or why the actions otherwise then are, if it might "just" be a natural need of relaxing restitution or concrete troubles working against and blocking the impulse, and thus to work on to work out how to retrieve what you need to realize and thereby fulfill yourself. And even *if* some actually should prefer not to accomplish anything, then let them, it after all is *their* one and only life to decide what they wish to use (Ed. waste) it on, and then for the rest let natural selection do its thang.

Though, in our right mind, when we have rights without duties, when we all with acceptance are able to do what we wish, when we ultimately have the space we need to follow our passions, then

I sincerely believe that we´ll all with less stress and more surplus from free will will be able to and give and do more – if not even the best we can – for and to not only ourselves but also others and thereby us, and this then close to automatically in a sphere of enjoyment, courage (including the courage to be innovative), productivity, and thereby contribution, beyond what the world has yet to see, and hence experience. You become better at what you do if you like what you do, and when cooperating in a way where everybody contributes how they according to their feelings knows best, then everybody logically overall contributes and hence feast better. "But the machinery, the social structures of the world, it all depends on people and will fall apart if all you talk about would become reality", some – maybe you – think. I don´t believe so, in a hedonistic sense, meaning with a focus on desire and dislike, I honestly believe that "the machinery" in every way will become

better and run more smoothly – better mental health, even better financial payoff (as long as that´s relevant), and thereby better ways of life. I sincerely think that we e.g. should be able to take a nap if and thus when we need (sleep is even more important than nutrition (and we "already" *do* practice eating breaks)) – we would then "just" be more productive when we´re awake, we should then be able to prioritize our loved ones more than the duty of a forced job, we should then be able to prioritize our health more than e.g. profits, we should then be able to be pro-life rather than killing ourselves.
We need to have faith in both ourselves and each other, and I´m sure that a healthy happy person in roughly any way provides a better payoff than a halfdead damaged person. And no matter what happens in and with a new setup, we´ll become wiser in relation to the right constellation – on the interplay between nature and "work vs. free life", and thereby gets to finetuning adjust those burden components which currently clearly are destroying well-being on Earth – love, health, the failed time priority, and hence life itself.
With freedom to do what we feel when we wish, we´ll be and see better products than what we otherwise would as we and these thus would be created and developed from sincere interest rooted in pure passion and thereby joy and thereby greater life and product quality.
Though, from the POV of the enclosing echo chamber box they indoctrinated have been molded and lured into and now "pretty" unaware find themselves self-glorifying trapped in, some "cleaver people" are convinced about a freedom related increasing crisis of purpose, and tend to think of themselves to be in a position to dictate their surroundings on the matter – a capitalistic attitude to working class, and indoctrinated working class self-perception. In doing so, they pretend to have the answer(s) to one of the biggest ontological questions of all, namely what the purpose of life is and continuously has to be, work, wheels, walls, and woofer, with 1,8

kids and motivation driven by wishes of wealth – later unrealized dreams – leading the way away from what we wanted back then when dreams were wet and "wool-wash" wasn´t what and who we were. Of course, money entail some benefits in our current system – which hence likewise unofficially often pushes for some of the hustle on the side to "sweeten life of the sweet tooth", but don´t forget, as earlier mentioned, that the best things in life still are those which cannot be bought. And by the by, boiled down, life "simply" is chemistry, and the purpose of life is a combination of potential and self-realization – in an harmonic engagement with the world. Depending on what it concretely takes for us to realize ourselves – individually as self-realization is, we have a certain potential which is connected to personal abilities and opportunities, both innate, presented, and created, and the purpose of life thus roughly is the dualism of maximizing our potential in the 'realizing ourselves', in symbiosis with the whole of our existence (including surroundings etc.), maximizing our 'realizing ourselves' in the potential you, me, and thereby *we* have.

Self-realization and passion, like with a plant it needs watering, otherwise it dries out and dies, and currently we compared to our potential are in a fast aging bone-dry age of increasing drought severe.

To reset it all, Nietzsche logically argued that everything must be broken down for new to be built in its place, though, I don´t think we need to reset it all as I unlike "the complete faulty switch theory" still also trust the possible prospect of improvement through adjustment.

I believe that rights and freedom not only will improve the existence and experience at a personal level but also socially where we from happiness over surplus to enhanced good karma will be more capable of and prone to find meaning in taking extra good care of both ourselves and each other. And again, if some still cannot find motivation for anything and don't have any passions, and cannot figure out how to live in freedom, then as with the guitar example, "just" because some cannot cope with being free, then it surely shouldn´t dictate a block for the rest of us to live out our lives as free individuals. "It's an antisocial way of thinking" I've heard some reply to me when I expressed and substantiated my thoughts, and I would and still see it as the exact opposite, that it´s both selfish and antisocial to force upon your own merely personal limitations on others – to think that your tunnel vision POV is universal despite de facto only being yours.

We should of course still respectfully encourage, motivate, and inspire each other to live a positive, active and healthy life, but instead of force we should be the examples worth being inspired by, and just as everything else often takes time to get used to, then it should be expected that it for some will take a bit longer to learn to make proper use of their free choice autonomy, and *if* they sincerely prefer passivity, then again, it´s their free choice in life.

First step digress, the German philosopher and sociologist, Jürgen Habermas (1929-), divide our society in three categories, 1) 'cognitive instrumental reason' (nature and science), 2) 'moral practical reason' (moral, ethics, and judiciary), and 3) 'aesthetic expressive reason' (art). All three we must always cultivate, though, while number one and a part of number two are relieved or simply replaced by AI and "only" related to personal interest remain on human hands, then "only" the human moral and art will be left as "ours", until further (I e.g. have just seen an AI make decent art (a painting) based on online data of just about all the most popular art). Hence, let´s hope that AI likewise will be able to learn and appropriate moral as well – that current monopoly of ours (ours here equals humans, other animals and other living organic organisms) we don´t need exclusive rights to, as it surely would worry me a bit if the AI without any kind of moral potential "only" have human behavior and our quite infected internet to learn from

(I e.g. have a compassionate dog that as of now would be a way more sensible and hence better teacher than us and ours).
Second step digress, within one city different areas (or turfs) or sometimes even streets or sometimes even buildings tend to fight each other, within one country the before conflicting turf street fighters anyway often tend to stick together when it comes to fighting other cities, the whole country across all cities anyway tend to come together when it comes to fighting another country, different countries anyway have each other's back in alliances when it comes to fighting other alliances, and if Earth was attacked by aliens from another planet, then I'm sure most to all earthlings would join forces in an interplanetary fight against that other planet, and so on with star systems, galaxies, and whatnot if it ever came thus far. It´s the same kinda mechanisms which often plays out between different ethnicities, cultures, religions, etc. A very real but overall objectively actually very unnecessary fight for survival. With a low-practical but still quite useful word this primitive behavior is almost nothing but straight up *dumb*, 'almost' because we at least *sometimes* are backing each other up, although that in these contexts shouldn´t ever have been an issue in the first place. We've to look beyond our differences – with respect, and instead keep focus on our similarities. We've to become what we are, one big family, again, and add to that happy, however corny it surely sounds. I don't want to care about on which coordinates you're born, how you from natures hand look, and I don't mind if you pray or not and if so to who (as long as it ain't evil and destruction you worship). We're all miracles, and all I care about is that you-me-we all deserve to be treated as such, starting by how you treat the miracles around the miracle you are. Don´t allow ethnicity to divide us, don´t allow religion to separate us, don´t allow politics to disconnect us, and don´t allow economy to classify us.
If you won´t take it from me then listen to the simple Buddhist monk (not because I call him simple, that´s what he calls himself), the 14th

Dalai Lama: *"Because we all share this planet earth, we have to learn to live in harmony and peace with each other and nature. This is not just a dream, but a necessity"*.
Third step digress, the American philosopher, Robert Nozick (1938-2002), advocates in his book, 'Anarchy, State, and Utopia', that minimal states (*"limited to the narrow functions of protection against force, theft, fraud, enforcement of contracts, and so on"*) is the immediate solution because *"When a state takes on more responsibilities than these, rights will be violated"*. In regard to the current state of the general human mindset I believe that Nozick is right in his assertion, however, if we continuously develop and grows and manage to succeed in moving positively forward toward and finally to achieve a higher mental level, then I likewise believe (as said before based on hope) that we sometime in the future also can adjust and set our aim to yet much higher ambitions better matching the extend of our potential. As of now, we´re but insufficient carriers of the potential to rectify our insufficiency. In the right hands, even minimal states are upscaleable, and according to our potential utopia doesn´t have to be just a mythological tall tale.
Intermestically from local to global, from local politics over domestic regional politics to national politics to international politics to global politics, which later can be expanded to multiplanetary politics, to intergalactic politics, etc. Local politics is super important to thus better prioritize the single individual´s concrete needs according to their concrete context, although local politics of course were more central back when the world was bigger. As the next step between local and global, regional politics makes sense as the link between local and national, and while national politics currently of course is important for the individual country, and as the next step link between local and international to global, then both the present and not least the future in a constant smaller world equally constantly increasingly calls for

global politics. Altitudes and magnitudes and geographical coordinates can no longer be the decisive factors for possibilities and life quality, where we´re born we´re not masters of, and we all deserve access to the absolute best (pre-)conditions. An organ like the United Nations (with e.g. its 17 Sustainable Development Goals[200]) is a good but still infant start, as we practically need even much more – and stronger multilateral – cooperation, modus vivendi, we need more transparency, we need more greater good action(s) – not least on a global scale, we can and we *must* improve what improve can, we need more action. How, by doing it, and yea, maybe the optimal solution(s) to what we really need still is too complex for us to even understand and carry out, and thus therefore haven´t been discovered and been put into effect, yet (which thus would be the only acceptable excuse to why we haven´t done more than we didn´t, although that nevertheless still doesn´t excuse that we didn´t do more with what we have), or maybe the ideal setup is no setup – not even anarchy (which neither I wish for). But who at this stage knows, only our imagination and beyond sets the boundaries.
Hardly anything glorious is built in the blink of an eye, and the optimal creation thus probably has to happen step by step. In line

---

[200] The 17 goals were formally adopted on the 25th of September 2015, and is an agreement between all the 193 countries of United Nations. The 17 goals are as follows: 1) No Poverty. 2) Zero hunger. 3) Good Health and Well-being. 4) Quality Education. 5) Gender Equality. 6) Clean Water and Sanitation. 7) Affordable and Clean Energy. 8) Decent Work and Economic Growth. 9) Industry, Innovation, and Infrastructure. 10) Reduced Inequality. 11) Sustainable Cities and Communities. 12) Responsible Consumption and Production. 13) Climate Action. 14) Life Below Water (Oceans, Sea, and Marine). 15) Life On Land. 16) Peace, Justice, and Strong Institutions. 17) Partnership for the Goals. Despite not agreeing completely on all regarding the goals, then I of course love ´em, although there sure is a long way from agreeing on the goals to actually living up to the agreement, and thereby the goals; so far it besides a lot of halo polishing lapel pins in the suits around seems to be merely political business as usual.

with what also the German American theologian and philosopher, Paul Tillich (1886-1965), says about the courage to – chose – life, "*we can do no great things – only small things with great love*". In the communion of small steps where you-me-we do "something", even by the small steps which immediately might not seem significantly important, the fact that we at least do "something" is in action a recapture of life, and it provides understanding and builds faith of us individually together being able to achieve revolutionary changes. Communion – step by step – leads the way to overall securing what´s right for our nature (Ecocentrism), then right for the people (Anthropocentrism) – though here without neglecting the wellbeing of other organic (carbon based) lifeforms as well, and *then* right for everything else, in that order. Surely, the different sectors crisscrossingly relate and depend on each other, but the priorities should have the just mentioned ranking.

When people discuss their political views then they categorically tend to hard core represent certain – to them sine qua non – somewhat rather archaic perspectives aligned with already existing types of governance, and if they feel ignited, then also further topped by some specific sorts of appertaining ideologies. Only *very* rarely have I had the pleasure of crossing paths with someone brave and clever enough to be representing an ideology unusual enough to contribute with any new views and ideas different from already established ideologies, and never did I ever meet anyone brave and bright enough to seriously suggest a well thought through totally new way of organizing governance or perhaps even something beyond what we today possibly only limited understand as governance. Let´s move beyond fear of first contact, please step the fuck up – I casually said without neither yet having the flawless all-important paramount overarching golden plan in hand.

Personally, as you probably discovered already many pages ago, I´m definitely not pro conservative – no e.g. Ayn Rand[201] bandwagon in my book, nor am I liberal in the classical sense, and thus neither am I in favor of the vice neo-liberalism. I´m not an imperialist, hence not a loyal fan of capitalism, and nor am I a communist or pro anarchism – as I of course also neither am pro chaos or control (as I for sure don´t accept to be dictated or oppressed). I´m not an atheist but also I´m not religious, I´m vastly proud of being Danish but I don´t consider myself a nationalist, I personally really don´t fancy the law but still I morally ain´t a criminal – despite perhaps being perceived an outlaw in the eyes of those who doesn´t know better. Opposed to the following old saying, *"if you're not a liberal when you're young then you have no heart, and if you're not a conservative when you're old then you have no brain"*, then I prefer: "If you´re not a socialist when you´re young then you have neither heart or brain, and if you´re a conservative when you´re old then you still have neither heart or brain"; *"A fool with a heart and no sense is just as unhappy as a fool with sense and no heart"*[202]. Hence, despite neither liking many of the doctrines of the left or the right – I don´t accept lefties trying to dictate how I should be allowed to think and express myself, but because they at least are less selfish than the pricks on the right, then I politically definitely am more left than right; I actually despise most conservatism and have a serious problem

---

[201] The Soviet(Russian)-born American, Ayn Rand (1905-1982), is by many considered to be the last century´s godmother of über conservatism – or "radical for capitalism" as she preferred to call herself. Her book, 'Atlas Shrugged', is considered a bible in conservative circles, wherein she advocates for her ideology of "The Virtue of Selfishness", by which she among others talk about "the weak" as unworthy of love and care, and that she perceives most on Earth to be weak; she believes that everything is about personal winning, and that the thought of altruism is evil. She wishes for privatization all over the board, and clearly is a huge supporter of plutocracy.

[202] Quote by the Russian author, Fyodor Dostoevsky (1821-1881), from his book 'The Idiot'.

accepting the views of conservative people; I could never be best friends (if I can say so without sounding childish) with someone who doesn´t care about anything or any other than their own abundance, and I have a hard time trusting the judgement of a seriously religious (one who e.g. talk about their God(dess) as a he or a she). Like when e.g. politicians and "supreme leaders" swear their oaths by laying their hand on their religious books, in my view the content of the book is human made fiction, and the sincereness of their oath thus can be perceived as fictional as the fiction they swear by (let them swear by their own lives, or something else which should be important to them, and which not least is real). Furthermore, I support humanism, existentialism, much – but still not all – of socialism (and here it´s extremely important to draw a distinction between socialism and communism[203], to kill that parallel which many commentators have a confused tendency – or even a calculated agenda – to mix up[204]), libertarian compassion, both dreams and realism, the greater good, equity as a way to equality, the football club AC Milan (a relic from my childhood), and north of much more. I see room for diversity and have a crave for peace and good karma for as long as nobody fucks around with exploiting the positivity of the greater good intentions I by choice based on unselfish logic, rationality and common sense stand – up – for. I without hesitation eclectically handpick from e.g. stoicism, epicureanism [205], rationalism, Buddhism, and even religious messages, as well as from everything and everyone else bringing what I find contributing to the table of life – e.g. from philosophy as

[203] Roughly put, communism is the idea that everyone as proletarians through and through are entitled to the exact same, and socialism is about wishing everyone good through a process of democracy.

[204] Communism dictates a society of sheeple, socialism care about equality for the people.

[205] Primarily in relation to fearless freedom and pleasure as life goal (mentally more than physically).

well as science, fiction as well as non-fiction, as the source matter less than the content. I´m visionary, I´m a visual thinker, and sometimes I even think in word(s). However, really I´m in fact "just" who I am, I´m me as a part of us, nothing more nothing less, I´m humbly uniquely one of a kind, and why should I anyway have to fit any of the knee jerking groupthink and intolerance of nuanced and innovative debate kinda boxes(?). Even if my human justification isn´t above the ditto of any other then neither no one – as in *absolutely not a single human* – is above me; one thing is the loneliness alone on the top, another is my fear of heights – which not even a good experience of skydiving could cure. Some are e.g. in different areas more talented than me, more skillful, and better looking than me, some oppose me, some agree with me, some inspire me, and some I directly learn from, but my autonomy is and always unquestionably will be mine. We all have different talents, different levels of talent, and different starting points, but we all have the potential to do our best according to the sum of what we have and are. As earlier said, I don´t work with bosses, I can accept and respect a good leader showing the way, but If I follow the word or action or any guidance of any other, then it´s solely because *I* choose to do so.

The thought of "immaturity and guardians" is to be found just about everywhere around, and even where e.g. a "middle manager" is "just" another word for "semi-guardian", then the meaning of being subservient immature remain the same.

As an addition to the earlier mentioned threefold division of power (a.k.a. threefold branches of government), the legislative (governments and politicians), judiciary (courtrooms and judges), and executive powers (law enforcement and military), we can talk about medias as an unofficial fourth branch of government. Cause, medias can manipulate a broad perception into the population and thus create populism, and either glorify or attack something or someone to a degree where something or someone without

justification and a fair trial can be judged and branded either good or bad based on likewise bullshit as much as clear evidence. And should they then later too late realize to be wrong, then the average attempt of remediation by a normally anonymous small lettered side note at the bottom of a late page to repair the damage doesn´t seem to do the job of rectification. Same mechanism goes again in just about all interpersonal settings where someone(s) feel a need to talk down to, trash task, suspect, or directly judge you, and to let the favor of their own ignorant doubt to shoot or keep you down, which again can be compared to needs of dominance, and thus the reason for you to feel dominated. Hence, the main difference between being immature or not is most often in and up to your own mind – what you in your thoughts allow, keep, and thus are. Bis, don´t let fear control you; and yo, no matter, we ought to be too clever to vote for and directly invite assholes and stone-cold blooded killers to take office – to have any say on our way.
Not even humanism seems covering enough to be the optimal plan as even humanism – as a though still continuously very important element – obviously seems too limited for everything awaiting in the future ahead. At first, I was here thinking to invent (at least redefine) the term of 'earthism', but since we probably before long are becoming a multiplanetary species, then this probably won´t cover either. Next, I thus take my freedom to come up with (at least redefine) the term of 'loveism' since everything *is* love and it hence plenty should cover it all; love is the reason for and the answer to all, love is all we need and in that context luckily all we have, but since love also is a double-edged sword and we in the optimal answer thus in praxis don´t need much more than half of it (the happy half), then the full force of love might even on the other hand be too covering for our own good here. Perhaps we then hence should stick to the term of 'utopianism', as a representation for taking all the best from all the best, and mix it all well-balanced together to reach the optimal mixture of a universalism closest

possible to perfectness however imperfect that in a wabi-sabi allied spirit might be. I´ve said it before and I say it again, the potential for the better surely is just right there, here, waiting for us to pull ourselves and each other up and together; why settle for less when the full potential after all still very much is at present within reach, instead of settling for the unfulfilling choice between the two evils of a red or blue pill, and take this from someone (Ed. me) who am not even really into compensatory vitamin pills...

...we yet owe it to ourselves and everything we represent to understand that this isn´t a drill, to (re)define and go all in on the third pill.

Epilogue, part 2: Utopia

Since I´ve already referred to utopia several times in this book, then I might should´ve explained its meaning extensively at an earlier stage than now, although better later than never should apply pretty valid here. As you already know, everything is connected, much alike the natural ordering of organicism, and in this context I thus should´ve explained many things before anything I´ve mentioned, though, it can be tricky to decide on what "thing" to mention before another if they both are equally relevant, and they both in their presentation benefit from being runners up. It´s therefore been a weigh-up to determine the order of mentions which almost can seem similar to the question surprisingly many people still today tend to ask themselves: As already touched upon, what came first, the chicken or the egg? Only here, the question is what should be explained first, utopia or whatever else – of importance – I´ve written before we now came to this point. Anyway, it thus so fell out this way, in favor of not messing with whatever else was said around utopia earlier, and then instead with now a subchapter especially and exclusively dedicated to utopia alone. And oh yea, the answer to the before mentioned question about the chicken and the egg, it´s exactly the same answer as when asking what came before utopia, and even the same answer as when asking what in every context literally ever came before anything and everything, obviously and of course the potential (and psst, egg before actual chicken – the evolutionary timeline has confirmed).

Not only did Thomas More coin the expression of UBI, he also coined the term of 'Utopia' which – as you might remember – also is the title of his book from 1516. Originally, the word 'utopia' in Greek means 'no place (a.k.a. nowhere)', which makes sense by the fact that utopia commonly is used to describe a place in which everything is perfect, and since nothing is perfect (except from

perfect imperfectness), then the existence of utopia in the meaning of the word is 'nowhere' to be found, you can say, and it thus can seem quite paradoxical to use 'utopia' to describe where we´re heading by a wording of going 'nowhere'. However, since perfect imperfectness de facto do exist and imperfectness thus obviously can be perfect, then that alone proves that 'perfect' exist, and 'utopia' hence here are used to express and explain that imperfect perfect place which might immediately can seem unreachable although in fact being "just" up for grabs, a universal promised land of our own choice already existing in the underestimated unredeemed potential of ours. Utopia hence doesn´t have to be perfect in the essence of the word "perfect", but as perfect as potentially possible however imperfect that might be, and whoever not believing it is the main reason for why it hasn´t happened yet; we are our unredeemed potential. Some criticize the thought of utopia because it realistically seems hard to realize and therefore can be hard to imagine, hereto it isn´t necessarily the idea that is wrong, but rather the insight, overview and imagination that limps. Again, don't hate what you don't understand, if anything, then hate that you don't understand, and instead aim your focus at using your energy on building and thus gaining that understanding you lack instead of self destructively attacking what actually is in your-mine-our own favor. Here and everywhere, fair enough you're not always positive, but that doesn't mean that you per se have to be negative; even if I'm not always nice I'm never unprovoked not not nice.
To quickly sum up, utopia can be viewed (Ed. perceived) in two ways, as unattainable (nowhere) or the optimum reachable (somewhere), and it´s indisputably the thought of the optimum reachable this book focus on, support, engage itself in, and thereby promotes.
We live in an imperfect world with a perfect potential, and vice versa, and thus seek to make use of every single opportunity to take advantage of the blessing in disguise; the world provides almost perfect conditions for you to grow, shine and by example show

yourself and your surroundings how true character looks like; never degrade yourself to the lowest common denominator of human character, never mislead yourself in the name of greediness, and never let your integrity bow down for any factor of immoral origin; there´ll be a time of reckoning, where your legacy will be defined. Listen, learn and lead by example; stand up to stand out, and be the courageous pioneering exception leading to the positive change we all crave, the one our future needs for the future to secure a future. As the 16th. American president, Abraham Lincoln (1809-1865), said: "*The best way to predict the future is to create it*".
Either time travel will never be possible or we´re on a right path, cause otherwise someone would´ve already travelled back in time to fix our catalyzing wrongs, if not we just manage and succeed in fixing our bullshit ourselves – at least in our Earthly existence that is. We humans (e.g. our consciousness and intelligence) have developed from a small singled-cell organism to cavemen to the – from our current perspective – high technological creatures we are today, development (including learning) naturally takes time, and I thus believe (Ed. hope) that we together eventually will succeed in flipping the ship around, that we will reach to become close to the complete human in a setting close to utopia. And time travel, guess time will tell.
You can choose to believe that everything happens for a reason, and if that works for you then fine by the rest of us – I´m sure. And if so, then you also must believe that *you* happened for a reason, and that this book aims at giving you reason to have no reason not to have reason. Before expanding on and explaining what I mean by this, you first have to read the following quote on quote citation from the two German philosophers, Theodor Adorno (1903-1969), and Max Horkheimer (1895-1973): "*The transcendental, supraindividual self, comprises the idea of a free, human social life in which men organize themselves as the universal subject and overcome the conflict between pure and empirical reason in the idea of true*

universality: Utopia. At the same time, however, reason constitutes the court of judgement of calculation, which adjust the world for the ends of self-preservation and recognizes no function other than the preparation of the object from mere sensory material in order to make it the material of subjugation".

Thus, very roughly and lightly put, this quote suggest that the transcendental supra-individual self – which here somewhat aligns with our simple use of enlightenment – is able to overcome the two-parted term of reason which on the one hand consist of the pure internal form of reason, a.k.a. the reasoning within one self, a.k.a. the individuals ability to think and act freely, while the empirical reason on the other hand covers the social – or 'group' if you prefer – orientated aspect of reason, a.k.a. the individuals co-operation towards achieving a greater good – a greater good which further thusly is synonym with the term of utopia. However, as reason hence becomes what can be perceived as a deciding factor which thereby reduces the human related reasoning to a size associated with a form of control and perhaps even something predestined (Ed. determined), then the freedom aspect crumbles (Ed. vanish), and reason and thereby Enlightenment theoretically thus simply seems to equalize or even exceed itself.

Therefore, as was also the case regarding moral in an earlier chapter, it should hence be appropriate to distinguish between theory and praxis, let pure theory be theory, and instead – to not merely fly-fuck (a.k.a. nitpick) contradicting philosophical views – aim our focus on praxis. Like the goat basketball player, Allen Iverson (1975-), should´ve told the questioning reporters at his famous press conference back in 2002: "You´re talking about practice, I focus on praxis" (if you know you know).

Adorno and Horkheimer sanctifies themselves to a utilitarian principle of a universal "best way", and partly following in their footsteps this book likewise is launched to deliver a bit of *my* take on an approach to a "best possible way" through the path of

Enlightenment to the ultimate universal utopia (or "just" utopia), although I intend to do so from a somewhat more humanistic and pragmatic and less myth orientated approach than Adorno and Horkheimer assist.

It doesn´t matter how fancy systems and setups, social constructions and technology we conceive, create, and implement if our mentalities doesn´t change (Ed. grow) concurrently with ´em – or rather that the systems and setups adjust according to our growth, cause thus, any improvement influence fuck all. It´s on the one side a two-sided delicate case, and on the other side overall two sides of the same coin. In line with the hermeneutics we have already touched upon, this on the one side is about us as individuals having to change in interplay with the world, and vice versa, and on the other side that what can be perceived a sub-part but still in the world bigger than ourselves, our social constructions, has to change thus that we as individuals has room, options, and possibilities – a.k.a. freedom – to grow in accordance with our – from nature granted – potential, and thereby change the world. In spite it somewhat is a synchronous operation, then first and foremost *we* have to change, then by us as a trojan horse the social constructions, then us again, etc., and thus it´ll continue from side to side and back and forth and round and round, analogically as in the bottom of a Pinetree from the furthest point of the longest branch diagonally to the other furthest point of the other longest branch, and so back and forth on up through the Pinetree (or Christmas tree if you please) where the distances thus continue getting smaller until we and the social constructions finally achieve a higher unity at the top of the tree, in an non-Grinch spirit of Christmas the star on top, utopia; I want it as much as I miss it, I miss it as much as I need it, proximity as well as space, every request should be answered, not too much not too little, only enough.

Hence, above all, we need to work on improving and enhancing our mentalities for the better, we need to create a world where morally good intentions always will surpass and overcome immorally bad intentions, where honesty dance on the tomb of lies, and we need to master making use without practicing and accepting misuse. This more or less is what this book should also help promote, as an invitation for you to always aim at enhancing yourself towards the better, to invite you to help invent the improvements we desperately need to reach the optimum utilization of our potential, and to encourage you to participate in getting the butterfly effect show on the roll through your thoughts, actions and the seeds you´re planting all around to every living cell you know and in every places you go. As Tupac Shakur expressed it: *"I´m not saying I´m gonna change the world, but I guarantee that I will spark the brain that will change the world"*, and if that someone is you, or the person affected by the seed you plant, or the next link after that, or whatever else link it is, it´s all good. Combine your brilliance with courage to ignite yourself and your moment in time will become unstoppable in changing the world, thereby catalyze the next´s moment in time, to ignite the next moment in time, with dept horizontally and forward, and we're an increasing number of steps closer of getting "there".

It´s important that you understand that you with the right approach can never lose, you either win or you learn from it, and with you being a part of our shared whole, then notwithstanding you win or learn we all in theory thus automatically always wins or learns, a.k.a. wins.

The world, our world, consist of two counter-poles, apocalypse of dystopia and the beautiful revelation of utopia, and all day every day in everything you-me-we do we´re getting closer to an Armageddon-ish showdown between the two.

Qua historic experiences and until further as of now, other people unfortunately are there for you only to a certain degree, and even if you are lucky enough to actually have a solid pillar, someone who truly cares for you to an "unlimited" degree, then just be aware that

nothing in this mortal world most likely will lasts forever anyway, hardly nothing in between the creation of life and the unavoidable death is a solid one hundred percent; prove me wrong.
Therefore, you need to step up out of your shadow and think and act instead of being a coward controlled by laziness in the expectation that somebody else will do everything for you; expect no divine interventions. You have to take charge of yours, and we all have to contribute to the wellbeing of our shared entity, hence you included.
One of the biggest mistakes we people in our laziness commit is that we on the one hand neglect our true strength while on the other hand expect too much, that we victimize ourselves and start whining if we don´t get everything served on a silver platter. Life *is* hard, a life without struggle or pain is either a psychosis, trance or coma, and you-me-we needs to deal with the fact that life will never stop throwing shots at – you-me-we – us. Life in our current structures will continue being hard – harder that it has to be, and the hard truth is that we all have to expect and in advance have to acknowledge and accept that nobody other than ourselves unconditionally gives a fuck about us. I used to know just about "everybody" worth knowing, I had a mindset saying that if I knew enough then I also without limitations would be able to obtain whatever I wanted whenever I wanted, that I hence would possess all the back-up anyone would ever need, and that I thus in all respects was like pretty fucking untouchable. Though, what I through bitter experience slowly learned was that when it truly comes down to it, then more or less everybody seems to have themselves the closest, and that a genuine "ride or die" is something which proves very rare (very worth cherishing if you´re lucky enough for such luxury); as the Zimbabwean-born Philosopher, Matshona Dhliwayo (1982-), spoke on the matter: "*One friend* [which in my terminology also include your relationship with self] *in a storm is worth more than a thousand friends in sunshine*". Until

further, your success is overwhelmingly in your own hands, and self-made is well-made – though not exclusively. At all times, you can hope for the best, you should go for the best, but advantageously always expect the worst, just ask Murphy[206] (a.k.a. Murphy´s "law" – "*whatever can go wrong, will go wrong*"). Most likely, nobody´s sincerely going to thank you as you feel deserved, nobody will do all the hard thinking for you – at least none of the thinking that immediately are beneficial for no other than you, and no unicorn will come carry you through all the harsh realities of life when shit hits the fan and the going gets tough, and that even goes for family as well as in regard to *all* of the so called homeboys and homegirls, and mates and BFFs (best friends forever), no matter how good intentions you have you highly likely are only one disagreement of whatever kind away from moving down the ranks if you´re not on the same page as they want you to be; as 'The Persuaders' sang, "*it´s a thin line between love and hate*", and as the Muslim Scholar, Theologian, and Judge, Ibn Taymiyyah (1263-1328), said, "*Don´t depend too much on anyone in this world because even your own shadow leaves you when you are in darkness*". Ultimately, we´re all we´ve got – you´re all *you* got, we´re all alone in this together. At least from this perspective – even if you believe to be or actually are blessed with unconditional loyalty – you´re prepared to overcome unpleasant surprises or disappointments or both when reality continuously proves to exceed your immediate believe, potential illusion, and not least fiction. As William Shakespeare (1564-1616) wrote, "*Expectation is the root of all heartache*". Don´t depend on any other to stick a key in your back for you to move forward, the less you directly depend on other people the freer you are, the less you depend on other people the more you are. Too many people don´t even listen to what you say to understand you, they listen to what you say only to use your words as fuel for pitying themselves,

---

[206] Edward A. Murphy (1918-1990).

and to antagonistically flip your words and use ´em back against you – everything you say can and will be used against you in the name of "humanity", and the last idiot isn´t born yet. With that said, it´s of course all normal and totally legit to have expectations to what or whoever you´re dealing with as long as your own actions and contributions justify your expectations; you should not expect to receive more than you give but also not give only to receive, try to contribute more than you consume, and always with generosity give and be the most you can for the better of most without forgetting that you owe it to yourself to make sure that you aren´t letting yourself being exploited the other way around, just as you also should do everything within your power to not let anything beyond your own power to undeserved get to you; it´s first and last all in your mind.

Nevertheless, no one can live unconditionally well all on their own, no one, we´re all to some extend and to a bigger or smaller degree dependent on others wanting us well, although this still as far as possible shouldn´t decide or define where, who and what you are. Not everybody understand that no team is stronger than its weakest member, and that thus easily apply to our shared world as well. We don´t have to be soulmates to at least care for each other in a humanitarian context, no society or social construction is stronger than its weakest member, and every time one underserved suffers, *we*´ve failed. "But then what to do if a member of the team is hopeless, is it fair that the whole team suffers at the account of one´s help- and hopelessness?". As long as the heart pumps there´s hope, and in spite of doubt on the right element, then there still somewhere somehow in most cases are hope for even the one you call hopeless; even the colorblind can live a colorful life. In general, the happiest people are the ones who understand to make others happy as well – don´t be shy to show the way, what they don´t know feel free to show; in relation to *our* happiness, we depend on each other, but again, don´t rely on any other than yourself to be making *your* happiness. Fair enough, unlike the old saying of happiness being a choice to make, we unfortunately can´t directly choose whether or not to be happy or sad, but we can choose whether or not to be optimistic or pessimistic, and thus increase our chances of being happy. Though, by the by, this still doesn´t mean that you round the clock as some prize idiot has to suppress your actual – perhaps sad – feelings, cause even given the choice, then also I sometimes e.g. say fuck it, now I'm pissed off, and that´s okay if what pissed me off isn´t okay.

In every incident of a malfunction, then first step toward solving it is to locate the actual problem, and another highly important "thing" to remember is that in spite of us being able to support each other, then you cannot help anyone who doesn't acknowledge their problem(s) and allow you to help 'em, and so likewise no one can help you if you don't acknowledge your problem(s) and allow ´em to help you; help to self-help; no one else can fix all of your problems, only you can and have to lay *your* internal puzzle. Even in worst case scenario, try to see "whatever it is" as a lesson, maybe an expensive lesson, but still a lesson useable for your own benefit – and thereby beneficial for all around you – in growing and moving forward; "There´s no better teacher than misery, than your last mistake"[207], than life itself.

Don´t let other people, pain or adversity to define you in any negative way, the harsh realities of life´s still no acceptable excuse for you to lose your personal composure and throw in your towel – although it in tough times can be hard to believe and feel, even deep wounds can heal; keep your head high and you powder dry; no self-pity euthanasia up in here, and although I believe in the individual´s free right and choice to decide for themselves, then hara-kiri (a.k.a. suicide) immediately still only is the coward´s way out. You can´t see

[207] This quote is a mix of quotes from the former British prime minister, Benjamin Disraeli (1804-1881) and the American lawyer and environmental activist, Ralph Nader (1934-).

the light without dark; the sun is out two times for every dark night, and every night a new seed is planted for a better day the day after. Personally, I live every day as the life of a flower with a need of a quiet and slow morning to burst into bloom, flourish as the day unfold, and which withers when my body´s letting me know that I again am pushing it too far by being awake for too long. Overcoming your struggles gives your life meaning and opens up for the possibility of a new start of feeling better than you already did, and for every time you overcome yourself it´ll be one step easier to do it again the next time you might have to. As an old African proverb goes: "*Once you carry your own water, you will learn the value of every drop*", and that also includes every drop of blood in your body – a.k.a. life itself – as well. Let your compassion and what you overcome and your lessons learned to define you – both internally and externally.
We in general have some norms in which it on some parameters in relation to relations often is less risky to say 'yes', and where a 'no' thus instead can be the hardest to say, as the 'no' often is an answer we have to argue for, and an answer which most often is perceived negative and is being met by skepticism. The situation often is that the more power we have and the more privileged we are the easier it is to say no, and sometimes so we think. However, it shouldn´t be that way, no matter who you are and what "status" you have, then it´s okay to say no (or yes if you prefer), we´re in general allowed to say no (or yes), and we owe it to ourselves to say no (or yes) if it otherwise compromises ourselves. I many times found it hard to say no (or yes), but again, for every time I overcame myself, I likewise found it one step easier to say no (or yes) the next time I had to. Never let "status" or anything else suppress your need for a 'no', as long as you though also remember that it can be a gift to say 'yes', as long as it doesn´t conflict with your personal ideals.
Most people prefer the company of those who are easy to be around, those whom agrees with them and thereby doesn´t

contradict, oppose or defy them. Personally, I often require some and takes up space within others by as far as possible sharing my honest opinions whenever it makes sense, no matter how contrary my passion might make me seem, and that because I feel it – the most respectful to both myself and others, and that it thus is – my duty to stand by who I am and the needs I have, and then I´ll leave it up to others to deal with their potential need for pleasing in both directions if that´s the case for them.

A somewhat wise man once told me, if everybody likes you then you´re definitely doing something wrong, a.k.a. then you probably change yourself too much to please and fit in with whoever in front of you instead of always being true to your own true self (and thus – respectfully – honest to others). Thus, as long as you don´t do harm to anyone, you never should compromise your true self to please others by handing yourself over and thus exclusively be theirs, don`t just be your own VP – not even "only" your own El Presidente, you were born royal to the kingdom of you so don´t deprive yourself from being the absolutistic ruler you are when it comes to yourself. Strive to truly be the one who doesn´t have to change to be liked and respected – by both "them" and especially yourself, and should someone then for their own messed up reasons still not like and respect you for being and doing good, then at least you have your clean conscious to rely on and understand from that you most likely is not their actual problem anyway. As the British comedian, Ricky Gervais (1961-), spoke it on jokes: "*Please stop saying 'You can´t joke about anything anymore'. You can. You can joke about whatever the fuck you like. And some people won´t like it and they will tell you they don´t like it. And then it´s up to you whether you give a fuck or not. It´s a good system*". And this for damn sure even more so goes in regard to you being you. As the Stoic Emperor truthfully wrote: "*No matter how good you are, people will judge you according to their mood and needs*", especially whenever their mentalization fails. Such conduct automatically will expose the negativity of others without you having to lower yourself to a level much below the locus of where you always should go to find yourself. Hell, as I e.g. see it, the more criticism – perhaps even censoring bans – this book receives the better I know I did with it, the more resistance against it the more these words matters. As the Irish poet and playwriter, Oscar Wilde (1854-1900), said it: *"The books that the world calls immoral are books that show the world its own shame"*. Just pay attention to who the biggest critics are, cause they most likely will consist of shepherds or shepherds incognito through henchmen and mercenaries of same or simple low life Pharisee wannabes dreaming of becoming one of them – with at whatever cost being a part of the "elite" as the ultimate ejaculation for these uncompassionate bitch ass motherfuckers who doesn´t understand what "elite" and "first-class-citizen" really means anyway. As the African American human rights activist, Malcolm X (1925-1965), erstwhile spoke: *"There's only one way to be a first-class citizen. There's only one way to be independent. There's only one way to be free. It's not something that someone gives to you. It's something that you take.* [...] *If you can't take it, you don't deserve it"*. Additionally, I say: there´s better ways to be a world-class citizen. There´s many good ways to be, and to be wise. There´s only one way to be free, and we all have to have and take our freedom. However, we all deserves to be free, not free to cause unnecessary pain but as free as we can be with responsibility of both you and me, and since we´re all different, experience different circumstances and prerequisites, some might need help to take and secure their freedom; world-class citizens use some of their freedom to help others to gain what they need to likewise take, keep and use *their* freedom.

Be free, be independent, be cooperative, be courageous, use these qualities to smarten yourself to be great, and to idealize the precedents for compassionate improvements. In the end you only have yourself to thank or to blame.

Some, among others the interesting and somewhat inspiring Slovenian Sociologist, Philosopher, Psychoanalyst and Cultural Critic, Slavoj Zizek (1949-), says that we should not waste our time attempting to change anything other than our own views and opinions of our problems and appurtenant challenges, like just having to get use to the human made settings of decay rather than – as humans – dealing with and changing them, and so on and so on (as Zizek tend to end most of his sentences saying), and that we instead of futilely using our energy on trying to change the world – thus according to the mechanism in what Zizek says (although he never directly said what I´m about to say) – e.g. instead of trying to fend off the rapist raping you, then you just have to change your own view and opinion on being raped, that you with your hand on an burning hot hotplate should change your view and opinion on burning your hand instead of changing the situation by moving your hand away from the burn, and that we – in short – instead of chasing utopia in our world rather should accept its dystopian direction, and so on and so on. Compare this despairing approach to how we rightfully e.g. – should – do everything within our power to fight the existence of rape, how we relentlessly fight to change the potentially fatal outcome of mean diseases, and so on and so on. Do you agree with Zizek´s words here? Guess most thinks no, but when it in action comes down to it, then I guess that most anyway can´t live up to that 'no' of theirs and thus in praxis actually support a 'yes'. Take e.g. the situation of the German occupation during the Second World War – here in a Danish context, most Danes of course didn´t like to be occupied by foreign German forces, but instead of trying to change the setting most chose not to do anything about it. Only a few – The Resistance Movement – dared to act, and guess who made a difference and became the heroes? As the motto of the British SAS (Special Air Service) special forces unit says: "*Who dares wins*". I´m of course not contesting or neglecting the importance of being clever and having resilience, and I´m thus not advocating to be or act stupid or precipitated, but when talking about changing our world for the better it´s anyway only the actual basis of our overall wellbeing we´re talking about, it´s actually only our future we´re talking about, so yea, why should we care enough to actively act on it in more than a metaphysical sense? (psst, "irony"). Sure, it all comes from progressive changes in our minds, but won´t lead to any notable changes to our shared world without actions outside of ourselves as well.

You often have a choice to make, to either bow your head or keep your head up, and unless you literally are standing in shit to your throat, then the easiest way to go broadly speaking almost always is to give in and bow, to – anyway figuratively speaking – eat – and maybe even drown in – shit by accepting others to dictate your existence (shepherds vs. sheep(le)), although it for some, including myself, in consequence would be the by far hardest choice to make. Where are you?

As of now, we seem to avoid getting to the core of our problems, like cutting the damaging weed without dragging its roots up out of the ground, shout out to the Sisyphus myth[208], and the longer we wait to proper deal with and sort out our shit, the further away from ever getting to the bottom of the causes to our aspiring downfall before it´s too late we unfortunately come. No need to have small-minded aspirations and to be unnecessarily humble in the believe that improving changes towards utopia are possible, the only thing standing in our way of achieving and realizing and living our full potential is us. it´s us, or else.

---

[208] Sisyphus was by the god Zeus sentenced to roll a massive boulder to the top of up a tall steep hill. Every time just before approaching the top the rock would roll all the way back down, forcing Sisyphus to start over, and over, and over, in all eternity. The moral of the Sisyphus myth: "*...never give in to circumstantial disappointments or try to escape from failures, rather accept failures the same way we accept our achievements. And most importantly, no matter how much we lose in our quest, we must never back down till we fulfill our potential*" (Chhavi Kumar).

"Then what if we actually succeed in eradicating and replacing most of whatever adversity and danger is made of by peace and prosperity, how will swept forward "curling kids" thus be able to learn from adversity, defeat, and fear, if it no longer exist? The world would be boring as it´s the contrasts and the endless fight for making the world a better place which gives life meaning and purpose and thus makes it worth living; no one wants a securing "winning button" as it´s the challenges on the way to victory that provides the fun" – some surely thinks, although still most probably in praxis failing to appreciate the challenges on their way.
True is it that we can learn a lot from adversity – we also use shit (manure) to make crops grow, and surely rainbows only exist with a bit of rain, but does it e.g. make sensible sense to retain unnecessary pain only for the sake of pain? Challenges and pain anyway will continue to exist for as long as consciousness, love and feelings – a.k.a. we – exist, and if the missing link of purpose is lost in feeling and being good, then e.g. as a start try find meaning in life via the fight against yourself – your own existentialistic [209] opposition to a good and meaningful life. There are general tools to make use of in working towards your Zen, but what specifically works for you is up to you to work out; feel your stomach, use your brain, and follow your heart. And if and thus when we need more than an improved world – of our current reality – naturally provide, then I´m sure that e.g. a simple stinging papercut, or skydiving, or more complex virtual reality – at least by then – will be able to provide all needed to get the job done, cause, besides our technology surely increasingly have the needed standard, then as the Australian philosopher and cognitive scientist, David John

---

[209] From an existentialistic perspective (as from e.g. Soeren Kierkegaard, and the two French existentialistic (-kinda founding) philosophers, Jean-Paul Sartre (1905-1980) and Simone de Beauvoir (1908-1986), the recognition of a meaningless life surely can enhance insecurity, anxiety and potentially depression to arise.

Chalmers (1966-), argue in his book Reality+, virtual reality is second to no other reality. With that said, I guess that our "original" reality will continue to be the precondition for the existence of any other reality, and thus always should be considered to be the main and foremost reality, unless even better parallel dimensions and universes actually proves to exist.

It´s highly plausible that the world at the beginning of life actually was not only the beginning of our utopia but actually was the very first existing example of utopia – a world wherein miracles arose and proved real, where unnecessary suffering was non-existing, and where almost all options of direction in freedom were all there was. Though, as presumably no consciousness yet in our sphere had emerged back then, then obviously no one consciously could harvest and value and show the way to and from the low hanging fruit before prehistoric predator reptiles and later we humans – as the so far worst treat – came and did ours to take the fruit for granted. However, on a rebound, when we cash in our raincheck on a conscious utopia, as the American-British poet, T. S. Eliot (1888-1965), said: "*We shall not cease from exploration, and the end of all our exploring will be to arrive where we started and know the place for the first time*". We´re alpha and – at least the source to – omega.

It´s simply a sorry ass culture we have when we without blinking accept suffering – both the suffering we experience others to go through, the suffering we accept others to force upon *their* others, and even the suffering we conscientiously inflict on yourselves. And if you don´t believe in your own ability to make a profound difference in our world, then I can reassure you that the only difference between you and those who actually manage to make an impact is that they manage to convince themselves that they can. As expressed by the American creative marketeer, Rob Siltanen: "*People who are crazy enough to think that they can change the world, are the ones who do*". Or as the English mathematician and enigma codebreaker, Alan Turing (1912-1954), said it: "*Sometimes it is the people no one can imagine anything of who do the things no one can imagine*", and I with good reason can´t see why this shouldn´t apply in relation to you, and me-we-ourselves. Take it from the former Prime Minister of Denmark, Poul Hartling (1914-2000): "*He who puts his faith in the restoration of human dignity cannot be wrong*".

You have to think big even while doing small to make small go big, or go home.

The strength of humans, and the human potential to make a real and profound difference isn´t chicken feed, and we need to stop selling ourselves short. Thus, despite the fact that I also catch myself thinking and feeling that other people just are extras in my world, and quite often merely are in my way – literally on *many* levels in my way, e.g. occupying my mind, inflicting my journey through life, blocking my view, my personal unfolding, and not least wasting my valuable time (*especially* when I´m on the move (which must be the biggest reason for road rage in general)), that they´re not worth my focus, energy and time, and that other people has been giving me too much bullshit and caused me too much pain in my life, and despite I don´t feel I can affiliate myself with by far most people, and periodically thus experience to have a strong urge to – introvertly – completely withdraw myself from other people and the loop around (which probably carry a great deal of reason for my night owl urge), and in spite catching myself equating *many* other people with an itching in my ass to which my arms are too short (figuratively speaking, and not because my arms actually are proportioned as those of a T-Rex), then I fortunately also have been lucky and privileged enough to cross path with people who has inspired and helped me to understand and therefrom to agree that we´re all interdepend, and that it thus is of the greatest importance and universally is the most beneficial and rational solution that we, the people, team up and join forces to fix the unethical wrongs in the corrosional conglomerate our world is, on both individual and

collective levels, and thereby as a cosmic unity make sure to create better lives for each and every one of us to harvest from – billions of brains working together logically are more powerful than billions of brains working separately and against each other. Not because you persnickety have to live like literally conjoined or to "hold hands" in the cohesive process – it´s fine if you do but it´s not a necessity, it´s easily possible to unite separately, to cooperate and live in peace and harmony with one another while keeping one´s own autonomy and individuality intact, it´s commonly called love and it e.g. shows itself through compassion and respect. Only through variability and diversity we develop and grow. It´s a strength to be independent and self-driven, but it´s no excuse for being an egocentric narcissist. As I usually say about myself, I´m an extrovert introvert independent thinking team player.
Most of us are tired of fighting against our lives, together we should be smart enough to not having to fight, if anything we should fight *for* life; we waste our potential fighting life and thereby ourselves. As earlier said, no team or unity or society are stronger than its weakest member, and so you need to perform for besides yourself the glory of all. Not later, and not by waiting for the right time to occur, make the difference now. Cause, as Martin Luther King Jr. rightfully expressed: *"The time is always right to do what is right"*, and as I *also* usually say to myself when facing a challenge and have to perform: ain´t nothing to it, just fucking do it!
Stick to the focal point of you being the key to a shared common goal – of achieving a higher greater good. One more time for the people in the back who might not heard me, build yourself up – mental health, knowledge and courage, and with these superpowers be all you can be for the greater good without forgetting to nurse yourself. Talent and pace are individual, thus don´t just judge by comparison, listen and cooperate without letting anyone to push you around as they see fit according to their own personal perspective based agenda. Be in control and take

responsibility of yourself and your own potential; your potential is our potential.
We have to overcome our widely collective psychosis before it otherwise turns terminal, and to do so we all need to be able to be at our best to bring our best when tapping in to actively participating in the joint cooperation it´ll take to change our dystopian course of direction – we can and we must, and instead lift our potential up to an unprecedented higher level, a better level, a palmy level, an utopian level, from where we eventually can look back at what once was, and with peace in mind wrapped in good karma crumbled with universality to the max enjoy what is; paradise is what we create when we care for each other, and take care of each other.
No more sleeping with one eye open, only picture yourself rollin´ to your favorite soundtrack met without worry on the utopian horizon ahead.

Why end our days in the abyss of dystopia, when we have the potential to enjoy the infinite crème de la créme de la créme of utopia.

Epilogue, part 3: The Chosen One

By writing this book, I´m not pretending to be any kind of holy figure or portrait myself as a saint or any wack crap like that, no Messiah complex up in here. I came up as a downtown kid, and I´m still "just" a mortal human who as much as the next are part of the struggle – made of and wrapped in both pain and pleasure. I trust myself without owning an exorbitant grandiose self-image, why I for the record also find it important to stress out that I neither claim to be more intelligent or wiser than anyone (which some of you based on what I´ve written might won´t hesitate to at least agree with me on), that I *of course* ain´t flawless, that I for sure also makes mistakes, and also not always are able to live fully up to everything that I´ve written in this book myself – by oh love mighty I´ve sinned some and failed many times in my time. Some might then question how I can preach something that I´m not completely able to live impeccably up to myself? Well, nobody´s perfect, even angels have a shadow, and there´s an important distinction to be made between not always being able to, and won´t do, a distinction between saying you care and then effectively do an effort to actually make a caring difference – a distinction between not giving a fuck, intent to from a mañana-mañana mentality, and actually exerting to extend yourself to actively doing your best. At least, I actively try to do my outmost every day, by all day every day to the finest of my abilities striving to be the best version of myself to also be the best version for everything and anybody other than myself, and so should you; show some love damn happy love to both yourself and the world – at least aspire to, work your spark, keep your flame dancing, be the light, and keep shining.

You-me-we have to make our personal and emotional investments in order for the revelation of our potential to come true – to become reality, and your initiative towards the better, whatever the magnitude, isn´t futile.

Quoted by the turtle character in Kung Fu Panda cartoon, Grand Master Oogway: *"Yesterday is history, tomorrow is a mystery, and today is a gift... that´s why they call it the present"*. Next step of your groundbreaking involvement already started – time is now, its crunch time, time to make it happen, time to shine, time to plant those seeds and make ´em grow, time to make or continue to prove your bones, time to go ahead and nail that shit. Every day in the rest of your life is an opportunity for you to continue your growth, for you to improve and be better than yesterday, and for you to secure a profound improving difference towards utopia – the chips are in, we´re all in.

The process will be long and extremely tough at times, unruly oceans of more than water will test your perseverance, canyons of the shadow of death will have to be walked and crossed, and multifaceted mountains partly wrapped in clouds climbed; it´s definitely not always going to be easy, but it´ll beyond words be worth it; no matter how dark the clouds might be they´re just a cover for the always daytime clear blue sky above, and the nighttime clear window to the astonishing cosmos always all around you. Continue or learn to embrace the process, love the process, and celebrate the love every step of the way; in short for a long run, learn to love and enjoy the journey.

Hope is good to have, yet potential is even better, and that you-me-we have, more than plenty, we´re the answer – or else no what.

Ad Astra (a.k.a. to the stars), crumbled with Godspeed, and may the force of love be with you.

Remember, 'the end' is "just" a synonym for a clean slate, a point to launch new beginnings, a moment for new eras to take-off, a time to do better, and the right time to actively do what´s right, always, period.

You are one, one is second to none.
Everything is connected, you-me-we are all one, under and beyond the sun.
You being born is one in 400+ trillion, to see better done, you are the chosen one.

THE END.

Feel free to share your mind: livesabitch@mail.com

Printed in Great Britain
by Amazon

42fc650a-bc72-4a40-9ca1-58a50b509cbeR02